W9-BTG-300

19756

JUST
ANOTHER
KID

JUST ANOTHER KID

TOREY L. HAYDEN

G. P. Putnam's Sons/New York

G. P. Putnam's Sons
Publishers Since 1838
200 Madison Avenue
New York, NY 10016

Designed by Rhea Braunstein

Library of Congress Cataloging-in-Publication Data

Hayden, Torey L.
  Just another kid.

    1. Mentally ill children—Education—United States.
2. Problem children—Education—United States.
I. Title.
LC4631.H39   1987   371.94   87-7229
ISBN 0-399-13303-8

Printed in the United States of America
1   2   3   4   5   6   7   8   9   10

CHAPTER ONE

It was a hodgepodge setup, that classroom, not unlike the rest of my life at the time. The room was huge, a cavernous old turn-of-the-century affair with a twelve-foot-high ceiling and magnificent large windows that looked out on absolutely nothing worth seeing: a brick wall and the chimney stack of the heating plant next door. A hefty chunk of the room had been partitioned off with gray steel industrial shelving units, used to store the school district's staff library. The L-shaped area that was left, was mine. Windows ran the length of the wide, long arm of the L, where the chairs and worktable were; the narrow, shorter arm of the L contained the chalkboard on one wall and the door at the far end. It was an adequate amount of space; I had taught in considerably more cramped conditions, but it was a quirky arrangement. The blackboard was useless because it couldn't be seen from the work area. And short of standing like a sentry at the junction of the two arms of the L, I could not monitor the door. Most eccentric, however, was the district's decision to combine a classroom for disturbed children with a staff library.

This was to be the first official self-contained classroom in the district for E.D.—emotionally disturbed—children since the mainstreaming law had come into existence back in the seventies. I was called a consultant resource person in my job description; the children were termed behaviorally disordered; and the classroom was known, on paper, only as The Center, but we'd come full circle. For me, walking back into the schoolroom that late August morning, having been gone from teaching almost six years, had provoked a sense of intense déjà vu. It seemed simultaneously as if I had been away forever and yet had never left at all.

I hadn't meant to be teaching again. I'd been abroad for almost two years, working full time as a writer, and I intended to return to my life in Wales, to my stone cottage, my dog and my Scottish fiancé. But family matters had brought me home, and then I'd gotten embroiled in the interminable red tape involved with gaining a permanent British visa. Every conceivable problem cropped up, from lost bank records to closed consulates, and one month's wait stretched out to three and then four, with no clear prospect of the visa's arrival. Disconcerted and annoyed, I traveled among friends and family.

A friend of a friend rang me one afternoon. I'd never met her, but she'd heard of me, she said. And she'd heard about my problem. They had a problem of their own, it seemed, and she was wondering if maybe we couldn't help one another out. One of their senior special education teachers had been taken unexpectedly and seriously ill. There were only ten days left before the beginning of the new school year, and they had no immediate recourse to another special education teacher. Would I be interested in some substitute teaching?

No, I'd said immediately. I was waiting for this stupid visa. If it came through, I wanted to be able to leave instantly. But the woman wasn't easily put off. Think about it, she said. If my visa did come through early, I *could* leave. They could find another substitute, if necessary. But otherwise, it would be a good way to spend my time. Just think about it, she urged.

Still I'd said no, but by the time the Director of Special Education contacted me, I had mellowed to the idea. Okay, I said. Why not?

Sitting there amid the paraphernalia accumulated for the start of another school year, I stared out the window at the smokestack, dull and gray in the summer sunshine. I was coming to the nettling conclusion that I wasn't a very well directed sort of person. I didn't have a career so much as a series of collisions with interesting opportunities. After ages away from teaching, an abortive Ph.D. attempt, several years in private research, a spell as a clinical psychologist, and time abroad spent writing, here I was again, sitting at a table converted by clutter into my teacher's desk. I enjoyed such unpredictability and diversity; indeed, I thrived on it. But I was also growing increasingly sensitive to how capricious my lifestyle actually was.

A knock on the door brought me sharply out of my thoughts.

"Torey?" a voice called. I couldn't see who it was from where I was sitting, so I rose. A secretary from the front office had her head around the door. "One of your kids has arrived," she said. "The parents are in the front office."

The old building was no longer used as a school, but rather it housed the district administration offices, most of which were on the ground floor. I had the entire upper floor to myself as the rest of the rooms were used only for storage. In fact, there were only two functional classrooms in the whole building, mine and that of the full-day program for educable retarded preschoolers two floors below, in the basement. So the halls were hauntingly quiet on this first day of school.

I followed the secretary down to the large main office, alive with clacking typewriters and chittering word processors. A man and a woman were standing in front of the chest-high barrier that served as a reception desk. They would have been a remarkable-looking couple in any circumstance. The man must have been at least seven feet tall, because I, at almost five feet ten inches, did not even reach his shoulder. But in spite of his size, he was soft and delicate looking, with gray hair in loose, tousled curls, like a child's. He appeared to be in his late fifties, and although not particularly handsome, he was attractive in the way aging men are, an attractiveness born more of confidence than anything physical.

The woman, who looked to be only in her thirties at the most, was startlingly beautiful. Indeed, I had never seen anyone up close who looked like she did. She was tall and angular, with chiseled cheekbones and a Kirk Douglas cleft in her chin. Her eyes were pale green, genuinely green, like cat's eyes, only lighter, and quite prominent, giving her an intense, almost arrogant appearance. Her hair was a dark, tawny blond and very, very long. Although straight, it was thick and unruly, flowing about her like a lion's mane. Hers was an elegant, assured kind of beauty, the sort one doesn't usually find outside fashion magazines, and it seemed rather out of place in real life, but it had an arresting effect on me.

"Good morning," I said and extended my hand. "I'm Torey Hayden."

The man reached forward and gave my hand a quick, damp shake. The woman didn't move. She was very casually dressed and made up, but there was nothing casual about her demeanor at all. Every muscle was taut. It made her beauty more impressive. She bristled with beauty, keeping it drawn up around her like a cloak.

Silence followed. I didn't have a clue as to who these two were.

"You'll have to excuse me," I said. "Mrs. Adams, who was supposed to be teaching this class, has gone very unexpectedly into hospital. I'm her replacement, and I just took this job a few days ago. I've got to admit—"

"We can't get her out of the car," the woman blurted.

"Oh."

The man was glancing around, as if not paying particular attention. The woman regarded me intently. While her expression was not precisely hostile, neither was it very friendly. She studied me with the kind of unabashed scrutiny not usually tolerated among adults.

"Let's just leave it for today," the man said, still gazing off. Languidly, he looked down at me. "Perhaps she'll feel more like it tomorrow."

Without any warning, the woman's eyes filled with tears. She blushed brilliantly, and all the muscles tightened along her jaw. *"No,"* she said through gritted teeth. Then she turned abruptly and bolted out of the office.

The man shifted his feet uneasily, and I half expected him to take off too, but he didn't. "My wife's a bit upset about this," he said softly.

"So I see."

A pause. The man looked down at me. He had blue, watery eyes. "I think we should just leave it."

"Why don't I come down and help? I'm quite used to this sort of thing. It's pretty normal. New teacher, new room, all that."

He shook his head. "No, let's just leave it. I'll bring her in tomorrow." And he turned and left before I could say more.

I gazed in stunned disbelief at the empty doorway. Turning, I saw the three secretaries watching me. We all burst out laughing, for lack of a better reaction.

"Can you believe that?" I asked. "I don't even know who they were."

"The Considynes," replied one of the secretaries. "They're our answer to *Dallas*."

My second student arrived shortly after I returned to the room. Mariana Gilchrist. With her was her mother, a young woman who couldn't have been more than twenty-five. Her hair was cut short and greased into thin, wet-looking spikes that stood up all over her head. Her eye makeup, a combination of heavy liner and pearly shadow, made her look like Cleopatra. By contrast, Mariana, in a red tartan jumper over a frilly white blouse, seemed sweetly old-fashioned.

"Am I the first kid here?" she asked. "Oh, goody. I get everything first. I get to pick everything I want first." She pulled away from her mother.

"You behave yourself in here," Mrs. Gilchrist said. "You got to behave. This here lady'll make you. You can't go effing around in here like in that other class."

"Where's my place?" Mariana was asking. She was at the far end of the room already. "Where's my place going to be?"

"I'm going now," her mother said.

"Are these toys for us kids?" Mariana had opened the cupboard under the sink and was hauling everything out.

"Good-bye. I'm going now. I'm leaving you in this here place."

The girl never looked up.

Mariana was eight and came with the kind of profile that was almost a cliché in this sort of classroom: borderline IQ, short attention span, overaggressive. She also had a history of precocious sexual behavior. Her entire short career at school had been spent in one special setting or another, and she had achieved virtually nothing. After three years, she could neither read nor write and could understand only the most basic math.

"Where's the other kids at?" Mariana asked suddenly. She rose, leaving a litter of puzzles, games and art materials behind her on the floor. "Who else is going to be in here? Will there be any girls?"

"Yes, one. There're only going to be three of you in here to start with, although I expect we will have others join us as we go along."

"What's the other girl's name? Is she eight too?"

"She's seven, and her name is Leslie."

"How soon's she going to be eight? When's her birthday?"

"Next spring."

"Well, we'll probably be best friends anyway, even if she is a bit young for me." Mariana took up a pencil and tried to drill a little hole into the Formica tabletop.

The door banged, and my third student entered.

I was well prepared for Dirkie. They had all told me about Dirkie. He was eleven and had spent virtually all his life in institutions. He had had an early childhood history too horrible to bear thinking about, a litany of abandonments, abuse and bizarre family acts. Then had come a long spell in the state mental hospital. Eighteen months earlier, a husband-and-wife team of psychologists had met Dirkie while they were working at the state hospital. They had fallen in love with him, with his curiously lovable ways, and had decided to become his foster parents in an attempt to give him some chance at a normal family life. Dirkie's problems, however, were rather more than love alone could conquer. He was diagnosed as having childhood schizophrenia and had a very poor prognosis for improvement. As a consequence of his truly amazing assortment of peculiar behaviors, he had not managed to survive the previous school year in a regular classroom and had ended up being taught at home.

Both Dirkie's foster parents came with him that morning, dragging Dirkie between them. He struggled and screamed. "No! No! No! Don't make me go in there! No! Help!" he yelled, nonstop.

I held the door open. Once inside, he broke free and bolted across the room. "Hoo-hoo-hoo!" he squealed with sudden glee, and leaped up on top of the table. Mariana's eyes grew wide with surprise.

"Come down from there, please, Dirkie," his foster mother said in a soft, patient tone. "Tables aren't for standing on, remember. Come down now."

"Hoo-hoo-hoo!" He was down from the table and under it.

I smiled at his foster parents. I felt an instant empathetic fondness for them. "I think we'll be all right."

The woman smiled back, and I saw her relief. I couldn't tell if it came from my confidence that we really would be all right or if it was the prospect of being free of Dirkie for six hours.

After his parents left, Dirkie remained under the table and hooted like a demented monkey.

"That kid's crazy," Mariana said seriously. "Did you know that? Did you know that kid was going to be crazy?"

I nodded.

"The other one's not going to be crazy too, is she? The girl, I mean. The girl's not going to be crazy too? She's going to be my best friend."

"I haven't met her yet, so I don't know. But she's not going to have Dirkie's problems, if that's what you mean. Everyone's different."

"Dirkie? *Dirkie?* Gad, what a stupid name. No wonder he's crazy. Hey, Turkey-Dirkie, how you doing under there?"

"Mariana . . ."

"Dirkie-Turkey. Dirkie-Turkey." Then suddenly she stopped short. She dropped down on her hands and knees to see Dirkie better through the tangle of chairs. "Gad. Look what he's doing, Teacher. He's rubbing hisself. Look, he's humping. He's humping that chair leg." She leaped to her feet.

I moved forward to take the chairs away and then reached down for Dirkie. "Hoo-hoo-hoo-hoo-hoo!" he squealed with excitement.

"Come on, Dirkie. Come out from under there. Here, take my hand. Let's sit up in a chair. I've got some interesting things in store for us today."

Rising, I dragged Dirkie out.

"Mariana!" I cried in surprise. "What *are* you doing?"

She had her jumper hiked up around her waist and was removing her underpants.

"Put everything back on this instant and pull your dress down. *Now!*"

"Ooooooh!" Dirkie said. Excitement brightened his eyes, and he slid off the chair like butter melting into a pan. The chair beside me began to convulse as he masturbated against it.

Beyond the shelving, the door to the classroom unexpectedly opened and shut, and before I could extract Dirkie from under the table again, Mrs. Considyne appeared with her hand clenched around the back of her daughter's neck.

"Good morning again," I said and smiled. I was acutely aware of Mariana, just beyond me, her underpants not yet up. Dirkie hooted maniacally.

Mrs. Considyne pushed her daughter forward. Her fingertips were white from the pressure of her grip on the child's neck.

"Hello, Leslie," I said. "I'm so glad you could make it after all. We were just preparing to start."

Leslie did not look at me but rather through me. Her expression was completely vacant.

"Here, come here. I'll show you where your cubby is. You can put your lunch box in there." I laid a hand on the girl's shoulder and gently eased her away from her mother's grasp.

Mariana materialized, fully dressed, at my side. "Hello, you," she said to Leslie. "I'm the other girl in this here class. You want to be my best friend? You want to sit with me?"

Leslie screwed up her face and slapped her hands over her ears.

"Oh, *shit*," Mariana muttered. "She's crazy, just like him."

I returned to Mrs. Considyne, who was looking fairly horrified. "I'm sure Leslie will be all right. Things are always a little hectic the first few days of a new year."

She said nothing, but rather looked past me, over my shoulder toward the children.

"I do appreciate your having gone to the trouble to bring her in, Mrs. Considyne. I realize there were problems, but it is probably a good idea that she comes on this first day."

She nodded. Looking down, she opened what I had assumed was her handbag. Instead, it was sort of a little medical kit full of bottles and cups. "Here are Leslie's things. The testers and the insulin and all that. I've put extra candy in, in case of shock. You *do* know what you're doing?" she asked, glancing up.

I hoped she meant regarding Leslie's diabetes. I nodded. "I've been shown. But Mrs. Whicker, the school nurse, is coming in to give the injections for a few weeks."

I put the bag on one of the upper shelves of the library to keep it out of the children's reach and then moved around Mrs. Considyne in an effort to encourage her to leave. Turning, she came with me.

"Oh, by the way," she said, as we reached the door, "I'm not Considyne. My husband's Considyne. My name's Taylor."

"Oh, I'm sorry, Ms. Taylor."

She shook her head. "Not Mzzz. I'm Dr. Taylor."

I felt myself blushing. "Oh. Okay. I'm sorry."

Dirkie sidled up. Standing beside me, he gazed up at Dr. Taylor for a long moment. "My," he said in a very solemn voice, "what big tits you got."

CHAPTER
TWO

Leslie Considyne was a very curious piece of work. When I returned from seeing her mother out, I found her in precisely the spot I'd left her. Taking out a chair from the table, I indicated it to her. She sat. There was nothing mechanical about her movements. In fact, she moved with a surprisingly fluid grace, but she appeared to have no one at home inside her body. The entire morning she acted only when instructed. Otherwise, she remained wherever she was, staring vacantly ahead, and without a muscle ever twitching. She would not look at me or at the other children. Even when I sat directly in front of her and lined her face up with mine, she continued to look ahead, straight through me, as if I were not there. I could tell she wasn't seeing me. What I couldn't tell was if it was a conscious effort.

Although I had been led to believe that Dirkie would be my most disturbed child, Leslie presented a more disconcerting appearance that morning. She was the only one of the three who did not speak and was not toilet trained. She also had brittle diabetes, which necessitated a harrowing round of injections midday. Even this got no reaction from her. The nurse came in, took her aside, injected her, and Leslie never flicked an eyelash. She never even looked down at what the nurse was doing.

When the children had gone for lunch at 12:15, I sat down at the worktable with the files. Having now met all three children, I looked forward to understanding more what had been written about them.

There was a quick rap at the classroom door and then it opened. I looked up. Once again, my view was blocked by the shelving, and I could tell that not being able to see the door from the main part of the classroom was going to drive me mad. "Come on in," I called and waited for someone to appear.

"Just me. How did it go? Okay?" It was Carolyn, the special education teacher from the class in the basement.

I nodded. "Pretty good."

She grinned. "You want to come to Enrico's with us? That's where everybody here goes at noon."

"Thanks, but I've brought my lunch. I need to catch up on all this stuff before the afternoon. Maybe I'll join you tomorrow."

"Who all have you got?" she asked, coming over and leaning down to look at the names on the files.

I liked Carolyn. I'd liked her instantly, which was fortunate, since we were the only two teachers in the building. She was about my age, still single and unabashedly concerned about it, easy-going, gregarious and inclined to speak before thinking, which gave her a refreshing naturalness.

Suddenly Carolyn whistled under her breath. "You got Considyne? Is this *the* Considyne?"

"I wouldn't know. Have you had Leslie too?"

"Oh God, no. *Thank* God, no. The kid is absolutely wacko, which is all right, because it makes her fit in with the rest of the family. You live here for any time at all and you'll know all you need to know about the Considynes. Or rather, Tom Considyne and *Dr.* Taylor."

"Yes, believe it or not, I've already had that pointed out to me."

Carolyn flipped open Leslie's file. Pointing to the father's name, she said, "He's an artist. Supposed to be famous, although I've sure never heard of him anywhere."

Then a wicked grin creased Carolyn's features, and she pulled out a chair and sat down. "You want to hear the gossip about them? It's pretty hot." She reached over and helped herself to my potato chips. "She's supposed to be this absolute genius; anyway that's what people say. She's a scientist of some sort. God knows how they met one another. But talk about a father fixation. She's like twenty-five years younger than he is. Anyway, she was working back East at some university or other and commuting back and forth. They had their own private plane, jetting all over creation and part of Canada. She was even in Moscow once. Then all of a sudden it stopped. She got fired off what she was doing; that's what I heard said. She has this fairly dramatic drinking problem, as you'll no doubt discover, and I'm sure that's what happened to her.

"So now *we've* got her, and she's a pretty lively case, believe me. She has all these affairs. She isn't even discreet about it. I know for a fact that she's had an affair with Dr. Addison from up at the children's clinic. It's got to be humiliating for Mr. Considyne, because everybody knows she's doing it. I suppose it must be because of the way she looks. I mean, if I looked like that, I'd probably have me a sugar daddy and keep a string on the side too." Carolyn laughed.

I regarded my cheese sandwich glumly. This was the kind of thing you liked to hear about people you didn't really know, not the parents of the children in your schoolroom.

"Trash with class, that's what it boils down to," Carolyn said. She leaned across the table and helped herself to my grapes. "She puts on all these airs. I mean, look at this silly business about *Dr.* Taylor. She thinks she's too good to even talk to the rest of us. She'll never even say hello. And who is she? What would she be if she weren't Tom Considyne's little bimbo? He's the one who's famous. He's got all the money. But he's nice. He's real friendly, if you run into him down at the Co-op or something. If he's been introduced to you, he'll always remember your name. If he's got any fault, it's that he's too casual about things. He tends not to follow through. He drove Rita wild last year. She was Leslie's first-grade teacher. She was always arranging things with him to try and help Leslie, and he was always promising to do them, but he never did. That, and also he never answers his phone. If their help's out, you'll never be able to contact him, short of knocking the door down. He's got a studio out in back of his house where he does his painting, and last year when Leslie went into a diabetic coma, Rita stood outside his studio knocking on the window, and he never even bothered to turn around and see who it was."

"This sounds like a soap opera, Carolyn."

"Ooooh, it's better," she said, with a gleam in her eye. "It's real."

I grimaced.

Carolyn smiled knowingly and pulled over the rest of the files to look at them. "You want me to fill you in on these too?"

"You know about them?" I asked incredulously.

She laughed. "No. But I'm sure I could think of something."

We both dissolved into giggles.

After Carolyn left, I opened the Considyne file. There was nothing in there that hinted at the steamy stories Carolyn had been telling me. Dr. Taylor was a physicist. Mr. Considyne was listed simply as a painter. The first time I'd read it, I'd thought it meant housepainter. The only thing to have caught my eye initially was Dr. Taylor's first name: Ladbrooke. The peculiarity of it had not struck me so much as idle curiosity over what, in intimate moments, one would call someone with such a formal name.

There was a fairly extensive sheaf of papers on Leslie and her disturbance. As in so many cases of severe handicaps of this nature, there was little certainty about exactly what her problem was and what had caused it. Apparently her birth and early infancy had been normal. She was a full-term baby and, while placid and not particularly responsive, she'd been easy to care for. Her progress past the usual milestones had been slow, but within normal limits. Then, somewhere around two and a half, she had begun to deteriorate. What little vocabulary she did have disappeared. What progress she'd made in terms of toilet training and self-care was lost. A futile round of doctors and psychiatrists started soon after Leslie was three. Autism, one report said. Mental retardation, said another. Childhood schizophrenia, said a third. No one seemed to know for sure, but everyone was willing to guess.

Amazingly, to my way of thinking, Leslie had had no special treatment program and, indeed, was kept in a regular classroom for two years. She had, in fact, spent more time in the classroom than had Mariana. There were a few acerbic jottings from Rita Ashworth, Leslie's previous teacher, about the challenges this presented, and I got the impression that in the end, Leslie had been left pretty much to her own devices.

There was nothing written anywhere to suggest how Leslie's parents had come to terms with their daughter's handicap nor anything about what the home situation was like. There was a brief mention of two older stepchildren and how the younger of them, a teenaged girl, had a poor relationship with Leslie, but there was nothing else.

The first week passed. The three children were very different from one another, and I did nothing more than scuttle among them those first days, trying to keep order. Both Leslie and Dirkie could have done with a teacher apiece. Dirkie was fairly advanced in comparison to many other schizophrenic children I'd encountered. He was toilet trained, could express himself quite well, could follow simple instructions, and even had mastered a fair number of academic skills, although at a level way below what would have been expected for his chronological age. However, he still needed virtual one-to-one teaching to stay on task.

Dirkie's worst problems came from an assortment of obsessions with things that were very commonly encountered, such as cats, hair, old men and women, fire engines and door hinges. Discharging the excitement generated by the obsessions took the better part of most days. First, an obsession would come to mind—perhaps he'd see a picture or hear a sound, and that would start him off. Then he'd become excited, then agitated, then frenzied, needing desperately to fulfill elaborate rituals before he could free his mind and think of something else. I became able to discern when one of the obsessions was overtaking Dirkie, because he would begin to talk in an odd voice. He spoke in a weird manner most of the time, with his voice deep and gravelly, like a child imitating its father, although

Dirkie did have a normal speaking voice, rarely used. However, when one of his obsessions overtook him, Dirkie's voice grew deeper and became urgent sounding, taking on a tone that made him sound permanently appalled. Then, as the excitement increased, he'd lose control and be unable to form words. He hooted instead. Hoo-hoo-hoo-hoo-hoo. No other sound, just that. And he'd begin to clap. Physical excitement took over from there, and he could no longer sit still. On his feet, he'd adopt a mincing, disjointed sort of locomotion, like a marionette with a very bad operator, and usually, he'd end up under the table, where he'd sit, clapping and hooting, and frequently, masturbating frantically on the table leg. Then calm would return.

Sometimes I could successfully interrupt the hoot-and-clap syndrome early enough to quell the frenzy and reorient Dirkie to the task at hand. More often, I couldn't. And if he'd gone beyond a certain point, he needed to continue, because otherwise, he exploded, screaming and yelling, kicking and slapping, tearing papers from the bulletin boards, magazines from the shelves, overturning chairs, ripping his clothes and banging himself against walls and furniture. But even without such cataclysmic conclusions, Dirkie's obsessions ruled us.

"Do you have a cat?" he asked me on the first day.

"Yes," I answered, not realizing what I had started.

His eyes grew shiny with excitement. "What kind is it?"

"Just a cat. Tabby and white."

But that wasn't enough information. "How tall is it? How long is its tail?"

Thinking to put him off, I explained it wasn't even my cat, but rather a cat on loan from my grandparents to keep me company. So I didn't know the beast too intimately. But this didn't put Dirkie off. Indeed, the novelty of the arrangement intrigued him, and he questioned me endlessly. "What color eyes does your cat have? When's his birthday? How long did your grandparents have him before you got him? Here," he demanded and gave me a piece of paper. "Draw a picture of your cat." When I demurred, he panicked. "Draw it! Draw it! Draw your cat! Draw your cat in his basket. Draw your cat in the bathtub. Draw your cat eating food," he screamed, his voice becoming louder with each demand. So I began to draw, and immediately, Dirkie quieted. "That's your cat. You're drawing your cat. You're drawing your cat sitting up." But when I finished, he thrust another sheet of paper under my nose. "Draw your cat lying down." The room was soon a veritable gallery of my rather undistinguished cat drawings.

Our whole relationship began to revolve around my cat. Every time Dirkie saw me, he had to query me exhaustively about my cat. This conversation could be repeated twenty or thirty times over the course of the day. All I had to do was go out of Dirkie's range of vision and return and he'd need to have a cat conversation with me. And if it wasn't my cat, it was other cats. Did Mrs. Renton, the secretary, have a cat? Was it a big, yellow tomcat? Did it weigh seven pounds? Did it eat from a green bowl? A white bowl? I felt ridiculous asking Mrs. Renton what color bowl she fed her cat from, but I did ask. It was either that or make it up.

Equally absorbing to Dirkie but with considerably less scope for conversation was the length of my hair. I had quite long hair, well past my shoulders, and this fascinated Dirkie. "You have long hair," he would say. "I like your hair. Are you going to cut it?"

"No," I'd reply.

"Don't cut your hair. Leave your hair long. I like it long. I like long hair."

This would be quickly followed by: "I need to touch your hair."

He was, I quickly discovered, much better off not touching my hair. On the occasions he did, it only fueled his excitement, and he'd run off in a full hooting session. He also tended to grab and pull *very* hard instead of simply touching.

But the conversation over long hair was repeated, if anything, more often than our cat conversation. Or perhaps it just seemed like it, since there were not many dimensions of my hair to talk about. Again and again he asked me about it. One morning I counted him asking me about my long hair fourteen times during one hour. By the end of the first day, I was tying my hair back. By Friday, I was ready to shave it all off.

Leslie proved to be only slightly less of a challenge than Dirkie, and in some ways, she was more. Being untrained, she left me with the distasteful task of wrestling wet diapers off her several times a day, made less pleasant by the need to root around in them with a dipstick to check her sugar levels. Changing her presented other problems. Either I had to leave the other two alone in the classroom while I rushed Leslie down the hall to the girls' rest room, or else I had to retire discreetly to the depths of the steel shelving and hope there weren't going to be any nasty surprises. Taking Dirkie and Mariana to the rest room with me was out of the question. Seeing Leslie undressed and my cleaning her proved too much stimulation for Dirkie. He would masturbate frenetically against the sink or toilet-stall doors and use incredibly descriptive language. This, in turn, would get Mariana going. Sexuality and sexual matters were very much a part of both children's disturbances, and I couldn't allow Leslie to be exploited in this way. But it made the logistics of changing her difficult to cope with.

In the classroom, Leslie did nothing. If I told her to sit, she sat. But if I didn't, she would remain stranded wherever I had left her. She did nothing without being physically oriented to it and told to do it, but once started, she would continue a task until physically stopped. For example, if I gave her crayons and paper and asked her to draw, she would begin making marks on the paper and continue until the entire page was covered and still continue coloring over this.

She was the most withdrawn child I had encountered. I had the impression some days of not only mental absence, but almost of physical absence as well, as if she weren't really there at all, as if I were in the company of a hologram.

On the other hand, admittedly, Leslie was no trouble in other ways. If left to her own devices, she got up to no mischief. She got up to nothing whatsoever, other than a little self-stimulation. She didn't speak. She gave no indication of being able to, although her file stated that she had spoken, when younger. She made no noises whatsoever except when she cried, which wasn't often.

In my opinion, Leslie needed very intensive work, the kind of one-to-one stimulation that was next to impossible within the constraints of my classroom. I had to leave her far too often quietly "disappeared." I compensated by using every spare opportunity to make physical contact, to hold her, to touch her, to cuddle her and keep her close. Even then, Leslie seemed to be not much more than a body with no child in it, but holding her was the only way I could reassure myself that she really existed.

Poor Mariana was in lousy company. Regardless of her own problems, compared to Dirkie and Leslie, she was a world ahead. Glumly accepting that she was going to have no best friend in this class, she took her folder of work each morning and sat alone at the far end of the table. She was just as hopeless at academics as everyone had said and could have used a whole lot more of my time, but her difficulties were neither serious enough nor dramatic enough to compete with those of the other two. I was grateful for Mariana's presence, however, from a purely selfish point of view. She was someone with whom I could have an occasional sane conversation. And I tried to reserve her some special, uninterrupted time, but with Leslie and Dirkie, that was a challenge. They couldn't be ignored, and Mariana was capable of understanding that sometimes I did have to ignore her. So she soldiered on without complaint.

I knew what I needed—an aide. Desperately. During most of my years as a teacher in special education, I'd worked with children at the severe end of the emotional-disturbance spectrum and had had some kind of assistance in the classroom. Even with my smallest classes, there had been an extra pair of hands. It made all the difference in the world. Someone to change Leslie or watch the others while I did, someone to oversee while I gave a child individual instruction, someone to provide feedback, to laugh with, to chew over the day's events, to compare bruises on the shins with—that was what I needed.

I discussed the matter with Carolyn. We had joined the local health club and started going down to the spa most evenings after work for a swim and a sauna, or a soak in the whirlpool. I quizzed her during those relaxed evenings. She had one full-time trained aide and two volunteers, who appeared regularly. Being so new to the community, I didn't have the resources necessary to locate volunteers. Where had she found hers? Did she know of anyone else who might be interested? Did she have any alternate ideas?

I also went to talk to Frank Cotton, the Director of Special Education. I got to know Frank much better than I had any previous director, which was the one advantage of having a classroom in the administration building. I saw him daily. He was one of the gang, taking his coffee breaks in the teachers' lounge with us, eating lunch with us at Enrico's, and this quickly put us on a genuine first-name basis, the way it is with friends.

"I'm beginning to think it's me," I said. We were in his office, a long, narrow room converted from a storage closet, chosen because it abutted the main office, a former classroom. "I've got only three kids, for crying out loud, but it's just not coming together as a class." I explained my feelings of constantly shuttling between Dirkie and Leslie and getting nothing else accomplished.

Frank leaned back in his chair. He smiled gently. "You're feeling out of practice."

I nodded and grinned. "Yes, I guess it is a bit of that. But I keep thinking, we're going to make a cohesive group out of this lot yet. I was always so good at that in the old days. I could make a group out of any sort of rabble. But it's not happening this time."

"It's early yet," Frank said.

"It still should be giving some sign of happening."

Frank continued to lean back. He fingered his lip. "Not enough kids."

"Quite enough kids, thank you."

"No, I mean it. Not enough to make a group of. You've always had bigger classes before, haven't you?"

I nodded. "But not much. I had only four when I was teaching at the state hospital, and we made a hell of a group there." I smiled in what I hoped was a very disarming way. "What I *need*, Frank, is an aide."

"Wish I could afford one for you."

I knew I couldn't have one, even before I'd said it, but it felt good to put it in words, to say it to someone in charge. "Any volunteers that you know of?"

He shook his head. "Not that I'm aware of. You should ask Carolyn. She seems to keep a secret supply."

"I've tried Carolyn already. No luck."

We continued to talk. Frank slowly diverted the conversation away from my aide business and on to other things. When a natural pause came into the conversation, he leaned forward. I sensed a change of topic. Clasping his hands together, Frank pressed them pensively against his lips a moment and stared at the orderly stacks of papers on his desk. His eyes rose to meet mine.

"That earlier conversation . . ." He paused, looked away, looked back. "It's going to make what I have to say now a little harder."

I wondered suddenly if I had done something wrong.

Frank smiled. "It's nothing major. It's just that . . . well, how can I say it? You're getting two more children next week."

"Two?"

"Yes. Sisters. Five and eight. They're from Northern Ireland."

"Oh."

"Their family's been embroiled in the trouble going on over there, and now the girls have come to live with relatives to get them out of all that, to give them a new start, that sort of thing. They've been up at Washington Elementary since school started, but it isn't working out. They're not integrating."

"I see."

"The younger one isn't talking at all, so I thought of you immediately. With your experience in elective mutism, your room seemed the ideal place for them."

I think I was too stunned to talk. Here I'd come in to complain about being unable to cope with the children I had, and I was ending up with two more.

If Frank sensed my benumbed state, he was ignoring it. "Like I said earlier, I think you need more kids to get organized. Three's not a group. At least those three aren't. Besides, it'll be better for Mariana Gilchrist." He smiled cheerfully. "This way, you can get the momentum going."

I didn't doubt that.

CHAPTER THREE

I remember, as a girl, hearing a newscast about the Troubles in Northern Ireland and asking my grandfather to explain the issue to me. When he had, it offended my child's sensibilities. A war between the Catholics and the Protestants? How could that be? I'd asked him. They wouldn't even be able to tell themselves apart.

They would and they could and they did. My few years in Wales, another Celtic country still chafing hundreds of years after English conquest, had given me more insight into the issue, into its remarkable complexity, into its lack of resolution. But more than anything, my time there had made me well aware that I still had no understanding of the matter. I remained an American, born and raised in a young country created from immigrant diversity. I had no resources upon which to call when it came to comprehending four-hundred-year-old memories of invaders and usurpers. I had no eye for seeing the differences that they saw among themselves and even less for appreciating their need to see them. As a result, I came back from Wales with nothing more than the knowledge that I didn't know. The only thing I did have a strong conviction about was the violence—too prevalent and too senseless. It destroyed my sympathies for both causes.

As a consequence, perhaps I was a particularly inappropriate choice of teacher for these two girls. Our community had a strong Irish connection and was openly pro-IRA. The story of the girls preceded them. Long before I ever met them, I heard about them in the grocery store and the gas station, their history being passed on word-of-mouth, like an epic saga. I came to recognize the sad expression and the sorrowful tone of voice that accompanied the telling; the children were made minor celebrities by their suffering.

According to the stories, the girls' father had been an active IRA man. About eighteen months previously, he was arrested by the Royal Ulster

Constabulary in a big sweep-up operation and accused of participating in some very serious acts, including murder. However, he was released shortly afterward. Rumor sprang up that he was, in fact, an informer, although no concrete evidence was presented to substantiate this. Soon, he and his family were being harassed, although no one yet seemed to know who was doing what. Was it the IRA getting back at their own? One of the splinter groups? Or was it the paramilitary wing of one of the Protestant groups exploiting the advantage of having an IRA man identified? Whatever, one night a petrol bomb was thrown through the letter slot in the front door. The house caught fire, and while the father managed to rescue his two daughters, his wife and young son died in the blaze. Within three weeks of the fire, the man was found hanged in his brother's garage, a suicide. The girls were shunted back and forth among relatives in the large, extended family until finally, in midsummer, they were granted American visas to come and live here with their father's sister and her husband.

After all this presage, actually meeting Geraldine and Shemona McCulley the Monday morning they arrived in my class was a bit of a disappointment. They were something out of a myth by that time, and I think I was expecting them to look the part. They didn't. They were two very ordinary little girls with moon-shaped, freckled faces and blue-gray eyes. Shemona, poignantly named after what her mother had believed to be a peace settlement in Israel, but which turned out to be a town victimized by the same kind of terrorism as Belfast, was the younger child. She had longish, rumpled-looking blond hair and grubby knees. Geraldine wore glasses with ghastly pink plastic frames that gave her the look of a fifties housewife. Her dark hair was cut in a short, blunt style that we used to call a Dutch bob when I was little.

Frank and the girls' aunt brought them in early, before the other children had arrived. The sisters entered meekly, the younger one clutching a well-worn stuffed monkey in one hand and her aunt's coattail in the other. Mrs. Lonrho indicated the chairs at the table, and both girls sat down primly, still in their coats, hands folded in their laps. Mrs. Lonrho knelt beside Shemona. She pushed the child's hair back from her eyes in a gentle gesture. "You be good here, okay? You do as the lady says. She's here to help you." Then she rose. She turned to me. "They're good girls."

Alone with them, I suggested they take off their coats and then showed them where their hooks were, and their cubbies. Back at the table, they sat side by side. I took out a chair opposite them. I'd made up folders for them to work from. Geraldine reached over and took first her own folder and examined it, and then Shemona's. The younger girl just sat, the stuffed monkey clutched against her, and did nothing.

"We work a little differently in here than in most classes," I said. "Everyone is in a different place, so each person has to be responsible for doing the work in her own folder. I come around and help you with it throughout the day, but sometimes I need to be with another child, and then you have to work on your own. Sometimes you'll get stuck when I'm with someone else, and I won't be able to come right away to help you. If that happens, you need to skip that part and go on to do something else until I'm free."

Geraldine nodded. "I can do these," she said and pointed to one of the papers. "I can do this work." She glanced briefly at her sister's folder. "And Shemona says she can do hers too."

Shemona sat, immobile. She gazed at me steadily, her eyes, like her face, veiled with an unreadable expression.

Mariana was delighted. "This here girl's going to be my best friend," she said almost immediately upon entering the room and seeing Shemona and Geraldine. She hauled her chair up next to Geraldine's. "You want to be my best friend? You want a Life Saver? And then you give me something nice and we'll be best friends. Okay? You wanna do that?"

Geraldine's face brightened at the sight of the candy and she accepted it eagerly, popping it into her mouth. Then she looked expectantly for more. "Shemona wants one," she said.

Mariana looked up.

"Give Shemona a sweetie."

"*You're* going to be my best friend. Not her. She's too little."

With a suddenness none of us had anticipated, Geraldine snatched the roll of Life Savers from Mariana's hands. She deftly popped a candy out and handed it to her sister.

Mariana burst into tears. "They're mine! My mommy bought them for me."

"Hey," I said and reached down to take the Life Savers from Geraldine. "None of this, please."

At that, Geraldine burst into tears as well.

Dirkie arrived at that point. "Who are they?" he asked, his voice going gravelly with excitement.

"Sit down, Dirkie. These are our two new girls. Remember, I told you last Friday that we'd be having some new children today. Now please sit down."

Geraldine snuffled.

Mariana still bawled. "They're mine, Teacher."

"All right. Here." I gave her back the roll of candy. "Now, what's the rule regarding bringing in candy?"

Mariana said nothing.

"You've got to *share*," Dirkie said with great feeling. He was cottoning on to the presence of the candy.

"That's right. You have to share. Now, if you gave Geraldine a piece, it's only fair that you give Shemona one. And Dirkie. Then put them away, unless you want to share them all out."

Mariana began to cry again. "That's not fair. My mommy bought them for *me*."

"I can appreciate how you feel. You like your candy and you want to keep it. But it also isn't fair to give a piece just to Geraldine. Geraldine was right to be concerned about her sister, although perhaps she needn't have snatched the candy in quite that way."

Mariana begrudgingly handed out a Life Saver to Dirkie and then returned to her seat to count how many were left. She squirreled the rest of them away in the pocket of her jumper. "What are you gonna give *me* now?" she asked Geraldine.

Geraldine shrugged. "Haven't anything."

Glumly, Mariana kicked the leg of the table. "Some best friend you've turned out to be."

Dirkie was mesmerized by the two girls. He spent much of the morning simply watching them. Then after lunch he took to circling the table, and it occurred to me what was so fascinating to him: It was Shemona's hair. Leslie's hair was longer and even Mariana's hair was quite long, and as I had never noticed Dirkie showing interest in either of them, I had assumed he was only preoccupied with adult hair. So I was a bit surprised and certainly dismayed to discover he was attracted to Shemona's. The only thing I could reckon was that Shemona, like me, was blond, while both Mariana and Leslie were dark. This lent a new dimension to Dirkie's obsession. Whatever was behind it, he could not leave Shemona's hair alone. Around and around and around the table he went, his body slightly crouched, his muscles tense with excitement. When he would get in back of her, he'd pause, quivering. If either Shemona or Geraldine turned to look at him, he would jump and then begin circling again. "Hoo-hoo-hoo," he was whispering under his breath.

"Dirkie, sit *down*," I said. I was holding Leslie on my lap and trying to work with her, so it was inconvenient to have to keep getting up to reseat him. And his circling was nerve-wracking.

Dirkie moved off, but within moments he was back, once again circling like a hyena with its quarry.

"Miss," Geraldine said, "Shemona doesn't like this. This boy is bothering her." "Miss" was the only thing Geraldine would call me.

"Dirkie," I said, "sit down. Now *sit*. You've got plenty of work in your folder, so please come here, sit down and get busy."

I pulled his folder closer to where I was sitting, and when he came over, I sat him next to me. Geraldine, farther down and across the table from us, raised her head to watch us.

"You're a girl," Dirkie said to her, his voice low.

"So?"

"She's a girl too," he said, indicating Shemona.

Geraldine rolled her eyes in an expression of incredulity and went back to her work.

"And she's a girl and she's a girl," Dirkie continued, pointing to Mariana and Leslie. "And *you're* a girl!" he said to me. "You know what that means?"

"Girls' pussies," Mariana supplied. She giggled.

Geraldine looked scandalized.

"Girls, girls, girls!" Dirkie said excitedly.

"Dirk, time to settle down. Here, let's get on with your work." I took a paper from his folder.

He studied Shemona, bent over her work. "And *that* girl," he said pointedly, "that girl there, that girl with the yellow hair, with the long yellow hair, she's a girl. She's got a girl's pisser, that girl with the long yellow hair."

"Dirkie, I mean it, settle down."

The excitement proved too much for him, and Dirkie was up once more, mincing around the table to Shemona.

"Mii-iissss!" squealed Geraldine in exasperation. "We're trying to work. Make that boy stop."

Putting Leslie off my lap, I rose and went to catch Dirkie. Taking him by the shoulder, I physically returned him to his chair and pushed him into it.

"That girl has long yellow hair. You have long hair. You have long yellow hair too. Are you going to cut your long yellow hair?"

"No, Dirkie."

"That girl, is she going to cut her hair? Is that girl going to cut her long yellow hair?"

"She might," Geraldine said waspishly.

"No, Dirkie, she isn't going to cut her hair either. Now come on. Here's today's math. Let's see if you can get it finished before recess. I'll help you get started."

But he couldn't reorient. "Hey, girl," he said, "girl with the long yellow hair, do you have a cat?"

Geraldine came over to me toward the end of the afternoon. "Shemona doesn't like that boy, Miss."

"Yes, he can be annoying, that's for certain. But if Shemona doesn't like him, all she needs to do is tell him to go away. And he will. He doesn't mean any harm."

Geraldine frowned.

"What about you?" I asked. "What do you think of him?"

"Shemona thinks he's silly. So do I."

I was grateful to see that particular day done. While nothing major happened, it had been hard work. I'd been nervous about these two girls with all their tragic fame, and it had left me on edge. The others were unsettled by the change. Dirkie, especially, had remained impossible all day long, and I was ready to skewer him by the last hour. In an effort to hasten the end, I agreed to let everyone out on the playground five minutes early to wait for their rides. It was a clear, sharp September day, and I knew the tensions would evaporate more quickly in the brisk air.

Mariana's and Dirkie's buses came. Then Shemona and Geraldine's aunt arrived to collect them. That left just Leslie, holding my hand.

"Where's your mama?" I asked. "It's not like her to be late." I scanned the length of the street for Dr. Taylor's dark blue Mercedes. Normally, she was extremely punctual, waiting at the wheel of the car when I brought the children down. She even occasionally came up to the classroom to get Leslie, if I ran a minute or two late.

We waited for a few moments longer, and then I took Leslie around the corner of the building to the playground and pushed her on the swing. She adored swinging. It was the single activity to evoke any kind of genuine response from her. She would close her eyes and let her head fall back, her long, dark hair fanning out behind her. While swinging, Leslie came the closest I had seen her come to smiling.

No doubt Leslie would have been happy to stay on the swing until dark, but I had a special ed. meeting at 4:45 in a nearby school, so my time wasn't totally my own. Ten, fifteen, twenty minutes slipped by, and still no Dr. Taylor. By four o'clock, I decided things had gone on long enough. I let the swing come to a stop and took Leslie inside to the office, where I telephoned the Considynes' home.

No answer. I wasn't sure what to do. Could I leave Leslie down here? Should I take her to her house myself and trust someone would be there by then? Or should I just keep waiting? I dialed the Considynes' number once more and let the phone ring and ring.

Upstairs in the classroom again, I got Leslie settled with some toys while I sat down at the table and looked over my notes for the meeting. As 4:20 approached, tension returned. The Considynes lived at the opposite end of town from where I was going; if I left with Leslie now, I wouldn't get back in time for the start of the meeting. And what if no one was there? What then?

Where the hell had Dr. Taylor gotten to? I went out in the hallway and down to the end, where I could see the street in front of the building from the stairwell window. I searched up and down the tree-lined road for some sign of the Mercedes. This was definitely atypical of her. I had previously been impressed with her Colditz-style precision. Leslie appeared and disappeared each day at exactly the right moment. She was always clean, neat and supplied with all the necessary accoutrements, which was no mean feat, considering the number of disposable diapers, needles, syringes, blood-sugar tapes and such that Leslie required. Dr. Taylor never troubled me with any discussion over things. Leslie and her paraphernalia were brought and collected without my ever exchanging so much as a "hello" with Dr. Taylor. It was formal, but efficient. So this unexpected lateness concerned me.

Leslie trailed into the hallway after me.

"Come here, sweetheart," I said, and extended an arm. "I'm not sure where your mama's gotten to, but I know she'll come. You'll get home all right." I hugged her against me.

In desperation, I took Leslie down to Carolyn's room. She was due at the same meeting I was and so was just preparing to leave. I explained what was happening and asked if she'd pass on the information. I'd try to get over as soon as I could.

I was also worried about Leslie's diabetes. She had a very strict regimen of snacks and meals, and I knew she was going to need to eat soon to keep her insulin level in line. Carolyn provided some crackers and milk left over from her pupils' snack time.

"Are you coming to the spa tonight?"

I nodded.

"If you don't make it to the meeting," she said, "I'll see you there. You can tell me all about this." And she gave me a demonic grin.

Back I went to the office and tried the Considynes' number. Still no answer. Was Mr. Considyne home and not answering? Or was no one there at all?

I returned to the classroom. Leaning against the radiator, I stared out the window. The door opened behind me, and my heart rose in anticipation. I turned to get Leslie's coat. But before I could, the footsteps disappeared into the library. Two voices muttered quietly to one another, the sound filtering indistinctly out to Leslie and me. I looked at her; she looked at me. I think she was disappointed too.

Pulling a chair out from the table, I sat down. Leslie, standing beside me, moved to get onto my lap. I closed my arms around her.

"Don't worry, lovey. Your mama wouldn't forget about a lovely girl like you. I'm sure it's probably just some little thing that's held her up. We just need to be patient."

Leslie relaxed against me. She was a snuggly child and burrowed in against my breasts. Her hair smelled of herbal shampoo. I rested my cheek against it.

The people using the library left, and all went quiet again. Five o'clock came and then 5:15. I decided I would wait until 5:30 and then ring Frank. I listened to each minute being ticked noisily away by the clock over the blackboard, and they all seemed to last forever. I gazed at the clouds in the sky beyond the window as they turned pink with the approaching sunset. Silent and motionless, Leslie remained in my lap.

Then, slam, bang went the classroom door and there was Dr. Taylor. I glanced at my watch. It was 5:25, nearly two hours since school had ended.

"I'm late," she said and that was all the explanation she offered. She had stopped at the corner of the shelving units and came no closer. Holding out her hand toward Leslie, she gave a slight jerk of her head. Leslie responded immediately, sliding off my lap and running to her mother.

What I noticed was that Dr. Taylor looked wonderful. She always dressed casually, but in a very fashionable way, the way I would have liked to dress if I'd had the money and the fashion sense. This afternoon it was all wool and denim and leather boots. Her complexion was ruddy, as if she had been out a while in the brisk autumn air, and it suited her. She had very fair skin, and normally she looked unhealthy to me. Momentarily mesmerized by her appearance, I forgot my irritation. But as I rose and came abreast of her, while she was bent, doing up the buttons of Leslie's coat, I realized abruptly that her ruddy glow was not due to health.

Dr. Taylor was drunk.

I was too shocked to react immediately. I just stood there, watching her fumble with the buttons, as the dark, oaky smell of whiskey wafted around us. The arrival of an inebriated parent wasn't a wholly novel experience for me, but this had been so unexpected that I was speechless.

Without so much as an acknowledgment of my presence, she finished the buttons, stood, turned and ushered Leslie toward the door.

"Dr. Taylor?"

She was at the door but paused to look back at me.

I didn't know quite what to say next, and the pause grew overlong. She turned away again and went on out.

"Dr. Taylor, are you alone?"

She was into the hallway.

"Wait," I said and went after her. "Dr. Taylor? Wait a minute."

No response.

She was a tall woman with a long stride, and I had to skip to get in front of her. "Dr. Taylor, stop."

"What do you want?"

"Are you driving?"

She pushed around me.

I quickly reached for Leslie's free hand. Both of them came to an abrupt halt. Leslie whimpered.

"I could drive you home," I said.

"No. Thank you," she replied and reached down, deftly disengaging my fingers from Leslie's hand. The smell of whiskey as she leaned forward was strong enough to make me step back.

She shoved Leslie ahead of her and approached the stairwell.

"Dr. Taylor, please."

No response.

I could negotiate the stairs faster. Stepping forward, I grabbed hold of the collar of Leslie's coat.

This brought a ferocious glare from Dr. Taylor. She was still a step above me, so she towered over me physically. In fact, she felt about eight feet tall at that precise moment. I moved a little to the side.

"I don't need your help, thank you," she said through gritted teeth. Her tone left nothing to the imagination.

I kept hold of Leslie's coat. "I'm not sure it's a good idea for you to be driving."

Her eyes widened into an expression of utter incredulity. It made me feel small, to be stared at like that, as if I'd said something so dumb as to beggar belief. But I kept my fingers around Leslie's collar.

"Leslie is my responsibility at this point," I said. "And I don't think I'd feel comfortable if she went with you."

Dr. Taylor said nothing but continued to fix me with that stare. She really was a remarkably beautiful woman. It was unsettling to me, because I couldn't keep from noticing it, even at a moment like this, when she made obvious the old adage about beauty being only skin deep. But ignoring her appearance was like trying to ignore a drastic deformity.

And she wasn't giving in. She had eyes like a reptile's. They didn't blink.

"Please, let's be sensible about this," I said.

"Let go."

"Please? Come on now, Dr. Taylor. Be reasonable."

"I said, let *go.*"

"Let me drive Leslie then. You go as you want, but let me take Leslie."

"Can't you hear me?" she asked.

"Come on now."

"*Let go,*" she said, her voice barely above a whisper.

"Please?"

Her eyes narrowed, and in a very calculated manner, she reached her hand toward mine. Ruefully, I uncurled my fingers from Leslie's coat collar and let go before Dr. Taylor's hand touched me.

The moment I did, Dr. Taylor and her daughter disappeared down the stairwell and were gone.

Carolyn laughed. She threw back her head and really howled. We were the only two in the whirlpool, but I slid down into the water until it was up around my neck so that the people over by the swimming pool couldn't see me.

"It's not that funny, Carolyn."

"She really laid it on you, didn't she? Well, it serves you right. It *does,* Torey," she said and leaned forward. "You think because you're new here, you're classless. You think you can mess with small-town politics."

"I wasn't messing with politics. The woman was stone drunk."

Carolyn closed her eyes and relaxed back against the side of the whirlpool. "You're better off leaving her alone. They're different from us."

"Oh, that's silly, Carolyn. What rubbish." I pulled myself up out of the deeper water and sat back beside her on the bench.

Carolyn remained in her relaxed pose. "It's not. They're rich. They've got a different kind of lifestyle than the rest of us. Different kinds of friends." She opened her eyes and looked over. "You know what happened to Carly Johnston, you know, the girl who runs the gallery on Rosten Street? She got invited out to one of Tom Considyne's big bashes a couple of years ago. It was a Christmas party, I think. Anyway, you know what they gave for party favors?"

I shook my head.

"Coke. Cocaine. Half a gram of coke."

I said nothing.

"I'm not kidding, Tor."

"I didn't think you were, but she wasn't high, Carolyn. She was drunk. Plain old booze, like you buy over the counter in the supermarket. And I'm not thinking of busting into her jet-set lifestyle. I'm thinking of Leslie." Carolyn didn't respond. She closed her eyes again and stretched out to let the whirlpool jets run against her arms.

Brooding, I remained upright on the bench. I looked over. "Did Dr. Taylor come to the school drunk like this last year?"

"Yeah," Carolyn said without opening her eyes. "I didn't see much of her. My room was on the far side of the building, and Leslie was in Rita

Ashworth's room. But she was drunk quite a lot. She drove Rita bonkers more than a few times with it. She'd be sober for ages and then come in absolutely blotto two or three times a week for a while. Rita never knew what to expect. It was worst in midwinter. It got to be a joke among us. You know how you get about things like that."

"Didn't anybody do anything about it?" I asked.

"Like what, precisely?" Carolyn half-opened her eyes and looked over at me.

"I don't know. But she's got to be doing herself a fair amount of harm. She's young. What age is she? Thirty? Thirty-five?"

"I mean really, Torey, who cares? She isn't exactly the poor-and-dying of Calcutta, is she? She's such an arrogant so-and-so. She couldn't give a fuck about you or me, if you'll forgive my French. So I'm not about to play Mother Teresa for her benefit. Nobody is."

I didn't respond.

Carolyn looked over. "Has she ever said more than two words to you?"

"No. Not really."

"See what I mean? Besides, we're schoolteachers, not social workers. Or psychiatrists, which is what I suspect the woman really needs."

"I'm thinking of Leslie."

"Leslie seems pretty unbothered. Lots of kids have alcoholic parents, Tor. I did myself. You survive."

Sighing, I leaned back and stared up at the open girders supporting the ceiling.

"Don't sound so defeated. She's not going to cause any trouble. She's one of those drunks who really doesn't do much more than just get snockered. When I said she drove Rita wild, I didn't mean to say she was trouble. She wasn't. Half the time I didn't even realize she was drunk. Just leave her alone. That was what Rita did in the end, and it worked out best all around. She wants no truck with us mortal folk anyhow. If you don't talk to her, you can be plenty sure she'll never talk to you."

"Still seems to me like she should have help."

Carolyn rose up out of the whirlpool. "To be honest with you, Tor, I really couldn't care less. I mean, what has she got to drown her sorrows over anyway? She's beautiful. She's rich. She's smart. She has a fantastic husband. She has the whole formula for happiness and look what she does with it. Parents of most of the kids in my room, what have they got? Welfare. Prison terms. No education. No money. No chance. No hope. Nothing. And she's got it all and goes around making a real horse's behind out of herself. No sirree. Don't look here for sympathy."

CHAPTER
FOUR

What a pair Shemona and Geraldine made. They were two halves of a whole, rather than two separate children. Shemona was truly mute, spending every day in total silence. She had one of the most closed, unreadable faces I had ever come across in a child. It was as if someone had stuck up one-way mirrors behind her eyes, because, while Shemona constantly watched me, I could never see anything in return. And she did watch me. Even when I turned to look directly at her, she never averted her eyes. She simply continued to study my face. At those moments it was hard to remember she was a five-year-old. There was no innocence about her.

Geraldine, however, was clingy, noisy and infantile. From the beginning, she insisted on being physically close to me whenever possible. If I sat down, there she was, climbing on my lap, hanging over my shoulder, fondling my hair and my face. If I was standing, she would come up and move very close to me. Everything I owned was a target for kisses and caresses: my hair, my hands, my belt, whatever she could reach. On one occasion, she actually kissed my shoe before I realized what she was doing. Being a physically oriented person myself, I was surprised to find how irritated I became with all this attention. I liked being touched, but Geraldine was another experience altogether. She treated my body as if it belonged to her.

On their own, their individual problems would have been enough to merit psychological intervention. However, it was the relationship between the two girls that made them both fascinating and maddening for me. Geraldine did everything but pee for Shemona. Whatever whim Shemona might have, be it for a pencil or a paper or a glass of water, Geraldine was off getting it for her without Shemona's ever giving an indication that I could perceive. At recess, Geraldine did up Shemona's coat with motherly care; she wrapped the muffler around her sister's neck, pulled the hat down over her ears. At lunch, Geraldine cut her sister's food, carefully leaving a bite on the fork when she'd finished. I seldom saw her more than three feet away from Shemona at any given time. She guarded Shemona; she attended Shemona; she spoke for Shemona. No one could have found a more effective bodyguard than Geraldine.

Shemona seemed fairly dispassionate about all these ministrations. She accepted them more than appealed for them, and I got the feeling that it was Shemona, not Geraldine, who was the dominant member of the team. Shemona behaved like a little queen. Geraldine was the toady.

The most noticeable problem, of course, was Shemona's muteness. I puzzled over what to do about it. During the seventies, I'd done an extensive amount of research with children who refused to speak, a psychological disorder called elective mutism. If Shemona had been any one of the legion number of elective mutes I had encountered during those years, I probably would have leapt right in with both feet, the way I always had. But here, now, I hesitated. Without an aide, I was unable to work with her in the uninterrupted one-to-one mode I was accustomed to. More specifically, I couldn't get her separated from Geraldine, and I knew full well that with the two girls together, I wouldn't stand a chance of getting her to speak. So the first weeks slipped by, and I accomplished nothing.

After the girls had been with me about three weeks, I asked Mr. and Mrs. Lonrho to come in and see me after school. To work more effectively with the sisters, I felt I needed to know more about their lives at home.

Mrs. Lonrho seemed relieved at the chance to talk about Shemona and Geraldine. She and her husband had four children of their own as well, all near in age to the two sisters, so they had expected no trouble in taking these, her brother's daughters.

"I'd met them in Belfast," Mrs. Lonrho said. "I've tried to get back there every couple of years or so. Most of my family's still there, and I want my kids to know their roots."

"Did the girls seem okay to you when you last saw them in Belfast?" I asked.

She nodded. "They were just kids, like any kids."

"Shemona was always the quieter," Mr. Lonrho added. He spoke with a broad western drawl. His wife, I noticed, was incorporating his accent. She still had the burring lilt of Northern Ireland in her words, but the vowel sounds were growing broad and flat.

Again Mrs. Lonrho nodded. "Yes, she was. She was always a self-possessed little thing. Independent, you know? She must have been about three or three and a half when we last saw her. She'd made herself a little house out of a blanket over a chair. Spent hours in there on her own. You never had to entertain Shemona. I remember thinking what a good quality that was for a child to have, because our four were a bunch of hooligans. Forever whining, wanting to do something, getting into trouble doing it."

"And Geraldine?" I asked.

"She was at school during the day, so we didn't see as much of her. But she enjoyed playing with our lot in the evenings."

"I don't remember much about her, to be honest," Mr. Lonrho said. "She was the sort of kid to blend in with the wallpaper."

"That was the thing," his wife said, "they were just ordinary kids. When all this other happened and we found the girls were on their own, it seemed only natural to take them. We didn't think two thoughts about it. You expect there to be some upset, but we assumed they'd adjust. Get them here, give them plenty of love, and they'd come out of it. We never expected it to be like this."

"Are they getting any outside help? Any psychological help?" I asked.

Mrs. Lonrho frowned. "They were. We had Shemona to see a guy over at the clinic. But she wouldn't talk. Eight weeks and she did nothing but sit there. And for their prices, well, I'm afraid she's going to have to do her sitting at home."

"Has Shemona been mute all this time?"

"Not a single word," Mr. Lonrho replied.

"I don't know when she started this," his wife added. "It's been going on a while now. The girls were with my sister Cath before coming here and Shemona wasn't talking there. And that was about a year ago. We didn't think anything much about it when Cath mentioned it. We just thought it was a kid's thing and she'd stop being so silly once she and Geraldine got settled."

"Does Shemona talk to Geraldine?"

Mrs. Lonrho shrugged. "I think she has to, but I've never heard her."

"We've tried everything we can think of," Mr. Lonrho said. "We've tried the psychologist. We've tried his ideas. We've tried the other school's ideas. We've talked to our priest. We've talked with Bet's sisters. I thought separating the girls would make a difference. Bet didn't agree with me. She thinks they need each other. Anyway, one weekend I took Geraldine down to see my mother, and it was hell. She screamed the entire time. And Shemona still never talked."

"How is it you decided to take Geraldine and Shemona?" I asked. "Surely you still have quite a lot of family in Belfast."

"My sister Cath's the only one who could take them. And most of hers are already grown and gone. And she's got a job to think of and everything.

Things just weren't working out. And we didn't want them in a foster home. They'd been in a foster home part of the time as it was. We just wanted to give them a fighting chance."

A small silence sprang up unexpectedly. Both of them had grown thoughtful. I was jotting notes, and when I looked up and saw them, I was unwilling to intrude on their thinking.

Then Mrs. Lonrho raised her head. "Shemona cries at night," she said softly. "It's the only time I hear her. Usually she does it after Geraldine is asleep, but if I go in to her, she falls silent. I put the light on and I see her lying there, her face all red and puffed up. I change the pillowcase. Sometimes I even have to change the pillow, it's so wet, but if I try to touch her, she moves away. She hates to be touched. She pulls away and faces the wall. You know, I ache to hold her then. She's so little. But I don't dare. You can tell by looking at her face that you'd better keep your distance."

The following morning when we were outside on the playground at recess, Geraldine and Shemona came to stand next to me, as was their custom. I was leaning back against the brick wall, hands sunk deep into the pockets of my jacket. Geraldine leaned too, her arm linked through mine, while Shemona was hunkered down fingering through the dirt at our feet.

"Do you miss Northern Ireland?" I asked.

Geraldine did not respond immediately; however, Shemona looked up from where she was squatted. She had a collection of tiny twigs in her hand. I studied her face and wondered if, at five, she knew what Northern Ireland was.

"Shemona misses it," Geraldine said.

"Do you?" I asked her.

Another pause and then she nodded slowly. "Yes, Miss."

She pressed close to me. She'd had only one arm linked through mine but now brought up the other. I extracted my hand from my pocket and put my arm around her shoulders, drawing her against me.

"Would you like to go back?"

She nodded without hesitation. "I *am* going back. Shemona and me both. When we're bigger. We're here because we're just wee girls."

"It must be very hard for you and Shemona to have lost your mother and your father and have had to come so far from home. Any one of those things would have been very upsetting to cope with, but to cope with all of them at once must be extra hard."

"Our brother Matthew died too, not just our mam and dad," Geraldine added.

"Yes. That must have been very hard. You've lost a lot. It must make you feel very sad sometimes."

Silence fell between us. Mariana had a ball and was bouncing it enthusiastically against the brick wall not far from where Geraldine and I were standing. The rhythmic thuds from wall to pavement and back again filled up the silence.

"Now Shemona is youngest," Geraldine said. "Used to be me, then Shemona, then our Matthew. Now she's youngest. And I'm the oldest. I'll always be oldest." A small pause. "Unless I get killed too. Then Shemona will be an only child."

The other parents I wanted to see were Mr. Considyne and Dr. Taylor. Leslie was making no noticeable progress whatsoever. Like Shemona, she suffered from my lack of auxiliary help. By the time I had finished diapering her, checking her sugar levels and injecting her with insulin, there was hardly any time left to work with her. What work I did do seemed to have negligible effect.

I wanted to know more about Leslie's behavior at home. Watching her interactions with her mother in the brief moments I saw them together, I got the impression that Leslie was more responsive to her mother than to me. Did Leslie interact more in general at home? Was she less withdrawn?

The other issue I felt I could no longer live with was Dr. Taylor's drinking. Just as Carolyn had predicted, Dr. Taylor went through a spell of arriving to pick Leslie up stone drunk more often than not. I was appalled both by the severity of her drinking problem and by everyone else's complete acceptance of it. I'd encountered alcoholic parents and some pretty spectacular displays of drunkenness over the course of my career, but nothing to equal the grueling, day-in, day-out consistency of Dr. Taylor's problem. And I had certainly never experienced anything equivalent to the attitudes of the people around me, when I expressed concern. I was treated as if *I* had the problem, not her.

It became clear to me that Dr. Taylor was the person everyone loved to hate. Her legendary aloofness went beyond the point of rudeness; her hostile arrogance was all the more bitter for its silence. More than a few people openly felt she deserved such a comeuppance. More to the point, however, she gave the impression of being a very dangerous woman. Rich, powerful and antagonistic, no one interfered with her because I suspect no one dared.

I didn't dare either. I thought about it a lot. I had fantasies about standing up to Dr. Taylor, but when it came right down to looking her straight in the eye and hanging onto Leslie, I never quite managed. On the other hand, I hadn't given up. Despite failing time and again to keep Leslie from going with her intoxicated mother, I was still prepared each afternoon to try again. I was still taking hold of Leslie's coat collar. Dr. Taylor and I were still having our daily battle of glares. I think even she knew by that point that, while I might not have the courage of a tiger, I had the tenacity of a terrier.

The meeting was arranged for very late on Friday afternoon, a time I chose because I knew the building would be relatively empty. When Dr. Taylor came to pick Leslie up after school, I reminded her of the meeting. With relief, I noticed that she was sober. But when the time arrived for the meeting, no one came. I sat, waiting, at the table. Neat piles of Leslie's work and my records lay beside me. I fiddled with them, stacking them and then restacking them, lining them up straight. The clock ticked noisily, and I couldn't avoid listening to it.

At last the door opened and closed beyond the shelves and, shortly, Tom Considyne's huge frame appeared around the corner. I rose and extended my hand to him and asked him to sit down. We exchanged a few brief pleasantries before he pulled out one of the child-sized chairs next to me and lowered himself into it in a surprisingly graceful manner.

"I'm afraid my wife isn't going to be able to make it," he said. "She isn't feeling well."

"I'm sorry to hear that. I'd just talked with her when she came to fetch Leslie at 3:30."

"It's her stomach. Incredible problems with it."

"Oh. I see." I opened Leslie's folder and began to take out examples of her work. I laid out other things, charts and graphs mainly, that I'd used to keep track of her progress. I explained my concern, because, as he could see, the progress had been minimal.

Even though Carolyn had filled me in, Tom Considyne startled me by being so friendly and garrulous. Having met him only that once, I had little personal experience to judge him on, but I'd assumed automatically he'd share some of his wife's distant reserve. Not so. Warm and expansive, he talked, listened, asked questions, gesticulated, joked and laughed heartily. He was also a bit of a flirt, using just enough sexual innuendo in his conversation to keep me slightly uncomfortable.

What surprised me more was the fact that he was uncommonly astute about the methods I was using with Leslie. Obviously, he had encountered them before and he'd paid attention. The methods he was less sure of, he studied in minute detail. It became apparent that he adored Leslie, in spite of her handicaps.

"She loves your class," he said at one point. He had one of her papers in his hand and smiled tenderly at it. "I take that as the best indicator of your abilities. She's always so anxious to get here in the mornings. Right out of bed first thing. She has no sense of time, you know. It's charming in some ways. Up at 3:30, dressing to come to school. She was like that Saturday. I'd told her at bedtime that there'd be no school in the morning, but she forgot. And so there she was, 5:45, in our bedroom, taking the covers off my wife, putting Ladbrooke's slippers onto her feet to make her get up. Leslie had her clothes on and everything. We had no choice but to take her into bed with us to get her back to sleep."

This all sounded like considerably more life than I'd ever noticed in Leslie. I couldn't imagine her dressing herself. I mentioned this to her father.

"She's not good with strangers. Like her mother in that respect, I'm afraid. A bit shy."

"It seems like rather more than shyness to me," I said. "She's virtually nonexistent some days." I didn't mention the fact that I hardly considered myself a stranger to Leslie.

He nodded. "Yes." A second nod, more resigned. "Yes, she does that at home sometimes too. She's rather unpredictable."

"What do you mean?"

He shrugged. "Sometimes she's okay. Depends. If she's interested in what you're doing, if it's food or something, she can be very responsive. Or if it's something she knows you don't want her involved in . . ." He grinned. "But . . ." The grin faded to be replaced by a wearier expression. "She's hard work some days."

"I can well imagine."

"It's just the way she is, though. I don't fight it anymore. We used to, you know. Christ almighty, we went to every professional in the book for a while. We turned ourselves inside out for them, but nothing worked." Then he shrugged. "No more. We've come to accept the situation. That's been the only way to handle it. Leslie's just different."

"Does your wife accept it as well?"

He went silent, rubbing the stubble on his chin in a pensive manner. Then he nodded slowly. "I think so. My wife doesn't have the kind of patience Leslie needs. Ladbrooke's a very—what would you say?—a very mental person. And Leslie, well, you don't really think about Leslie. You *feel* Leslie. Leslie *is.* You do Leslie by instinct. My wife has a hard time with that kind of thing. She finds Leslie difficult to cope with some days. I guess we both do, occasionally." He smiled gently at me. "Saying that I can accept Leslie for what she is doesn't mean that I always find her easy to live with."

I nodded and relaxed back into my chair. "Are there any areas where Leslie's particularly hard to cope with?"

He thought a moment. "I think we get into the most trouble at night. Leslie doesn't seem to need much sleep. It's incredible, really. She can go to bed at eleven and then be up at three and never go back again. Other times, she goes to bed easily enough but wakes up every hour or two, right through the night. You get up six or seven times with her. And this has been going on for years now. You can't really believe what it's like until you live with it. Nothing works. We even tried drugs at one point, but unless you knocked her right out twenty-four hours a day, she still woke up."

"Does she stay in her bedroom when she wakes up?"

"No, not really. I must admit, I can't come to terms with the thought of locking a child in somewhere. That appalls me every time someone suggests it. Leslie seems to need this chance to go through the house when there're no other distractions. She needs the security of checking in all the drawers and cupboards and seeing everything is still there. I think that helps her define her life in some way."

"What do you mean exactly, when you say 'checking in all the drawers and cupboards'?"

"Well, when she gets up at night, she likes to open the cupboards and dressers and things. She goes in the kitchen and the bathroom mainly and takes things out. You know, just to check they're all there."

Astonished by the thought, I pursued it. "You mean Leslie gets up in the middle of the night and goes around taking everything out of the cupboards?"

"Oh, she's very careful. She's not destructive; she almost never breaks anything. She just takes things out and leaves them."

I was trying to imagine what it must be like to live in a house with a child doing that sort of thing nightly. I had visions of my own apartment, of waking in the morning to find the contents of my cupboards and drawers removed.

Mr. Considyne seemed unaware of the curiosity value of such behavior. "About the only problem we have with her is over smearing things. She does love to rub things around, you know, like jam or ketchup or toothpaste. Anything spreadable. Sometimes I take her out to the studio and let her use my paints." He paused. A smile crossed his lips, and he chuckled. "Boy, did she make a beaut of a mess a couple of weeks ago. She got up and no one heard her. The next morning we went downstairs to the kitchen and found she'd opened the freezer and taken every single item out and laid it on the floor. She'd taken the lids off the ice cream, and it was spread all over the tiles. God, you never saw anything like it."

There was an oddly indulgent tone in his voice. I think I would have been a bit more appalled to lose the contents of my freezer in that manner.

"What does your wife think of all this?" I asked.

"Oh, it was her fault. She didn't remember to lock the freezer."

"No, I mean, in general. Doesn't she mind that Leslie does this kind of thing?"

He shrugged. "Ladbrooke gets impatient with the mess sometimes. But like I said, Ladbrooke isn't the world's most patient person. She has no real understanding of kids. I try to explain to her that Leslie needs this. I think it's expression for Leslie. Besides, Ladbrooke has household help. She doesn't need to worry about the mess. I wouldn't stick her with that."

"I see."

There was a small silence. Mr. Considyne looked down at his hands and then over in my direction without looking directly at me. He smiled sheepishly. "I'm rambling on, aren't I? You'll have to forgive me. I don't get a chance to talk about Leslie very much. Most people don't understand really, do they? Most people aren't very interested."

"That's all right. I'm definitely interested. This gives me a much clearer picture."

"God, I love that child," he said. "It's hard to explain to people. All they see are her defects. But if I had to admit it, I'd say I love her more than my two normal kids. She's so pure. So untainted. She just feels and does. There's no inhibition. No fucking intellect. Just purity. A completely natural person." Then he paused and shook his head. "But that's not to say she's not a challenge some days."

"I don't think most people realize what living with a child like Leslie entails," I said.

"No," he replied in a very heartfelt way.

A small silence came. I could hear the wind pick up beyond the window. I'd opened it slightly after school to let in a little fresh air, and now the silence was filled with a greedy, sucking sound.

"Do you have help specifically for Leslie?"

"We have Consuela. She's not really just for Leslie. She's a cook and housekeeper, in fact, but she spends a lot of time with Leslie."

I nodded.

"Consuela's been with us forever. I don't know what we'd do without her. She makes the difference between sanity and insanity around our place more often than I'd care to admit. I'm afraid Ladbrooke isn't exactly what you'd call domesticated. We'd all fall apart without Consuela. And she has the patience of Job with Leslie, with all of us."

"Does she sleep in Leslie's room?"

"No. No, she has her own rooms at the other end of the house."

"Who gets up with Leslie then, when she does all this waking?"

"We do. My wife and I."

"And this is every single night?"

He nodded.

I scribbled a note of this on the upper edge of Leslie's file.

"I suppose, if I'm honest, I have to admit Ladbrooke does most of the getting up. I'm a pretty heavy sleeper. Most nights I never hear her."

Another small silence intruded. Mr. Considyne reached out to finger one of the papers on the table.

"When did your wife give up her work?" I asked.

"Quite a while back now. Three and a half years, maybe."

"What made her decide to stop?"

"Her project ended. She's a physicist, you know, and she was doing some experimental work with some other people at Princeton University. But they needed to meet quite often, and she found commuting too much, especially with Leslie to think about. And their funding kept giving them trouble. It always had. When the new administration came in in Washington, she knew they weren't ever going to get any increase in their grant. It was going to have to end sooner or later; so, she just wound up her involvement in things."

I studied his features as he spoke. All along I was thinking how different his version of his wife's circumstances was from Carolyn's. I wondered who was right. Or if either was.

"And she's not worked since?"

"No. Leslie started getting very bad about that time. My wife has a full-time job with her alone." Then, as if to amend the way that sounded, he added, "Anyhow, it wouldn't be feasible for her to go back to work. Isn't much call for someone in her profession in a place like this, is there?"

I shook my head.

"Was Leslie planned?" I asked.

He smiled in a very knowing way. "Oh no. Not at all, believe me."

I nodded.

"That's not to say she isn't loved. Or wanted."

"No, I know."

He smiled, his features creasing into a tender expression. "You could say Leslie's been one of life's unexpected pleasures."

Silence came, and this time it stayed. Neither of us spoke. I glanced at my watch. Mr. Considyne, appearing comfortably draped over the small chair, gave no indication of preparing to leave. I was wishing he would. If he went now, I'd have an excuse to say nothing more. But he just sat, unperturbed by the silence.

My stomach knotted. The tightness started around my navel and worked its way upward, tensing muscles all along my trunk. I thought absurdly of the image of being squeezed by a python.

"I'm finding it sort of hard to say what I'm going to have to say next,"
I murmured.

He looked over. "What's that?"

The python was up to my neck. "It's regarding your wife."

"You mean the fact that my wife's an alcoholic?" he asked, his voice
as casual as it had been all along. He remained in his relaxed pose, but
his eyes had left my face and gone to gaze on the steel shelving and the
posters I'd stuck up on them in an effort to disguise their presence. "Is
that what you're trying to say?"

"Yes," I said softly.

"It's no secret, love. Wish that it were, but it's not, least of all to my
wife and me."

"Has anyone encouraged her to join AA or something like that? Has
anyone talked to her seriously about her problem?"

A derisive smile came to his face. He laughed slightly. "You obviously
don't know my wife."

"No, I don't. That may be one of my problems."

Still the sneer. He was looking back at me now, and I could feel the
mood changing almost imperceptibly. The pleasant camaraderie we'd shared
was slipping away.

"There are a lot of good programs around these days. I'm sure if she's
not interested in AA, there's still something suitable available. There are
plenty of alternatives. I'd be quite glad to find the information for you."

"Thank you," he said, and there was a patronizing tone to his voice.
"It's sweet of you to be concerned, but I doubt Ladbrooke would be
interested. She's not a joiner. She's really not into that kind of thing at
all."

He was still looking over at me. His eyes were very watery, giving him
a look of permanent tearfulness, but the expression in them had hardened
and they had become veiled in much the way I'd seen Shemona's do. He
turned away finally, scratched his head, then shrugged wearily.

"Look," he said, his tone gentler, "it *is* sweet of you to be concerned.
I'm sure you mean well. But we're used to it. The way I see it, you've just
got to accept certain things about people. I wish Ladbrooke didn't drink.
I wish, if she did, she wouldn't feel obliged to make such a public ass out
of herself in the process. I wish she could just pull herself together, once
and for all. But it's like with Leslie. You've got to accept people for what
they are, not what you wish they'd be."

"This is perhaps a little more acceptance than is good for either one of
them. I'm scared to death every time your wife comes to pick Leslie up.
I'm terrified that sooner or later someone is going to get killed. I know
I'm going to upset your wife something terrible if I interfere, but one of

these days I'm going to have to. I'd feel entirely responsible if anything happened to Leslie as a result of my letting her go with her mother."

"Don't worry about Ladbrooke's driving, if that's what you mean. It's only two-and-a-half miles, and I've gotten her a good, safe car. She's never had an accident. I doubt she ever will. She's a very reliable driver."

I didn't know what further to say.

Tom Considyne reached across the table for his coat. "I don't know," he said softly. "In a way it'd probably be better if she did have an accident. It's going to take something like that to wake her up."

"Or kill her."

He shrugged. "She's doing that to herself anyway."

CHAPTER
FIVE

On Monday morning Mrs. Lonrho came in, carrying Shemona. Geraldine was home with the stomach flu. Shemona had been sick over the weekend and was now recovered, but she wasn't feeling very enthusiastic about the idea of coming to school by herself. I shut the door before Mrs. Lonrho set Shemona down. From the expression on her face, Shemona was considerably less than enthusiastic.

I, on the other hand, was tickled pink. Here was just the opportunity I needed. After Mrs. Lonrho left, I took Shemona over to the table and opened her folder. She sat silently beside me while I reviewed her morning's work.

"Where's that other girl gone?" Dirkie inquired when he arrived. I had never heard him ever refer to anyone by name. We were all simply girls, boys, ladies and men to Dirkie.

"She's home sick today and won't be here."

"It's just this girl then," he said and grinned. "This girl with the long yellow hair." He leaned way over the table toward Shemona and her folder. Shemona shot a hand out and swiped at him in an irritated way. Dirkie hooted.

"You got a girl's pisser," he said.

Shemona pursed her lips to spit.

"Hey, both of you," I said. "None of that."

Mariana leaned forward. "Shemona doesn't like that boy, Miss," she said, in a perfect imitation of Geraldine.

Once I had Dirkie and Mariana settled with their work and Leslie listening to a cassette, I took Shemona around the corner of the shelves into the area by the chalkboard. It was gloomy there. The steel shelving blocked off the light from the windows and the overhead fluorescents. Taking out a stick of colored chalk from its box, I handed it to Shemona.

"Make me a seven," I said.

She did.

"Good job. Now, draw a set of seven squares."

She drew carefully, making each square precisely and coloring it in. As I had hoped, the colored chalk appealed to her immensely.

We went on like this for several minutes, making numbers and corresponding sets of objects. I drew some too, and had her make lines to connect the sets with their numbers. Shemona was good at numbers. I wanted to relax her, to involve her in the pleasure of this new medium, to please her with her own expertise. It was a trick I'd often used with other elective mutes that had always been very effective, because once involved and relaxed, the child took readily to my increasing the speed of the activity, of making a racing game of it. I then took over more and more of the game, so that I did most of the writing and most of the answers. I verbalized what I wrote. I speeded the pace up even more. And if I did things right, the excitement became enough that when I eventually asked a question and didn't answer, the child would. It was a simple trick that had worked so often for me with elective mutes that I'd videotaped it and used it in presentations of my research. One colleague, intrigued by the results shown on the tape, maintained it was a kind of hypnosis. I'd never thought of it that way. To me it was simply mental sleight of hand.

It took effort to get Shemona going. She was more interested in drawing with the chalk and wanted to make her drawings carefully. She would erase with her finger and try again in an effort to make her triangles exactly straight or her circles exactly round. So, in the end, I had to take the chalk from her and tell her she could use it afterward.

"Show me an eight. Show me a four. Show me an eleven. Twelve. Six. One. Fourteen. Zero." I went faster and faster. Shemona was getting caught up in the process by this time. Some of the numbers were written a bit too high for her to reach, and she had to jump to point to them. This pleased her and she giggled. "Six. Nine. Three. Thirteen. What's this? Five. What's this? Seven. What's this? Two. What's this? Fifteen."

On and on and on. Faster and faster and faster. The whole board was covered with my quickly scribbled numbers, and Shemona was panting to keep up with me. She was smiling and giggling loudly enough that I could hear sound.

"What's this? Four. What's this? Ten. What's this? Eight. What's this?"

Silence.

The next answer was six, and Shemona knew it. She'd already leaped up to point in that direction, waiting for me to say six. When I didn't, she fell back abruptly, her arm still raised. She was panting. An expectant smile was still on her lips, and I was reminded of my Labrador dog and the same enthusiastic, expectant expression he had, when I paused, mid-game, with the ball in my hand.

"What number is this?" I asked, pointing to the six.

She looked at it. The smile faded and she regarded the number a long moment, as if it were written in a foreign script.

"What number is it?" I tapped the board.

She continued to gaze at it.

"What number is this?" I knew the impetus was gone. I knew I had failed. If I hadn't caught her in the excitement of the moment, I knew I wasn't going to now. I smiled in an effort to keep the good feelings between us. "It's a six, isn't it?" She gave a half-hearted little jump to point to the six, wanting to keep the happiness in the situation as obviously as I did.

I handed her the box of colored chalk. "You did that really well, didn't you? You know all your numbers. Here. You may use these until recess time."

Carolyn and I had worked up a system whereby we alternated playground duty at recess. Because of her aide, Carolyn wouldn't have needed to stay down on the playground during the fifteen-minute recess period. I did, as there was no one else to look after my children. However, Carolyn, understanding the pressures of this sort of job when there was no break, had offered to alternate with me, watching my kids as well as hers. So every day I had a fifteen-minute break, either in the morning or the afternoon.

Usually, I used the period to catch up on miscellaneous tasks, such as running off the children's worksheets on the mimeograph or setting up art projects. Some days I did no more than collapse in the teachers' lounge. On this particular morning, I'd gone to get the keys from Bill, the janitor, to open his cleaning closet on my floor so that I could wash out the mucky tray from our easel. I had the tap running, and dirty water was gurgling noisily down the drain, so when Leslie appeared in the doorway of the closet, I jumped with surprise.

My first reaction was to glance at my watch, because I was suddenly alarmed to think I'd lost track of the time and my children were back in the room. But there were still five minutes remaining of the break.

"What are you doing here, sweetheart?"

Leslie was red cheeked from exertion and looking a whole lot more alert than usual.

"What do you need?"

She turned her head and looked down the hallway.

"What is it?" I stuck my head out of the closet and glanced in the direction she was looking.

Back and forth between me and the stairwell Leslie glanced. Her body was taut with excitement.

"You shouldn't be up here, you know," I said. "You're supposed to be down on the playground with Miss Berry and Joyce. Do they know you've come up here?"

She raised one hand and pointed down the hall, then she grunted. It was the first intentional sound I'd ever heard Leslie make.

Again, I looked around the corner of the closet door. "What is it?"

"Crying," she said hoarsely.

"Crying? Who's crying? Can you show me?"

Leslie took off. I followed her down the hallway, down the stairs, through the fire doors. As we came out of the stairwell, I was accosted by noise. A general hubbub filtered up from the area around the main office.

Carolyn was just inside the office door when I reached it. She had hold of Dirkie by the collar of his shirt and Shemona by her coat. Dirkie was crying angrily. Shemona was hysterical. She twisted and turned, all the while screeching at the top of her lungs.

"Oh, thank God," Carolyn said when she saw me. "I thought you'd gotten lost."

"What's happened?"

"She tried to kill me!" Dirkie shouted. "That girl, that girl with the long yellow hair, she tried to *kill* me!"

"Dirkie was just being Dirkie," Carolyn said. Letting go of him, she reached over the top of the barrier to grab a handful of tissues. She held them out to Dirkie. "You were being a bit annoying, weren't you, Dirkie? You kept wanting to touch Shemona's hair. I asked you several times to leave her alone."

"She tried to *kill* me!" He displayed a scratched cheek.

"I was about to kill you myself," Carolyn replied. "How many times did I ask you to leave her alone? Five? Ten? It's not surprising she got fed up."

Shemona persisted with ear-splitting screams, making it nearly impossible to continue the conversation. Moreover, the other children were milling around inquisitively.

I looked over at Carolyn. "Do you suppose you could spare Joyce to watch my gang for a moment? There's an art project all laid out up there. Maybe to be on the safe side, you could take Dirkie down with you. But I'd like a private moment to deal with Short Stuff, here."

Carolyn nodded. Getting a good grip on Shemona's jacket, I dragged her, still kicking and screaming, off in the direction of the teachers' lounge. Once there, I shut the door firmly behind us, then pulled her across the room to the sofa and sat down.

"Do you want to sit here beside me?" I asked.

She simply continued to scream.

"Would you like to sit in my lap?"

"No!"

"Oh, all right. Very well. The thing is, however, I can't let go of you. I need to hold on so that you don't hurt yourself in here. Or hurt anything else. When you look like you're more in control, I'll let go of your wrist."

This brought a new spurt of anger, and she struggled savagely, clawing at my arm with the fierceness of a tiger cub. Grabbing her free hand with mine, I hung on and said no more.

Shemona screamed. And screamed. Tiredness eventually crept into her voice, but she still managed to carry on shrieking in monotonous, syncopated bursts. Then exhaustion finally overtook her, and her screams faded to squawks and then grunts. At last she was hoarse. Genuine tears filled her eyes at that point, and when she looked at me briefly, I saw the anguish. Sinking down first to her knees and then all the way down, she sat on the rug at my feet. I let go of her wrists.

I smiled. "That was hard work, wasn't it?"

She gave no response.

"I'm tired now. Are you?"

She fingered the red marks left on her wrists by my grip, then she snuffled and wiped her nose on the sleeve of her blouse.

"This must have been a hard day for you. It must be scary, having to come to school without Geraldine. You must miss her."

Very slightly, Shemona nodded.

"Geraldine takes good care of you, doesn't she?"

Tears came back to her eyes. Her lips quivered, and she sucked them between her teeth to keep from crying.

Noisy silence enveloped us. The refrigeration unit on the pop machine came on. The Xerox machine whirred. The heating plate under the coffeepot clicked. The clock jumped the minutes with an audible *tink.*

"Would you like to sit up here beside me?"

She shook her head.

"It's very soft, see? They're nice cushions, these, just the kind for relaxing against. You'd probably find them nicer than the floor."

Again she shook her head.

"I was a bit upsetting too, wasn't I? Playing that game with you at the chalkboard. Did you think I was trying to trick you into talking? I didn't mean it to be a trick, you know. Just a help. Just something to get you over the first time, because it's the first time that's so hard."

She stared at her hands.

"And then there was Dirkie. What an annoying boy he can be. He wants to touch my hair all the time too, and I don't like it either."

The tears had begun to run down her cheeks. They dripped off her jawbone and onto the collar of her blouse. She did nothing to stop them.

I leaned forward, elbows on my knees. "Come here, Shemona."

She shook her head.

I watched her. She watched her feet.

"I'm kind of thirsty," I said. "Are you? I would think so, after all that screaming. Shall we split a can of pop?"

Lifting her head, she looked at me through her tears.

"What kind would you like?"

No response.

Standing, I pulled a handful of change from my pocket and went to the machine. "Coke? Shall we share a Coke?"

She nodded.

I put the money into the machine, and the can rattled noisily down into the tray. When I turned around to bring it back, Shemona was sitting on the sofa.

I sipped the froth off the top of the can and then handed it to her. Shemona reached up eagerly and put the Coke to her lips. Several seconds were lost in greedy gulping. Then finally she lowered it.

"What do you say?" I asked.

"Thank you."

That was no breakthrough with Shemona. At best, it was détente. Once back in the room with the others, the veil came down again, and she retreated into silence. It had been a worthwhile time in the teachers' lounge because it had forced her to acknowledge me as someone to be reckoned with, but I hadn't made her talk. Exhaustion and loneliness made her talk. That and the Coke. I had the sense to know it wasn't me.

On the other hand, there *had* been a major breakthrough, which had been almost entirely eclipsed by Shemona's tantrum. And that was Leslie. When she had come to me in the janitor's closet, that had been the first time Leslie had ever made even so much as a communicative grunt. It had startled me beyond reaction when it had occurred, and then I'd become too embroiled in Shemona's mess to acknowledge it afterward. But once things settled down, I was astounded by the implications. Could Leslie actually talk? Could she control her speech? I'd been so accustomed to her silence that I'd just accepted it as part of her. I had assumed that the deterioration of her speech had been part of her general disturbance and had thought no more of it. That sort of thing was fairly common in children with Leslie's kind of handicap. But could Leslie really talk?

After school, I waited up in the room with Leslie in an effort to lure Dr. Taylor out of the protection of her blue Mercedes and into the classroom. Within five minutes of the other children's departing, Dr. Taylor was there.

"Do you suppose I could speak to you for a few moments?" I asked.

Her brow furrowed and her expression grew wary. I wondered if she thought I was going to get after her for having missed the conference on the previous Friday. Or perhaps her husband had clued her in about what we'd discussed.

There was a long, expectant, thoroughly uncomfortable pause in which we regarded one another. When I didn't look away and she couldn't stare me down, she finally dropped her gaze. Almost imperceptibly, she nodded.

"Let me take Leslie downstairs to stay with the other teacher here." I guided Leslie toward the door. "Do you want a cup of coffee? I'm going to stop and get myself one on the way back."

Dr. Taylor shook her head.

Back upstairs, I sat down at the table. Unlike her husband, Dr. Taylor did not sit down next to me. Instead, she sat across the table and three seats down in the chair nearest the doorway. I couldn't have touched her, even if we'd both extended our arms.

"I'm sorry you couldn't come the other night. I had everything out to show you then, and I'm afraid I don't now. This was a sort of spur-of-the-moment idea, asking you in. But it helps me tremendously to talk to both parents. Also, we had a most extraordinary thing happen in here today, and I was curious to find out how it compares with Leslie's behavior at home."

Dr. Taylor simply sat, regarding me as I spoke. She had the most disconcerting ability to maintain eye contact, and she had the most exceptional eyes, which increased the discomfort caused by her staring. While her eyes were not unusually large, she had a way of widening them that made them seem enormous to me. The whole iris became visible, giving her that kind of cold, unblinking expression reptiles have. Or perhaps it came more from the crocodile color. Whatever, her gaze made me feel continually obliged to look away, and I was annoyed with myself for doing this.

"How is Leslie at home? What's she like to live with?" I asked.

This caused Dr. Taylor to finally take her eyes off my face. She looked down, up, around, then back to me. She shrugged slightly. "Just Leslie."

"Listening to some of the things your husband was telling me on Friday, I get the feeling she must be quite a handful sometimes."

Another shrug.

"Do you find the going a bit hard sometimes?"

A pause, then a slight nod.

"Can you tell me in what ways?"

Another shrug.

"Your husband says she doesn't sleep very well."

She shook her head.

"What happens?" I asked.

"She gets up."

"Then what?"

"Wanders around."

This conversation was like pulling teeth. In all my other encounters with Dr. Taylor, she gave me the impression that deigning to talk to me was something that she just couldn't bring herself to do. It felt less that way now. I wondered if she was feeling threatened by this situation, or if she was guarding her private life.

"Who gets up with Leslie when she wakes?" I asked.

"I do, mostly."

"Do you just put her back to bed?"

"If she'll go."

"And if she doesn't?"

"Then I need to stay up with her."

"How often does this occur?" I asked.

She shrugged slightly. "Every night."

"*Every* night?"

Another shrug. "Every night I can think of."

"More than once a night?"

Another shrug. "Sometimes."

"How often did you get up with her last night?"

"Three times."

"That sounds exhausting," I said.

Dr. Taylor nodded slightly.

"Do you do all the getting up then? Or does Mr. Considyne help sometimes too?"

"He doesn't usually hear her."

"So let's see if I'm getting this right," I said. "You correct me, if I'm not. You get up every night, two or three times. Sometimes you just resettle her. Sometimes you have to stay up with her."

"Well, not all night. Just until she goes back to sleep."

"I see. How much sleep do *you* get?"

A shrug. "Enough."

"What if you just left her alone, instead of getting up each time to put her back to bed?"

"She makes a big mess."

"I see. Have you considered using something like a Dutch door or a screen door to confine her to her room?"

"My husband feels Leslie needs to do this. He says it makes her feel secure."

"Do you agree?"

She shrugged. "I guess so."

A pause came into the conversation. I glanced down at the notes I'd hurriedly scribbled on my pad.

"We had something unusual happen in here today," I said. "There was a fight out on the playground this morning. I wasn't down there because it was my break; I was upstairs. Then all of a sudden, there was Leslie. She'd come all the way up to get me, which alone would have been a surprise to me, but more extraordinary, she actually spoke to me. Meaningfully. It was just one word, 'crying,' but it was very appropriate to the situation. That's what two of the other children were doing, and she wanted me to come down."

Dr. Taylor, who was watching me, displayed no change of expression whatsoever, as I told her this. She appeared neither surprised nor delighted.

"She does that sometimes," she said finally.

"She does? I had no idea she talked at all. No one's ever mentioned it to me."

"It isn't very consistent."

"But she does speak?" I asked.

"If that's what you call it."

"How often?"

Dr. Taylor wrinkled her nose and thought a moment. "Once a month, maybe. I don't know."

I contemplated the matter. It had suddenly begun to rain outside, and I was briefly distracted by the sound against the windowpane. When I looked back at her, Dr. Taylor was staring at me again.

"I think there's a whole lot more to Leslie than meets the eye," I said. "I wish I could work with her more intensively. I'm absolutely desperate for some auxiliary help in here. With all the cuts and everything in education, there doesn't seem to be a way that the district can afford me an aide, which is a crying shame, really, given kids like Leslie. And unfortunately, I haven't managed to track down any willing volunteers yet. But when I do, Leslie's going to be right at the top of my list for some one-to-one work. I think she's got more potential than she's letting on."

Dr. Taylor had begun chewing vigorously on her thumbnail. She still regarded me steadily, and I had the impression that she was intending to speak, but seconds slipped by and the silence began to grow noticeable.

"Did you want to say something?" I asked.

This appeared to unnerve her. She looked away quickly and snapped her hand down from her mouth in the gesture of someone suddenly aware of indulging in a bad habit. She shook her head slightly.

Another pause intruded. She was no longer watching me, so I took the opportunity to study her. In spite of her guarded aloofness, I was finding it harder to dislike the woman. There was something vaguely pathetic about her, sitting as she was, nearly the whole distance of the table away from me. Shoulders hunched, arms in close around her body, her steely beauty gilded over her like chain mail, she looked less the aggressor than the victim.

"I was wondering," she said very quietly, "what you thought might cause Leslie's problems."

"You mean her handicap in general?"

She nodded.

"It's hard to say. There's a lot I don't know about Leslie."

A slight nod, as if I'd given her an answer.

"My gut feeling is that it's some kind of organic dysfunction. Like autism. Her behavior's somewhat similar to that of other children I've worked with. But I don't really know for certain."

Her long hair had fallen forward against the side of her face, and she took a strand and twisted it. She glanced over briefly. "What's that mean?"

"What? Organic dysfunction?"

She nodded.

"It means that something isn't working right physically. Because we still don't know much about these things, we don't know why handicaps like Leslie's happen, but evidence seems to indicate it's an inborn matter. It's not the result of an emotional disturbance." I looked over at her. "I don't mean to say such children don't have emotional problems. Often they do. These are inordinately hard kids to live with. They can upset even the most well-adjusted family, simply because it's so difficult to accommodate their needs. I mean, look at your case. From my reckoning you've had about five years of continually broken nights. No one functions well under such circumstances, so it's fairly understandable when things get in a twist, as a result."

She looked down, and for a flicker of an instant, I felt she was near to tears. It was just a sensation I had, more than anything concrete in her behavior. She was still twisting her hair around her fingers, releasing it, twisting it again.

"We're coming out of an era of psychiatry and psychology that has been very cruel to the parents of children with these kinds of handicaps," I said. "There's been too much emphasis on whose fault it is when the child has a problem, and I don't think it's done anyone any good. Blaming's a pretty fruitless exercise all the way around, to my way of thinking. I don't care what did it. It's happened and become history. What I care about is the present. What's the problem now? What can I do to help make it better? That's all I'm really interested in: making it better."

She nodded slowly without looking up. "I was just wondering."

CHAPTER SIX

✸ "You're going to kill me," said Frank, as he came into the classroom.

"Why's that?"

"Because I'm going to tell you you're getting another kid."

"You jest."

"Nope," he said. "'Fraid not. Moreover, it's Irish Kid, Mark III."

Pausing from my activities, I looked over. "Oh, come off it, Frank. You must be joking."

"Nope. Sorry. The Lonrhos seem to have acquired another one."

"What is this? Some kind of import business they're starting?"

"Seems that way."

"I didn't think there were any more," I said.

"This is a cousin or something. A boy, thirteen."

"And he's coming in here? Into this class?"

"Well, from the sound of things, he does definitely have problems."

"Good heavens, they do pick 'em."

Frank grinned and reached a hand out to thank me chummily on the back. "Cheer up, Torey. Mrs. Lonrho specifically asked that the boy be placed in here with you. She thinks you're brrrrrilliant," he said in an exaggerated Irish accent.

"Oh, thanks."

Shamus, or Shamie, as he preferred to be called, was the son of Mrs. Lonrho's sister Cath. Mrs. Lonrho came in to see me shortly before Shamie's arrival. His school records weren't going to be forwarded on for some time, she said, so she hoped she could help me prepare for the boy. And she did help. From her came a picture clearer than anything I would have gotten from a school file.

Shamie was the last of eight children, a gentle, artistic boy who'd been doted on as the baby of a large family. He wasn't what could be called a bright lad, Mrs. Lonrho said. None of Cath's were geniuses. But he was good hearted and hardworking.

Shamie's family, like Shemona and Geraldine's, was deeply embroiled in the politics of Northern Ireland. Two of his brothers were "Provies," members of the Provisional IRA, complete with prison sentences to show for it. His mother still worked in a pub that had been bombed twice in the previous four years by opposing groups of loyalist and republican supporters. Shamie's family had been close to Geraldine and Shemona's. They lived only a few hundred yards apart on the same street, and indeed, it had been in Shamie's garage that his uncle had committed suicide. Shamie himself had been very close to this uncle. He had intended to apprentice into his uncle's electrical business when he came of age, and he had spent a lot of time at his uncle's house, helping him with his work. Thus, after the uncle's arrest and release, the boys at school had begun taunting Shamie and calling him an informer too. It was nothing serious, Mrs. Lonrho said. They wouldn't have really hurt Shamie, but he'd always been an oversensitive lad. He took it seriously. He began to suffer bouts of depression, insomnia and restlessness. He became convinced that he and his family, like his cousins' family, would be killed.

While listening to Mrs. Lonrho, I developed great sympathy for Shamie. To be taunted as a traitor in a place where people were killed for doing no more than selling building supplies to the opposing side would give me a fright too. Where did the abusive mouths of schoolboys leave off and the real threats begin? Shemona and Geraldine and their family lived only three houses down the street from Shamie. His fears seemed fairly realistic to me.

In the end, Shamie decided that he too wanted to come live with Auntie Bet and Uncle Mike in America, as Geraldine and Shemona had. He wanted to get away from Belfast altogether. And immediately. He couldn't wait, he'd told his parents. He couldn't last it out until school-leaving age at sixteen. He said he knew he'd be dead by sixteen.

Shamie arrived in my room six days later. He was a thin, bony boy, looking considerably younger than thirteen, with black hair cut in a style reminiscent of *Star Trek*'s Mr. Spock. His features were soft and feminine, the femininity accented by the thickest, longest eyelashes I'd ever known not to originate in a drugstore. The dark lashes seemed to overpower his eyes, which were a nondescript bluish color, giving him a dreamy, almost sleepy look.

"This is our cousin Shamie," Geraldine announced with tremendous pride. "He's come all the way from Belfast. He was just there last Friday. Weren't you? He's our Auntie Cath and Uncle Joe's Shamie, who lives just three doors down, at 44 Greener Terrace. That's his address. Our house is 38 Greener Terrace."

"It isn't now," Shamie said. "You don't live there now. Your house number is 3018 Scenic View Drive." He smiled, pleased with his knowledge. What I noticed, listening to him, was how much of her accent Geraldine had already lost. She sounded broadly American against Shamie's thick brogue.

"I'm going back," Geraldine said. "When I'm grown up, I'm going back to live at 38. And Shemona too, huh, Shemona? Shemona and I are going back to live together at 38 Greener Terrace."

"Can't do. It's sold."

"Shall do, Shamie. We shall buy it back."

"How silly. You haven't any money."

Geraldine's lower jaw jutted forward in a defiant expression. "Shemona and I," she said with great importance, "we shall get jobs. We'll earn bags of money and buy 38 back."

"It'll be all different anyhow, Geraldine," Shamie replied.

"We'll make it just as it was. And we'll live there like before. Shan't we, Shemona?"

I stood by, bemused.

"Well," said Shamie with a shrug. "You can, if you want. I shan't go back. I shall never go back. I'm staying here forever."

Following the brief after-school conversation with Dr. Taylor, I felt more at ease in her presence, although I obviously hadn't disarmed her any. She still continued to be aloof and uncommunicative when we encountered one another; however, I ceased to take it personally. I perceived it less as directed hostility and more as just an unfortunate personality trait, and that helped me. I was no longer frightened of her.

What helped even more was that she stopped coming to school drunk. I had been on my guard for the first week or so after the conference with Tom Considyne, but I think he must have said something to her, because from then on, she showed up sober. I flattered myself by hoping that perhaps our after-school discussion might have helped. Indeed, I went so far in flattering myself as to think perhaps she was now frightened of *me* and didn't dare come to school drunk. It was a warming thought, and I relaxed considerably.

Then the second week of November arrived. It was a Tuesday afternoon, and Dr. Taylor was sitting at the wheel of her car. As had become our custom, she did not get out. Instead, I opened the rear door and helped Leslie into her seat belt. But that afternoon, when I opened the door, I was assaulted by the smell of licorice breath candies and alcohol.

Now what?

For lack of something better to do, I hastily unbuckled Leslie's seat belt, pulled her back out of the car and shut the door. Then I stepped back up on the curb with Leslie, who was looking perplexed but stayed calm.

The window on the passenger side lowered with an electric *whirr.* "What are you doing?" Dr. Taylor asked, irritation naked in her voice.

I said nothing and did not lean down so that she could see my face. Instead, I turned Leslie around, and we started back for the school building.

The far-side door opened, and Dr. Taylor got out of her Mercedes. "What *are* you doing?" she asked, over the top of her car.

I paused and looked back at her. "I'm going to take Leslie into the office and call a taxi for her."

The alcohol certainly didn't impair Dr. Taylor's reflexes any, because she was around the car and up in front of Leslie and me faster than I probably could have done it sober.

"Just what the hell do you think you're doing?" she asked. "This is *my* child. I'll take her anywhere I damned well please."

"Let's not make a big deal out of it, okay? I'll get her a taxi. You go meet her at the other end."

She glared, crocodile eyes widening. "Give her to me." The words were said very individually, each emphasized carefully.

"No." I'd crossed the Rubicon and I think we both knew it. There was a very, very long exchange of glares between us. "Move aside, please," I said.

But Dr. Taylor gave no indication of backing down. Her eyes narrowed, taking away some of the frightening reptilian coldness but making her look a whole lot angrier.

"You do this," she said, "and I'll see you destroyed."

Not much to say to that.

"You can be assured that the first phone call I'll make when I reach home will be to my lawyer." Her voice was very low and quiet.

I swallowed.

"I don't know who you think you are," she said, "but I can tell you right now who you aren't. And that's a teacher in this school. Because you're never going to teach in this town again. Believe me."

Not having any other way to defend myself, I simply stood silent and stared at her. It was a bluffer's trick, something I'd learned from my elective mutes. She must have learned it somewhere too, because she stared steadily back, completely untroubled by my silence.

Outstared, I finally had to look away. Dropping my gaze, I studied the sidewalk beneath my feet for a few moments and wondered what to do. I was weighing the possibility that she might try to stop me physically, if I tried to move. She was as tall a woman as I was, if not a little taller, and I didn't want to chance that kind of thing. I raised my head and glanced around to see who else was nearby. Inside the school doorway, I could make out two of the secretaries standing there, watching us. I could just imagine what they were saying.

Taking a deep breath, I turned slightly, took Leslie's hand and, making a wide circle around Dr. Taylor, I walked toward the school building.

Mercifully, Dr. Taylor did not try to stop me. Instead, she stormed back to her Mercedes, got in, slammed the door resoundingly, and roared off, leaving a frantic swirl of fallen leaves in her wake.

My knees were like so much Jell-O. I wobbled into the office, and by the time I dialed the taxi company, the shaking had extended to my voice. What the dispatcher must have thought of my several attempts to speak correctly, I would hate to guess.

Throughout all this, Leslie had remained curiously composed. When the taxi came, I put her in and paused to hug her. "Don't worry, sweetheart. Everything's okay. Your daddy and Consuela will be there on the other end to meet you. Probably your mama too." I hugged her again. Then I dug into my pocket and handed the fare to the driver.

The rest of the day passed very unpleasantly indeed. Dr. Taylor overshadowed every thought I had. Her normal, everyday demeanor was so hostile that I hated to think what she'd be like genuinely angry, but I had no doubt she could make a formidable foe. Was she serious about the lawyer business? If so, could she actually do anything? Had I been wrong in any way? My stance seemed fairly clear-cut to me, but I had heard of stranger lawsuits than this.

If Dr. Taylor's intention was to give me a thoroughly nasty time, she succeeded splendidly. I couldn't eat my supper. I couldn't concentrate on what I was doing that evening. Once in bed, I couldn't sleep. Over and over and over the whole incident played in my mind.

Things didn't improve much in the morning, because by then, along with everything else, I was tired. Carolyn had a dental appointment, and her class was being taken for the morning by a substitute, who seemed unable to maintain control. As a consequence, I felt obliged to stay and eat lunch with her children to settle them down. Dirkie was more obsessive than usual, pacing after Shemona and her hair, frantically searching for cat pictures in not-very-promising places, like *The Journal of the American Academy of Child Psychiatry*, spending most of his time hiding under the table and hooting softly, like a forsaken owlet. Leslie had a huge, smelly bowel movement in her diapers, and we were all left gasping for air, the windows wide open into the November rain. And returning from morning recess, Shemona tripped over an untied shoelace while coming up the stairs. In a fit of pique, she ripped off the shoe and threw it down the three-story stairwell. I insisted it was too late to retrieve it; we needed to get back to class. So I made her leave it where it had fallen until lunch. This infuriated Shemona and, in turn, Geraldine, as Shemona's protector. Both girls sat grimly through the rest of the morning, except for the times Geraldine mercilessly pestered me to return the shoe. Only Shamie and Mariana seemed to be having a passable day.

The first half of the afternoon went little better than the morning had, so I took corrective action at recess. I organized a couple of fast, hard-running games and then ended up with a version of dodgeball, where the children, including Carolyn's bunch, stood around me in a giggling circle and did the avoiding, while I did the throwing. Even I felt considerably better after half a dozen attempts to flatten Dirkie with the ball.

Back in the classroom, I tried to assure that everything restarted smoothly. Shamie had reading instead of his dreaded math. Geraldine had a paper she and Shemona could work on together. I collected the other three and sat down to play a game of lotto with them. Peace reigned until about 2:45. Then slam! *Bang!* went the classroom door.

Startled, I looked up. When no one appeared, I excused myself from the game and walked around the corner of the shelving units. There stood Dr. Taylor.

CHAPTER
SEVEN

Seeing Ladbrooke Taylor standing there in the gloom of that part of the classroom was like seeing an incarnation of some mythical creature—a Valkyrie or a Fury or something like that—beautiful, ferocious and slightly unearthly. Her hair was loose and wind-blown, flowing around her wildly. Her cheeks were suffused with color. And the fierceness of her expression left me in no doubt that I was meeting an avenging angel.

She was also very, very drunk.

"I've come for my daughter."

I could sense the children collecting behind me. Glancing over my shoulder, I shooed them away, but they retreated only as far as the corner of the shelves. "Back to your seats," I ordered. "Back to work." None of them moved.

I reached around Dr. Taylor for the doorknob. "Let's step out into the hall."

The children persisted in staring.

"Shamie?" I said.

"Yes, Miss."

"This is just Leslie's mom. I need to have a quick word with her, and we're going out into the hallway. Do you think you could keep an eye on things for me? You may get out the storytelling tapes, if you'd like. I'll be back in just a jiff."

"Yes, Miss."

Dr. Taylor was so inebriated that she was unsteady on her feet. I hadn't realized she was *that* drunk, but as I did, a lot of my initial terror diffused. I found an inordinate amount of reassurance in the knowledge that whatever was going to happen, I'd be faster.

"I want to take my daughter home," she said, as I ushered her out into the hall and firmly shut the door behind us. "And I want her now."

"It isn't quite the end of the school day yet, Dr. Taylor. Leslie won't be finished for another forty-five minutes or so. Why don't you go home and wait for her. All right?"

"I want her *now.*"

"Yes, I know. But this is her time to be in school."

She glared at me. Tall as she was, she could look me very squarely in the eye. As had happened on the previous day, I found myself wondering about the likelihood of being physically attacked. I couldn't very well let her back into the classroom but was not looking forward to the prospect of keeping her out if she became insistent about Leslie.

"Perhaps you'd like a cup of coffee," I said. "We can go down to the teachers' lounge—"

"Would you stop your goddamned patronizing?"

"I'm not patronizing you, Dr. Taylor. I'm trying to get back to my class. I'm a teacher and I'm supposed to be in there teaching."

"Then let me have my daughter. *Now.*" She was growing angrier.

Then, unexpectedly, she made a lunge past me for the door. I moved to keep her hand from the doorknob, but I needn't have worried. Her reflexes were shot. The sudden motion overbalanced her, and she thudded first against me and then heavily against the far side of the door frame before sliding down to her knees.

"I know what you're thinking," she said, when she looked up at me. "You're thinking that a person like me ought to be taking my poison some other way, right?"

Not exactly. I was thinking more along the lines of what a vapid fool she was making of herself.

I leaned forward and took her shoulder. "Get up, Dr. Taylor. Come on. You can't stay here."

"You're not human," she replied.

"Come on. Get up."

"You don't have any reaction to anything, do you? What are you anyway? Some kind of robot? You certainly aren't human. What are you?"

"Sober. Now, I mean it. Get up. Come on."

But she didn't quite make it. Rising part way to her feet, she suddenly collapsed like a puppet whose strings had been cut. Plop. Down and out.

Oh, shit. I stood a moment, completely overcome with horror. Subdued panic rose in my throat. What was I going to do now? I couldn't very well just leave her in a heap on the floor. What the hell was I going to do with her?

I knelt down and touched her, hoping she'd rouse out of it. "Dr. Taylor?" I jiggled her shoulder. "Wake up. You can't lie here. Come on now, wake up. Please?"

No response.

The only possible thing seemed to be to drag her into the classroom. Putting my hands under her armpits, I tried to lift her, but she was an absolute deadweight. This was the kind of thing you saw people doing on TV all the time, and it looked a piece of cake. Yet, here I was, no weakling, and I could hardly shift her. Pulling open the classroom door, I stuck my head in. "Shamie? Shamie, come here a minute."

When Shamie came to the door, he went white and gasped. Then immediately he crossed himself.

"For crying out loud, Shamie, she isn't dead."

"What's the matter with her, Miss?"

"She's drunk. Passed out, that's all. Nothing nearly so romantic as death, believe me."

"I thought you'd killed her, Miss."

"*Shamie!* For pity's sake." I bent down. "Now listen, give me a hand. I want to get her into the classroom."

Even between the two of us, it was an awkward job. Once far enough inside to close the door, I let go. "This is good enough."

"Should we go get Mr. Cotton?" Shamie asked.

I considered the suggestion but then shook my head. "No. I don't think so. She'll come out of it on her own. I think."

"She doesn't look very comfortable, Miss. Do you think we ought to fetch her a pillow?"

"This isn't the Hilton, Shamie. She'll be just fine."

Dirkie abruptly rounded the corner of the shelves. His reaction was the same as Shamie's had been initially, only much louder. "You killed her! She's dead!" he shrieked.

"You *guys*. Good grief. Do I look like I go around killing people? I haven't killed anybody. She's not dead. So hush up."

"She's *dead*," Dirkie said, appalled.

"She'll be all right in a bit, if we just leave her alone. She's *not* dead, Dirkie, believe me." Approaching him to turn him around and get him back to work, I extended my hand. Dirkie jumped and ran around the corner of the shelves.

Shamie remained standing over Dr. Taylor.

"You too, Shamie. Come on. Let's get back to work."

He looked over, a slightly bemused expression on his face. "It's like having Sleeping Beauty in the classroom. She's like a fairy person, she's so beautiful."

"Beauty is as beauty does, Shamie. Now, come on."

Of course, it proved utterly impossible to get back to work. The children were already stirred up. Everybody knew Dr. Taylor was over there. Moreover, she made noises. They were fairly stuporous sounding, and she never managed to rouse herself completely, but every time we heard her, we all jumped. Mariana, Geraldine and Shemona found the whole episode hysterically funny and giggled nonstop. Dirkie remained convinced that I had done her in. Shamie persisted in getting up every few minutes to check around the corner of the shelving to see if she was still there. Unfortunately, she always was. Only Leslie seemed unconcerned. Perhaps she had seen it all before.

After twenty minutes or so of irritatedly trying to keep the children on task, I gave up. There was very little class time left anyhow, and it just didn't seem worth the aggravation. So, I told the children to collect their belongings and then took them downstairs. Carolyn had music during this period, and I knew she wouldn't mind a few extra voices. Besides, I figured she owed me one for having supervised her kids at lunch.

"You are never in a million years going to believe what's going on up in my classroom," I said, as I ushered my lot through her door.

"Yeah," said Dirkie brightly. "There's a dead lady up there."

Back in the classroom, I knelt beside Dr. Taylor and gave her a good, bone-rattling shake. She responded this time, moaning and rolling over onto her side.

"Get up," I said, all guise of politeness gone.

Slowly, very slowly, she managed to bring herself into a sitting position. She clasped either side of her head with her hands.

"All the way up. On your feet. *Now.*"

This proved harder, and I realized suddenly that I wasn't going to be able to simply open the door and evict her, as I had intended. Supporting her to keep her steady, I guided her around the corner to the table and pulled out a chair. She collapsed into it, hunching forward, elbows on the tabletop, hands over her face.

"Well, this is a hell of a mess," I said. "What are we going to do with you now?"

She made no response.

"Shit," I muttered and turned away, walking over to the window. I was really fed up. Why me? Thrusting my hands deep into the pockets of my jeans, I leaned against the radiator and stared outside. I studied the brick wall, the asphalt yard, the chimney stack for several minutes. Then I turned back.

She hadn't moved.

"Are you okay?" I asked. Seeing her as she was, I had a split-second sensation that she wasn't.

And I was right. Because the next moment, she was sick. Not slightly, not politely, but appallingly, all over the table, the chair, the floor and herself. She must have brought up a whole week's worth of food, because it went everywhere.

I squawked and jumped.

Then my mind went absolutely blank for what must have been only a moment or two but seemed like eternity. Paralyzed, I did nothing.

She retched again. Locating the wastebasket, I thrust it into her hands. "Here, use this. I'm going to find the janitor." And I beat a hasty retreat.

Bill was in the teachers' lounge with his coffee and the newspaper. "One of your parents?" he asked incredulously. I just rolled my eyes and asked if he had anything in his closet that I could use to help her clean herself up. He tossed me the keys. "Leave it open," he said. "I'll be up in a minute." And he drained the last drops from his coffee mug.

Upstairs in Bill's closet, I could find nothing but a stack of floor cloths. They looked clean enough, and from the way they were stacked, I assumed they'd been washed and not yet used. I sniffed at a couple. They'd do.

Back in the room, Dr. Taylor had not moved. She'd vomited again, and the wastebasket was between her knees. There was an ungodly odor.

Going over, I opened all the windows to the chilly November air. Then I went back to the sink and took out a plastic dishpan from the cupboard underneath. Running water into it and adding a generous amount of baking soda, I threw in the floor cloths.

"Are you going to be sick again?" I asked.

She shook her head.

"Are you sure?"

She nodded.

"Well then, come over here in this chair."

She rose, came over and sat.

I washed her. As if she were one of the children, I took the wet floor cloths and simply got on with it, doing the best I could to get the vomit off her clothes and off her. I had no idea what her current mental state was or how capable she was of cleaning herself up, and I was in no mood to inquire. She seemed considerably more sober than earlier but was perfectly willing to let me take care of things. Neither of us spoke a word. I knew when all this was over, the embarrassment was going to be excruciating for both of us, but for the moment all proprieties were suspended. A word from either of us would have broken the spell.

Bill came in, pushing his clanking mop bucket. Smiling at us, he produced a canister of Vomoose and sprinkled it blithely around. Then he went to work with brush and dust pan. Then the mop. He was whistling

"Oh! Susanna," and cleaned up the mess as casually as if it happened every day. The sour smell of vomit was soon overpowered by the almost equally nauseating odor of floral-scented disinfectant.

"See you around, Tor," he said and marshaled the mop bucket out of the door.

Bill's cheerful ordinariness displaced some of the tension in the room. I took the dishpan and cloths back to the sink and rinsed them out. Dr. Taylor turned her head to watch me. The color was coming back into her cheeks.

"Would you like some water?" I asked.

She nodded slightly.

All I had back there was my used coffee mug. Rinsing it out, I filled it and brought it over. She took it from me but then drank very little, pausing after only a few sips and lowering the mug. I folded the floor cloths and laid them on the table. The box of baking soda was still to be put away. I held it up.

"This is good stuff," I said. "It takes the smell away." Carefully, I pushed the little three-sided flap back down to close it. "I always keep some around. With the kids, you know. It's very good for getting rid of that horrible odor, and it tends not to hurt your clothes."

She very briefly caught my eye. Immediately, she looked away and then down. There was a moment of acute discomfort between us as the last seconds of obligatory intimacy melted away. I was as embarrassed about all this as she was, which no doubt had produced my sudden commercial for baking soda.

She stared down at her hands. "You're disgusted by me, aren't you?" she said, her voice soft and matter-of-fact.

"Well . . ." I shrugged and smiled self-consciously. "I'm sure you didn't come in here intending to do this."

She kept her head down.

"It was just one of those things," I said.

"I'm sure you must hate me."

"No," I said. "I don't even know you."

Her chin quivered.

"I must say, however, that I do think you need to get some help with your drinking. This kind of situation isn't doing anybody any good."

Bringing a hand up, she covered her eyes a moment, pressing against them in an effort to keep the tears back. "Some days I want to kill myself," she said.

Unexpectedly, I found myself feeling intense compassion for the woman. Her distress was suddenly so powerful that it filled the air around us. I could have touched it with my fingers. My feelings were intensified, as I watched her struggle so desperately to keep the tears back. After all the humiliating things she had already done, this rather minor loss of control seemed to be the one troubling her most. In an odd way, that moved me.

"Can I help you?" I asked.

She shook her head.

"I don't mean just here, now. In general. Is there something I can do to help?"

Again she shook her head.

Bringing her hands down, she snuffled back unfallen tears. She groped in her coat pocket for a tissue.

"I'm sure things must be hard for you," I said quietly. "From all I've heard about living with Leslie, you're under a lot of pressure. Coping must be very difficult in such circumstances."

"I don't know what to do."

"Perhaps I could help you with Leslie," I said. "If you want, I think I could probably make it a little easier for you."

She shook her head.

"You don't want that?"

"It's not Leslie, it's me. I just wish I could kill myself."

Concerned, I regarded her.

"I can't sleep. I lie in bed and think about how I'm going to do it. I make lists in my head."

"Lists?"

She shrugged slightly. "Of the people to call. You know, the lawyers and such, the things you've got to arrange."

I didn't know quite what to say.

"I lie there and think about those things," she said. Her voice was very soft, almost apologetic. "I'm scared to death of screwing it up. Tom'd never forgive me."

"I see."

"I think about it all. And then I go downstairs and I think, I'll just have one drink to give me courage to do it. But one drink isn't enough. I'm still too chicken."

Her facial muscles tensed; the tears reappeared but still did not fall. "And then Tom comes downstairs and he looks at the clock. It's maybe like 6:30 in the morning. And he says, 'What a disgusting bitch you've turned out to be.' "

CHAPTER
EIGHT

I collected Leslie and drove her and her mother home. I was reluctant to let Dr. Taylor drive as I had no idea how much alcohol was still in her system, and I was even more reluctant to leave her to her own devices. The journey was fairly long and took place in virtual silence. The change in location from the classroom to the car had broken the last of our intimacy. I could feel her defenses being put back into place, and I became a stranger again.

At last, I pulled into the long drive and came to a stop in front of the Considynes' house. It was a magnificent affair, sprawling in all directions, set in a literal forest of trees. But there was little sign of life. Dr. Taylor fumbled at the side of the car door, trying to find the handle to open it.

My mind had been racing during the trip over in an effort to come up with something to say. "Dr. Taylor?"

She did not answer, did not turn toward me, but she paused in her efforts to get out.

"Can I help you in some way?"

No response.

"I know this afternoon has been a pretty dreadful experience and I imagine you never want to see my face again, but I mean it. Is there something I can do?"

"Like what?"

I smiled apologetically. "I'm not sure. Could we perhaps just talk again?"

She nodded very slightly. The car door opened. "Thank you for everything," she said, her voice barely audible. Then she got out. She opened the back door for Leslie, and I watched as they walked up the drive to the house.

*　　*　　*

Dr. Taylor didn't take up my offer to talk. In fact, over the next few days she seemed to studiously avoid me. Tom Considyne brought and picked up Leslie, and I didn't see Dr. Taylor at all for the rest of the week.

Initially, I was disconcerted. I didn't know how seriously to take her talk of suicide, but I didn't necessarily think it should be ignored. On the other hand, I was unsure what I, personally, could do. At the time, it had seemed most important simply to get her to return, because until she was willing to do that, any offer of help from anyone would go unheeded. But if she did return, I didn't know precisely what I intended to do about her situation. I did make the effort to collect a few brochures on AA and other locally available programs for alcohol treatment, but beyond that, I hadn't done anything.

However, as time passed, the sense of urgency in the situation diminished. The immediacy of that horrific afternoon in the classroom receded, and ordinary day-to-day life with the children began to take precedence again.

My expectations of Shamie, Shemona and Geraldine were different from what reality was proving to be. I'd never dealt directly with children who had been on intimate terms with serious political strife or guerrilla warfare. It all seemed such a horrendous thing to me that I'd assumed it would somehow permeate every fiber of their beings. I had expected them to exude the tensions of Northern Ireland like breath, so that we would never be free of it. Indeed, I suppose I was as naïve as all those who had spoken to me of the girls before their arrival, because I expected their sad saga to overwhelm the children themselves. In fact, it didn't. They were, for the most part, very ordinary children, filled with very ordinary concerns. Certainly all three had suffered as a result of their previous circumstances, but they had suffered in the way all children suffer—in bewildered silence. Only their accents and their occasionally strange-sounding phrases reminded us of their foreign origins. Geraldine, alone, brought Belfast directly into conversations. She was undeniably homesick and couldn't keep from comparing her life here with her life there, but they were commonplace comparisons, of foods or different ways of doing things. They were the kinds of comparisons any homesick child would make. Belfast could have been Buffalo.

As the weeks passed and I grew more familiar with the children as individuals, I found their behavior very, very similar to that of severely abused children. They had that same quiet wariness about them, that same faint air of lost innocence, but they accepted their lives as normal and never raged against what had been stolen from them. Only on brief, incidental occasions did I glimpse the gray, gaunt specter of the abuser.

Geraldine, I discovered, was quite unwilling to mix with the other children on the playground. She stayed completely clear of Carolyn's kids, which I could understand to a degree, as their ages and handicaps made them fairly unsuited to an eight-year-old's activities, but she also refused to play with Mariana or Dirkie. Indeed, she didn't even play alone. Instead, she spent the entire time standing with me or with Carolyn, depending who was on duty, and because she did, so did Shemona. The only way to get the girls to join in was to join in myself.

Geraldine was making a general nuisance of herself one morning when we were out. She was swinging on my arms, hanging on my clothes, stepping on my shoes. Then she was in back of me, arms around my waist, face buried into my down jacket.

"Look over there," I said. "Joyce has gotten a game going. Why don't you take Shemona over and see if you can play too?"

"Don't want to," Geraldine breathed into my jacket.

"It looks like fun."

"They're all babies. I don't want to play a baby game."

"Mariana's over there. It looks like they're playing Duck, Duck, Goose. If you were there, Mariana would probably choose you."

Geraldine hugged me tighter. "Shemona wouldn't like it, would you, Shemona?"

Shemona, standing beside us, looked up but gave no response.

I reached an arm around to disengage Geraldine's bear hug. "Would it help if I went over there too?"

"Don't want to, Miss."

"Why not?"

"Just don't want to."

Shemona sat down on the asphalt and began to play with the Velcro fastening on her shoe. Over and over, she undid it and did it up again with an irritating rip. Geraldine pushed her hands into her pockets and stood beside me.

"Are you afraid of the other children?" I asked quietly.

"I'm not afraid of anything," Geraldine replied, just as quietly.

Then silence. We watched the other children playing. Everyone was over there, including Shamie, and the game was growing exuberant.

"Do you know what they did to me once?" Geraldine said, her voice soft.

"What's that?" I said, not knowing who or what she was talking about, but, noting the faraway tone of her voice, not wanting to ask.

"They put me in a dustbin."

She drew nearer to me. I extended my arm to pull her in.

"I was up on the High Street. I wasn't supposed to be there. Mammy didn't let us go there by ourselves, but I had some money and I wanted to buy some sweeties at the newsagent's. But when I saw their school uniforms, I knew I shouldn't go in there, so I turned around and crossed the street and went down between the houses. But those boys saw me and they started to chase me."

I looked down at her.

"I was running as hard as I could, but they were bigger than me, and they caught me. This one boy held me down and took my money. Then he and the others picked me up and put me in a dustbin. They sat on it and wouldn't let me out."

I pulled her close against me. "None of the children here would do a thing like that, Geraldine."

She didn't respond immediately, but Shemona rose to her feet and moved closer to us.

"I don't know," Geraldine said softly. "I've never gone to school with Prods before."

On the following Monday, Tom Considyne again brought Leslie to school. Then, in the afternoon when I took the children down to their rides, there was Dr. Taylor's familiar dark blue Mercedes. She got out of the car when Leslie and I approached, but she remained on the street side of it.

"Hello," I said, and smiled politely. Bending down, I opened the rear door and helped Leslie in. I fastened her safety belt.

"I'm sorry I didn't come in again last week," Dr. Taylor said, as I straightened up and shut the car door.

"That's all right."

"I meant to."

"That's okay. Don't worry about it."

There came a small moment's hesitation. She had her eyes averted. Feeling uncomfortable in the situation, I stepped back and prepared to return to the building.

"'Bye, Leslie," I said, leaning down to wave to her. "See you tomorrow." I looked over at her mother. "Good-bye, Dr. Taylor."

"No, wait," she said.

Opening the car door, she retrieved something off the seat. "I'm no good at talking about things," she said in a weary voice. "That's why I didn't come in. This is all I could think of." And she slid a green-covered spiral notebook across the roof of the car toward me. I had to move quickly to keep it from sailing off onto the ground.

She said no more. Getting into the car, she shut the door, started the engine and drove away.

I flipped through the notebook. It was a diary.

Going back upstairs, I returned to the classroom and sat down at the table. The notebook was completely filled in, from one edge of the page to the other, with no margins, each page, front and back. Virtually every line was covered in small, tight, very precise handwriting. The diary spanned a period of several months during the previous year. From glancing at its last page, I assumed it must continue on in another notebook.

> Consuela's gone to her mother's for the weekend. I make Leslie supper. She throws it on the floor because I forgot to put on her red bib first. While I am trying to scrape it up, Leslie has a b.m. and it gets all over the kitchen chair. Tom comes in and yells at me because I haven't gotten her to the toilet. He says I should know by now when she is going to go. He gets angry because the creamed corn has gotten all over the new carpet and the cat is licking it up. I say, if you don't like it, you can help. But he slams the door and goes to the studio. He doesn't come in for supper, so I have to give Leslie her bath and put her to bed alone. She hates this and does not go to sleep until 12:30 AM.

"What's that?"

Startled, I jumped and slammed the notebook shut. Carolyn was standing behind me. I'd been so engrossed, I hadn't heard her come in.

Carolyn craned her neck, curiosity brightening her expression. "What's that?"

"Just something someone gave me to read."

Carolyn grinned wickedly. "Must be interesting."

I grinned back. "It is."

"Is it dirty?"

"Not so far."

"Anybody I know?"

"Couldn't say."

She eyed me a moment to see if I'd give in and tell her, but when she realized it was unlikely, she shrugged. "Anyway, I came to find out if you wanted to go to that do over at Jefferson. It's Madge's thirty-umpteenth birthday, and the girls in the office got her a cake."

I shook my head. "No. I've got a ton of work to do."

"Goodness," Carolyn replied. "That thing *must* be interesting."

I reopened the notebook after Carolyn had gone.

> The house reeks of urine. There is no way to keep up with all the wet clothes and carpets and furniture. I'm sure the man from the

carpet cleaners thinks we're a bunch of deviants out here, because he's cleaned so much pee off our things. But Tom keeps insisting it's wrong to put Leslie in diapers because, he says, she can't pull the diapers down fast enough and it makes her frustrated. I tell him Leslie's constant messes frustrate me. I tell him he can clean the shit off things for a while. He tells me if I were more vigilant, I'd get her to the toilet when she needs it. He tells me if I'd been a good mother, we'd never have been in this spot to begin with.

It's Tom's turn to take Kirsten and TJ. I don't know how I am going to put up with Kirsten and TJ, as well as Leslie, for two whole weeks. Kirsten calls Leslie "Queero Baby" all evening. I go in the bathroom and find that Leslie has opened the childproof lock on the cupboard again. This from a kid who can't master the tapes on disposable diapers. She has spread Kirsten's moisturizer all over the mirror and then drawn through it with Kirsten's eyeliner. Everything is in chaos. Kirsten is livid. She is going out with Sam-the-Bam this evening and now maintains Leslie has wrecked her life. I tell Kirsten she can use my makeup. She looks through it and then knocks the whole works on the floor. Oooh, it's an accident, she says. I get angry and then Tom comes to see what's going on and gets angry at me. He says I am as bad as the kids, that I am stupid for always letting Kirsten upset me. She is only fifteen, for God's sake, and I am thirty-two and ought to know better. I start to cry. I don't mean to, but the bathroom is such a mess and everything is everywhere and half of it is broken and Leslie is covered head to toe and will need her hair washed. And all I wanted was to go to bed early. Kirsten is smiling. I tell Tom he is doing just what Kirsten wants by taking sides against me. Tom says I am doing just what Kirsten wants by getting so upset. The way it seems, we all do just what Kirsten wants. When I finally go to bed, there is a little note folded in between the sheets. It has been written in eyeliner pencil and says, "Cry baby cry/Punch you in the eye/Tie you to the bedpost/Leave you there to die."

I've got the pills. 271. That should be enough. I get a bottle of scotch and sit down with them. I divide them into groups of five. I think I can swallow five at a time. But then I stop and put the bottle back. I get to thinking about something I read once about how a lot of people vomit pills back up if they use alcohol, so I decide to use water. My stomach's so shot anyway. Some days I throw up just brushing my teeth. Garson comes in. He jumps on the desk and walks over the pills. He wants to be petted and is very insistent. He rubs against my cheek and jumps back up when I put him down. His purr is very loud and urgent. He *must* be petted. I tell him what a nuisance he is and throw him on the floor. But he keeps getting back up. He keeps purring and trying to get cuddled. I start to cry. I think, What will happen to Garson? Tom'll have him put to sleep if I am gone, and this makes me hate Garson. I hate him because I love him. It makes me cry harder. I end up getting the bottle of scotch back out. I feel like a real turd. And stupid Garson has knocked the fucking pills everywhere.

I closed the notebook after reading that. It was by no means the last entry. There were pages and pages more. But at that point, I couldn't read any further. Elbows on the table, chin resting on my clasped hands, I sat and stared at the very ordinary-looking green cover.

When Dr. Taylor came in with Leslie the next morning, I took the notebook down from the shelf and handed it back to her. "Look," I said, "will you come in and talk with me?"
She lowered her head.
"There are some real problems afoot, aren't there?"
No response.
"I appreciate your having given this to me," I said, "because it makes it a lot easier for me to understand, but I can't do much if we don't talk."
She kept her eyes averted. Watching her, I was reminded of one youthful summer in Montana when I'd had a young, partly broken horse. My free time was devoured, trying to catch him. Quiet and reassuring as I always attempted to be, he remained wild-eyed and skittish, his trust in me always failing at the crucial moment. He wanted to come. I had the oats bucket on my arm and I could see the longing in his eyes. Occasionally he found the courage. But more often than not, he would approach, come within a few feet of me and then lose his nerve, rearing back and galloping off; and we'd have to start all over again. Dealing with Dr. Taylor was proving to be an exercise on par with wild-horse catching.
"Why don't you come in this afternoon, after the school day is done. Say, about 3:45? We'll just have a chat, okay? Nothing more. Just you and me."
Still no response.
"Give me a chance, okay?"
She nodded very slightly.

And she did come, sober and subdued. She was very, very late. It was almost 5:00, by which time I'd lost faith and had already gone on to other tasks. So she found me at the table, midst plan book and strewn-out papers.

Surprised to see her, I smiled. "Hi. Come on in."

She slid into the chair opposite me. Looking like a chastened schoolgirl, she kept her coat on, her hands stuffed deep into its pockets. I had the distinct impression that she, like my horse of long ago, would start and flee at the slightest wrong move on my part.

I smiled again, in an attempt to ease things, but she wasn't looking at me. Within moments I saw her cheeks awash with tears.

Disconcerted, I shifted in my chair and reached to clear away the things on the table. "Would you like a cup of coffee?"

She shook her head.

"Are you sure? It isn't any trouble. I think I'm going to go get myself one."

"No. Coffee upsets my stomach."

"Oh, I see. Would you like something else? Tea? A soft drink? Juice? I think there's juice down there."

"No. I'm all right. Really. It's just that this is so hard for me to do."

I smiled. "I can appreciate that. From reading your notebook, I get the impression things are fairly rough at home."

She nodded.

"Leslie sounds like an extremely wearing child."

Again she nodded.

"But from what I gather, Leslie isn't the only child you're coping with. It sounds as if your husband's two children are over a great deal."

Another nod.

"How often?"

"Every other weekend. And all the school vacations."

"The whole vacation?"

"Usually."

"How old are they?"

"Kirsten's sixteen. TJ's seventeen."

"I get the feeling that they're difficult children in their own right."

She shrugged.

"Do *you* feel like that?"

"I guess."

"Can you tell me in what specific ways?"

She gave a little half-shrug.

"I can see you're finding it hard to talk, but don't let it upset you. It isn't bothering me."

This renewed the tears.

I leaned back, attempting to look relaxed in my rather unrelaxing wooden chair.

Dr. Taylor took tissues from the box on the table and wiped her face. Several minutes passed in silence as she recomposed herself. Laying the tissues on the table, she leaned forward and took off her coat. That was perhaps the most positive sign yet.

"Do you find you usually have trouble talking with people you don't know very well?"

She nodded.

"Just nerves?"

"I guess. I don't know."

"Well, don't let it worry you in here, okay? It's not something that's going to bother me any. I've spent a lot of my career working with people who don't talk easily. There's a special problem called elective mutism that interests me very much. It happens to kids, mostly; they *can* talk but won't. Anyway, working with them has made me very comfortable with silence."

A few minutes passed, and she didn't say anything. Then she tipped her head and grimaced. "It bothers my husband," she said quietly.

"What does? Your not talking easily?"

She nodded.

"Yes, he seems the kind to like a good chat."

"I just can't talk like that with anybody. You know, make small talk."

"Does it make him angry?"

She nodded. "He used to give these parties. He was famous for them. But he's stopped now, because of me."

I remained silent.

"His first wife was very good with his parties. You know, what's the word? A hostess. And I think Tom just assumed I'd be the same. You know, put on a great dress and . . ."

"And you weren't?"

She shook her head. "No, I wasn't. I hid in the bedroom sometimes. I'd shut the door and lock it and stay in there until everybody went home. It made Tom furious.

"Other times I just drank," she said. "That was the other way to get through those parties. To get too drunk to care. I could take them then, mostly because I never remembered what happened."

Silence.

"Have you had a drinking problem for long?"

She shrugged.

"Have you gotten help specifically for it at any time?"

"No."

I regarded her. She looked over then, and our eyes met briefly.

"I'm not really into that sort of thing, into those kinds of programs like AA. I went once to an AA meeting and I had to have a drink afterwards to get over it."

There was something about the way she said that which made me think she was pulling my leg a bit, so I smiled.

"It isn't funny. They aren't for me, those kinds of things. I think I'd rather be an alcoholic."

"There are a lot of alternatives," I said.

"I can stop if I want to."

"I see."

"I *can*. I mean, sure, I get drunk occasionally, but when I've done it, I've meant to. It didn't happen because I couldn't stop. I wasn't really out of control."

"Oh."

"Everybody gets drunk sometimes."

I looked at her.

She looked down at her hands in her lap. The tears reappeared.

I realized I needed to back off. She wasn't kidding anybody and she knew it. But I could tell that if I pressed the issue, she'd only grow more defensive and most likely simply get up and leave.

"Do you have any family out here? Any of your own family?"

"I've only got one brother. But he lives back in Pennsylvania."

Our conversation continued in much the same way, and it was bloody hard work the whole time. Dr. Taylor wasn't exaggerating her difficulty in making conversation. Even when she relaxed, it didn't come any easier for her. Indeed, she was one of the most inarticulate adults I had ever encountered. If I asked a question and it could be answered with a gesture, it was. If that wouldn't work and a single-word response would suffice, she opted for that. Had I not known ahead of time that she had had an education, nothing in her conversational abilities would have clued me in. I never in a million years would have guessed she had a doctorate in anything.

However, our conversation did progress. With excruciating slowness, I was given bleak insight into the workings of the Considyne household. Gilded by the ostentatious trappings of wealth, the whole family sounded emotionally bankrupt. They lived like a group of threatened hermit crabs, each person entrenched, isolated, untrusting of the others. Interestingly, the only one apparently to prosper in this setup was Leslie.

I was getting an extremely different picture of Leslie than I'd had initially. At the beginning of the year, I'd perceived her as the stereotype of a neglected child. She was so sweet and docile, so withdrawn, that I had endeavored to give her every spare moment of warmth and attention I could afford, occasionally even at the expense of the other children, in an effort to bring her back to life, as if she were some emotional Sleeping Beauty. However, during the conference with her father, I'd had my first inklings that things were different than they seemed. Now, talking with her mother, I realized Leslie was *not* suffering from lack of attention. Far from it!

Indeed, Leslie was the hub of the Considyne household. It ran to her specifications and hers alone. She ate when and where she pleased; she slept when and where she pleased; she even eliminated when and where she pleased. She indulged in her "self-expression," as Tom Considyne put it, getting into everything at any hour of the day or night and leaving behind her messes that could take literally days to clear up. No one endeavored to stop Leslie in any of these activities. When required to conform to more conventional behavior, Leslie sharply reprimanded those around her by withdrawing and giving nothing.

The clock on the wall worked its way around past six, then 6:30 and finally seven. My stomach was growling, and I had to lean against the edge of the table to make it inaudible, but the conversation was winding down too, more from fatigue than anything else. About 7:20, a weary silence came at last and lay down between us. I didn't have the energy to shoo it away.

Dr. Taylor looked over at me. Her anxiety had gone completely over the course of the two hours, and she now regarded me in that peculiarly thorough way she had. It was a very searching look, as if she expected to locate something and absorb it from me. To be examined like that was disconcerting.

Dr. Taylor finally looked away. She had a tissue in her lap and she fiddled with it. "You know what I want?" she asked quietly.

"What's that?"

"I want to be a better mother. I don't want Leslie to wind me up like she does." She paused and glanced over. "I want to be like you are with her."

I smiled slightly.

"I watch you on the playground. You're happy with her. Can you teach me to be like that?"

"Well, I expect it's a little easier for me. She isn't mine."

She ducked her head, looking down into her lap for a few moments, then a quick glance across to me again. "Can I ask you something?"

"Yes, of course."

"I've had an idea in my head," she said softly. Her voice grew cautious sounding. "But I didn't know how to ask you about it."

"What is it?"

"Well . . ." she hesitated, head down.

"Can you tell me?"

"You're going to think I'm being silly."

"I can't really tell, until I hear. What have you got in mind?"

"Well . . . well, you know how you were saying . . . that first time we talked. After school. You were saying how you never got enough time to work with Leslie. Remember that? After school in September?"

"Yes."

She was talking mostly to her lap. "You were saying you needed an aide, but the school district couldn't afford one. Well, I've been thinking about it ever since." She blushed brilliantly at that point and lowered her head even further. "Would you take me?"

I was genuinely stunned.

She instantly took my surprise as rejection.

"It was a horribly stupid idea. I'm sorry I've put you on the spot. I mean, I know I'm not the most . . . I mean, I . . . well, I don't know anything about this kind of work. It was dumb of me to ask."

"No, it's not dumb. You just caught me off guard, that's all. It's a good idea. I am still desperate for an aide. But the thing is, do you really want to *do* it?"

She nodded and still did not look at me. "I've been thinking about it for a while, but I just didn't know how to ask you. I mean, I know I don't know anything about this kind of work. But I thought I could learn."

There was a small pause.

"I thought maybe it'd help," she said. "Tom keeps telling me what a lousy mother I am, and he's right. I've got no patience for Leslie. I just don't seem to be able to treat her the way he does. So I was thinking that if I learned to do that better, maybe it'd help. And you seem to do it all so effortlessly."

"But you have to remember, Dr. Taylor, that I'm none of these children's mother. It's a lot easier to do this and then go home to freedom and a full night's sleep. Besides, regardless of how effortless it may look from where you are, it very often isn't. I screw up a whole lot in here. I can often be very, very wrong."

"That's okay," she said. "I learn from mistakes too."

CHAPTER
NINE

"You've lost your ever-loving mind," Carolyn replied. "Ladbrooke Taylor? In your classroom? What is this? Not enough nuts in your fruitcake already?"

"It was her idea."

"Her last idea, as I recall, was to come and upchuck all over your table."

"Look, I'm thankful for another pair of hands, whatever form they come in."

"For pity's sake, Torey, that's like Attila the Hun's volunteering to teach Sunday school. What does she know about any of this anyway?"

"She doesn't need to know. She just needs to be fit and hardworking. Besides, there's no one else volunteering, is there?"

"You're not getting help, Torey. What you're getting is just one more kid, a lot bigger and a lot ornerier when crossed. What are you going to do when she comes in drunk?"

"Turn her around and send her back out again," I replied.

"And you honestly think you're going to make an aide out of her? Look at the way she dresses, for pete's sake. You think she's going to come in, Guccis and Puccis and all, and crawl under the table after Dirkie?" Carolyn suddenly giggled.

"I'm serious, Carolyn. She's coming back in tonight, and if she still wants to try, I'm going to let her."

"Get your head examined. You need it."

On this occasion, Dr. Taylor was not late. At the arranged time, she appeared at the corner of the shelves. She stopped there.

I looked up from where I was sitting at the table and grinned. "You haven't chickened out, then?"

"No," she said, without even the hint of a smile.

I tried the grin a second time. "Okay. Come on over. Sit down, and I'll show you what we do in here."

She came around the table and pulled out the chair next to mine. She smelled tweedy, and I couldn't tell if it was cologne or just the scent of her hair and clothes. It was pleasant and outdoorsy. As ever, she was dressed with relaxed elegance: silk blouse, suede jacket, designer jeans. I wondered how she found the time to shop with all her drinking. I was sober and could never find anything that looked like that on me. But then again, I didn't have a body like that to put it on.

Passing the children's folders over to Dr. Taylor as I talked, I tried to tell her a little bit about each one. I mentioned Mariana and her sexual precocity, Dirkie and his obsessions. I talked about Shemona's and Geraldine's symbiotic relationship and Shemona's refusal to speak. I spoke of Shamie, sweet and gentle, but so immature.

I also mentioned Dirkie's fixation with long, blond hair. I didn't want to make it sound too dire, but I did suggest that it would be better if she kept hers tied back, at least in the beginning. Why? she asked. To keep him from touching it, from needing to touch it. For the first time genuine concern came to her eyes, and I could tell she was having second thoughts about us.

Afterward, I went over the pattern of our day. I explained the kind of jobs aides usually got stuck with and talked about the kind of relationship I'd had with most of my previous aides and what I hoped we could develop, if she found the work suited her. In the beginning, I would try to make her tasks all fairly specific and supervise them carefully, since she had no experience, but it was a gut-level occupation, I said, and I hoped she would come to the point where she felt comfortable enough with us to go without strict plans and simply fill in where the need was greatest without my having to direct her to it. I preferred a team member to a subordinate.

The one child I did not want her to work with was Leslie. I felt very strongly about this, explaining that Leslie already had her own little niche in here. It would be unfair to take that away from her. So, while I didn't want Dr. Taylor to ignore her daughter, I preferred to be responsible for most of Leslie's day myself.

"How's this all sound?" I asked, when I'd run through most of my notes.

"Okay."

"Is it what you expected?"

Her lips quirked up on one side. "I don't know what I expected."

I smiled.

"I think what I expected was for you to tell me I couldn't do it."

"I've had several parents working very successfully as volunteers in the past. And one of the best aides I ever had was a migrant worker who'd done nothing but pick asparagus before he came into my class. It's a vocation. Either you'll love it or you'll hate it. And you'll find that out soon enough."

She nodded.

"But it *is* hard work. Make no mistake about that."

"Hard work's never put me off before," she said, sounding slightly indignant.

I glanced down at my notes. "There is one other thing. I sort of hate to bring this up, but I think I need to. And that's your drinking."

She turned her head away from me.

"You've got to be sober in here all the time. I'm afraid I am going to have to be very strict about that. As you'll quickly discover, we need all our wits about us here. So, if you drink, if you want to drink, if you've been drinking, I'll ask you to leave. Understand that I won't be angry with you. I won't hassle you. I'll understand that you need to be gone. But in here, all the time, every time, you need to be cold sober. That has *got* to be a ground rule. Okay?"

She nodded slightly. A small pause followed. "What time do you want me?"

"Well, your hours are pretty much your own. As a volunteer, it's easiest if you set your own schedule and then just let me know which hours you plan to be here so that I can arrange things around that. How often do you think you might want to come in?"

She regarded me. "I thought I was going to be here every day," she said, her voice sounded a little surprised, as if this were a foregone conclusion.

"Well, yes, I suppose, if you want to be."

"When do you come in?" she asked.

"About 7:30 most days."

"Well, can I come in then too?"

"That's probably a little too early. The children don't start until 8:45. I'll tell you what, if you're thinking of working mornings, why don't you arrive about eight? Then we can use the extra time to go over plans."

"Okay." Pushing back her chair, she stood up and reached across the table for her coat.

"Oh, there is one other thing, Dr. Taylor," I said.

"What's that?"

"Do you have something less formal that we can call you in here? I tend to avoid titles. Seems more egalitarian to me."

"Sure," she replied, "it's Ladbrooke."

I reached a hand out to her. "I'm Torey."

Abruptly, she smiled in a very disarming way. It was the first genuine smile I'd ever seen cross her face. "Maybe this will work out after all," she said cheerfully. "We've both got screwball names."

It wasn't until I got home that night that I questioned what I'd just done, accepting Ladbrooke Taylor as an aide, and unexpectedly, I found myself awash with misgivings. What the heck had I just let myself in for? How had I gotten from this woman threatening to sue the life out of me to giving her full rein to share my days? The degree of impulsiveness in all this was pretty hard to ignore. My intention had been to simply direct her to someone somewhere who could help her and then get back to my own life. How had I gotten sidetracked into accepting her as a volunteer? My God, I thought suddenly, she wasn't even a recovering alcoholic. She was still in full swing. What on earth had I thought I was doing?

To her credit, Ladbrooke was punctual. She arrived the next morning precisely at eight o'clock. While she hadn't quite managed to shed the designer image, she'd obviously tried. The jeans were Levi's. The fashion boots had been replaced by a rather seedy-looking pair of jogging shoes.

Sitting at the table with my chin braced in one hand, I regarded her. "You're going to have to take off the jewelry."

She glanced down at herself.

"You can put it in the top drawer of the filing cabinet. That locks. But you're not going to want anything that dangles in any way."

"Why not?"

"So that you don't get hurt if somebody grabs you."

"Oh."

"And can you braid your hair back or something?"

She touched her hair uncertainly. It was still loose. She'd clipped it back with large barrettes so that it stayed behind her shoulders, but I knew that wasn't going to be enough to deter Dirkie.

"There're rubber bands over there on the top shelf."

She nodded. Sitting down across from me, she opened her handbag and took out a comb. She unclipped the barrettes and let her hair fall loose. Shaking it free, she pulled it around over her shoulder and began to braid it. She never spoke.

I hadn't said much to the children. I had intimated that we might be getting some help, but because I was unsure if Ladbrooke was going to follow through, I hadn't prepared them in any substantial way. This was a fairly flexible group of children, so I didn't think that would matter much. However, it did cause some unforeseen problems for Ladbrooke. The last time the children had seen her, she was passed out by our door.

Thus, the children were rather more interested in her than either of us had anticipated.

"Are you quite well now?" Shamie inquired, when he was introduced.

Ladbrooke glanced in my direction, a questioning expression on her face. It occurred to me that she might have little memory of that part of that day.

"He means when you were here. At the beginning of last week." I gave her a knowing look.

Ladbrooke blushed a brilliant hue. "Yes, thank you," she replied.

"Are you our new teacher?" Geraldine asked.

"She's our new helper. Your old teacher is right here," I said.

"You're pretty," Geraldine said to Ladbrooke. "You should be the teacher. You're prettier than she is."

Mariana bounced around the corner of the shelving and came to an abrupt halt. She regarded Ladbrooke a long moment and then smiled in a friendly way. "I know where I saw you last," she said brightly. "You were laying on our floor."

Another flush of color to Ladbrooke's face.

And, of course, there was Dirkie. When he rounded the corner into the main part of the classroom and saw Ladbrooke, he screamed as if someone had just plunged a knife into him.

"It's the dead lady!" he shrieked. "That dead lady is in our *room!*"

I knocked over a chair in my scramble to catch him before he bolted out of the classroom door. I just managed to snag him, hooking my fingers into the collar of his shirt and pulling him up short.

"Dirkie, she's not dead. She never was dead. I told you that before."

"You killed her."

"She's perfectly alive, Dirkie. Now calm down."

"I ain't meeting no dead lady. Let go of me!"

I pulled him back around the corner and into the main part of the room.

"Make her go away! Make that dead lady go *away!*"

To say Ladbrooke was looking horrified at this point was a vast understatement. It was doubtful, as I dragged Dirkie up to her, which of them was more likely to run screaming out of the room first.

With my free hand, I grabbed Ladbrooke's bare arm. "Here Dirkie, feel her arm. Touch it."

"I'm not going to touch no dead lady!"

"*Touch* it. Feel her arm. See? See how warm her arm is. Feel mine. Feel your arm. They're warm, see? How can she be dead? Dead people are cold, aren't they? Ladbrooke's just as alive as we are. Feel how warm she is."

I had to physically place Dirkie's hand on Ladbrooke's arm, but as I had hoped, the connection was instanteously successful. The human warmth of her skin was too obvious. Dirkie's hand relaxed against her arm. He touched his own arm then. And mine. And back to Ladbrooke's. His other muscles relaxed. I loosened my grip on his shirt.

Dirkie looked up at Ladbrooke. Then he scanned the rest of her body. It was a a very thorough bit of scrutinizing. Then he touched her bare arm again.

"That's enough touching, Dirkie."

"Hoo-hoo-hoo," he said, and a maniacal little smile came to his lips.

"Dirkie? I mean it. That's enough touching. People don't like to be stroked like that."

If possible, Ladbrooke's expression was even more horrified than before. Every muscle had tensed. She seemed frozen, unable to pull herself away from Dirkie, who was touching her arm in an increasingly provocative manner.

"Take your hand off her *now*, Dirk. I mean. it." I reached over and removed his hand. "That is *not* appropriate."

"Hoo-hoo-hoo."

I maneuvered Dirkie away from Ladbrooke and toward his chair.

"She's got big tits!" Dirkie said with loud enthusiasm.

"Yes, but you're not going to say anything to her about them, are you? Remember what I've told you about personal remarks, Dirkie? People don't like them. They get upset. And we don't want to upset Ladbrooke on her first day, do we?" I fixed him with the evil eye. "Do we?"

"But they're *big!*"

"Just like the trouble you'll be in, if you don't take your seat."

As had long been my custom in special classes, I opened the day with "discussion." Discussion began with a "topic"; topics traditionally explored areas that persistently got the children in trouble, such as cause-effect behaviors, feelings and moral questions. Occasionally the period was used for problem solving. At the beginning of the year, I usually had to introduce the majority of topics we discussed, but as time progressed and the children became used to the procedure, they themselves supplied most of the topics. We set a fifteen-minute limit on the length of discussion of the topic, and everyone was encouraged to participate. Afterward, each child had a few minutes to recount what had happened to him or her in the interim since we'd broken up the previous afternoon and to share any interesting news. Then I passed out the work folders, gave a brief outline of the day's events, and we knuckled down.

Over the years, I had accumulated a box of props that the children liked to use during discussion. There was a collection of photographs showing people in numerous situations and with countless expressions on their faces. There was an extended family of tiny, plastic dolls and some dollhouse furniture. There were six hand puppets: two girl puppets, two boy puppets, a witch puppet and a knitted dragon. And there was a large set of plastic animals. All the children liked using them.

"I've got a topic today," Mariana announced, extracting two girl dolls from the box. She stood them up and made them move toward each other in mincing steps while the rest of us arranged ourselves comfortably on the floor pillows. But once we were sitting and attentive, she stopped playing with the dolls and held them, one in each hand, and stared at them.

"Do you want to go ahead, Mariana?" I asked.

She regarded the dolls. "I brung in my special eraser yesterday. The one that looked like a strawberry. And somebody's tooken it." She did not look up. Instead, she caused one doll to beat the other over the head.

"You've looked carefully for it? You've searched right to the back of your cubby?" I asked. "And you're certain you didn't leave it at home?"

Mariana nodded. "It was my strawberry eraser that smelled like a real strawberry. I showed it to you yesterday, remember? Then I put it right back into my cubby to keep it safe. Now it's gone. And I know who stolded it." Mariana glared in Geraldine's direction. "She did. That little fucker over there."

Silence reigned for a brief moment, then Dirkie hooted softly. He leaned toward Ladbrooke and said sotto voce, "She lets us say words like that. *Swear* words. Fucker, fucker, motherfucker."

Glancing in his direction, I raised my eyebrow, and he sat back demurely. "Hoo-hoo," he whispered.

Back to Mariana. "You know we don't use discussion as a time to accuse people."

"But Geraldine *took* my strawberry eraser. It's gone and she stolded it and I know she did. I'm not accusing her. I *know*."

"We'll handle the matter later, after discussion."

A crashing silence came down around us, and it became apparent that the children weren't going to orient to another topic. Shamie, Geraldine and Shemona were all huddled together, like a group of covered wagons preparing for an Indian attack. Mariana glowered at them from across the circle. Dirkie was studying Ladbrooke's assorted attributes. Leslie, beside me, sat silent and motionless.

"Why do you suppose people steal things?" I asked.

"Because they're dumb fuckers," Mariana replied.

"Why else?"

"Because they want things and they don't have them," Shamie said.

"Has any of you ever stolen anything?" I asked.

"She has!" Mariana retorted. "Ask *her*. She has."

"Has any of you ever stolen anything?" I asked again.

No response.

"I have," I said. "I remember once when I was eight, I took a magazine from my classroom at school. It had Halloween projects in it, and I really wanted to do them. But they weren't the kind of thing a teacher would let you do at school, so I stole the magazine and took it home with me."

Everyone looked scandalized.

"Did you get caught?" Mariana asked.

I shook my head.

"Did your conscience bother you?" Shamie asked.

"At the time, no, not very much. I wanted to do the projects too much. And I can remember doing them. One was making this paper-clip skeleton, and it was quite good. But afterward, I was left feeling disappointed. I couldn't share the projects with anyone. I had to do them alone and then put them away without showing them to anyone. That ruined it for me. The consequences, even though I didn't get caught, were enough to make me not do it again."

I looked at the others. "Has anyone else had an experience like that?"

"I steal sometimes," Mariana said. She still had the two dolls clutched in her hands. "When Daddy Jack comes over and him and Mom get to sitting around and drinking, I get mad and I steal tapes out of his car. I steal 'em and break 'em. Then he spanks me. But I don't care. Him and Mom, they get six-packs and put them on the back porch, and then they sit in front of the TV and drink and drink. They don't get me or Markie no dinner or nothing. Then I have to make Markie scrambled-egg sandwiches, because that's all I can cook. 'Cept I can't now, 'cause the stove's broke. You know what Markie did last night?"

"What?" asked Dirkie, enthralled.

"He wee'd in the sock drawer. I said, 'Markie, you stupid ass, don't do that.' But he did. So I had to take all the socks out and wash 'em. I washed 'em in the bathtub, but there was other junk in there already, so I thought I better wash that junk too. So I got some soap and I washed it all and hung it on the furniture to dry. And Daddy Jack and Mom were down watching TV, and he says, 'Hey, Mariana, what the fuck you doing up there?' And I says, 'Nothing.' And he comes up to see and he says, 'What's all these goddamned socks doing everywhere?' I wasn't going to tell him Markie did that, so I snuck out the back door and hid under the porch till he was done being mad. But I was mad myself. So later I went and got all the tapes out of his car and broke 'em. And I don't feel bad. I'm glad I done it. I think he deserves it."

"So you steal to get back at your Daddy Jack," I said.

Mariana nodded.

"And what about you, Geraldine?" I asked, turning in her direction. "When you were little, did you ever steal anything?"

Geraldine shook her head.

"Liar!" Mariana shouted.

I touched Mariana's arm.

"Geraldine's lying," she said. She had risen to her knees, and tears came to her eyes. "My mommy bought me that strawberry eraser because I was a good girl last weekend. It smells like a real strawberry, and I want it back. It's mine."

Unexpectedly, Shemona leaned forward and snatched away the two dolls that Mariana had been holding. Then, extracting one of the girl puppets, she put her hand inside and began pounding the dolls. Bang, bang, bang she went, in silent fury.

Geraldine became agitated by her sister's unanticipated actions. "Oh, Miss," she cried. "Shemona's trying to tell you she took it. She took Mariana's eraser. And she's really, really sorry. Aren't you, Shemona?"

Shemona's behavior abruptly deteriorated. Grabbing up the dolls, she smashed them down. Then the hand puppet became a weapon to flail things with. She picked up the dolls and hurled them like missiles.

"Hey." I rose to my knees to catch hold of her. The other children scattered to safety.

When I grabbed Shemona, Geraldine panicked. "Don't smack her, Miss! Don't smack her! It's in my bag. I've brought it back. Shemona took it, but I've brought it back." Geraldine was on her feet and across the room to her cubby.

I lifted Shemona high up over the other children.

"Please don't smack Shemona, Miss. Here's the eraser. Here it is." Geraldine had begun to cry too. She threw the eraser at Mariana as if it were a hot coal.

"I'm not intending to smack anyone, Geraldine," I said, letting Shemona down. When I released her, she bolted to the far end of the room and crouched down midst the pillows. "I don't smack kids." Geraldine ignored me and ran to Shemona, flinging her arms around her sister.

The place was in chaos. Leslie was flapping her arms with excitement. Dirkie had dived under the shelves. Shamie, appearing on the verge of tears himself, wrung his hands nervously. Ladbrooke, too bewildered to move, simply stood in the middle of everything. Only Mariana, her beloved eraser in hand, seemed composed.

"Okay, everybody," I said and went to the table. "Work time. I'm going to start passing out folders. I'll count to ten and then I want to see everyone in his or her seat." I counted slowly, then took down the stack of folders from the top of the file cabinet. "Come on, Dirkie. Come out of there." I squatted down to peer at him, lying flat on one of the shelves. He crawled out slowly and took his folder.

Shamie sat down and accepted his work. Mariana sat. I had to hold Leslie for a few minutes before she quieted enough to sit.

"If you have any questions about your work, you can ask Ladbrooke. She knows what each of you is doing."

I then went over to Geraldine and Shemona, still in the corner. I put a hand on Geraldine's shoulder. "Come on, sweetie. Let's go back to the table now and get you started on your morning's work."

"Shemona didn't mean to take it, Miss. She wasn't being naughty on purpose. I don't know what got into her."

"I understand, Geraldine. Now, come on. Stand up."

Geraldine stood. Shemona still huddled on the floor. I reached down and lifted her to her feet. She was trembling. But as usual, she pulled away from my touch. So I herded them together back to the table and pulled out chairs for them. Taking their work folders, I sat down with the two girls and went over their work with them.

Forty-five minutes or so later, when I was at the sink in the back of the room with Leslie, Shamie came back to wash his hands.

"You know Geraldine took that wee eraser, don't you?" he asked in a very soft voice.

I nodded. "Yes, I know."

CHAPTER
TEN

I was determined to do something about Leslie. All I had been waiting for was some auxiliary help, and now that I had it, I was able at last to get around to the kind of one-to-one work with Leslie— and Dirkie, as well—that I'd wanted to do from the beginning. But my perceptions of Leslie had changed so drastically over the previous few weeks that I was more desperate than ever to intervene with her.

Although I remained convinced that the major basis for Leslie's disturbance was physiological, I'd gained a great deal more insight into the layers of manipulative behavior that had grown up around it. The indepth discussion with Ladbrooke had been invaluable; my entire perception of Leslie altered. She took on a Helen Keller aura to me, another example of a brilliant, handicapped youngster who wasted her energies tyrannizing an indulgent family. The annoying thing was, Leslie had achieved pretty much the same sort of relationship with me. I'd cuddled her and coddled her and assumed, like everyone else, that the poor little dear wasn't capable of much more. The quieter and more withdrawn she was, the more cuddles were forthcoming. She was nowhere near the little dictator here that she was at home, but she still had my personality quite accurately figured out.

One morning after discussion, I sat down with Leslie's folder. As usual, she climbed into my lap. Normally, Leslie's folder didn't include much, as she was unable to work on her own at all and was generally unresponsive to being worked with in a group. However, this morning I'd included one of Shemona's worksheets. On the left side of the paper were a series of colored shapes. On the right side were the same shapes in different order. The object of the exercise was to draw a line from the one on the left to its mate on the right.

"Look what I've got for you today," I said, as Leslie adjusted herself in my lap. "You have a worksheet, just like everyone else. Isn't that something? A big girl's work. You and I are going to do it together."

I took the sheet out and laid it on the table in front of us. I explained what was to be done. Leslie sat, motionless.

"Here. Here's a pencil."

No response.

I looked down at her and saw she wasn't even looking at the paper. She stared vacantly ahead. I tilted her head down. Then, taking up her right hand, I carefully inserted the pencil and wrapped her fingers around it. It fell out and bounced along the floor. I retrieved it and once again pressed her fingers around it. Again it slid out and rolled away under the table.

"Well, no, that's not going to do," I said. "You need to hold the pencil. Here, take it in your hand. Hold it. Or else you won't be able to draw the lines."

She had completely evaporated. I was left with just the shell of a kid, flimsy as a paper sack.

"Oh, I see. You aren't quite in the mood to work. Okay." I lifted her down from my lap, stood and went over to Shamie. He was practicing his spelling, so I took up his list and began to help him.

Leslie remained standing, frozen into the position I had left her in. Not a muscle twitched. Her eyes were unfocused, her face expressionless. She stood that way for the entire hour and fifteen minutes between my getting up and the start of recess, when she joined the other children as they left the classroom.

After recess, I approached Leslie again. Or rather, she approached me. Coming up to me as I was sitting with Mariana and Geraldine, she attempted to get into my lap.

"Oh, good, you want to work too," I said. "Just a minute. Let me get your paper. I reached over and pulled her folder across the table. I lifted Leslie into my lap. "Here." I handed her a pencil. She didn't take it. Once again, I took her hand and pressed the pencil into it. The pencil dropped out.

"You don't feel like working?" I asked.

Leslie had evaporated.

"Oh, well," I said and put her off my lap. "I'm afraid you can't sit here then. I'm busy with girls who are doing their work." I slid my chair closer to the table, so that my abdomen was right up against the edge. Then I proceeded with Mariana and Geraldine.

This registered with Leslie. She didn't blank out entirely, but rather watched us, her forehead slightly wrinkled.

After a few moments, Leslie lifted one leg and attempted futilely to wedge herself onto my lap in spite of my closeness to the table.

"Oh no, I'm afraid you can't sit here, Leslie. I'm busy. If you want to do this paper with me, then you may stay. Otherwise, I need to get on with Geraldine and Mariana."

In her own noiseless way, she became quite insistent. It was the first time in all these months that I'd seen her truly engaged in an interaction with me, other than that one occasion in the janitor's closet. With persistence, she attempted to make room for herself on my lap. She got one leg up across mine, which left her in a precarious position. I did my best to ignore her, as she stood like a stork, hopping on one foot. The other two girls were having a harder time.

"Why are you being mean to Leslie today?" Mariana asked.

"I'm not being mean. I'm just busy. She wants to sit in my lap, and I don't have time for that right now. I'm busy with people who are working hard."

"Leslie can't work," Mariana replied earnestly, clearly concerned at what she was perceiving as maltreatment.

"Leslie *can* work. Everyone can work. And when she's feeling in the mood, she can sit on my lap and I'll help her. In the meantime, I'm busy with you two."

Leslie, still caught with one leg lodged between mine and the table, balanced silently. When I scooted my chair back, she fell down. I rose and walked off. She didn't move.

Leslie realized the gauntlet had been thrown down, and she hadn't gotten where she was through a weak spirit. One day, two days, three days passed wth no change, other than the worksheets. Each day I approached her, and she went vacant. Each day she approached me, and I refused her access to my lap. Sometimes three or four times a day we went through this, both of us insistent on things going our own way.

I did hope I was doing the right thing. My spirits were flagging after the third day. I was dreadfully conscious of having Ladbrooke in the room. She never said anything, but by the same token, she certainly didn't ignore us. Every time I looked, she was watching us intently. That horrific encounter we'd had in early November, when she'd threatened to sue the life out of me, was never again mentioned. Indeed, I suspected that it might have been something lost in the alcoholic mists of her memory, but I sure hadn't forgotten it. I kept thinking about it each time I saw Ladbrooke's eyes following me as I once again pushed her child off my lap. Even worse than Ladbrooke were the other children, particularly Mariana, who were very vocal about the sudden change in my relationship with "poor Leslie." It was their comments, more than any other thing, that made me realize how much we'd all come to accept Leslie's withdrawn behavior as normal.

On Thursday afternoon of that week, I went down after school and had a long talk with Carolyn. Had she ever come across anything like this? Did she think it was possible for a child to manipulate withdrawal in this manner? Was I expecting too much out of a poor little mite who couldn't understand what was going on? Was I depriving her of the warmth and security and physical contact she had come to depend on as a vital part of our relationship? Would I hurt more than help in the long run?

Carolyn hadn't come across anything like this, but she was reassuring and supportive. Keep trying a little longer, she said. Give it a week and see how it goes.

We got to the following Tuesday and there *was* a change. We'd started the morning the same way as the others. Again I had the matching-colors worksheet for Leslie, again she refused to cooperate. So I'd put her off my lap and gone on to the other children. It was a hectic morning all around, and I soon became absorbed in what I was doing. So when I turned around just before recess to see what Leslie was doing, I found her gone.

I glanced around the room. Getting up from the table, I went around to the blackboard area. No Leslie anywhere.

"Where's Les?" I asked, coming back to the table.

Everyone turned and looked.

"Has anyone seen her?"

Then all of a sudden there came a loud *rrriiiip* from deep within the library shelves. Going around the corner from the table, I plunged into the long, narrow aisles of the library. There was Leslie at the far end. She had next to her a whole pile of shredded journals. When she saw me, she looked me straight in the eye and tore another long strip from one of the magazines.

"Young lady, what's this?" I pulled her to her feet. Bits of *Psychology Today* fluttered everywhere.

"This is *not* what we do with magazines."

Leslie glared, not at me but simply straight ahead. Her forehead furrowed, her eyebrows formed a grim line.

"Go get the wastebasket so we can clean this up."

She did not move.

"Go get the wastebasket, Leslie."

More furrows on the forehead.

"Go. Now."

"No!" she shouted and ran down the long aisle with her arm held out, causing every single journal she touched to fall on the floor. At the far end, she paused, grabbed what she could reach and flung it everywhere.

I leaped over the things strewn in my path and caught hold of her. She screeched with a volume I'd not anticipated, writhed and sunk her teeth firmly into my hand. I let go of her, more from surprise than pain.

Leslie shot off around the corner and into the main part of the classroom. Wiping blood on my jeans, I shot off after her. Everything she could get her hands on, she threw down. Work folders, books, coats, art materials all went crashing to the floor. With a final lunge, I caught up with her in the far corner, grabbing hold of her clothes. I lifted her physically off the floor by the back of her overalls and, wrapping my arms tightly around her in a confining bear hug, I sank down to the floor.

She was not screaming, not crying, just fighting. Grunt. Gasp. Flail. Kick. Twist. Turn. She kept at it and at it, trying to break my grip, so I enveloped her further, bringing my knees up to pin her in closer to me. We wrestled for a matter of minutes before she finally gave in. In the end, she collapsed wearily against me. I let go of her then, and she fell from my arms to lie, panting heavily, with her face against the brown-and-white linoleum.

I rose and went over to the quiet chair, a large wooden chair in the back of the classroom. Mostly, I sent children to sit there until temporarily lost tempers were recovered, but I also used it for plain, old time-out. "Leslie, sit here," I said.

She looked up at me, and for a moment, I knew she was weighing the challenge. But in the end she rose and came over without further urging.

"I'm going to put the timer on for five minutes. When it rings, you may get up and rejoin the rest of us. Until then, sit here."

I turned and came back to the others. Blood from where Leslie had bitten me had gone all over my blouse. I went over to Ladbrooke, who was sitting white-faced and wild-eyed at the table. She was trembling. "I'm going to go down to the office and get a couple of Band-Aids. I'll be right back."

"No. Don't go," she said.

"I'll be right back." And I was, even before the timer had gone off. I returned, sat down with Dirkie and began to help him with his work. When the bell rang, I looked over to Leslie. "You may get up now."

She didn't. Her body remained on the chair; the rest of her had disappeared.

At recess time, Leslie got off the chair when the other children started putting on their outdoor clothes. She headed for her cubby and her own jacket but hesitated as she passed her usual place at the table, where her work folder still lay open. Without so much as a glance toward the rest of us, she reached over, took up one of Mariana's pencils and drew unfaltering lines between the colored shapes. Then she put the pencil down and continued on to get her clothes. I said nothing, neither to Leslie nor to Ladbrooke, who was bent down beside me to help Shemona with her jacket. But I did smile.

Both boys developed fairly obvious crushes on Ladbrooke during the course of her first weeks with us. Ladbrooke's beauty was the sort of thing one didn't acknowledge noticing, but it wasn't really possible to ignore. However, lumping it into that broad category of things which people can't help about themselves, I'd not given it much more thought. I suppose I should have weighed the matter before allowing her into the classroom with pubescent boys, but the wholesale silliness I was letting us in for never really crossed my mind.

Shamie's reaction was that of any red-blooded male. He was besotted, plain and simple. Making calf eyes, trying to sit next to her at any opportunity, falling over himself to accommodate her every whim, he did nothing more than make a lovable nuisance of himself.

Dirkie, on the other hand, was something else again. He kept wanting to touch Ladbrooke. This was particularly unfortunate, as Ladbrooke, I soon discovered, was uncomfortable even with normal amounts of physical contact. She couldn't bring herself to casually touch the children and she barely tolerated their touching her. She'd go motionless, all muscles tensing, and wait breathlessly for the child to take his or her hand away. So Dirkie got to be a bit of a menace.

Dirkie's reaction was to stroke himself, which was, if anything, more embarrassing to Ladbrooke. "Oh, beautiful lady," he'd say, running his hands down the sides of his face. "Beautiful lady, beautiful face." Which was a whole lot better than his "Big tits, big beautiful tits," while he caressed his shirt.

But of course, Dirkie's worst problem was with Ladbrooke's hair. I had to admit, she did have the kind of hair that would attract almost anybody's attention. Thick and shiny and always slightly uncontrolled, no matter what she did to it, it invited touching. I knew sooner or later I wasn't going to intervene in time.

Leslie's explosion that morning set us all on edge. Even after lunch, when things had pretty much returned to normal, the children were hard to settle. Dirkie, as always, was the most sensitive to disturbance, and as a consequence, he'd spent most of the day hooting quietly from under the table.

After lunch, he came into the classroom hyped up. He giggled and laughed and clapped, all the while mincing around the room on the tips of his toes, like a drunken ballerina.

"Dirk, sit down, please," I said. The children were making paper chains in preparation for Christmas, three weeks in the future.

Dirkie went to his chair and sat, reaching for a handful of construction-paper strips. But within minutes, he was up again, dancing around. He minced over in Ladbrooke's direction.

"Dirkie," I said, my tone sufficient warning, or so I hoped.

He had his hand out, just the tip of his forefinger touching a strand of Ladbrooke's hair. Half the problem lay with her. She just could not abide the need to keep her hair braided or otherwise bound firmly back, and I don't think she appreciated how much time I wasted, intervening. I felt petty, reminding her again and again, and resolved to let natural consequences take their course; but when in the classroom, seeing Dirkie on the move, I could never bring myself to just sit by and watch. On this occasion, Ladbrooke didn't have her hair completely back. The bit around her face was pulled back and held with a barrette but the majority lay loose down her back and over part of the chair she was sitting in. It was this, the bit sticking out over the back of the wooden chair, that was too much temptation for Dirkie. He minced away on his toes and then returned. Another finger went out, and he touched the hair again.

I rose, walked around the table and took him by the shoulder. "Come back here with me," I said, and sat him down beside me. I gave him part of my paper chain to work on.

"You got nice hair," he said and reached up to stroke mine.

"No," I said and put his hand down. "That isn't appropriate. You don't touch people's hair without asking permission first."

"You've got nice, long hair. Are you going to cut your hair?"

Geraldine across from us groaned. "Doesn't he ever say anything else?"

"Are you going to cut your hair?"

"No, Dirkie. Now help with the chains."

But he couldn't. "Hoo-hoo-hoo." And then he slipped off the chair and under the table. "Hoo-hoo-hoo." He began to clap.

After Leslie's explosion, I didn't like provoking Dirkie into something similar; and I knew I would, if I kept at him. So, instead, I let him stay under the table.

We worked for some time in relative peace. The chain making was an enjoyable activity. Christmas was far enough ahead that the mania hadn't set in, but the festive spirit was becoming apparent. The children talked animatedly among themselves about presents, traditions and the things they liked best about Christmas.

Shamie, who was sitting next to Ladbrooke, lifted up his chain to see his progress. He'd been beavering away and now found he couldn't stretch his arm high enough to display the entire length, so he shook it to straighten it out on the table. That sent a flurry of paper strips scattering into Ladbrooke's lap and down onto the floor.

"Oh, I am sorry," Shamie said.

"That's all right," Ladbrooke replied and leaned down to retrieve the fallen strips beside her chair. That was her fatal mistake. As she bent down, her hair fell forward, and Dirkie, waiting under the table like a lurking piranha, couldn't resist the opportunity presented him.

I didn't realize what was happening at first. Ladbrooke had been sitting across from me, then there was a sudden shriek and she just disappeared off her chair. Astonished, I rose up and leaned across the table. Chaos followed. The other children on that side of the table were jumping aside. Chairs went everywhere. Paper chains and construction paper flew about us.

"Dirkie?" I was still leaning over from my side of the table, still not altogether sure what had happened. Then I pulled my chair back and knelt down to see under the table.

Really serious chaos was going on down there. If Dirkie had wanted hair, he had certainly managed to find it, because Ladbrooke's hair was all over him. He was clutching huge fistfuls of it, rubbing it frantically against his face and writhing in ecstasy. He hooted hysterically.

Ladbrooke was almost as hysterical as he was.

I crawled under the table in an effort to separate them. "Out. Out the other side. Move. Ladbrooke, move back."

"I can't! I can't! I can't!"

"Dirkie, *stop* that! Now move."

Neither of them did. I kicked out the chairs from around the table to give space, but I couldn't actually move the table much. It was huge and heavy, and there wasn't much spare space in the room to move it to, but I did manage to slide it back enough to give me easier access to Dirkie.

Not knowing how else to stop him, I climbed on top of him and physically pinned him to the floor. It meant having to climb on Ladbrooke's hair as well, but I was past worrying about causing her any more pain than she was already experiencing. Sitting firmly on Dirkie's stomach, I smashed his wrists against the linoleum. Moving a knee onto his elbow, I took one hand and began doggedly prizing his fingers apart and unwrapping the hair from his hand. It was a slow process, because by that time the hair had tangled upon itself and around the buttons of Dirkie's shirt and even into my clothing. Moreover, we were still half under the table, so I had to hunch forward to keep from hitting my head.

"If I ever, *ever* catch you doing this again," I said, as I worked, "I'll make dogmeat of you, Dirkie. I promise you, I will. This is cruel. It hurts."

He was growing calmer as I sat on him. The hooting stopped, and he lay silent.

At last, I had all the hair disentangled from our clothes. Ladbrooke pulled back and disappeared, while I stayed astride Dirkie.

"Have I made myself clear to you?" I asked. "I don't want to ever catch you doing this again. Not with Ladbrooke. Not with Shemona. Not with anybody. Is that registering?"

Solemnly, he nodded.

I eased back and stood up. "Okay, get out from under there and go sit in the quiet chair."

"Are you mad at me?" he asked.

"Yes."

Dirkie, with an injured expression on his face, rose from under the table and went to the quiet chair. I shoved the table back where it belonged and started replacing chairs. Then I looked around for Ladbrooke. Shamie jerked his head in the direction of the blackboard arm of the room. "She's over there."

I went around the corner of the shelves to find Ladbrooke at the far end, leaning against the wall. I put an arm around her shoulders. "You okay?"

She nodded. There were tears in her eyes.

"I know. It hurts. I've had it happen to me," I said.

She nodded again.

"Listen, there's not much time left before recess. Why don't you go on down and relax in the lounge for a bit. I'll meet you there once the kids are out."

"Okay."

By the time I got down to the teachers' lounge, Ladbrooke had recovered enough to try untangling her hair. I bought myself a Dr. Pepper from the machine and drank deeply of it. I regarded her over the top of the can. By this point, I was beginning to see the funny side of the situation, and it was hard not to smile, but I didn't. Ladbrooke wasn't overendowed with a sense of humor, even on the best of occasions.

She fought irritably with the snarled hair. "I look like a witch," she muttered, as I came over.

"Do you want some help?"

"No, it's okay. I'll get it."

"Do you want a drink?" I asked, holding out the can of pop.

"God, I could do with one, believe me," she said, her tone heartfelt.

I smiled.

Clearly still a little overwrought, she dropped her hands in frustration, when the bit of hair she was working on refused to untangle.

"It's going to take you forever that way, Ladbrooke. Here, give me the brush. I can do it more easily from behind you."

She hesitated a moment.

"Come on, give it here."

"All right," she said wearily, and passed the brush to me.

Going behind the sofa, I lifted her hair up and over the back. I paused to try and tease a bit of it free with my fingers, but I couldn't. It was in a frightful state, and I wasn't too sure where to start. Pulling over a nearby empty wastebasket, I upended it and sat down. Then, carefully, I started at the bottom and began working my way up.

For a considerable time neither of us spoke. The teachers' lounge was empty except for the two of us, and the quiet atmosphere was soothing.

"I'm not used to anyone doing anything with my hair," she said.

I concentrated on a very snarly bit. In the end, I had to pick it apart with my fingernails.

"I've never liked that sort of thing," she said, "people all over me, touching me."

"I've noticed," I said.

"I just don't like it."

Again I teased apart a nasty tangle with my fingers. I could have done with a rat-tailed comb, or even an ordinary comb, because Ladbrooke's brush was not very effective against such tangles as these.

"Golly, that hurt when Dirkie did that," Ladbrooke said. "It really surprised me how much."

"Yes, I know. I've had it happen myself. Never as bad as this, but enough to give me plenty of empathy."

"I think I've got your point now—about putting my hair back," she said, her tone rueful.

I smiled. "Carolyn and I go down to the spa at night and sit around in the whirlpool, comparing bruises. You get so you can go down your legs like a road map. This one's from Shemona, when I made her get ready for lunch. That one's from Mariana, when she pushed the swing into me. It's the main reason I wear pants all the time. My legs are a mess."

"You're really laid back about all of this, aren't you?"

"Doesn't bother me, if that's what you mean," I replied.

"It's more than a case of simply not bothering you, Torey. You really get turned on by it, don't you? All this blood and guts."

I smiled. "Yes, I suppose."

Finally, I got to the point where I could brush most of the hair out in long, straight strokes. Ladbrooke slowly began to relax. Taut muscles along her neck and shoulders loosened, and she leaned back into the saggy sofa cushions. I ran my fingers through the hair to see if I missed any tangles.

"Yes, I like all this," I said. "Not this particular part, mind you. I mean, I don't like seeing anybody get hurt, but in a relative sense, I like all this. I like the unpredictability, the volatility. I like the sense of living on the edge that's always there."

"And the people part," she said. "You like that."

Again I smiled. "Yes, and the people part. I like all of that. I think because it's real. I know what I'm doing's real. I know I'm alive."

This made Ladbrooke come the closest yet to smiling. "Yes," she said and tenderly touched her head. "After this episode, I'm pretty convinced I'm alive as well."

CHAPTER
ELEVEN

Christmas fever struck during the first full week of December. Since we were not in a regular school, with all the excitement of other classes preparing for the season as well, and the traditional round of parties and performances, I hadn't anticipated much of a brouhaha. Carolyn and I had discussed having a small last-day-of-school party for the two classes combined, before the Christmas break, but that was all. And by and large Carolyn's children were not much of a source of stimulation. Being two floors away from us, they were too far removed physically, and being mentally handicapped four- and five-year-olds, most were not very aware of what was going on anyway. However, regardless of all these deterrents, my lot still caught the contagion.

When it became apparent that Christmas was becoming a major topic of conversation in the classroom, I tried to discourage the excitement from fermenting into full-blown delirium. We put up our paper chains and a few placard Santas, but otherwise, I restricted art projects to fairly abstract areas and kept the Christmas-related stories/films/activities to a minimum.

All this effort at life-goes-on-as-usual went unappreciated. Shamie was the worst one for upsetting the equilibrium. He kept asking when we were going to do this thing or that thing. He stirred up the others into a frenzy with tales of what went on at his school in Belfast. And of course, it was he who brought up the whole business of a Nativity play.

We were all sitting together at the table one morning, supposedly working, except that Mariana had developed an annoyingly loud case of the hiccups; which provided just enough distraction to keep anyone from concentrating. Finally, I sent her back to the sink to get a drink of water.

"Are we going to have a Nativity play?" Shamie asked, right out of the blue.

"We don't usually have them in American schools," I replied.

Geraldine's brow puckered. "But you've got to have a Nativity play, Miss. Else it wouldn't be Christmas, would it?"

"We've got enough people for the parts," Shamie said. "Geraldine and I, we were talking about it at home. We could have one of us boys be Joseph, and then there'd be Mary and the Angel of the Lord, and then there could be one shepherd and one Wise Man."

"There's supposed to be three Wise Men," Ladbrooke put in.

"Well, yes, I know. There's supposed to be more shepherds too. But we could just pretend." Shamie ducked his head. "I'm sort of big for this kind of thing anyway. I told Geraldine that. It's for the wee ones. But I wouldn't really mind doing it. Shemona hasn't ever had any Nativity plays. We should have one for her."

"Miss, we've got to have a Nativity play," Geraldine insisted.

I grimaced and shook my head. "No."

"Please?" Shamie asked.

"It'd be too much work, Shamie. And how would you include Leslie and Shemona, when they don't even talk? How could we make it work out? It's a nice idea, but we'd need more children."

"We wouldn't, Miss."

"More importantly, we'd need an audience. And we don't have an audience."

"Sure we do," Shamie replied, warming to his subject. "We could invite Miss Berry's class. We could invite the secretaries. And Mr. Cotton. And Bill, the janitor. And we could invite our families. That'd be enough. Come on, Miss, please? Do it for Shemona's sake. She's never had a Nativity play."

"Do it for *your* sake, Shamie," I replied.

He giggled self-consciously. "They're fun, Miss. I like them."

At this point, Mariana rejoined us. "What's a natibby play?"

"You know. With Mary and Joseph and Baby Jesus," Geraldine said.

"I could be the director," Shamie offered.

"You'd have to be director, scriptwriter and actor all rolled into one," I said.

"Please, Miss? It wouldn't be Christmas, would it? I mean, that's what Christmas is all about."

Shamie and Geraldine had obviously discussed this at great length before bringing the subject up, because for every reason I had not to do it, they had a counter reason for doing it. The other children quickly caught their enthusiasm, although I doubt any of them actually knew what was being discussed. Mariana clearly had no idea what the whole thing was about.

Dirkie just wanted to do what everybody else was doing, whatever it might be. But soon there was a small, pleading chorus.

"Okay, look," I said, "if you want to play, Shamie, this is what we do. *You* write the script. You may use the time you usually have for English to do it and you can have Geraldine or anyone else you want to help you. But you can't waste time. This'll have to be done quickly. Probably by Friday at the latest. Okay? And then we'll see if we can make a play out of it."

"Hooray!" Shamie cried, throwing his pencil way up into the air. "Hip-hip-hoo-goody-ray!"

By that week in December, Ladbrooke had been with us for nearly a month, and she was proving to be a real experience. I hadn't taken her very seriously when she first started. My concern for her and her difficult circumstances was genuine enough, but I must confess that deep down I'd felt she wouldn't be worth two hoots in the classroom. Part of my feelings were no more than pure prejudice. I found it hard to look at someone like her and really take her seriously. There was just too much of the glitzy, upper-class bimbo about her. And part of my feelings were based on past experience. This was demanding work, both emotionally and physically, and as a consequence, very few people found it really suited them. Volunteers had a habit of coming and going with monotonous regularity. That was just a fact of life. So, once the going got tough, I expected we'd lose her.

We didn't. On Ladbrooke's second day, she showed up at precisely 8:00 A.M. just as she had the first. And so she did the third day and the fourth and the fifth. Every day, exactly at eight, there she was. I kept assuming she'd go home sooner or later during the day, but she never did that either. Once arrived, she stayed through the morning session, through the lunch period, through the afternoon session, through my after-school prep time and right up until I myself clocked out at five. She never left a moment before I did.

This caused me no small amount of surprise. The entire first week I did nothing whatsoever except wait for Ladbrooke to leave. I'd never envisioned having a full-time colleague, and it took me a while to adjust to the fact that I suddenly had one. Yet I didn't really know how to go about inquiring into the matter without sounding ungrateful for such a generous donation of time.

Ladbrooke squashed what other prejudices I might have had by proving to be a remarkably hard worker. Within hours of her arrival on the first day, she was already locating materials for me, putting things away, responding to the children. I never had to tell her twice that a thing needed doing. Indeed, Ladbrooke demonstrated a disconcerting ability to anticipate what I needed, sometimes even before I was aware of it. Suddenly, there were no more piles of unsorted papers, unassembled materials or uncorrected work. The files in the filing cabinet became alphabetized, color coded and filled with the things that belonged in them. I found myself in a hitherto unknown state of wonderful organization.

Ladbrooke had more difficulty falling in naturally with the teaching side of things. Her drive to be useful often overwhelmed her sense of timing, and as a consequence, we stumbled over one another a lot, both figuratively and literally. I think it was caused mostly by the lack of experience, because otherwise, Ladbrooke appeared to have the instincts of a natural teacher. She was comfortable with the children, talked to them without talking down, showed respect for their individual differences. More importantly, in our circumstances, she was able to maintain a modicum of discipline if I needed to have a private moment with a particular child.

Ladbrooke's real contribution, however, came from her expertise in mathematics. I knew how numbers worked; Ladbrooke knew why. A chance question would bring diagrams on the chalkboard or little three-dimensional constructions out of erasers, pencils or even borrowed journals from the library. With a handful of building blocks, she gave Shamie more insight into long division than I had managed all year long. Whatever else the gossips might have said about her, they'd been close to the mark on this occasion. She was a fair genius in math.

In light of such substantive contributions to the class, it would have been nice if Ladbrooke's advent into our lives had been smooth. Unfortunately, it was anything but. Along with her industry and abilities came Ladbrooke's personality as well, and that was another matter entirely. Tense, guarded, and anxious, she proved more of an emotional challenge to me some days than the children did.

I could appreciate the fact that Ladbrooke wasn't going to feel immediately at home with us. She and I had a negative relationship to put behind us. She was in a field she wasn't confident in and she was working in a subordinate, low-status position. And of course, there was the usual amount of apprehension among strangers. But in her case, it all ran rather deeper than that.

Ladbrooke's most glaring problem was her extraordinary defensiveness. She seemed to operate under the belief that everyone's raison d'être was to do her harm. And clearly, she felt the best defense was a good offense, because she was on the offense a fair share of the time, day in, day out. Either that, or if very upset, she bolted for the safety of the girls' restroom or some other isolated location. I found this continual fight-or-flight attitude very tiring to cope with for long stretches, but whatever difficulties such behavior might have caused me in the classroom, they were only hiccups compared to her problems with strangers. Appearing devoid of all the usual social minutiae one takes for granted in minor interactions, Ladbrooke reacted to every arrival at the classroom door as if personal attack were imminent. Someone would appear and, instantly, she'd clam up. The cold crocodile stare would return, and she'd emanate a bristly, hands-off kind of hostility that was so manifest it was almost palpable. This, of course, gave her the charm of a porcupine. Within days of her arrival, she had so thoroughly turned off the rest of the staff that no one dropped by the room any longer just for a chat. Indeed, no one came at all, unless absolutely necessary. It was like sharing quarters with Typhoid Mary.

Eventually, this behavior spread to me, in a knock-on effect. Being in a group with Ladbrooke, when she was so purposely alienating, was sheer hell for me because she upset everyone. Feeling responsible for having introduced this social monstrosity into our midst, I had to retreat. Although I continued taking my daytime breaks in the teachers' lounge, I refrained from going in there before and after school, when it was likely to be crowded. And I gave up on Enrico's entirely. My stomach just couldn't cope with that kind of tension. So I ended up eating packed lunches in the classroom, alone, except for the company of this cuckoo I'd allowed into the nest.

Honestly, I didn't know what to do with Ladbrooke in such situations. In the classroom she was nowhere near as antagonistic as she was in public. Certainly her defensiveness remained a huge problem for us, but it was fairly superficial. Once reassured, she usually relaxed the bristly guardedness and became tolerable again, but in public, absolutely nothing seemed to reassure her.

Ladbrooke's other major shortcoming was her poor verbal ability. What I had initially mistaken for a nervous reaction, I soon discovered was a fundamental part of Ladbrooke's character. Even in the best of moments, she was a taciturn person. There was none of the pleasant chitchat I was accustomed to in my relationships, particularly with other women. There was none of the quiet sharing of thoughts and feelings which usually accompanied familiarity. Instead, we would often spend the entire ninety minutes of prep time after school without exchanging more than a handful of words.

While obviously a good part of Ladbrooke's silence was her particular personality, I also suspected some of it sprang from genuine inarticulateness. When she did talk, even in relaxed and familiar circumstances, Ladbrooke seldom expressed herself well. She had a poor speaking vo-

cabulary for someone of her apparent intelligence. Indeed, in most in-
stances, she didn't seem to command many more words than Shamie did.
And she could be quirkily unfluent. Quite often she would grind to a halt
right in the middle of a conversation, or she'd come up with peculiar
responses which, while close to the subject at hand, were strangely out
of context. These had a most disconcerting effect, because while they
sounded like non sequiturs on one hand, they seemed more like Freudian
slips on the other. And on a few occasions, she said things that made
absolutely no sense whatsoever. The words would be transposed or completely incorrect, and I'd be left baffled, yet Ladbrooke never heard them.
When I kept asking her what she meant, she seemed to feel I was playing
a poor joke on her.

But, in spite of everything, we did manage to survive one another.
Loath as I was to admit it, Carolyn had been right. Ladbrooke, weighted
under all her emotional baggage, had more in common with the children
than with me. Good sense told me on more than one occasion to move
her on, and I probably should have, but I didn't. I'd gained what I needed
most: a committed, hardworking aide, and I let that justify my actions.
The truth, however, was that she had the same compelling impact on me
the kids did. By the end of the first month, I was hooked. If she'd left us
then, I would have missed her.

The next Monday got off to the kind of start only Mondays seem to be
capable of. The hot water in my apartment gave out mid-shower, leaving
me to finish washing the shampoo from my hair with cold water. The
zipper on my jeans broke, and I hadn't been to the laundromat yet that
week. On the way to school my aging Fiat expired with a shudder in the
middle of a five-way intersection, causing me to come struggling into the
classroom only minutes before the children.

Dirkie, Leslie and Mariana all came at the usual time, but the other
three did not. We waited for them, because I couldn't imagine all three
were ill at once, but Mariana grew restless and Dirkie grew tiresome, so
I finally collected everyone together and we had morning discussion. Just
as we were finishing, there was a terrible noise from Leslie's direction.
Worse followed, as diarrhea came out around the cuffs of her disposable
diapers and all down her legs. Ladbrooke squawked in surprise and snatched
Leslie up to make a run for the girls' rest room.

In the midst of the excitement that followed, Geraldine, Shemona and
Shamie arrived. I was in the back of the room washing off the chair.
Dirkie was hooting from under the table. Mariana was pounding on the
top of it, using two rulers as drumsticks. Leslie had begun throwing clean

disposable diapers out of their box and onto the floor. Ladbrooke was scurrying back and forth, trying to distract Leslie, trying to reorient the others, trying to tell me that Leslie had been just fine before school or else she wouldn't have let her come.

Geraldine walked up to me. "You know why we're late, Miss? Our pussy got killed right out in the street, while we were getting into the car. Zoom comes this car. Bang, right on our pussy."

I glanced quickly over my shoulder in the direction of the others. Shemona was putting her coat away.

"Where's Shamie?" I asked.

"Over by the door. He won't come in. He's crying," Geraldine replied.

"Shamie?" I called. Drying my hands on my jeans, I went to find him.

He was just inside the door. Hands over his face, he leaned against the wall.

"I'm so sorry, lovey. Geraldine's just told me." I put my arms around him and drew him close to me.

"Why did it have to happen?"

Beyond us, I could hear chaos. Mariana was relating Leslie's accident in loud, graphic detail. Dirkie was hooting and clapping, and from the sound of it, leaping up on the table.

"Why did he have to do that?" Shamie wailed. "Of all the stupid places for him to go. We live practically in the country. He had all that nice field next to the house. Why did he have to go in the road?"

"Torey?" Mariana shouted. "Leslie's just gone poopy again. It's all over her dress. Come quick!"

"Poopty-doopty-poop!" Dirkie shouted, careening around the corner of the shelves to where Shamie and I were standing. "Poopy! Poopyface!"

This was hardly the atmosphere for giving comfort to the grieving. I gave Shamie one last hug and let go of him. "Stay here a minute, sweetheart. Let me get things settled."

Back around the corner, I found Ladbrooke struggling unsuccessfully to bring about order. Leslie had made a horrific mess. Mariana was up on the radiator, dancing in a provocative manner and rubbing her fingers enthusiastically between her legs. Shemona had her hands clamped over her ears. Dirkie swirled around us like a dervish. Only Geraldine, looking stunned, was in her chair.

"Take Shamie out," I said to Ladbrooke, as I caught hold of Dirkie and shoved him into his seat. "Take him down to the teachers' lounge until he's feeling better."

Ladbrooke looked alarmed.

"He just needs a good cry. And this certainly is no place for him."

"What'll I say to him?"

"Anything," I replied, and put a hand on her shoulder to encourage her in the right direction.

"But what?" There was a note of agitation creeping into her voice. "I'll stay here, Torey, okay? You go."

"*I* need to be here. Just take him down to the lounge. No big deal."

She did not move from my side.

I was beginning to feel a bit frantic myself. The noise level was deafening. The smell in the room was overpowering. We couldn't stand here talking as if it were Sunday afternoon.

"Look, Lad, don't worry about this so much. Just do it. He's too concerned with how much he hurts to listen to your actual words. Little, kind, caring noises will be enough. Just duck."

"I can't."

"You *can.*"

"I can't."

I dug into my pocket for a couple of quarters. "Here. Buy him a Coke."

"What?"

"Buy him a bloody Coke. Take him down there and buy him a Coke and don't worry about saying anything to him. Just get him out of this bedlam." Taking her hand, I slapped the quarters into it and left before she could protest further.

Shamie and Ladbrooke managed. By the time they returned, about twenty minutes later, I had the class more or less sorted out, and everyone was at the table working. Shamie was fairly composed. He'd had the Coke, which had pleased him, and he'd had Ladbrooke's undivided attention, which, as I'd assumed, had pleased him even more.

Unfortunately, it was just one of those days. Things refused to stay quiet for any length of time. Shemona, too, was upset by their cat's demise and spent much of the day hiding from us. The remaining time, she covered bits of paper with harsh, heavy crayon strokes. Any effort on my part to comfort her was met with angry snarling. Of the three children, only Geraldine seemed unfazed by the cat's death. I've seen people dead, she told me, why should seeing a dead cat bother me?

At lunchtime Dirkie got into a fight with one of the lunch aides and was sent back to the room to finish his meal with Ladbrooke and me, which ruined ours. In the early afternoon, Mariana tipped two jars of mixed tempera paints over Geraldine in what Mariana maintained was a simple accident. At afternoon recess, Shemona fell off the swings and cut her lip. And there was a slip waiting in my box in the office saying that the garage had phoned about my car. I rang back to discover it needed repairs that I could ill afford.

My mood deteriorated progressively as the day went on, and I was feeling absolutely grim by 3:30. On top of everything else, I had a particularly boring meeting coming up at a nearby school. After taking the children down to their rides, I had to return to the room for my belongings and then hightail it over to the other school on foot.

Upstairs, I found Ladbrooke hard at work, stapling dittoed worksheets into packets. "I've got to leave right away," I said. "It's going to take me that long to walk over to Millington. Can you lock up all right?"

"Could I give you a ride?"

"No, it's okay. The walk'll probably do me good."

Ladbrooke went back to her stapling. I noticed her hands were shaking, and it was making getting the papers together evenly a harder task.

I had seen Ladbrooke's hands shake on other occasions. True to her word, she had been sober with us every day, but I had no idea how much drinking she was doing otherwise. Feeling as out-of-sorts as I did just then, the thought that she was not controlling the problem irritated me.

"You ought to get help with that," I said.

She looked around, not sure what I was talking about.

"It's not working out, is it? You really should see a doctor or something."

Realization dawned on her, and she jerked her hands back out of sight. "Look," she said, "I'm coping. You don't want me to drink in here, I'm not drinking, am I? Okay? Don't get on me about it. I'm coping."

There was sudden silence. Momentarily overcome with the relief of making someone else as miserable as I was feeling, I turned away to get my things.

"Look, Torey," she said, "I'm *coping.*"

"Okay, okay," I said, not bothering to look over.

When I didn't turn to acknowledge her, she flung down the stapler noisily against the table. Storming past me, she left the room. Bang went the door. Bang went my moment of wicked relief. Bang went my sense of self-righteous superiority.

Realizing that I had no alternative but to apologize, I went to find Ladbrooke. She was in the girls' rest room, standing in front of one of the sinks, wiping tears off her face with a paper towel.

"I'm sorry," I said. "I was stupid back there."

She bristled. I had no intention of coming closer; I knew better. But she moved a step away from me, just to make certain.

"It's been a lousy day. I know that doesn't really excuse me, but it's been bloody atrocious, and I've ended up taking it out on you. I'm really sorry."

"Well, you're right. I can't do this. I'm not coping."

"Oh, you're coping just fine. I wasn't even thinking, when I said that. I was just being stupid, that's all."

She lowered her head. Her hair, which had been braided back into one long plait, was working loose, and long strands fell forward to obscure much of her face from me. "I can't do this job. It isn't working out," she said softly.

"Don't talk like that, Lad. I've been rude, and you're justifiably upset. It has nothing to do with your work."

"I can't do what you expect of me. I can't get in there and do what you do. What do I know about telling some kid his cat's gone to heaven? I couldn't even put my arm around him."

"I was probably wrong to force you into that situation," I said. "I just needed help badly at that moment and didn't know what else to do."

"*You* can do it!" she cried angrily. "You just go up to him, to any of them, and hug them. Christ almighty, you can even hug me. I sat there for ten fucking minutes trying to make my arm go around him. It was like it wasn't even part of my own body, like it had a mind of its own. I couldn't do it. Here's this poor little boy, sobbing his heart out, and I just sat there, having an argument with my fucking arm." She whipped another paper towel from the dispenser and pressed it to her face. And she began to cry. She'd been teary all along, but now she cried in earnest, head down, one hand up to her face. Like Shemona, she made almost no noise.

I stood, two sinks away, and studied my rather grubby hands.

"Why do you make me cry so much?" she muttered bitterly, and took down another towel to wipe her face. "I've cried more since I've known you than I've cried in all the rest of my life put together. I just look at you and I cry."

I smiled in spite of myself.

"It's not funny."

"I'm not laughing at you, Lad. But that's a heck of a comment on my character."

"It's not funny. I hate crying. It makes me feel so helpless."

"Yes, me too."

Silence.

"Do you really feel like you want to quit?" I asked.

"No," she said quietly. "Yes. No."

I smiled slightly. "Not quite sure?"

She shrugged.

"I think you've been doing really well. Maybe I haven't said it as much as I should have. I just assumed you knew, because it's so obvious. Considering that you've never done anything like this before, you're really quite remarkable. I'd be unhappy if you left us now."

Silence again. Ladbrooke, looking down, discovered a hair caught in the band of her watch. She pulled it out, straightened it to its full length and stared at it, appearing momentarily mesmerized. Then she dropped it and watched it fall into the sink.

"I haven't had a drink since I started in here," she said softly. "I don't want to go to AA. All that spilling your guts to a room full of strangers, that's not my thing. So I thought I'd just prove to everybody that I can stop."

I studied her profile. "Has it been hard?"

She nodded.

A pregnant pause came.

"I'm not being quite truthful," she said then, her voice low. "I haven't had a drink during the week since I started in here, but I haven't quite completely stopped. I've been trying, but I did have a drink over the weekend. I didn't get drunk, but I did have a little drink. I managed to stop it before it got worse. I went over and poured the whole rest of the bottle down the sink to stop myself. But it was a hard weekend. I needed a drink."

Raising her head, Ladbrooke looked at her reflection in the mirror above the sink. She studied it a long time. "When it gets hard, like it did then, I think about the kids. I think about what Shemona and Geraldine have gone through. Or Dirkie and all those terrible things that were done to him when he was little." Ladbrooke continued to regard her image. "I want to be like them. Strong."

I smiled gently. "You already are. But I think you're just expecting a little too much of yourself too soon."

Lowering her head, she shook it.

"You're expecting to be me, Ladbrooke. You're expecting to have naturally what it's taken me about ten years to acquire. You're expecting this to be easy, when no one ever said it would be."

Silence returned.

Ladbrooke opened both taps on the sink and washed her hands. She splashed cold water on her face.

"I've got a headache," I said. "You want to go get something to eat with me?"

"You're going to be horribly late to that meeting."

"I'm going to miss that meeting. Or rather, I won't miss it—believe me." I smiled. "Why don't we go get a sandwich? Maybe at that place over on Second Avenue. Then afterward, you can drop me off at the Fiat garage."

Thoughtful a moment, Ladbrooke looked back at her reflection in the mirror; then her lips slowly quirked up in the hint of a smile. She looked over and nodded. "Okay."

CHAPTER TWELVE

A little unvarnished nepotism was at work in creating the Nativity play. By Friday, Shamie and Geraldine had finished the script and had automatically assigned the best parts, those of Joseph and Mary, to themselves. Shemona was a little harder to accommodate. They clearly wanted her to be Angel of the Lord, but because she wouldn't speak, the part had to go to Mariana. Shemona, they decided, would be a shepherd. Dirkie was cast in two parts, as the innkeeper and a Wise Man. This latter assignment even tickled Ladbrooke, and she had to put a hand up to smother a giggle. Leslie got to be the zoo, playing a sheep in the fields with Shemona and a cow in the stable with Joseph and Mary.

Friday afternoon was devoted to the first rehearsal. Shamie had carefully written out all the parts on little slips of paper and gave them out to each child with much fanfare. We shoved the table back as best we could to make the center of the room into a stage. Geraldine and Shamie were obviously old hands at this business, because they knew precisely what props were needed and where to put them. Shemona, too, was involved serving as a gofer to the other two. In her usual telepathic manner, she responded to her sister and cousin, finding and fetching various things they needed to set the stage. One of the art boxes was emptied and set in the middle to become a manger. A chair served as the location of the inn. The pillows at the back of the room became the Judean hills.

Geraldine went to the toy cupboard and took out a well-played-with, unclothed doll and wrapped it up in a rather grubby receiving blanket. She laid it carefully in the cardboard box. "This is going to be Baby Jesus," she said to us. "And this is His manger. On the day we give the play, I think we ought to make it look nicer. We can maybe get some real straw."

Shemona went over and snatched the doll out.

"Shemona?" Geraldine said, not too good-naturedly. "That's Baby Jesus. Put Him back."

Shemona didn't. Instead, she unwrapped the doll and chucked it back into the toy cupboard.

"Shemona? What are you doing? Now I said that was going to be Baby Jesus." Geraldine went around her sister and took the doll back out.

Shemona grabbed the doll's legs.

There was a sudden, silent confrontation between them, eerie to watch, because neither said a word, neither moved. They just stood, eyes locked.

"No, you can't," Geraldine said finally. "We're going to do it this way."

Grimly, Shemona hung on to the doll's legs.

"*No.* This is me and Shamie's play. And I want to use this for Baby Jesus."

Baring her teeth, Shemona refused to let go.

"Miss, tell Shemona to stop it. She won't let me put this doll in for Baby Jesus. She's holding everything up."

I rose to my feet. But before I could intervene, Geraldine let fly with a clout of her hand, thunking Shemona soundly on the side of her head. Shemona screamed.

"Hey, you two, we'll have none of that." I grabbed Geraldine's shoulder. "Over in the quiet chair, please."

And so the first rehearsal ended.

That evening, Carolyn and I met at the spa. I'd arrived a bit before Carolyn and had already done my mile's worth of laps. I was waiting for her to finish hers so we could go into the sauna, but she'd grown sick of it and hauled herself out of the water to sit on the edge with me and catch her breath. We got to discussing the Nativity play. Originally, we'd had no plans for any special Christmas program, but now, with the play, I needed to get definite arrangements made. We discussed having Carolyn's class in the audience, inviting parents, and staging.

"You could use the auditorium," Carolyn suggested. "It's not very big, but it does have a stage with curtains and lights and all that."

I knew the building had one, but since the conversion to administration offices, it hadn't been used. "What condition's it in? Does everything work?"

"Don't know. I assume so."

"We'd have to scrub it out," I said, with ghastly visions of cobwebs and hard labor.

"There's not that much junk in there now. It'd be nice for your kids. They could do their little play right. You've got to give them credit, Torey. That's a sweet idea, wanting to put on a play for everybody."

I kicked at the water. "I suppose I could send Ladbrooke down to have a look at it. Maybe she and Shamie could shift some of the things."

There was a small pause.

"How's your protégé doing?" Carolyn asked.

"You mean Lad? She's okay."

Carolyn didn't reply.

"It's been so much easier having someone to do all those gruesome little tasks."

Carolyn reached down and ran her fingers through the water. "Ladbrooke was out at the Blue Willow over the weekend. She was drinking."

"Who's telling you this?"

"Me. I was there."

I shrugged. "Well, I suppose it's her choice."

"She was with some man, and he certainly wasn't Tom Considyne." Carolyn leaned down to dabble in the water a moment. Then she sighed. "*I'd* be satisfied with Tom Considyne." She straightened up. "But she's *with* all these other men. All the time. It's no secret."

I nodded.

"I think it's a bit much," Carolyn said. "I mean, she is a married woman with a child."

"Yes."

Carolyn looked over. "Doesn't it bother you? I mean, she's not changing."

"I don't think it's my business, really. She's a consenting adult. It's not the way I'd run my life, but I don't see where that gives me the right to condemn what she does with hers."

Carolyn eased herself back down into the pool. "Be careful that what you think of as tolerance doesn't become lack of judgment."

The next morning was cold and wintry, and all the children arrived bundled up. I was busy sorting out some papers when I noticed that, although Shamie, Geraldine and Shemona had been in the room for some time, Shemona was not taking off her outer clothes.

"Do you need some help with your clothes?" I asked, as she was particularly well wrapped against the frosty weather outside.

At this, Geraldine flounced over and solicitously began unwinding Shemona's muffler. Shemona jerked away.

"She doesn't want any help, Miss. Shemona's being awkward today. Auntie Bet says she got up on the wrong side of the bed this morning."

"Well, Shemona, whatever the problem, you need to get busy taking off your jacket. It's almost time to start discussion."

I then picked up the papers I'd been working with and went around the corner into an aisle of the library where I'd cleared one top shelf to store prepared work. As I was standing in the narrow aisle between the two tall shelving units, Shemona, still fully wrapped, came sidling up.

"*Do* you want help, honey?"

She began to take off her mittens. Then came her muffler and hat. her long hair tumbled out in disarray. She attempted to undo the zipper of her jacket. Being such a young child, she was still often clumsy with zippers, and it was a slow, concentrated process. Finally, she managed to get a good grip and carefully unzipped the jacket. Inside, against her blouse was tucked a small, stuffed monkey. Very gently, she removed the toy. She lifted it up to me.

"This is Curious George," she said in a gravelly whisper.

"Oh, he's a fine one, isn't he? I remember you bringing him to school with you that very first day you came here."

She nodded. "He's a boy. A girl doll shouldn't be Baby Jesus. Here, Miss. This is to be Baby Jesus."

I knelt down and accepted the monkey. It was a small, cheap toy, wearing a sewn-on cap and shirt, emblazoned with "Curious George." The fur on the feet and hands had been loved off.

"Yes, this is a much better idea, Shemona. Jesus wasn't a girl, was He?"

Shemona had the same kind of quirky half-smile on her face I had seen so often on Ladbrooke's. "I sleep with him. My mammy gave him to me when I was a baby. He's bare there, on his hands, but we could wrap him up. It wouldn't show."

"That's very kind of you to share Curious George with us."

At just that moment Geraldine materialized at the head of the narrow aisle. "Oh, there you are," she said brightly, and began to come down toward us. Then abruptly, she froze, her gaze riveted on the toy.

"What have you been doing, Shemona?" she asked, her voice growing loud.

"Shemona's brought in her Curious George to be Baby Jesus in the play."

An angry flush came to Geraldine's face. She shoved her glasses up onto the bridge of her nose in a rough gesture. Her eyes narrowed. "Gimme that," she said.

Shemona edged closer to me.

"Gimme that, Shemona!"

I still had the toy in my hands, and before I could react, Geraldine rushed at me, ripping the monkey from me. "You little bleeding traitor!" she screamed at Shemona, who had taken refuge behind me. "You little bleeding traitor!" And she attempted to scale me in an effort to get at her sister.

I was still kneeling, when Geraldine attacked, and was hard put to avoid being kicked and punched as I attempted to quell her. Ladbrooke appeared and grabbed Geraldine from behind, but in the confined space, it was hard to restrain her. Magazines flew. The shelving units shuddered as the three of us thrashed against them. As we struggled, the monkey fell to the floor and Shemona snatched it up. Running to the far end of the aisle, she pushed out stacks of journals and slid to safety by squeezing through the shelves.

Geraldine just would not give up. She was all arms and legs. Her glasses came off, and I kicked them to safety under one of the shelves because I didn't dare take a hand off her to pick them up. She socked Ladbrooke in the mouth, and blood went everywhere. It made Geraldine's skin slippery and harder to hold.

Slowly, we maneuvered her out of the library and around the corner into the classroom. Dragging her across the room, I snagged the quiet chair with my foot and dropped her into it. Ladbrooke pinned one of Geraldine's arms behind her in a wrestler's hold. I let go.

Geraldine was still furious, still crying, still raging wordlessly against us. But she didn't make any effort to get out of the chair. I gestured to Ladbrooke, who slowly released her grip.

"You stay sitting in that chair until you've calmed down, Geraldine," I said. "I don't want you out of it until you've stopped crying entirely and are ready to come work."

She simply shrieked at me.

Geraldine sat the better part of the whole morning in the quiet chair. Ladbrooke had to remain in at recess with her because she was still not ready to rejoin the other children. And even when she did, she was still angry. Taking her work folder, she sat down at the table and glared over at her sister.

"You just wait till we get home, Shemona," she said, her voice barely above a whisper. "When you're not watching, I'm going to take the scissors and rip your Curious George to bits."

CHAPTER
THIRTEEN

At last came the big day, the 22nd of December, when we had our party and put on our play. I don't suppose there was a play anywhere that had been more rehearsed, more clucked over, more thought about than this one. We did decide to use the auditorium. With the lights turned on, it proved to be a shabby little room, painted penitentiary blue, with an equally shabby little stage and literally moth-eaten curtains. Even in its heyday, it must not have been much. But the curtains and the lights did work, after a certain amount of adjustment, and it was a real stage.

Cleaning the auditorium was just as gruesome a job as I'd feared it might be. Ladbrooke and Shamie devoted several recess periods to furniture moving, but it soon became apparent that we'd never have it ready in time, spending only fifteen-minute periods on it. I allowed the children to stay after school a few afternoons, and in the end, Shamie asked to come in on the final Saturday to finish the task. Then Geraldine wanted to join him and then Mariana, so I felt obliged to come too. Ladbrooke, seemingly unable to accept that we could cope without her, showed up unexpectedly. She and Shamie appeared to have the same need to make this all perfect, and together, they tackled the grittier jobs of vacuuming down the cobwebs backstage and scrubbing the stage itself. Mariana and Geraldine and I contented ourselves with wielding spray polish and dusters.

By the last week, the play had taken on a life of its own. It had gone far past the point of being simply a Christmas play. We were obviously out to trap something more elusive. Because of this, the need for perfection reached a fevered pitch and, as a consequence, tempers began to fray. Curious George, who had remained in protective custody in the locked filing cabinet when off duty, had to have a stand-in during rehearsals because Shamie and Geraldine treated him so roughly when they argued. I needed to call regular time-outs to get everyone to settle down. Incessant bickering over who did what, who wore which costume, who said which lines when, went on through lessons, recess, lunch and free time. I counted the hours until it was all over.

As could be expected from this kind of buildup, when the 22nd finally arrived, the children were all too strung out with anticipation to do anything constructive in the morning. Geraldine, Mariana and Shamie quarreled nonstop, all three ending up in tears at one point or another. Dirkie hooted, clapped and constantly annoyed Ladbrooke with suggestive behaviors. Shemona withdrew to the far corner of the room and curled up in a fetal position. Leslie twirled, twiddled and flicked her fingers in an unending pattern of self-stimulation. Acknowledging that the morning was a lost cause, I threw away the plans and let the children go down to the auditorium, where we went though half a dozen more rehearsals of the play.

At lunchtime, I went home and changed clothes, putting on a skirt and makeup, my concession both to the parents and to the specialness of the occasion. On the way back to school, I stopped at the supermarket and bought six bars of chocolate with almonds, one for each child. Only after I was out in the parking lot did I remember that Leslie couldn't have one, so I went back in and got her a small bag of diabetic candy from the special foods section.

Back at school, my change of clothes was greeted with astonishment. Mariana, looking genuinely stunned, came running over.

"Teacher," she said with great feeling in her voice, "you've got *legs!*"

Dirkie, already clothed in his innkeeper's costume, came over too. He bent down and with one finger gingerly touched the pantyhose over my shin.

"Dirk, as a general rule, it's best not to touch people's legs without asking."

"Just looking," he said and stood up again. He regarded my face, his gaze searching. "It looks like you've got caterpillars on your eyes."

"It's mascara, Dirkie."

"What's it there for?"

"To make me look nice."

"Oh. When's it going to work?"

I smiled. "Perhaps you ought to go see if you're needed somewhere."

Ladbrooke appeared. She'd stayed through the lunch hour with the children and was beginning to show the wear and tear of stage management. Wiping perspiration off her forehead with one hand, she too gave me the once-over.

"You say one thing about the way I look and you're going to be doing this on your own."

"Should I have changed? That's what I'm wondering." She looked down at herself. The designer image had been shed quite some time back. She was clad in jeans, dirty at the knees, and a plaid shirt with the sleeves rolled up.

"I wouldn't worry about it."

"I'll stay backstage anyhow. I don't want to get out there with all the parents. You can do that part."

I nodded.

"Do you know where the frankincense and myrrh have gotten to?" she asked.

"Did you look upstairs on top of the filing cabinet?"

She nodded.

"On the shelf where we kept it before?"

She nodded again.

"Then look in the teachers' lounge. I put the chocolate coins in there to keep anybody from eating them. Maybe the rest of it's in there too."

"Okay," she said and departed.

Soon after, the parents began arriving. Mrs. Lonrho showed up, wildly overdressed in a fur coat and spiky high heels, as if attending a Broadway first night. She looked charmingly out of place in the shabby auditorium. Mariana's mother came in a leopard-skin outfit à la Sheena, Queen of the Jungle, and had glitter sprinkled in her hair. Tom Considyne represented the other end of the continuum. He shuffled in wearing a pair of frayed Levi's and a Western shirt with a sheepskin vest over it, giving the impression that he might need to dash out to round up the cattle at any moment. He was the only father to attend. Indeed, he was the only man in the room, and with his great height, he was impossible to miss.

My entire group was behind the curtains on the stage, so I was left with sole responsibility for welcoming everybody. I went among them, making the obligatory small talk and pointing out the refreshments. Carolyn's children tore back and forth, squeally and overactive with excitement. Her parents mixed with mine, chatting amiably.

I felt obliged to go over and talk to Tom Considyne, who looked decidedly ill at ease. He was next to the refreshment table, absorbed in the task of choosing cookies. He took two and nibbled them, then took two more.

"You know," he said, as I approached him, "it took me about three weeks to discover this was where Ladbrooke was disappearing to every day." He reached for a fifth cookie.

"She's making all the difference in the world here," I said.

"She's never done anything like this before in her life."

"She's super with the kids. Very sensitive to them."

"I can't imagine it. She hasn't figured Leslie out in seven years."

"Maybe it's different with kids who aren't your own. I don't know. But she's been a lifesaver for me."

He helped himself to a cup of punch and drank it all in one go, then set down the empty cup on the edge of the table. "It surprised the hell out of me when she told me. I'd never thought of her as the type to do charity work." He shrugged. Then he smiled down at me. "And I must say, I'm damned curious to see this play."

I went from Tom Considyne to Mrs. Lonrho, who was sitting in one of the seats in the front row. "I think we're going to be done with Curious George this afternoon, when the play's over. Perhaps the best thing would be for me to give him directly to you, and you can take him into safe-keeping."

Mrs. Lonrho nodded.

"I don't know if Geraldine still feels as strongly as she did. She hasn't said anything since that episode I told you about, but I haven't wanted to take a chance."

"I don't honestly know what to do with Geraldine some days," Mrs. Lonrho said. "She's so sweet and biddable most of the time, and then you go and cross her and she's so vindictive."

"Well, I think the matter may have settled down. But you might still want to keep an eye on Curious George for a while. Geraldine doesn't seem to forget about things easily."

"No," Mrs. Lonrho said. "One thing Geraldine doesn't do is forget."

I rose and went up onto the stage and parted the curtains. Behind them, a bevy of costumed figures was scurrying about. I slipped in and shut the curtains behind me. Ladbrooke, red faced from the heat, came over. She had a piece of green Christmas tinsel slipped through the rubber band holding her hair back.

"You don't belong here," she said, and smiled.

"No, you don't belong here," Shamie joined in. He had a beard drawn on his face wih eyeliner pencil. Taking hold of my arm, he attempted to push me back to the other side of the curtains. Geraldine and Mariana laughed and came to join him in pushing me out.

"*We're* going to do this," Ladbrooke said cheerfully. "You go sit down in the audience and enjoy yourself. We're in charge now." She laughed and so did the children. They pushed me merrily back onto the apron of the stage and closed the curtains in my face. So I returned to the front row and sat down next to Mrs. Lonrho.

With the help of a scratchy Christmas record, the play was heralded in with a lusty rendition of "What Child Is This?" Shamie and Geraldine marched on. Geraldine had a costumed broom between her legs to represent the donkey. Her veil was crooked. The gold tinsel garland that was meant to be her halo was attached to a pair of feelerlike deely-boppers that bobbed and bounced as she walked.

Dirkie was hanging out of his cardboard window, waiting for them to get across the stage to him. "Go away," he shouted to them, when they were only halfway to Bethlehem. "There's no room in my inn."

"But we've traveled a long way," Shamie replied. "And my wife is heavy with child. Please, give us a place to stay. We can't go any farther."

"There's no room," shouted Dirkie again, and he leaned farther out of his window. Then, *crash*, the whole works fell over.

Shamie, with the aplomb of a seasoned actor, looked down at Dirkie, lying at his feet and said, "See, God smote you for that."

"Okay, okay, you can use my manger. Out in the garage," Dirkie replied.

Curious George dutifully appeared, wrapped in the receiving blanket. He was laid into the art box, overflowing with straw. The scratchy record came on again, and Shamie and Geraldine belted out "Hark the Herald Angels Sing," while Mariana stomped across the stage to Leslie and Shemona.

"Okay, you guys, go see Jesus now," she said.

"That's not what you're supposed to say," Shamie whipered loudly.

"Say: 'Behold, I bring you good tidings,' " came a voice from behind the curtain.

Mariana turned and looked offstage. "Say what?"

"Behold, I bring you good tidings."

"Oh, yeah." Mariana turned back to Shemona and Leslie. "Behold, I bring you good tigers. Now, you guys go see Jesus." Her halo had become disengaged from its deely-boppers and it fell across her eyes. She shoved it back, so that it hung from one of the bouncing projections, like a quoit on a peg.

Shemona rose and dragged Leslie to her feet beside her. Shemona went over to Mary and Curious George, while Leslie burst into laughter and tore offstage. The scratchy record returned, and Shamie and Geraldine belted out "We Three Kings of Orient Are." Geraldine kicked Mariana, and she joined in the singing. Ladbrooke's hand appeared, shoving Leslie back onstage.

Dirkie, wearing a cardboard and tinfoil crown, walked in, carrying a basketful of bath salts, incense sticks and gold coins, or at least the gold paper was in the basket. Even from where I was sitting, it was pretty easy to see the chocolate stains around Dirkie's mouth.

There's something about innocents portraying innocence that is impossible to take with a dry eye. I'd been too involved to watch most of the plays and performances in my career, but seeing this one and knowing what had gone into it, I went soggy as a bowl of cornflakes. My eyes misted over about the time Mariana lumbered onstage and they never cleared. I felt idiotic for being so sentimental and was more than a little concerned that I might actually cry and somebody'd notice. But that twenty minutes embodied so many hopes and dreams that I couldn't help feeling them.

Afterward, while Carolyn's children were onstage doing their party piece, I went back to where my children were changing out of their costumes.

"Well, what did you think?" Shamie asked. He still had his drawn-on beard, in contrast to his Sunday school white shirt and black wool trousers. "Was it good? Did you like it? Did our Auntie Bet like it?"

"It was gorgeous. It really was, you guys. You did an all-out job."

"Dirkie just about spoiled it," Geraldine said scornfully.

"But he didn't, did he?" Ladbrooke said.

Wrinkling her nose, Geraldine turned away.

Dirkie was hugging me. I hugged him back. "No, you didn't, did you? It was perfect. It was a perfect play." Then I lifted up my bag of candy. "Here's a present for everyone." I gave Leslie her special candy and then a chocolate bar to each of the other children. "Merry Christmas."

"Merry Christmas, Teacher," Mariana said.

"Yes, Happy Christmas, Miss."

"Happy Christmas."

I looked into the bag at the extra candy bar. Reaching in, I took it out and handed it to Ladbrooke. "Merry Christmas, Lad."

She was smiling, her features open and relaxed. She reached forward and accepted the chocolate bar from me. "Thanks. Thank you, Teacher."

CHAPTER
FOURTEEN

✳ After school that evening, I loaded my car and made the three-hour journey to my family home in a neighboring state. It had been years since I'd been home for Christmas, and this return was a warm, nostalgic experience. The entire season was bitterly cold, so I dug out my old ice skates from the attic and spent large chunks of each day skating on the lagoon near my home, as I had done so often when I was a child. I drove out into the mountains and took long walks through the snow-covered countryside. I enjoyed the company of people I'd been friends with since second and third grade. At home, we ate the same meal, had the same arguments, and were left with the same bloated, sated feeling as every other year; and as always, we all sat around afterward, swearing never to buy/eat/trouble ourselves so much again, knowing full well that in another twelve months, we'd be joyfully ready to do it all over. Thoroughly loving every moment of it, I stayed the entire two weeks of vacation and didn't return to my apartment until late the day before school reconvened.

And then I was back. Seven-thirty Monday morning I was fiddling with the fat, old-fashioned key in the keyhole of the classroom door. It clicked finally; the lock moved back and I pushed open the door and turned on the lights. The room smelled stale and closed up. The Christmas decorations seemed suddenly very out of place.

I set about opening the windows and watering the plants. I waited with the decorations until after 8:00 so that Lad could help me, but eight came and went and Lad didn't show up. This surprised me, as she had never been a minute late since she'd started, so I kept checking the clock and listening for the door. But she never came. By the time 8:45 rolled around, the children began to arrive. But no Ladbrooke.

Leslie arrived. She'd been traveling by taxi since her mother had started with me, so that wasn't much help, but at least I knew the Considynes were not out of town. I pondered going down to the office at recess to ring Ladbrooke but decided against it. My only conclusion was that Lad was ill, so I felt she wouldn't need me disturbing her.

What surprised me even more than Lad's absence was how much I missed her. I'd been looking forward to seeing her again after the holidays. So often when I was at home I became aware of storing away thoughts I was intending to share with her when we were back together. Now, suddenly, she wasn't here. The room seemed very empty without her.

We had the usual traumas involved in getting back to routine after a major disruption. Everyone was unsettled that day. Leslie was vacant. Dirkie hooted. Mariana was full of horror stories about sleeping in the back seat of her mother's boyfriend's car during below zero weather, while the adults barhopped. Shamie and Geraldine argued nonstop about the merits and lack thereof of an American Christmas. Shamie loved it here. Geraldine hated it. The only one not to trouble me was Shemona, who was home with chicken pox.

When Ladbrooke didn't show up the second day, I grew concerned. After school that day, I rang the Considyne residence. No answer. I rang again that evening after I got home from the spa. Still no answer. I dropped the receiver down noisily, annoyed with their peculiar phone-answering habits.

Wednesday came and still no Ladbrooke. Concern turned to worry at this point. I even went so far as to ask Leslie, a futile exercise, if ever there was one. So, once the school day was finished and all the children had gone home, I packed my things up early and drove to the Considynes' house. Somebody would have to be there to meet Leslie, and even if it was only Consuela, I reckoned she'd be able to tell me what had happened to Lad.

Consuela was the one who answered the door when I rang the bell. I'd never met her before. She was small, birdlike Mexican woman with a no-nonsense expression.

"I'm Torey Hayden, Leslie's teacher at school. I've come to see Ladbrooke. Is she here?"

"No ma'am. I'm sorry." And she began to shut the door.

"Wait a minute," I said, and put my hand on the door. "What about Mr. Considyne? Is he here?"

A long pause followed and it was obvious that one of Conseula's primary tasks was vetting people. "He's working in his studio, ma'am."

"Do you suppose I could have a quick word with him?" I asked, and when it looked unlikely she was going to try to find out, I added, "Just a very quick word?"

Slowly, she nodded. "Wait here." And she disappeared, shutting the door in my face.

A few minutes later, she reopened the door. "Yes," she said. "His studio's the small building at the back of the house. When you get there, just knock on the door."

Following her directions, I was greeted by a blast of icy air as I cleared the corner of the house. Beyond were three double garages and a large tennis court. Dusk was already closing in, and lights were on in the studio. I knocked loudly on the door.

There was no immediate answer. I had memories of Carolyn's story of how Rita Ashworth had banged fruitlessly on Tom Considyne's studio window to get his attention when Leslie had gone into a diabetic coma. That had seemed a bit far-fetched at the time, more like just one of Carolyn's stories. Now, standing in the freezing twilight, I found it alarmingly real. I knocked again, even louder.

"Just a minute," he called. So I waited.

The door to the studio opened, spilling bright light out onto me, standing on the step.

"Hi. I've come to inquire about Ladbrooke."

He was wiping his hands on a paint-stained rag. "She's not here."

"Yes, I know. Consuela told me. Where is she? She hasn't been at work these last three days, and I was beginning to get concerned."

He continued to wipe his hands on the rag, running it over each finger individually. "I don't know where she is," he replied, his voice casual.

The warm air of the studio felt marvelous as it rolled over me there in the icy evening gloom. "Do you know when she'll be back?"

"Like I said, I don't know where she is." He finally took his attention from cleaning his hands and looked down at me. "Go ask one of her lovers, if you want to find her."

That left me pretty well speechless.

"Look, she's not here, okay? She's not been here for days. I haven't the faintest idea where she's at and, frankly, I don't care. If you want to find her, you're going to have to look somewhere else."

What did I say to that? Now what?

My bewilderment appeared to touch Mr. Considyne. He smiled suddenly in a very disarming way and stepped back, extending his arm into the studio. "Come on in. I'm being a terrible host. You must be freezing out there."

I entered the studio, and he shut the door behind me.

"You want a cup of coffee?" he asked. "Or a drink?" He shrugged slightly. "That's one of the advantages of having Ladbrooke gone. I can have a guilt-free drink." He pushed back the cover of an old rolltop desk to reveal a vast assortment of bottles and drink-making equipment. He took out glasses.

"No. No thank you," I said. "I'd be satisfied with coffee."

"Oh, come on. Just a wee drink. So I don't have to drink alone. The coffee's been in the pot quite a while anyway."

"No thanks."

Across the room was the huge canvas he was working on. Beyond it was a wall of small-paned windows. I could just make out through the descending January darkness a lawn receding down to a lake.

"Do you like it?" Considyne asked. He came over to stand next to me.

I regarded the painting. It was enormous in size. Even with his height, he would have needed a stepladder to reach the top part of it. It was done all in grays and muted gray-greens, a slightly abstract picture of distant trees against water. A pale, misty-looking sun, or maybe it was the moon, shone faintly yellow in the gray-green sky.

I nodded. "Yes, I do."

"That's a trick question, isn't it? You can't very well answer no."

I grinned. "Probably not. But I do like it. I've seen your work before."

"Well, then that puts you ahead of most of the cretins in this neck of the woods." He went up to the painting and touched a small part of it with one finger. "You know what they always say about prophets in their own land. I came back here because I love the place. Because I always thought I owed it something. Because, basically, they've got no one from here who's ever done more than shit in a bucket. But I might as well never have bothered. I was much better off in New York."

Then he turned around and looked at me. He smiled. "But I've got a soft spot for lost causes. And underdogs. And failures. As you probably know."

We both fell silent. I sipped my coffee. He went back to the desk and renewed his drink.

"So," he said, "You want to know about Ladbrooke."

"I was concerned because she didn't show up at school. I was afraid she might be ill, because this didn't seem like her."

Tom Considyne guffawed. "Seem like her?"

"She's been very dependable. She's never missed a day. She's never even been late."

"Now *that's* not like her. *This* is, Torey."

I said nothing.

"You don't believe me, do you? You know how long she's been gone? Ten days? Eleven days? I've lost count."

"Aren't you worried?" I asked. I was flabbergasted. This was the kind of story I'd expect from Mariana, not Tom Considyne.

"No, she'll come back. Like the proverbial bad penny, Ladbrooke always turns up."

A silence followed, and for a long moment, he studied me. "I think she's done a sell job on you. She's been a good girl in there with you, hasn't she? She's made you believe her."

I said nothing.

He continued to study my face. "You've got to look at it from my point of view, Torey. You ever lived with an alcoholic? Do you have any idea what it's like to be around someone who has to get up to puke halfway through your Christmas dinner? Who can't remember if she sent out the Christmas cards or not? My kids were here for Christmas this year, and Ladbrooke spoiled it for everyone. She ruined it for my kids. Jesus, they won't even visit me half the time because of Ladbrooke."

I nodded.

"I remember coming to that conference of yours back, when was it? September? October? Whenever," he said softly. "I remember running on and on about Leslie, saying how hard it was never having anyone to talk to about her. But I must confess, it's not Leslie. It's Ladbrooke. I could manage with Leslie. But who the hell is going to straighten out the mess with Ladbrooke? Who on earth is there to talk to about her?"

He paused. "I keep thinking that I ought to be able to talk *with* Ladbrooke. But I might as well try talking with Leslie. Ladbrooke doesn't talk. Have you noticed that? She does *not* talk. You need to be telepathic to have a decent conversation with Ladbrooke, and I'm afraid I'm not."

"Have you considered marriage counseling?" I asked.

He rolled his eyes. "You've got all the answers, don't you? It was AA last time, as I recall. Haven't you cottoned on by now? If Ladbrooke's not going to talk to me, she's sure the hell not going to talk to strangers, is she? Besides, we hardly need marriage counseling. We haven't got a marriage."

I stared into my empty coffee cup.

"It's all such a hell of a mess," he said wearily. "I never saw it coming. God knows why I didn't, but I never did. She never could communicate anywhere but in bed. Spread her legs, that's the only kind of response she's ever known how to give."

I hadn't meant to get into all of this. Glancing around the room, I looked for some way to politely extricate myself.

"She's a hopeless mother. Hasn't the slightest clue as to what to do with Leslie. Never has had. Not one whiff of maternal instinct. She was back working at Princeton when Leslie was three weeks old. We got into screaming fights over it. I told her she ought to be home with her baby, that she was doing Leslie irreparable harm, but she wouldn't listen. Christ, if it hadn't been for me, sitting there with my Dr. Spock, Leslie never would have known she had parents. Ladbrooke could have listened. Jesus, I've been through it all before. I have two kids of my own. But no, not Ladbrooke. She wasn't going to get into all that touchy-feely business with babies. A bit too human, that. She needed the cold comfort of all her little numbers. And I got Leslie. I keep telling her, if she'd listened to me, if she'd just tried to be a decent mother, Leslie would never have had all these problems."

I shook my head. "I'm afraid I can't agree with you. I think most of Leslie's problems are quite separate. From a professional point of view, I have to say Leslie might well have developed her problems, whatever kind of mothering she had."

"Yes, but Leslie wouldn't have been the way she is. She might have had some tiny little problems, but not all of them. Right?"

"I think she still would probably have had some great big problems."

"But not all of them. Right?"

"I don't know. That's all speculation."

"But you're a professional. You've got to admit that a lot of Leslie's problems are purely emotional. Right?"

"What I'm saying is that there is no point in continuing to blame Ladbrooke for what happened years ago and is over and done with. She can hardly breast feed Leslie now."

"But a lot of Leslie's problems *are* emotional, don't you agree?"

"But continuing to blame Ladbrooke isn't very productive."

"But a lot of Leslie's problems *are* emotional. Right?"

"But what I'm saying is that continuing—"

"*Right?*"

"Well, yes, okay. A lot of Leslie's problems are purely emotional. But what I am saying is that it's pointless to waste precious time allocating blame for things that happened years ago when what we need to do is *solve* the problems."

"But I'm right," he said firmly. "You've said so yourself. You're a professional in the field and you've agreed with me that Leslie's problems are purely emotional. Ladbrooke's destroyed Leslie."

I sat back and shut my mouth. I was getting a far better idea of what Ladbrooke had to put up with in attempting to argue with Tom. As inarticulate as she was, I could imagine it must be hell.

Several seconds passed in absolute silence, and I let the silence collect around me, as I waited for some indication that he was easing off. At last he took a deep breath and relaxed back into the cushions of the couch.

"It's a waste of everybody's time to dig up the past and pick through it like a pile of old bones," I said. "Whatever's caused Leslie's problems, she's got them. We can't roll the clock back and make her a baby again. And whatever's caused Ladbrooke's problems, she's got hers too. The only crucial thing, the only thing that matters is that both of them manage to improve. Neither one seems to be living a decent life at the moment."

"It's because of Ladbrooke that Leslie has her problems," Tom said. "Ladbrooke needs to see that it's because she's the way she is that all the rest of us are living in such hell. Ladbrooke is the most self-centered person I've ever come across. She thinks nobody has problems but her. And if you try to talk to her, if you try to help her, what does she do? Scream at you. Slam doors in your face. Drink herself puking sick. *You* try and do something with her. You try and tell her she needs to change."

"This all seems a bit heavy on Ladbrooke."

"But it's true. If any of the rest of us is going to get better, Ladbrooke has to change. I can hardly make my kids treat her better if she's going to go around acting like a boozed-up harpy all the time. I can hardly improve our relationship if she's out fucking every pair of trousers in town."

I sighed.

"It's true. Right? How can we change if she doesn't? Don't you agree?"

"Yes, but—"

"But don't you agree? We can't change unless Ladbrooke does."

I wasn't going to get into this again, so I said nothing. He waited a long time, watching my face intently. I could tell I was irritating him by not answering.

"What kind of qualifications do you have?" he asked suddenly. "Are you a doctor of some kind? Are you a certified psychologist? Here you are, making psychological assessments of people, interfering in people's lives, like it's your born right. This seems a pretty far stretch from teaching to me. I mean, you are a teacher, aren't you?"

"Yes, I'm a teacher."

"Aren't you overstepping yourself a bit here?"

I shrugged. "Well, for what it's worth, I am certified. I am legally qualified. But that's not the reason I'm sitting here. I'm here because I'm the one who's been conned into all of this. Your wife picked me, not the other way around. It's my life she's decided to share for eight hours a day."

Silence came again. He rose to renew his drink. Then coming back, he leaned over and peered into my coffee cup. Without asking, he took it from me and refilled it.

"Have you considered getting a divorce?" I asked.

He didn't answer immediately. He'd returned to the couch, where he sat regarding his drink. The glass, filled with ice, had become wet with condensation. Reaching for the paint-stained rag he'd been wiping his hands with earlier, he began to carefully wipe the glass. Then finally, he shook his head.

"No. No, I've been through all that before. It doesn't solve much. Besides, I wouldn't do it because of Leslie. I've lost my other two kids. If you don't live with them, you lose them. You lose all the little moments. I wouldn't ever want that to happen with Leslie. Especially not Leslie."

"I'd think a judge would be quite lenient toward you. If Ladbrooke's been as incompetent as you say, it doesn't seem as if she'd necessarily win custody."

No response. He continued to regard his drink.

"A lot of that's changed in the past few years. Fathers get custody quite frequently. Regardless of the mother's competency."

He shook his head. "No, Ladbrooke'd put up a hell of a fight. She wouldn't let me do it."

"Ladbrooke doesn't seem a vindictive person to me."

"No, she's not, I suppose. But she loves Leslie. Whatever else I might say about her, I know she loves Leslie. She may be a lousy mother, but her heart works."

"Yes, but fathers still do get custody."

Again he shook his head. "No, you see, there's more to it than that. Leslie isn't my child."

"Oh."

Tom Considyne rose and went to turn on a small table lamp near me. The night had come completely, and darkness was pressing in around us. I sighed, wishing there was some way I could gracefully leave. I was tired and hungry and wanted to go home.

He looked tired too. I wondered idly if, now that Ladbrooke was gone, he was having to get up in the night with Leslie. But studying his features, I could tell it was a deeper tiredness. It had worn lines into his face.

Bastard that he was, I still found myself having a sort of grudging admiration for Tom Considyne. He had a lot to cope with. I knew I probably couldn't live with Ladbrooke. She was indeed on her good behavior with me, and I knew it. We had our difficult moments, but I was very aware of her efforts to mind herself. But day in, day out with Lad, intense and troubled as she was, would be grueling. That Tom Considyne persisted and that he managed to want to keep the marriage going, impressed me.

"So," he said after a lengthy silence, "what's Ladbrooke doing when she's in with you? Is it therapy?"

I shook my head. "No. She's just helping with the children. I needed an aide and she volunteered. It's all fairly straightforward."

"Honestly, I *am* amazed," he said and shook his head. "I cannot picture Ladbrooke reading little books about kitties and bunnies and wiping a lot of retarded kids' snotty noses."

I smiled slightly. "It's not exactly like that."

"Well, you know what I mean. I can't picture it."

Silence again. Tom Considyne got up for his fourth drink. Clink went the ice cubes. He was adding them in a very careful fashion, peering into the glass intently, as if it mattered that there be just so many.

"How did you and Ladbrooke meet?" I asked.

He shrugged. "In pretty much the usual way." He came back to the couch and sat down. "I was out with friends. I was living in New York at the time, and we were cruising the bars, just to see what was going on. We were down in Greenwich Village. And there she was."

Then he smiled and the smile grew inward. Pensive, he was no longer looking in my direction. "Here I was in this bar. And I looked over and there she was. And believe me, you couldn't miss her. She was young— what—twenty-three? You know, fresh face and all that. The way girls are at that age. And God, the way she looked. She looked wild. Untamed. She looked like a lioness. With all that hair, that coloring. The way she moved. You ever watch Ladbrooke move? Her muscles, under her skin up here particularly," he said, gesturing to his shoulder area. "She moves in a very feline way. I see Ladbrooke and, every time, that still comes to mind. Only now I think of her being a lioness trapped in human form, not the other way around, because being human certainly doesn't come naturally to Ladbrooke."

He shrugged, smiled slightly. "Anyway, there I was in that bar and I saw her and I remember telling my friend, the guy I was with, I remember saying, see that girl over there? She should be free somewhere. In the wild. She didn't belong in a place like that, in a bar in New York City. I also remember telling him I was going to have her. If ever there was love at first sight, it was then, with Ladbrooke."

He looked at me and laughed. "You're thinking what an old fool, aren't you? Old fools fall hardest, believe me." He laughed again. "Anyway, I got up and went over and talked to her for a while. I should have been forewarned, because she was drunk then. But sweet drunk, you know, the way girls get. And I talked to her. Or, rather, I didn't really. There was this other girl with her, and I talked to her most of the time. Like I said, I should have been forewarned. But this other girl kept saying what a whiz kid Ladbrooke was, how she was doing this Ph.D. in physics. I was bowled over. Brains as well as beauty, I mean, what a combination. And Ladbrooke was all embarrassed, you know, really cute about it. I just kept looking at her and thinking, I've *got* to have her. So I did."

There was a pause, and he looked at me. He smiled faintly again and then looked away. His attention turned to the massive painting. He studied it a long time. "I appreciate physical beauty. More than most people do, I think. I must have it around me. I could never love a plain woman, no matter how wonderful she might be in other ways. I need total perfection."

He continued to regard the painting.

"Ladbrooke's beautiful. She's the most beautiful woman I've ever seen. So I married her, simple as that. I wanted to be able to touch her, to smell her, to watch the way she moves. I wanted to wake up each morning, knowing she was mine, to have her forever to look at any time I chose."

He grew quiet. Dropping his head, he looked down at his hands. "It probably doesn't seem like much of a marriage to you. I know it doesn't to a lot of people. I know we have more than our share of problems. But I love Ladbrooke. In spite of everything. I mean, if you had a Rembrandt, you wouldn't want to sell it just because it clashed with your wallpaper."

CHAPTER
FIFTEEN

Friday morning, and there was Lad at eight o'clock. She looked terrible. Under normal conditions, she had pale skin, but now it had gone virtually translucent, giving her an unhealthy bluish cast. There were dark circles under her eyes. She'd lost a noticeable amount of weight.

"Hi," she said uncertainly from the corner of the shelves.

I was at the table and looked up. "Hi."

"Do you want me back?"

"Of course I do. Come on in." I pushed the chair across from me out with my foot. "I'll show you what we've been doing."

I didn't ask any questions. For the moment, it seemed best just to get on with things as usual, which proved no small challenge as the day progressed because Ladbrooke was in even worse shape than she looked. Her stomach was terrible. She got sick immediately after lunch and then several times thereafter through the afternoon. And she remained slightly out-of-sync with all the activities, being ill prepared and feeling too unwell to improvise. Thank God for the children, who were charmingly open about their pleasure in having her back. For them, she kept going.

Both of us, however, were relieved when the end of the school day came. It had been hard work, keeping a cheerful face on things, and toward the end, she was out of the room being sick more often than she was in.

I took the children down to meet their rides. When I came back up, I found Ladbrooke settled at the table with a glass of water, a packet of mints and her notebook. She was paging through my plan book, reviewing what we'd been doing since the resumption of school after vacation.

"Do you want to go home early?" I asked.

"No."

"You want to talk about it?"

"No."

"Okay." I got up and went over to find the children's folders in order to correct their work. Bringing them back to the table, I sat down again, uncapped my felt-tipped pen and prepared to work. I glanced over at her.

"Are you sure you don't want to go home?" I asked. "You're looking miserable. If you want to go, Lad, I don't mind."

She shook her head. "I don't want to go home."

I suddenly realized she was very near to tears. Not wanting to make her cry, I opened Shamie's folder and searched through it for his current work. Then I settled down to read it through.

I corrected the papers in all the folders, put them back and returned the folders to the top of the filing cabinet. Then I took the plan book and began the next day's plans. Throughout the entire time, Ladbrooke did no more than sit across from me. She ate the mints, one by one, keeping her arms folded on the table when she wasn't taking a mint out of the packet. Beyond that, she just sat.

The clock edged around to four, to 4:15.

Finished with the plans, I got out construction paper and brought it back to the table to make an example of the next day's art project.

"You must hate me," she said at last. She had been silent so long that I had become thoroughly absorbed in my folding and cutting. Her voice startled me slightly.

I looked over. "No. Of course I don't, Lad."

"You don't have to be nice to me, you know. You don't have to pretend to like me."

Frowning, I regarded her. "What kind of talk is this? I'd take it as an insult, kiddo, if I thought you really believed I've been pretending all this time. There's no pretending involved. I like you. Plain and simple."

She twiddled a piece of paper off the mint packet.

"You're really feeling down, aren't you?" I said.

She nodded slowly. Lower lip caught between her teeth, she kept her head bowed and nodded again.

"Why? Because of this . . . whatever it was, this binge?"

She shrugged. "I don't know. Just everything. I'm down about everything."

"Don't worry about what I think, if that's what's troubling you. Like I said back in November, if there're slips, there're slips. I'm not going to fall apart over it. Don't you either. Let's just pick up the pieces and try again."

She nodded faintly.

"Is that what's bothering you?"

She shrugged.

Silence once more. I looked down at my work. I stared at the silly-looking spider I was making. It stood, provocatively faceless, on seven little pleated legs.

"What caused the problem?"

She shrugged again. "I don't know."

I began to make the spider's eighth leg, folding it carefully into accordion pleats.

She shrugged once more. "I was so happy. That last day. It went so well. I thought the feeling was going to last me the whole two weeks."

"That day did go well. It was fun."

She nodded. A small pause followed, but then she shook her head. "I hate Christmas."

"Why's that?" I asked without looking up.

One more shrug. "I don't know."

I lifted the spider body up and attempted to attach the eighth leg. Silence intruded, and it grew very, very long. Minutes passed. I turned the spider over to see if it would stand up. With seven legs, it did. With eight, it didn't. The legs splayed and the body fell flat against the table. I picked it up, twiddled it, tried again. Once again, flat on the tabletop it went. Lifting it, I pinched in the legs, held it the other way around, and then, on impulse, made it dance along the table. Looking over to Ladbrooke to see if it got any sort of smile, I made the spider dance again. I grinned.

Ladbrooke was watching what I was doing intently, but she never reacted.

Leaving the spider lying on its back with its incompetent legs waving in the air, I started to make a second one.

"Can I tell you something?" Ladbrooke asked softly.

"Yes, of course."

But nothing came. She took in a deep breath and exhaled it, making the hairs around her face flutter.

"I don't know where to start. I don't know what to say. Now I've got you anticipating something and I don't know what to say."

"Don't worry about it."

She stared at the tabletop.

I snipped construction paper into long strips.

"My mom . . ." She stopped again. "My mom . . . my mom had . . . problems, I guess you'd say. She drank. My mom drank. She was an alcoholic."

Another pause. Ladbrooke was sitting with her hands on either side of her forehead, fingers intertwined through her loose hair. I could see her fingertips with their badly bitten nails turning white as she pressed them against her head. She still stared at the tabletop.

"There was this one Christmas. I was seven. I remember it really well. I got into a fight with my brother on Christmas Eve. I have two brothers. Well, I had two brothers. One of them's dead now. Anyway . . ." She fell silent again.

I had paused in what I was doing and was reluctant to restart lest I frighten her out of her story.

"Anyway my brother Bobby and me, we got into this stupid fight over which of us got to turn the Christmas tree lights on. It was Christmas Eve. Did I say that?" A sudden pause. She looked over without really raising her head. "I'm boring you, aren't I? I'm telling you too much junk you don't want to know. I'm terrible at telling about things."

"You're doing fine," I said. "Don't worry about it."

"I'm being boring."

"You're not, Ladbrooke."

Silence.

She rooted into the packet of mints and took one out. She regarded it and then offered it over. I accepted it. She then took out another one for herself. Several seconds of silent mint sucking followed.

"Well, anyway, my mom and my stepfather and a lot of people were there that night. They'd been drinking, and everybody was pretty far gone. My mom got really volatile when she drank, so you had to be careful what you said, because she always took it the wrong way. And you had to be careful what you did. Anyway, my brother and I got to fighting. So my mom said, that's it. If you're going to fight, there's no Christmas for you. And she sent us off to bed. I wasn't too worried about it, but when we got up the next morning, there was nothing. I mean, *nothing*. The tree was taken down. Our presents were gone. Everything. There weren't even any pine needles left on the floor. Even my little brother, who was two, even his presents were gone. And Bobby said, 'Where's Santa Claus?' He was only five then and he still believed. He'd written his letter and everything that year. He couldn't figure out what had happened. And my mother said, Santa doesn't like you any more. He doesn't like bad boys and girls, and you were bad last night, so he's come and taken everything away with him, back to the North Pole. And my brother started crying. But me, I knew better. I knew she'd done it. And I said, 'Where's Kitson's things?' Kitson was my little brother. I said, 'It's not fair of Santa to take Kit's things too. He wasn't even awake when Bobby and I got in trouble.' And I said, 'Where's the present I bought Bobby?' Because I'd gone out and spent all the money I had on buying my brother one of those Matchbox cars, and I'd wrapped it myself in this gold and red paper and put it under the tree. I said Santa had no right to take away my present to Bobby. I said Santa hadn't done it anyway. I said she'd done it. And she whalloped me right across the mouth. My mother very seldom hit us kids, but boy, when she did, you knew she'd done it. And then she took me out and made me sit on the back step. She sat me out there, like I was a dog."

Ladbrooke paused. Bringing one hand down, she ran her fingers along the edge of the table. Back and forth, back and forth, with hypnotic slowness.

"The weird thing, the thing I remember most clearly about that Christmas wasn't that we didn't get toys or such. It was sitting out on the back step. From where I was sitting, I could see across our backyard to the houses on the other side of the alley. It was the middle of the day, so everyone had their curtains open, but it was wintertime and overcast, so they had their lights on, and I could see right into their houses. I could see Christmas trees and I could see moms going back and forth in the kitchens, making Christmas dinner. I could see the little kid who lived right in back of us come out in his backyard to play. He was maybe two or three, and he'd gotten one of those riding toys a kid sits on and pushes with his feet. It was a little car. And he got on it and rode back and forth for hours. It was a marvelous present for him. He loved it. So I watched him and the others until it got dark and my mom let me in again."

Silence.

"I can see where that might put you off the idea of Christmas."

Ladbrooke shrugged slightly. "It hasn't really. That's the weird part. If anything, it's made me want Christmas more. I keep sitting out there year after year, still waiting to be let in. Every Christmas, I think, this one's going to work out. This one's going to be as nice as all those Christmases in other people's houses. But I keep finding myself back outside on the step. It's sort of an annual nightmare."

I nodded.

Another long silence came then, and Ladbrooke fell deep in thought. Not wanting to shatter the moment, I sat very quietly, regarding my half-constructed spider. Lifting my eyes, I looked beyond her to the window. It had begun to snow.

"My mom really had a lot of trouble with drinking," Ladbrooke said quietly. "She was always thinking these crazy things. I remember once when I was about five, she got really mad at me. I was in the bathroom by the sink—I remember that—but what exactly I was doing in there, I don't recall. Anyway, she came in and she was really, really angry. She had this funny idea that I was trying to come on to my stepfather. It was a persistent thing with her. I didn't even know what she was talking about. I mean, I did. She didn't leave much to the imagination. But I didn't know why she thought I was doing it."

Ladbrooke paused. As I watched her, I could picture what she must have looked like as a little girl. I remembered seeing a photograph of Brooke Shields as a small child, and I could imagine Ladbrooke's having the same kind of infantile sexuality about her, although that was hardly the type of thing to threaten an adult woman.

"Anyway, there I was in the bathroom, and she came in, absolutely furious with me. I had long hair at the time, and it was loose. Usually, I had it in two braids, but it wasn't that day. And she grabbed me by my hair, grabbed me so hard she lifted me off the floor. She told me to look at myself in the mirror, to look at my kind of face. She said the Devil'd have me, the way I looked. And she took the scissors and cut my hair. Not just short, but right off. I had about half an inch of hair when she got done."

I looked down at the table. "She did all this because she thought you were making sexual advances toward your stepfather?"

"I guess so. And because she was drunk."

"Was there anything going on with your stepfather? Did he ever make advances toward you?"

"No. I was five, for God's sake."

"Well, it does happen. And it's not the little one's fault, no matter how much sexual provocation adults might read into it."

"No. Not with my stepdad. He was really good to me. I wished he had lasted longer in the family. He was better to me than any of the others. Sometimes, he'd come in, after my mom had had one of her do's, and he'd take me on his lap and just hold me. It was nice, like. He'd tell me not to mind my mother, that she was just that way and I'd have to forgive her. But everything he did was innocent."

Silence. Ladbrooke exhaled noisily, scratched her head, ran her fingers through her hair.

"The thing that kills me," she said, "is that my mom drank. She was so terrible. She made me feel like such dirt all the time. I spent my whole childhood running after her, trying to please her, placating her, taking care of my brothers, because she never did. I ended up hating her. And I swore I would never be like her, that I'd never make anybody suffer the way I had. But look at me. Look at me now."

I said nothing.

Ladbrooke lifted her eyes and regarded me for the first time during the conversation. There was a long moment's eye contact between us before she looked away.

"Do you hate me now?" she asked softly.

"Of course I don't."

"I do," she said wearily.

"I know."

She sighed. Elbows on the table, hands interlocked, she rested her cheek against them. "What am I going to do with myself, Torey?"

"Stop drinking."

"How?"

"By not taking the next drink."

She sighed again.

Silence.

"I've never told anyone about any of this," she said. "Never. Not a word. Even Bobby and I never discussed it. It's why I don't want to get into AA or anything like that. I don't want to have to tell them about my mom. I mean, part of me blames her for my ending up like this. But part of me tells me that I have no justification for talking about what she did when I've done no better. And part of me says, what the hell, why bother? I'll just fail."

"I can appreciate that maybe a group setting like AA wouldn't be the best choice for you. I think you'd probably feel better in a one-to-one situation. Have you ever considered therapy?"

She nodded. "We had to go. About four years ago. Both Tom and I had to go. It was part of the whole deal when Leslie was being diagnosed."

"And?"

"I don't like to even remember it."

"Why?"

"Because it was horrible. I was frightened of the therapist. I didn't know him, and it was hard for me to talk. He kept saying I *could* talk, that I wasn't talking because I wanted to keep him out. I wasn't talking because there wasn't anything in there I could manage to say. But he wouldn't believe me when I said that."

"How long did you see him?"

"For about six months. I had to quit after a while. I started getting sick from about Monday on. The appointments were on Wednesday, and I'd be throwing up for two days out of every week. But Tom kept going. Tom went for about a year and then got fed up too."

She put another mint into her mouth and sucked it thoughtfully.

"I got angry this one time. I said it wasn't that I didn't want to change. I did. But people were always expecting me to do it all on my own. I said, 'You want me to change, but you never meet me halfway. To help me.' I said, 'Some days it's going to be harder for me, and you're going to have to meet me seventy-five percent of the way, because I'm only going to manage twenty-five percent. And some days, you're going to have to go ninety-five percent. And just occasionally, you may have to go all the way, all one hundred percent of the way, and carry me, because otherwise, I'm not going to manage to get anywhere. Someone is going to have to carry me sometimes and not just stand around waiting for me to do it all myself because otherwise, I'm simply not going to make it.' And he said that was my whole problem in a nutshell. I expected other people to do all the changing for me."

I looked over.

"Well, that's not what I meant when I said that." She raised her eyes to meet mine. "You understand what I meant, don't you?"

"I think so."

"Am I wrong?"

"No, not necessarily. The problem is, some of the hardest changes, no one else can do for you."

She nodded. "I know that. It's just that, well, doing them . . . Well, I just want . . . I need . . . What's the word I'm looking for?"

"Support?"

She shrugged. "I guess so . . . no, not exactly. Not support. Help. Help to keep control. You know. In those times when I can't do anything right, when I can't keep myself together any longer, then I need someone else to take over."

I regarded her.

"I'm still not saying it right. It still comes out sounding like I want someone else to do my work for me, and that's not what I mean. It's not like that at all. It's like . . ." A very long pause followed while she thought. "Well, it's like with you and the kids. Like the other day when Geraldine got so upset and out of control. She just went to pieces. But you were there, saying not to worry and picking up the chairs. That's what I mean. I need to know it's just me that's fallen apart and not the whole universe. I'm so weak. I need to know there's someone out there's who's stronger, someone still in control. That's what I'm talking about. Like what you do for the kids. Like what a mother does for her child."

CHAPTER
SIXTEEN

Back to work. These were my favorite months: January, February and March. Undisturbed by major holidays, vacations or good weather, I had a nice long stretch in which to work uninterrupted. We were far enough from the beginning of the school year to be settled in and acquainted with one another's idiosyncrasies, yet far enough from the end to be able to see through what we had started. Now was the time to apply myself. I was a winter person anyway, thriving in the cold weather and the short, gray days. This time of year always made me feel energetic, ambitious and motivated.

After the initial week's chaos, the children all settled down well from their long Christmas break. This was an unusual group in that respect. Change and disruption of routine did not bother them in the way it had my other classes through the years. I was never sure exactly why, but assumed it stemmed primarily from the fact that most of the children came from warm, stable homes. Only Mariana had a truly horrific home life, which was offset by the fact that she was one of the less disturbed children in the class.

The hardest person to resettle was Ladbrooke, who returned not only filled with emotional turmoil, but had some dramatic physical problems to contend with as well. She vomited constantly, seldom making it through the lunch hour with me. Her weight dropped even more. Her hands shook. Her skin had a dryish, loosened look. And always there was that distinctive sickish color to her face.

I wished fervently that she would see a doctor, and I urged her numerous times to go, until in the end, she told me she had. So I eased up on her some, but not because I believed her. I didn't. I think I knew as well as she did that she'd be hospitalized if she saw a doctor. However, there seemed little point in pressing her to the point where she lied to me to get me to leave her alone.

All during this time Ladbrooke said she wasn't drinking. I had no way of verifying that, but I felt perhaps she was telling the truth. I think this was all just recovery from the two-week binge over Christmas, because slowly, slowly, she did improve. As January progressed, she finally got to the point where she no longer needed to bolt from the room to be sick. The dark circles under her eyes faded. Her skin color improved. She grew more energetic. And I relaxed.

When it came to the kids, Leslie was at the head of my list for some serious intervention. Since my first concentrated efforts in November, I had made slow but steady progress with her. She would now sit down with me and do a few manipulative tasks or simple worksheets, but it was still hard going. She needed constant reorienting and total teacher involvement. Leslie wasn't the kind of child you could teach with five others present.

She still resorted to her disappearing act quite frequently. Particularly when angry, she could go maddeningly vacant and refuse to do a thing. However, I made it clear to her that sitting with me, being in my lap and being held, were all privileges and not rights. If she wanted to withdraw and do nothing, she did it on her own, because it just wasn't sociable. If she was responsive, she could have all the advantages that went along with it. And as I suspected, Leslie had no trouble understanding this.

Once Leslie confirmed to her own satisfaction that she could no longer control us in the classroom by her customary methods of withdrawal, she began to experiment with a wider range of behaviors. Many of these were distinctly less pleasant to put up with than the withdrawal had been. Sudden outbursts of temper became a regular, daily feature. UFOs took to the air. Worksheets and art projects met untimely ends. Wastebaskets appeared upside down, their contents strewn. And boxes of tissues, a particularly favored target for Leslie's energies, were being shredded on a near-daily basis, leaving the room looking as if a snowstorm had happened by. And Leslie grew much noisier. Although she still used only the very rare meaningful word, she now began to scream and shout and otherwise demand attention vocally.

As unpleasant as many of these changes were, I took them all to be signs of definite progress. They also confirmed my now long-held suspicion that Leslie's withdrawal had been purely a conditioned response and not a parameter of her disturbance. Once it was no longer rewarded in the classroom, it disappeared with amazing speed.

Once Leslie reached this noisy, rebellious stage, I felt more certain about the value of undertaking major changes. There were three areas in which I felt it imperative that Leslie show some improvement, both for her own future good and for the sanity of the people around her. One was to gain some form of communicative speech. Two was to achieve toilet training. Three was to diminish her bizarre midnight activities. I now felt improvement in all three areas to be within Leslie's capabilities.

Although Leslie did not apparently exhibit this new negative way-wardness at home to the extent she did at school, her behavior there was changing as well. Ladbrooke was trying to apply some of my more successful techniques in that setting. Particularly, she tried not to reward Leslie for her continuing withdrawn behavior and to not play into Leslie's long-established struggle to control the family. Unfortunately, well meaning as Ladbrooke was, she was not yet very competent at controlling Leslie's behavior, as indeed, even I wasn't in the classroom. Predictably, this was having dramatic effects on the family dynamics in general, and they weren't especially positive ones.

By the latter part of January, I could see we all needed to get together for another conference over Leslie, so I arranged for Tom to join Ladbrooke and me after school one afternoon.

Tom Considyne was definitely underwhelmed with Leslie's "progress" and spared no words whatsoever in telling me so. When I explained that evidence showed Leslie's withdrawal to be simply a form of manipulation, that it got her what she wanted when she wanted it, and that this now angry, disruptive child was simply one finding a more appropriate way of relating, he was unimpressed. If she did what she did to make us hug and cuddle her, he said, then she *should* be hugged and cuddled. Nothing manipulative in that. She needed hugging and cuddling or she wouldn't go to such extremes to get it, and he pulled out the hoary old chestnut about Ladbrooke's maternal coldness. She had driven Leslie to such bizarre lengths. Poor Leslie. We should hug and cuddle her more, he said, not deprive her of it. I tried to explain that, yes, of course, Leslie needed to be hugged and cuddled. I wasn't advocating otherwise. I was simply saying there were more appropriate ways of getting hugs and cuddles from other people than blackmailing them into it.

As the discussion progressed, it grew heated. Tom was angry with me for creating a little monster. I was angry with him for seeing Leslie as an abstraction of a child rather than an actual human being. Ladbrooke sat apart from us at the far end of the table, her head down, her hands against her face, and never said a word.

Leslie needed to change, I said. She was a real child living in a real world. Being hugged and cuddled and coddled and allowed to do whatever she wanted, whenever she wanted, was probably just fine by Leslie and probably always would be, but it was cheating her. We were shirking our responsibilities. She wasn't Peter Pan. One of these days she wouldn't be seven any more. She'd be seventeen. Or twenty-seven. Or forty-seven. Who'd be wiping her bottom then? Which backward staff member would the job fall to?

This, of course, made Tom Considyne furious. I was sullying Leslie. She was pure and innocent and natural, and he felt she herself was the only valid judge of what was good for her. Left alone with her purity, she could only be beautiul. But I was destroying her, destroying her innocence, taking a dream and making it into a nightmare.

This was extremely hard reasoning for me to deal with because it made absolutely no practical sense at all. Yet arguing with him over the matter was frustrating because, as I heard myself talk, all my justifications sounded so dreary and banal. How did you argue reality against dreams of beauty and innocence?

Ladbrooke began to cry. Right out of nowhere. I just happened to glance over mid-discussion with Tom and I saw the tears washing over her cheeks as she sat, chin in her hands. Tom, too, looked over when I did.

"Don't you have anything to say?" he asked. "This is your child."

She shook her head, got up and left the room.

I told Tom that I intended to persevere in the classroom with what I was doing. Speech first, I said. Then toilet training. And if there was still time, I wanted to see Leslie, if not sleeping through the night, then at least staying in her room so that other people could sleep.

Tom looked scandalized. Leslie can't do those things, he said. If she could do them, she would do them. It was criminal to force a child like Leslie.

I said I had no intention of forcing Leslie. I intended, rather, to teach her. She wasn't doing them, I felt, because she had never learned the necessity of doing them. But she could. I was convinced of that. She was a bright child, in spite of her handicap.

I studied his features, his gentle, watery eyes, and I knew I wasn't succeeding. He wasn't in the least convinced that I was doing right. He loved Leslie's feyness. In a way, I suspect he loved her feyness more than he loved the child herself.

Back in the classroom with Leslie, I got underway. I brought up an old desk from the basement and two small wooden chairs. These I put in the blackboard area of the room, up against the chalkboard. I then arranged the daily schedule so that Ladbrooke could handle the other children, allowing me an uninterrupted half hour a day with Leslie.

Although not normally given to highly disciplined approaches, I chose one for Leslie. Reckoning she needed to be taught to speak, rather than made to speak, as in the case of children with purely emotionally based speech problems, I decided to give Leslie small, concrete rewards for any attempt she made to create appropriate sounds. Food was the most obvious reinforcement, although with Leslie's diabetes, this was difficult. I had to look around quite a while to come up with something that she might like well enough to work for that wouldn't interfere with her regimen. In the end, I settled on chopped up bits of raw Jerusalem artichoke. Hardly high on most people's lists of popular foods, they weren't an obvious choice, but they were available, permittable on her diet and reasonably cheap. My real advantage was the fact that food of any kind was a novel reinforcer for Leslie. She had such a tightly controlled diet that she seldom saw food outside highly structured eating times.

I made up three flash cards with pictures of things with simple, single-syllable names—ball, man, dog. I knew Leslie was familiar with all three words and could recognize and identify them on sight.

I laid the cards on the desk between us. "Okay, lovey, can you point to the picture of the dog?"

She did.

"Good job." I gave her a piece of Jerusalem artichoke. This intrigued her. She held it up, examined it, smelled it. "Eat it," I said. She did, then gestured for more.

"Point to the picture of the man."

She did. I gave her a second piece of the vegetable. This time she popped it into her mouth immediately and crunched noisily. She reached across the desk for the plate. I removed it, holding it out of her reach.

"Eh-eh," she said.

"No, not yet. You'll have more as we go along. Where's the ball? Good. Here, have this. Where's the man? Good. Here, have another piece. Where's the dog? Good." Over and over the three pictures we went, and for each correct answer, I gave her a chunk of Jerusalem artichoke.

"All right, something different," I said, and picked the three cards up off the table. I shuffled them and then laid only one back down. "What's this, Leslie?"

She stared at it.

"Man," I said, forming the sounds very carefully. "Look up here, Leslie. Look at my mouth. M-a-n. What is it? M-a-n. What is it?"

Her brow furrowed slightly and she studied the picture.

"Look up here again. See my lips? See how I make the sounds. Give me your hand. Put your fingers here against my lips. M-a-n. Now, fingers on your lips. M-a-n."

She averted her eyes.

I held up a piece of Jerusalem artichoke enticingly. She reached out for it, but I kept it just out of her grasp. "M-a-n, Leslie. What's this picture? What is it? M-a-n." With my other hand I gently pushed her lips together to sound the letter M. "M-a-n."

At last she grunted. It wasn't a word. It wasn't even an M sound, really. Just a grunt. But I grinned. "Good girl. Here." And I gave her the piece of Jerusalem artichoke.

The other child I was increasingly concerned about was Geraldine. As the months passed, I realized her problems were much more complex than I'd initially perceived. While on one hand, she was by far the most compliant child in the group, usually presenting a clingy, babyish desperation to please; on the other hand, she nursed an almost unbelievable vengefulness. She could extract cruel, very personal revenge without showing any remorse for the act whatsoever.

I didn't know what to do with Geraldine on either account. Her whiny, clinging behavior drove me to distraction, irritating me and making me not want to be with her at all. Her darker side was unnerving because it was so secret and I didn't ever seem to be able to get effectively at it. If anything, she seemed to be getting worse as the year progressed. More and more often she was caught stealing, lying or inciting Shemona to carry out hostilities on her behalf. When confronted with any of this, Geraldine categorically denied all involvement, even in the face of very obvious evidence. I tried every approach to dealing with these infractions that I could think of, from totally ignoring them to treating her misdemeanors very strictly indeed. Nothing gave me the results I was looking for.

Once I had Leslie in hand and was working easily with her each day, and once Ladbrooke was fully back into the swing of things after her Christmas disruption and able to cope well with the children, I decided it was time to carve out a bit of special time for Geraldine.

The antisocial behavior was far and again the most serious of Geraldine's problems, but I didn't know quite how to approach that directly. So I turned my attention to the clinginess. I hated that behavior to the point that it was disrupting my relationship with the child. It brought out the very worst in me, since I lost patience with it so easily. Certainly I had to acknowledge that the problem was as much mine as it was Geraldine's, because this was just one of those things that personally got right up my nose. My preference was for rowdy, gutsy, aggressive kids, the sort with that desperate bravado against all of the odds—which was lucky, because these kinds of kids made up probably 95 percent of most of my special education classes. I also liked the quiet, troubled, complex ones who stayed in my thoughts after hours, who kept me thinking about them days and weeks and sometimes years after meeting them. But for the clutching, grasping, whining little toadies, I had no affinity whatsoever. This made me feel obligated to work overtime with Geraldine, because I was conscious of needing to compensate for my testy irritation.

So one January day during recess, I brought a rocking chair into the classroom and set it in the long, narrow blackboard arm of the room near Leslie's desk. And I didn't have to wait long to try the chair out. Later that same afternoon, the children were all gathered around the table, doing their individual work. Sitting across from Shamie, I was giving him words for his spelling test. Geraldine and Mariana were making scrapbooks in connection with their reading work. Back and forth they went between the table and the back of the classroom to get magazines for pictures. Geraldine kept stopping to put her arms around my neck. She caressed my hair.

"Honey, please don't," I said. "You and Mariana have your own work to do. I'm helping Shamie right now."

"Mariana's got the glue. I need more glue."

I slid my chair back to see where Ladbrooke was. Geraldine sat down in my lap. She put her arms around my neck and nuzzled against me. "Go ask Ladbrooke to get you some more glue. I need to finish with Shamie." I gently pushed her off my lap.

"Noooo," she whined, still clinging to my neck. She slipped back onto my lap before I could scoot closer to the table.

"Geraldine, please get off. I need to finish with Shamie; he's waiting. Take your glue pot over to Ladbrooke."

"Noooo. I want to sit here. With you, Miss."

I pushed Geraldine off my lap and unhooked her arms from behind my neck, then quickly slid in against the table so she couldn't reseat herself.

"Geraldine, we've talked about this. This isn't appropriate, and it's making me cross. I'm working with Shamie right now. If you need something, ask Ladbrooke."

Shamie, across the table, groaned with annoyance. "Mii-iisss? Next word?"

"No, Geraldine. Don't put your hands there. *No*. Stop it, please. This isn't a time for kissing. I don't *want* to be kissed. I'm working with Shamie."

It was like fighting off a giggling octopus. As fast as I disentangled her from one part of my body, she reattached to another. Lad materialized behind me and unhooked Geraldine's arms from my neck. This interference irritated Geraldine, and her laughter turned to a snarl. She elbowed Lad's stomach.

"Hey," I said, turning in my chair.

Shamie drummed his pencil impatiently on the table.

Geraldine obviously expected to end up in the quiet chair for that, because she was already halfway there before I'd managed to hand Shamie's spelling words to Ladbrooke and get up.

"Geraldine, come here, please," I said. She returned to the table. I put a hand on her shoulder and guided her around the corner of the shelves. I knelt down to look her in the eye.

"How many times have you and I discussed your hanging all over me?" She averted her eyes.

"How often?"

A shrug.

I waited.

"A lot," she muttered.

"Yes, a lot. It bothers me. When you climb on me and hang on me and kiss and touch me all the time, I feel angry with you. It's my body, and I don't like people using it without my permission."

Geraldine studied the floor.

"But my telling you how much it upsets me doesn't seem to be making much of a difference. You still do it. And sometimes I get fed up enough with it to make you sit in the quiet chair, but that doesn't seem to make much difference either."

"I don't know I'm doing it, Miss," she mumbled.

"You do know, Geraldine. You're inside your body. You know what it's doing."

She shrugged.

"So I've decided we need to try something else. You want to touch people and you need to make people touch you, and I'm beginning to think that's so important to you that the consequences of people getting angry with you don't matter. So I'm thinking maybe we need to set aside a special time especially for you—for me to hold you and for you to cuddle. What do you think?"

She shrugged.

"Let's make a deal. Let's arrange things so that you make an honest try not to hang on me quite so much, and in exchange, we'll set aside a special time for holding and hugging. See the rocking chair? What we'll do is sit together in the rocking chair at the end of the day, just you and me. We'll have a special time just for ourselves."

I stood up. "Come here. We'll try it out right now." I went over, adjusted the position of the rocking chair and sat down. Geraldine, with a disconcerted expression on her face, remained standing by the corner of the shelves.

"Come here, Geraldine."

"I'm too big, Miss."

"Too big for what?"

"Too big for sitting in your lap, Miss."

"You were sitting in my lap a few minutes ago, Geraldine. Right around the corner in the classroom."

She regarded me.

"Come here, Geraldine."

She shook her head.

"Would it be better if I brought over one of those chairs from Leslie's desk, and I could sit in that and you could sit in the rocker? Then we could just sit side by side."

She shook her head again. "No, Miss, I don't want to."

"Why?"

"I'm too big, Miss." She turned. "I'll go sit in the quiet chair instead."

CHAPTER
SEVENTEEN

Shamie's notes and files arrived from his school in Belfast the final week in January. They confirmed what I had pretty much concluded all along, that Shamie was not much of a scholar. My experience with him in the classroom showed that he was behind in virtually all subjects and would need resource help in math and probably in reading in a normal junior high.

I was hoping to mainstream Shamie part days at a nearby school within a month's time. He was neither sufficiently disturbed nor sufficiently dysfunctional to merit full-time placement in special education, so I was trying to give him as many experiences close to those of a regular classroom as possible.

One area in which Shamie did excel was history. He was fascinated by the past, and history was the only area in which he could be enticed into doing extra reading. I'd put him on a course of studying medieval Europe and then tried to coordinate as many other activities to the subject as possible. We did tied-in math projects, spelling lists and art activities. We even created a special medieval meal one lunchtime for Shamie to serve to the other children.

One morning, he arrived carrying a book about castles. His assignment had been to read three books of interest relating to the medieval topic, and this one he had located in the public library. It was a beautifully illustrated book, full of incredibly intricate drawings of every possible aspect of castle building.

"Can I read this book for my assignment?" he asked, showing it to me. I paged through it.

Ladbrooke was beside me, and she leaned over my shoulder. "May I see it?" she asked, when I closed it.

I handed it to her. Laying it down, she leaned forward, one hand braced on the edge of the table, and turned the pages slowly. "You know what we could do?" she said, her voice thoughtful.

"What's that?" Shamie asked.

"We could make a model of this castle."

"How do you mean, Miss?"

Ladbrooke considered one of the pictures. "We could take some cardboard and a protractor and a compass and then build this. See, like this. You'd measure that bit there and then transfer it, because, see, it says here that these are scale drawings."

"Could we?" Shamie asked, awed. Then he turned to me. *"Could* we, Miss?"

The classroom suddenly became a depository for every conceivable bit of paper rubbish there was, as Shamie collected together enough material to build his castle. In the beginning, it took form on the end of the table, which was generously large and could accommodate the eight of us with plenty of room to spare. But the castle quickly outgrew these lodgings. Very carefully, Shamie disassembled it, piece by piece, and reassembled it on the floor, back by the sink.

Ladbrooke wasn't satisfied, however, with the way the castle was taking shape. She arrived one morning with a set of what looked like architect's tools, including a compass that should have been classed as a lethal weapon. Cutting open one of the cereal boxes, she flattened it out with the unprinted side upward. Taking the castle book down on the floor beside her, she found an explicit picture of a rampart and tower. "See this," she said to Shamie. "Here's how we make it." And she proceeded to show him how to take precise measurements and transfer them exactly to the cardboard.

The castle became an exercise not only in medieval history but in mathematics. Ladbrooke had an eye for detail and a need for precision that led her to long periods on her hands and knees with Shamie, measuring, cutting, measuring again. Ladbrooke didn't simply go at it with ruler and scissors the way I did. She had to use the protractor and the architect's curve and the craft knife to get a perfect edge. And Shamie, because he loved Ladbrooke, learned to love these things too. She got after him if he wasn't precise enough. She made him measure over, cut again, retape, and he did it without protest. He would probably have done it for her regardless, but he was also enough of a perfectionist himself to appreciate Ladbrooke's need for precision a bit more than I did. The castle became an exact scale model of the one in the book. Although still constructed chiefly of cast-off boxes and bits of Styrofoam packing material, it was no longer a makeshift affair. It became a real, recognizable castle.

Mariana and Geraldine were drawn into the process too. Dirkie wanted to help, but he was relegated to the ignominious tasks, like painting bricks on the cardboard walls, while Shemona watched wistfully from the sidelines. Sometimes Shamie let her paint the cardboard gray before Dirkie drew on the bricks, but for the most part, she was deemed too small and too incompetent. This was a "big-kids' project," as Mariana put it. So Shemona and I used "castle time" for doing other things together.

The castle grew. It had inner walls and outer walls, ramparts and turrets. Inside were stable blocks and feasting houses and grain stores. For more than two weeks, its construction dominated our lives. Ever spare moment became "castle time." In fact, it even began to intrude on life after school. I came back from a meeting one evening to find Ladbrooke flat on her stomach on the floor, peering in through the castle entrance, trying to insert a small portcullis made out of floral wire. Up, down, up, down she moved it, trying to get it to lift on its own with the aid of a small piece of dental floss. She was too absorbed to talk to me. I came over and thumped the soles of her jogging shoes as they waved in the air.

"Are you going home?" I asked. "It's quarter after five."

"Just a minute. I want to fix this."

I stood, waiting. I had to lock up, because by this time Bill would have already gone.

Ladbrooke, still on her stomach, slid her hand through the cardboard doors. I knelt to see what was going on.

Up, down, up, down went the portcullis. Ladbrooke's forehead puckered with concentration.

"This could probably wait until tomorrow," I said.

"I want to get it done tonight. I told Shamie I would."

"I'm sure he'll understand." I stood up again. Raising my arm, I glanced at my watch.

"I won't be that much longer," she said.

I stood, waiting.

Finally, Ladbrooke took her hand out of the castle entranceway and held it up, without taking her attention from the fiddly portcullis she was holding with the other.

"What do you want?" I asked, thinking she needed scissors or something.

"The keys. Just give me your keys. I'll see you in the morning."

I left then, not finding out until weeks later that Ladbrooke had stayed until almost ten o'clock at night, making Shamie a cardboard and floral-wire portcullis that could be raised and lowered.

"I had a letter from my mam yesterday," Shamie said. It was approaching morning recess and we were all sitting around the table together. "She said that they killed a policeman in our street last Saturday. Right out in front of Curran Maris's house. He was laying on the pavement right by the Marises' flower bed, where Mrs. Maris grows her gladioli."

I looked up.

"You know," he said, "I think it's wrong. I think it's wrong for them to keep killing everybody like they're doing. I don't care whose side anyone's on. I don't think there's anything worth killing someone over."

"It was revenge," Geraldine said, her voice soft. "For Ireland's sorrow."

"Aye, revenge. But I still think it's wrong, Geraldine. That man didn't do anything except walk down the street."

"He did. He was a Prod. And a policeman."

A small silence came. Shamie lifted his left hand and examined the fingers. Thoughtfully, he bit off a hangnail.

"There's nothing worth killing someone for, Geraldine. I think maybe Uncle Paddy was right. I think he should have told the police about things. There's got to be some way to stop what's happening, because pretty soon there won't be anybody left. They will've all killed one another."

Geraldine's eyes narrowed. She regarded Shamie intently. "Are you saying our daddy was a tout, Shamie?"

"What I was saying is that I think maybe it wouldn't have been so wrong if Uncle Paddy did tell them. I think what's going on is terrible and it has to end."

"Our daddy was no tout!" Geraldine shouted suddenly. Dirkie, next to me, startled violently at the unexpected volume, his pencil flying out of his fingers and across the table.

"Geraldine, I was saying—"

"You take that back! Our daddy was no tout! Our daddy would've never told!"

Seeing the need to intervene hastily, I rose and went around the table to Geraldine's chair. "Okay, everybody. I think it's nearly recess. Put away your things now and get your coats." I had my hands on Geraldine's shoulders.

"He was no tout!"

Geraldine began to cry. I knelt down next to her and put my arm around her, but she didn't want my comfort. Pushing me away roughly, she escaped out the other side of the chair and then shot off into the safety of the library.

"I didn't *mean* Uncle Paddy was a tout, Geraldine," Shamie shouted. "I know he wasn't. I wasn't saying that."

"Bloody, rotten liar! I hope you die. I hope you fall down the stairs and get killed and go to hell!" Geraldine shouted back.

I put an arm around Shamie. "Let's just leave it. She's upset, and it's not a good time to try to reason with her."

"But I didn't say—" he protested.

"I know you didn't. But this isn't the time to pursue it. Get your things and go on out for your break."

"I'm sorry, Geraldine," he hollered.

"I hope you die!"

Ladbrooke took the children out, and I stayed there in the room with Geraldine, who refused to come out of the library. Once everyone was gone, I entered the long, narrow aisle where she was hiding. She was sitting at the far end, huddled against the wall. Her face was awash with tears.

I knelt down near her. "I don't think Shamie meant to say your father was an informer, sweetheart. I think he was just talking in general terms."

"He wasn't. He said our daddy told the police. And Daddy *didn't!*"

"No, I don't think that's what Shamie said. Besides, he wouldn't know anyway, would he? He wasn't there."

She wiped her tears with the sleeve of her blouse. "Go away," she muttered.

"I know it's a difficult issue, Geraldine."

"What do you know about it? You weren't there either."

"But I know it's difficult."

"You're a Prod too. Go away. I don't want to talk to you."

Rising back to my feet, I stood over her a moment. I pushed my hands into the pockets of my jeans.

Geraldine mopped furiously at her tears.

"Come on, sweetheart. Let's go out and join the others."

She bared her teeth. "I said go away. Now, go away."

During the lunch hour, Ladbrooke and I sat together at the table and munched our sandwiches.

"What do you think Shemona thinks about all this?" Ladbrooke asked.

"You mean the Irish issue? Or about what was going on between Shamie and Geraldine?"

Ladbrooke shrugged. "Either." She studied her sandwich. "I mean, when I was five, I didn't even know what state I lived in, much less people's politics."

"I don't expect she understands much about all that."

"No, I don't either."

"In fact, I can't imagine she understands about this business with her father being an informer. Or what he was informing on."

Ladbrooke put down her sandwich and struggled to open her carton of milk. "I can't think Geraldine understands that much about all this either. What's this crap about Ireland's sorrow? For pity's sake, the girl is eight years old. Ireland's sorrow. *She's* Ireland's sorrow. She and Shamie and Shemona and the likes of them. They're Ireland's *shame.*"

I nodded.

Ladbrooke fell silent for a moment.

"But what about Shemona?" she said at last. "She's the one I'm always thinking about. I keep wondering how all this must seem to her. She never talks about it, but I know she must be thinking about it."

I nodded. "Oh, yes, I'm sure she thinks about it."

By afternoon, Geraldine appeared to have forgotten her earlier upset. The time until recess passed quickly, with all the children hard at work. During our free break that afternoon Lad and I went down to the teachers' lounge for the fifteen minutes. Lad needed to make a phone call, so she excused herself after ten minutes or so. I stayed on and talked with two of the school psychologists, who were also in the lounge.

"Torey?" Frank stuck his head in through the door.

I looked over.

"I think Ladbrooke wants you. I can hear her calling from the stairwell."

Baffled, I rose and emptied the dregs of my coffee into the sink before going out. I could hear the commotion then.

"I'm right here, Lad. I'm on my way up," I called, as I reached the stairs and bounded up them two at a time.

Ladbrooke had Shemona by the back of the neck. As soon as she saw me on the stairs, she shoved Shemona ahead of her back toward the classroom.

"Just wait till you see this," Ladbrooke said, as I came abreast of her.

The room was a catastrophe. Things had been knocked off the table, off the shelves, off the windowsill. More pointedly, Shamie's castle had been totally destroyed. It had been systematically walked on, all its careful details ruined beyond recognition. Most disgustingly, a generous amount of dog feces had been smeared over the remains of the castle's cardboard walls and along the radiator.

"I came up to get money to make the phone call," Ladbrooke said, "and I found Shemona in here."

"Alone?"

Lad nodded.

I looked down at the child. She had begun to cry, her face covered with her hands. I glanced around the room again. What puzzled me was how she had gotten back into the building unnoticed, particularly as she had to be transporting a fair amount of dog shit. This wasn't consistent with my experience of typical five-year-old wiles. Moreover, I was amazed by the extent of the damage. Shemona was given to frequent tantrums and occasionally destroyed thing in a fit of rage, but they'd always been small, impulsive acts. This was calculated.

"Did you do all this?" I asked Shemona.

Hands still over her face, she just cried.

I knelt and pulled her hands down. "Shemona, did you do all this by yourself?"

She kept her eyes tightly shut and her chin down against her chest. The tears dripped down onto her blouse, making dark spots on the material.

"This was a very, very unkind thing to do. Everyone has worked hard on that castle, even you. It belonged to all of us. Everyone is going to feel very badly when they see what's happened to it."

Just then, the other children burst through the door. "Pooey!" Mariana cried from the doorway. "Leslie's gone poopy in her pants. It stinks in here." Then she rounded the corner of the shelves. An audible gasp escaped her. "Oh, Shamie, don't come in," she warned.

The moment he saw the castle, Shamie burst into tears. If hurting him had been the intention, as I suspected it had, it was successful. He let out a long, low wail and went running over. Down on his hands and knees, he began picking up the pieces and pressing them to him, oblivious of the dog shit. He sobbed wordlessly.

Geraldine appeared beside Ladbrooke. "Shemona!" she cried in an indignant voice. "You naughty girl! Look at what you've done. You naughty, naughty girl. Miss will be very cross with you now. Look how you've upset Shamie." Geraldine looked over at me. "Shemona's like this, Miss. She does these things. Our Auntie Bet says, must be the Devil gets in her."

I cast a long, sideways glance at Geraldine.

"You're a very, very naughty girl, Shemona." And Geraldine bounced on by and over to her place at the table.

I pulled Shemona around the corner of the shelves for a little privacy. She was crying so hard at that point that her body shuddered with sobs. Tears and snot and saliva were running everywhere. I'd intended for Ladbrooke to keep order with the others, but her initial anger dissipated, she seemed concerned for the child's distress. Bringing over the box of tissues, Ladbrooke knelt and very gently wiped Shemona's nose and mouth.

"You want to take her in the rocking chair and give her a little cuddle?"

Finishing with the tissue, Ladbrooke rose. "No. Go ahead. I'll get the others settled."

Lifting Shemona up, I carried her to the rocker and sat down. She remained tense in my arms, never relaxing against me. I began to rock. Several minutes passed with Shemona perched on my knee.

I rocked and rocked. Slowly, the tears subsided, leaving the child quivery. With a handful of tissues, I helped her clean up.

"I'm having a hard time believing you did that," I said as I wiped her face."That doesn't seem like something you'd do."

She lowered her head.

"Did you really do it?"

She nodded.

"I see."

I rocked a few more moments.

"We're going to have to do something about it, aren't we?" I said.

Head still down, she nodded again.

"If you did it, I think you're going to have to clean it up. Does that seem fair?"

Another nod.

I leaned forward in the rocking chair. "Ladbrooke?"

Lad appeared around the corner of the shelves.

"Would you please take Shemona down to Bill's closet to get a bucket and some rags? I want her to wash the mess off the radiator and straighten things back up as best she can."

"Okay." Ladbrooke held out her hand for Shemona. Slipping off my lap, Shemona accepted Lad's hand and they headed for the door.

Geraldine appeared at my side when I returned to the other children in the main part of the classroom. "I got my project," she said cheerfully, and put her arm around me. She held up a small bag of yarn with the other hand. We'd been given a very small loom meant for weaving hot pads and the like, and Geraldine was desperate to try it. "You said you were going to show me how to do it this afternoon, remember?"

I regarded her. There was a long moment's silence between us, as we sized one another up. I was almost positive she was behind this whole episode. Even if she had not actually come up to the classroom to do it with Shemona, I still reckoned she had orchestrated the destruction. But I knew if I confronted her, she would only deny it, and I had no cold, hard proof.

I think Geraldine knew I knew. Our whole five months' relationship could be summed up in this one moment's exchange of glances.

"I'm afraid I can't work on your project with you today, Geraldine. Ladbrooke has gone to help Shemona get things to clean up this mess that's been caused, and without Ladbrooke, I'm afraid I haven't got the time to help you with your project."

Geraldine's forehead wrinkled as she eyed me.

"That's really too bad, isn't it? This was such a thoughtless, unkind thing to have happened. And it's not only gotten back at Shamie. It's ruined the time you and I meant to spend together as well."

Geraldine turned and, without saying anything more, threw down the bag of yarn and disappeared around the corner of the shelves into the blackboard area. When I stuck my head around, I saw she had gotten into the rocking chair by herself and was rocking quietly. I felt it was best to leave her as she was.

Not until I was putting things away after school in preparation to go home myself did I notice words etched into the pine seat of the rocker. I came closer and leaned down to see them.

"I hope you die, Prod bitch," they said.

CHAPTER
EIGHTEEN

The episode over the castle left me deeply troubled. I was having to face the fact that, as with Leslie, my initial assessment of Shemona and Geraldine was way off the mark. These two girls' relationship with one another was radically different than I had first perceived it. This was no simple matter of symbiosis, where a strong-willed elective mute controlled her weaker, more ineffective sister by manipulative silence. Despite her apparent cool self-possession, Shemona was not in control at all. Geraldine was the real mastermind. With what bordered on sociopathic detachment, she used Shemona to express her own hatreds, while staying clear and clean and cool herself. I'd seen this happen on previous occasions to a lesser extent and with the same result; however, it was this incident that drove home the seriousness of the matter. The other incidents had been minor; this was not. Most chilling was the fact that Geraldine showed absolutely no concern that her sister, as well as being set up, was going to bear the punishment for something not her fault.

Shemona herself didn't help matters much. Her silence and her persistent dislike of physical closeness kept her isolated from the rest of us. It slowly dawned on me that Shemona probably didn't actually know what was going on most of the time. She was a pawn and nothing more. This shouldn't have surprised me so much, I suppose, since she was, after all, only a five-year-old child; but her silent self-possession had made it easy to project onto her knowledge and understanding that she probably never had.

Considering these things threw Shemona's mutism into a very different light. Elective mutism involving a symbiotic relationship had been very common in my research of the problem. The vast majority of children displaying such behavior used their silence as a method for manipulating a weaker personality, usually a parent, although I had experienced several cases involving sibling relationships. So it had been easy for me to assume that I knew what was going on. Ruefully, I realized that it was probably precisely the amount of expertise I had in the area that tripped me up. Less experienced, I might have accepted what I saw rather than reading into it what I didn't see.

Reassessing the matter, I realized there wasn't a symbiotic relationship at all. I was becoming increasingly convinced that it was Geraldine, not Shemona, who kept Shemona from talking, I felt there must have been some sort of mental thuggery being carried out, and I wondered what kinds of things Geraldine might be telling Shemona when they were alone. I worried about how she kept control.

As I drew these conclusions, I was confronted with the need to radically alter my approach. Ideally, I would have liked to separate the two sisters into different classrooms. But where? Both of them clearly needed a specialized environment. Shemona, with no speech, few academic skills and nonexistent social behavior, would drown in the hubbub of a normal classroom. She'd already proven that with her kindergarten experience at the beginning of the year. Geraldine, whom I was starting to suspect could, like a rat, survive anywhere, needed the confinement of my kind of room. She was the one showing the genuinely pathological behavior, and I didn't think it would have been to anyone's benefit to ignore that. Unfortunately, in this small, rural district there just weren't two classes available for the girls to go into. This left me with the need to create something within our own environment.

"You know, I've finally had an idea regarding Shemona," I said. Ladbrooke and I were together at the table after school. We'd finished the next day's plans, and I was correcting papers. Ladbrooke had a mimeograph stencil in front of her and was transferring a math game onto it.

"Oh? What's that?" she asked, not looking up from her work.

"I want you to work with Shemona."

"What do you mean?" She was still involved in what she was doing and wasn't paying complete attention to me.

"I want you to get her to talk."

This did make Lad look up. "What do you mean?" she asked again, her expression perplexed.

"I've been thinking and thinking over this business with her and Geraldine, and I just can't figure out what else to do. I've got to separate them. If I can't do it physically, then I'm going to have to do it psychologically. And this is what I've come up with. I want you to work with her, individually, like I do with Leslie."

"Doing what?" There was a disconcerted look in her eyes.

"I want to get her into a good, solid relationship with an adult. We need to do that if we're ever going to drive a wedge into Geraldine's control."

"You want *me* to do that? I'm not sure I know how to do that sort of thing, Torey. I don't know how to get her to talk. Why me? Why not you?"

"Because I think you've got a better relationship with her than I do."

"Me?" Ladbrooke's eyes widened. "*You're* her teacher."

"That doesn't give me exclusive privileges. You're the special one. She always chooses you when she has the chance. I think it'd be advantageous to use that."

This all seemed novel to Ladbrooke. Her expression was still one of disconcerted perplexity. She looked away for several seconds, staring into space, then she looked back. "What would I do with her?"

"I'm thinking of just having you take her aside individually for a set period, like I do with Leslie. I'm not too fussy about what goes on. She doesn't really need academic help. It's the relationship I'm interested in. I just want you to form a good relationship with her."

Ladbrooke's expression remained wary. "I'm not sure I know how to form that kind of relationship."

"Don't worry. I'll help."

Ladbrooke remained remarkably nervous about the arrangement. Despite my having developed a tightly structured, easy-to-follow program for the first couple of sessions, Lad didn't relax. She couldn't eat her lunch the first day, and I think without much effort, she could have talked herself into being sick. I went over and over the material with her in an effort to reassure her, and in spite of her nerves, I was increasingly convinced that this was the right idea. She did have a better relationship than I had with Shemona; Ladbrooke wasn't going to fail in that respect. And she had something I couldn't offer: a keen understanding of the economics of loneliness.

Geraldine, as might be expected, was intensely curious about what was going on around the corner of the shelves when Ladbrooke first took Shemona.

"Miss, what's Shemona doing over there?"

"She's working with Ladbrooke. They're going to be working together every day at this time."

"But what's she doing? Why's it taking so long?"

"They're just doing some schoolwork. Like her papers in her folder," I replied.

"How come she can't do them out here with us?"

"Because I want her to do them in there with Ladbrooke."

"Has she been naughty?"

"No."

"Is it because she made mistakes on her worksheets yesterday? Does she have to have extra help?"

"No, Geraldine. It's just something they're doing together."

"Why? When's Shemona coming back?"

"In about twenty minutes. Now get busy with your own things, please. You haven't even started your notebook yet."

"But why's Shemona in there? Does she need help? I could help her."

"Ladbrooke's helping her, Geraldine. Now, please, do your own work."

"But why? Shemona isn't going to like it, Miss. She's not going to want to be in there by herself."

"She's not by herself. Ladbrooke is with her."

"But what if she needs something, Miss? Shemona's not going to want to do this. She'll get angry. She'll have a tantrum."

"Shemona'll be just fine. She'll be back at a quarter of two. In the meantime, please, just do your own work."

Geraldine frowned and looked down at her pencil. "Shemona isn't going to like this."

As I had anticipated, Ladbrooke and Shemona got on with no problems at all. The time went quickly for them, and there were still plenty of things they hadn't gotten to when I came around the corner of the shelves to tell them it was 1:45.

By the end of the week, both Ladbrooke and Shemona were openly anticipating the sessions together. Ladbrooke continued to need help in preparation and a generous amount of feedback. After school, she needed to recount every moment of the thirty-minute session in minutest detail. Was this okay? Did she do right with that issue? Did I mind if she did this? We often took more time discussing them than the sessions themselves took, but she spoke eagerly of them. She wanted to make her own plans, writing them out in careful detail on a yellow legal pad in much the same format as I used in my plan book.

And Ladbrooke's involvement paid off. She was an astute observer, and within days she was describing nuances in Shemona's behavior that had eluded us in the hurly-burly of the classroom.

"She's tense," Ladbrooke said one afternoon after school. "I notice that she always hangs on to the edge of the desk when we're working. I can see the ends of her fingers going white. I was watching her at the table after recess, and she does it then too. Have you noticed?"

I hadn't really.

"It's like she's holding on. To keep control."

Ladbrooke was pensive. "I was thinking . . ." Her voice trailed off. "I mean, if my aim is to get her to talk, to get her comfortable with me, I need to . . . well, relax her."

"What did you have in mind?" I asked.

She shrugged. "I don't know. Say, for instance, she *is* holding on to the table to keep control. I mean, what if that's literally true? What if she has to stay really tense and tight to keep from talking, to keep from doing the things Geraldine wouldn't want her to do?"

I regarded her.

"Well, then my job would be to make her let go of the table, wouldn't it?"

"Yes."

"I mean, that's supposing I'm right."

I nodded.

She thought a moment. "I was thinking maybe . . . well, maybe if I borrowed your colored chalk . . . we could draw with it on the board. She could move around."

I nodded again. "That sounds good."

Ladbrooke regarded me. "But am I right?"

"I don't know. But it's worth a try."

On Friday of the second week, when Ladbrooke and Shemona had been working together for about ten days, I had my first real surprise. It had been a rather raucous day, and no one was being particularly quiet. Shamie was working with a little electronic learning toy that beeped and whistled and chattered back to him in a tinny computer voice. Mariana and Geraldine were listening to cassette tapes, and although they had earphones on, the mutter of the tapes was still audible. I was with Dirkie and Leslie, doing number work with little colored cubes, but Dirkie was having one of his days and kept masturbating against the edge of his chair.

It was at that point that I heard the laughter. I paused and turned to look in the direction of the blackboard area. Even with the open shelving, the view was obscured by stacks of journals.

Shamie, distracted from his toy, turned his head. "What're they doing over there, Miss?" he asked, a half smile on his face.

"I'm not sure."

Fits of giggles.

Shamie and I exchanged bemused looks. "They sound like they're having fun," he said.

I nodded. Curiosity was getting the better of me. I didn't want to disturb them by going around the corner, but I wondered if I could see through the shelves. When I got up, Shamie got up too.

"I know where you can look through," he said. "Over here. This is our special spy place." He grinned at me. "That you don't know about!"

"I do now."

He laughed. Going to the edge of the long shelving unit, he pointed through the stacks of journals. "See. Here."

Shemona and Ladbrooke were sitting together with their backs toward us, Shemona in Ladbrooke's lap. Ladbrooke had her handbag open on the small desk and a tiny makeup mirror propped against it. The clips holding her own long hair back had been taken out and were now in Shemona's hair. Ladbrooke wielded a wide-toothed comb, pulling Shemona's hair up on top of her head and clipping it with one of the large barrettes. She lifted up the mirror for Shemona to see, and Shemona dissolved into giggles, her laughter tinkly, like small shards of glass falling on tiles. Moving off Ladbrooke's lap for a moment, she climbed back on, facing Lad. Running her fingers through the hair on either side of Ladbrooke's head, she pulled what she could catch up into a bunch and held it. Neither of them was saying a word, but again, Shemona laughed and then so did Ladbrooke.

Enchanted, I watched them. In all these months I had never heard Shemona laugh.

Then quietly, I withdrew. "Come on, Shamie. Let's get back to work."

"Are they supposed to be doing that?" he asked.

I nodded.

"But they're just playing."

"They're supposed to be playing."

"Lucky them."

CHAPTER
NINETEEN

✸ Just as February arrived, so did my permanent visa. There in the mail when I came home one evening was the thick, official-looking packet, containing my passport, my birth certificate and all the necessary papers I had waited so long to receive. Overwhelmed by sudden relief and excited beyond containment, I immediately phoned Ken, my fiancé, even though it was the middle of the night, his time. In fact, I spent a bomb on phone calls that night. Soon after talking to Ken, I rang my best friend in Wales, whose cottage was only a few hundred yards down the road from mine, and told her I was coming home at last. After a few drowsy moments of surprise from her end, she greeted my news with the expected joy. We hadn't talked to one another the whole time I'd been gone, and despite all our letters, there suddenly seemed a world of catching up to do. We nattered on as if we were still only yards away. Afterward, I called my family in Montana and finally another girlfriend out of state. My euphoria went unabated. After all these long, long months of waiting, it was *over.* I could return at last to Wales as a permanent resident. I could go home.

Only after all the phone calls and a nostalgic look through the photo album did I begin to return to reality. As I was making myself a late supper, I got to thinking about all the things that needed to be done before I could pack up for Wales. There were accounts to close. Things to get from my family's house in Montana. Selling the car. I went through a suprisingly long list before I thought about the class and the classroom. But then I did.

Frank had known all along that this was not a permanent placement for me, nor had he ever intended that it should be. Both of us had initially believed it would be a whole lot less permanent than it, in fact, had turned out to be. In the early weeks, I'd anticipated every mail delivery eagerly, expecting the visa to turn up. Frank had actively pursued finding a qualified special education teacher to take over the position when I needed to go. But as the weeks became months, the class became mine. I ceased to think of it as a temporary job; I ceased to think of the time when I would not be there. It had been ages since I'd inquired how Frank was doing. To my knowledge, he had never found another teacher. I wasn't sure he was even looking anymore.

What now? I desperately wanted to get home. As involved and interested in my work as I was, I was lonely without Ken and my friends. And there was so much to do. Ken and I were planning to be married in June, but before then, I also wanted some time in Wales to tidy up the last aspect of my single life. My best friend and I had made so many elaborate plans for climbing the Welsh peaks, hiking the Pennine Way, bicycling in France and all the other things I knew we'd probably never get around to doing together once I was married. We'd intended to do most of them through the course of this particular winter and spring. If only I'd had this last eight months there . . . Confronted with the knowledge that I could, at last, go back, I was overwhelmed with homesickness for everything I had been missing—from Ken and my friends to the ivy growing on the garden wall.

But how could I leave at this point? After five months together, I was fully aware of my responsibilities to the children and the class. I had more projects going, more work in progress, more things half-started than at any other point thus far. The program was in full swing, my influence on it substantial. Could someone else pick up at this point? Could he or she carry on without losing any of the children or any of the progress?

Still, I wasn't indispensable. I knew that. Maybe new blood would be good. Maybe new blood could make a difference to those children and circumstances I was failing, like Geraldine and her antisocial behavior or Shemona and her mutism.

I was full of mixed feelings the next morning when I went in to work. After putting my belongings in the classroom, I went in search of Frank to see just exactly where I stood. If he didn't have a replacement lined up, there was going to be a wait, whether I decided I wanted to go now or not. On the other hand, if he did have another teacher ready, it was going to shift all the decision making onto me.

Frank wasn't in his office yet. I stopped for a cup of coffee and a quick chat with some of the front-office people and then returned to the room, where I found Ladbrooke just arriving. She was removing her coat. The cold weather had given her a very ruddy glow and made her nose run. She snuffled and smiled cheerfully when she saw me.

"Hello."

"My visa came last night."

A puzzled expression crossed her face.

"My visa. My British visa. I can go back now. I called Ken last night and told him to get ready."

Ladbrooke knelt and pulled off her boots. Taking her jogging shoes out of the bottom drawer of the filing cabinet, she slipped them on and knelt to tie them. "What are you talking about?" she asked.

"You know. I've told you, haven't I, about all that hassle I had getting a permanent visa to live in Wales?" And suddenly it occurred to me that I probably hadn't told her in any substantial way. She had arrived too late on the scene to have been part of my earlier efforts. By November, when Ladbrooke joined us, I was already resigned to an eternal wait. And crucial as the matter was to me, it, like most of the other occurrences in my personal life, was not something I seemed to get around to talking about with Ladbrooke.

I gave her a brief summation of the convoluted story.

Ladbrooke had remained kneeling over her shoes as I talked, but when I'd finished, she slowly rose. Her brow puckered. "What do you mean, you're going? When?"

"It depends on things. Mostly on whether or not Frank has a replacement lined up for me."

"You mean, *now?*"

I nodded.

She grew wide-eyed with disbelief. "Oh, you can't mean that, Torey. You don't mean now, do you?"

"Well, I don't know. Probably not. It all depends on Frank, really. You have to understand, this hasn't been a permanent job for me. We've all known it was just until my visa came through."

"But what's going to happen if Frank does have somebody? Are you going then? Are you leaving?"

"Like I said, I don't know. I'm just going to have to wait and see."

"You *can't* leave. It's right in the middle of everything. Look at everything we're doing. You can't leave the kids at this point, can you?" Her shoulders dropped in a desolate gesture. "Can you?"

I smiled warmly. "Well, let's not worry about it for the moment, okay? I need to talk with Frank, and until I do, there's no point speculating."

"That's easy for you to say. You have nothing to worry about."

It was a difficult day. I had made a serious mistake in talking to Ladbrooke when I did. I hadn't stopped to consider how she might feel about it. Overcome with my own excitement, I had simply blurted everything out without thinking. But the news upset her, and she remained defensive the whole day. The children had a rotten day as well. I don't know if they were reflecting Ladbrooke's and my conflict, or if it would have been a bad day in any case. Whatever, every minute was damned hard work. This certainly did not decrease my longing to leave. If anything, I ended the day feeling that probably anyone could do a better job with this lot than I was doing.

Not until after school did I catch up with Frank. When I did, I discovered that he'd found a replacement. She was a behavioral specialist living in a nearby community and working there as a substitute special ed. teacher. He showed me her credentials. They looked impressive. She was available at two weeks' notice.

I slouched down in the big chair across from Frank's desk. I hadn't wanted to hear that. As I listened, I realized I'd been hoping he would tell me he hadn't found anyone. That would have saved me from being responsible for the consequences.

"Do you want me to contact her?" Frank asked.

I stared down at my hands in my lap. "I don't know which way to go, to be honest," I said.

"Perhaps it would be best if I did get hold of her. Two weeks isn't long, but if you want to leave . . . If we just let her know she might be needed, then, if you decide to go, she'll be prepared. Maybe she could even come over and look at the class while you're still here."

I sat, weighing the matter. How on earth was I going to be able to leave? Of all the times for my visa to come through, why now? If it had been earlier and things weren't yet started, I could have gone. If it had been later and things were finished, I could have gone. But now?

I sat a long time without answering. Finally, I shook my head. "No, don't get hold of her yet, Frank. Okay? Give me a few days to think it over."

Frank was grinning. I think he already knew I wasn't going.

I think I already knew too. A heavy, jaded feeling descended on me. I dreaded the thought of phoning Ken to tell him of this change in plans. I dreaded the disappointment I knew I was going to feel when I was in my apartment, alone, without the distractions of school. Here, now, it was easier to accept the idea of staying. There, on my own, it would be another matter.

Back in the classroom, I found Ladbrooke at work at the table. She did not look up when I entered, but, rather, continued to write. I took my own work from the top of the filing cabinet and came over to sit down.

"What did Frank say?" she asked, her tone conversational. She still continued to write.

"He has someone. An E.D. specialist from Medicine Bow. Her name's Muriel Samuelson."

"Oh." Ladbrooke was looking at me then, although she hardly lifted her head. Her examination was thorough but brief, and then she returned to what she was doing.

"I don't know what I'm going to do," I said wearily. "What a lousy predicament."

Ladbrooke paused, lifting her pencil from the paper. For a long moment she regarded what she'd been writing. I watched her. I could feel the tension still between us, as it had been all day, but I didn't know what to do to diffuse it. With Ladbrooke, it was sometimes better to carry on and pretend everything was all right than to back her into a corner by confronting her. I let her be and prepared to start the next day's plans.

Ladbrooke laid down her pencil and pushed back her chair. "If you'll excuse me," she said, got up and left the room.

Supposing she'd gone to the toilet, I didn't think much about her leaving. However, when ten minutes or so had elapsed and Ladbrooke still hadn't returned, I looked around in the direction of the door. Groaning, I got up and went after her.

Can of Coke in her hand, Ladbrooke was leaning against the wall at the far end of the girls' rest room. She was sipping the pop slowly, the elbow of one arm braced in the hand of the other. When I pushed the door open, she frowned.

"Go away, Torey," she said, her voice low.

"This is childish, Ladbrooke. If we've got a problem, for pity's sake, let's talk about it, like two adults."

"I'd rather be alone for a while. Please, go away."

"I'm not a lot more in the mood for this than you are, Ladbrooke. It hasn't been one of my better days either."

"Then leave me *alone.*"

Shoving my hands into the pockets of my jeans, I turned and leaned back against one of the sinks. "Is all this over my visa?"

No reply.

"Can't you appreciate the position I'm in, Lad? Can't you empathize, even a little bit?"

Her chin was trembling. She drew her lower lip in between her teeth to stop it. Suddenly, she seemed very young to me. She seemed no older than the kids.

"This is a hard profession. You get close to people. You come to love them as a natural part of it, to love them dearly. And it makes it hard."

"Is that all we are to you? Your profession? Your three hundred bucks a week, or whatever it is? So you can just give up and walk out on us any time you feel like it?"

"No, of course not. That's not what I'm saying."

"Well, what do you mean then?"

Without warning, I found myself on the verge of tears. The day had been so difficult and the situation so complex. I didn't know how to defend myself in this kind of argument. It was all proving a bit too much for me. Lowering my head, I studied the fabric of my jeans. Not trusting my voice, I didn't answer immediately.

Then finally, I shrugged. "I don't know. The thing is, I do have this other life. And I get lonely for it."

Ladbrooke set the Coke can down noisily on the tile windowledge.

"What do you want me to say to you?" she replied angrily. "That I'm sorry for you?"

I didn't answer.

"Or do you want me to admit how much I need you? Is that what you want?" And then her own tears came, and she couldn't stop them. "*Shit,*" she muttered bitterly, and turned away.

A sudden, tense silence fell between us.

"You are the only person in the world who's ever made me feel like maybe I'm worth something," she said, her voice low. Her back was still to me. "For the first time in as long as I can remember, I actually want to get up in the morning. I have somewhere to go that *I*, as a human being, matter." The way she said it, it sounded like a condemnation.

Letting my shoulders drop, I sighed.

Ladbrooke turned back around and glared at me. "I know how these poor kids feel now, being tugged and pulled, their whole world manipulated and nothing they can do about it. You're damned well mucking about in other people's lives, Torey. You come in here, all high and mighty, like God, and you *muck about.* Maybe you don't love us, but you've made us love you. You've made us believe you *care.*"

"I *do* care! Good grief, Ladbrooke, lay *off* me." Try as I had, I couldn't keep from crying myself. "I do care. That's the whole bloody problem. Are you so thick you can't see that?"

My tears bewitched Ladbrooke. She froze, staring at me, studying my face intently, and I felt acutely embarrassed. It was like crying in front of one of the children. Reaching for a paper towel, I dampened it and wiped my face. Neither of us spoke.

I glanced in Ladbrooke's direction. "I'm probably not going," I said softly, "I'll probably wait until the end of the school year. I've pretty much said that to Frank already. I was *trying* to say it to you, if you'd only given me half a chance."

Snuffly silence.

I took another towel and did a final clean-up job. The cool water felt good. I kept the towel pressed against my eyes for a few moments, then I took it and the other one and threw them into the waste bin.

Turning, I looked over at Ladbrooke. She was still watching me, her own eyes still teary.

I smiled wearily. "God, would you look at us? We're a couple of proper dames, aren't we? Just look at us. I'll bet when Butch Cassidy and the Sundance Kid had a falling out, they never ended up bawling in the men's room like this."

A hint of a smile touched Ladbrooke's lips. "They didn't have men's rooms in those days. They just peed in the bushes."

I grinned. "Maybe that's our problem. No bushes."

A pause.

Looking at my reflection in the mirror, I ran my fingers through my hair, pulled out the clips, replaced them. I hitched up my jeans, smoothed out my blouse, grimaced at my reflection. Ladbrooke remained leaning against the wall. She too was watching my reflection.

"Look, I'm sorry I upset you," I said. "None of this was intended to hurt you. I just got caught up in my own personal mess. I didn't think."

She shrugged. "I didn't mean to hurt your feelings either."

"Don't worry about it."

"I'm sorry. If you really do want to go back . . . I didn't mean to sound selfish. I'm sorry you're missing everyone. I do understand, sort of."

"Don't worry about it." I turned from the mirror to leave.

"Where are you going?" she asked.

"Back to the room. I haven't got anything prepared yet for tomorrow."

"Are you angry?"

I smiled then. "No. Just tired. Come on, kiddo, you too. Let's get back to the room. There's a ton of work waiting there."

CHAPTER
TWENTY

■ The decision to stay was still difficult to make. In explaining to Ken why I was staying an additional four months, I could no longer shift the blame to the British consulate or the vagaries of Frank and the school district. It was my decision. Accustomed to drifting along pleasantly and meeting what came, I found this sudden need to steer a direct course a hard thing to do. However, I knew I had to stay. Ladbrooke's outrage had some legitimacy. I *was* mucking about in other people's lives. My method of intervention relied fairly heavily on personal charisma, and I knew full well it did. Successful as the method could be, this was one of the drawbacks. I was not justified in using it if I intended to walk out in the middle.

The decision not to go home left me depressed for some days afterward, and, like a bad cold, there didn't seem much to be done about it, other than bear with it. I threw myself into work at school in an effort to distract my thoughts, and that was just as well, because we went into a skid. Everyone's behavior deteriorated.

I had been trying for some time to arrange an alternate placement for Shamie. It had been apparent almost since his arrival that Shamie did not need a class like mine, yet he'd remained, mostly because I'd had my plate full with other problems. When we came back from Christmas break, I had endeavored to remedy the matter by arranging a part-time placement for him at a nearby junior high school. Shamie was to come into my class in the mornings and then go over at lunchtime to the other school, where he would have three regular classes.

Within a matter of days it became apparent that the whole thing was an unmitigated disaster. Shamie couldn't cope with the junior high routine of changing classes and teachers. He was frightened by the normal rough-housing and teasing of the other children. The work in the classes was far from what he was used to with me. It wasn't harder, but it was more formal and impersonal. Plus they used different books, different layouts and different methods of testing. Worst of all, he just didn't fit in. Although a slow learner, he was a studiously inclined boy, and the relaxed, rather nonacademic attitudes of some of the other students in his classes affected him tremendously. He hated every moment of every afternoon. After two weeks, I gave up. Obviously, something was wrong with the whole plan. Shamie returned full time to my room.

Dirkie went from bad to worse. He'd always been on a considerable amount of very powerful medication to control his more outlandish schizophrenic behaviors, but this now seemed not to be sufficient. Adolescence and the accompanying metabolic changes suddenly upset the delicate balance, and he needed to have his medication adjusted to accommodate this. What seemed in conferences with his consulting psychiatrist and his foster parents a fairly simple procedure turned out to be nightmarish in the classroom. Dirkie became drastically uncontrolled, and we spent a very miserable month indeed.

Geraldine and Shemona didn't change one way or the other. No matter what I tried, Geraldine kept up her steady stream of petty antisocial acts and her clinginess, while Shemona kept up her silence. I was blatantly aware of the fact that I had no control over either girl, that I had thus far made no impact on either's behavior.

Leslie was slow going. She did start to talk in her own peculiar fashion. She developed a fetish for letters of the alphabet and would go around the classroom all day long, shouting "M!" "C!" "Y!" at the top of her lungs, until I wanted to throttle her. But she never said anything else. She never said anything that made sense. I was getting her to produce sounds during our sessions, but they were just attenuated grunts. After half an hour of pressing her lips together with my fingers to force out the *"mmmmmm"* sound of "man," I'd let go, her lips would fall apart, and she'd look at the picture of the man and happily say, *"uh."*

Only Mariana seemed on an upward course. Bless her little heart, she plodded along steadily, learning with agonizing slowness to read the first-grade primer. I had wanted to mainstream her, too, into a regular classroom for part of the time, but I couldn't imagine whose, as Mariana would need to avoid math, reading and spelling to have any chance at success. And that was before I went down to the girls' rest room just off the lunchroom one day and found Mariana and one of Carolyn's boys in a toilet stall together. Even I was embarrassed by what they were doing.

Then to cap it all off, we were struck in the latter part of February by a stomach bug. I dreaded stomach bugs in these kinds of classes, because I was always guaranteed a few really disgusting days. And we certainly had them. Shemona got it first and was sick everywhere one afternoon, with no warning whatsoever. Within the next two days, three different children had vomited on me, including Dirkie, who had been sick on me, gone home for a day, come back and been sick on me again.

On Thursday of that week, Ladbrooke came up just before morning recess.

"I've got to go home, Torey," she said.

The moment I saw her, I knew she'd caught the bug too. Her face was the color of cold oatmeal.

"I'll be back tomorrow. It seems to be just a twenty-four-hour thing."

"Look, Lad, don't worry about it. Stay home until you're well. All right? Now go take care of yourself." I gave her a pat on the shoulder, then turned and went back to the children.

Ladbrooke didn't return on Friday. I wasn't surprised. I hadn't expected her to. The bug was so virulent and her stomach, even under normal circumstances, so touchy, that I'd assumed the combination would prove more than twenty-four hours could cure. However, when Monday came and Ladbrooke still wasn't there, I was immediately concerned. It *was* a virulent virus. And she really should have been under the care of a doctor for the kind of gastric problems she had. She'd shown me once where areas of her teeth had been damaged because she'd vomited so frequently over the previous few years that the stomach acid had dissolved parts of her tooth enamel. It had all come about as a result of her alcohol abuse, and for that reason, I knew Ladbrooke was reluctant to get help for it. However . . .

The moment I thought about her alcoholism, all my other thoughts, all my concerns deadened. Ladbrooke wasn't still sick. She was on another bender. After five days, it was unlikely that she was still home with a bug. No, she was gone again. Like the last time. Gone. Out. Drunk.

My instant reaction was anger. The clock was edging around toward class time. I stood below it, watching it, and I felt rage. *The stupid idiot.* This was the last thing in the world her poor, abused stomach needed. It was the last thing *she* needed. All the heart-tugging misery she was feeling in January, and she could just turn around and let it all happen again so soon? What the hell was the matter with her, anyway?

Uncharacteristically, my anger proved to be long lived. It didn't pass off as the children arrived and the day started. I was still actively fuming at recess, when I stayed in the room and stapled up worksheets, a job Ladbrooke normally did. The whole time I was preoccupied with all the horrible things I was going to say to Ladbrooke when she finally did manage to limp back. I wasn't going to have the same kind of patience I'd had in January. What kind of patsy did she take me for?

*   *   *

I was sound asleep Tuesday night when the telephone rang. The noise fit absurdly into my dream, and I didn't waken immediately,. When I did, I was momentarily disoriented. Groping for my alarm clock instead of getting out of bed to answer the phone, I tried to make out the numbers in the dark. I couldn't, so I turned on the bedside lamp: 2:10.

When I finally picked up the receiver, Ladbrooke was on the other end.

"Do you know what time it is?" I said.

There was a pause. "Were you sleeping?"

"Good grief, Lad, of *course* I was sleeping."

Another pause.

"What do you want?" I asked.

"Could you come get me?"

"Where are you? What's going on?"

"I'm in a phone booth."

"Where?"

"Poplar and Seventh Avenue."

Consciousness was slowly returning, which didn't make the conversation less bewildering. "What are you doing there? Are you safe?"

"Yeah, I think so." A pause. "But I'm cold. And I need somebody to pick me up. I don't have enough money for a taxi."

"Okay. Hold on a sec. Let me get a pencil. Now tell me precisely where you're at so I can find you straightaway. Are you sure you're safe there? Can you wait till I come?"

I dressed and went down to bring my poor old car to life in the bitterly cold February darkness. There were four or five inches of old, graying snow underfoot, and it squeaked as I walked on it.

I wasn't familiar with the part of town Ladbrooke was calling from; however, Lad's directions were clear, and I found her with no trouble. She was standing inside a dimly lit booth, arms tight around herself. She had no coat on.

For the first time I became genuinely concerned about what was going on. Up to this point, I think I must have been still half-asleep, because I didn't question it. I was too concerned with finding her. But now that I had, the peculiarity of the circumstances struck me. What the hell was she doing out at two o'clock in the morning, with no coat, no money and no one around? What was she doing in this part of town, bereft of night spots, bereft of everything except industrial complexes and office buildings? A truly horrible thought went through my mind. Was she engaging in prostitution?

I pushed the car door open. "Lad?"

Tentatively, she opened the door on the telephone booth.

"Lad, it's me. Get in the car."

"I'm *freezing* to death," she said, as she got in on the passenger side. She slammed the door.

"I can very well imagine you are. It's below zero out there. Where on earth is your coat?"

No answer. Her teeth were chattering. Pushing the heater up as far as it would go, I turned the car around and started off.

"Don't take me home," she said.

"Where do you want to go?"

Saying nothing, she clasped her arms tightly around herself to stop the shivering.

"Where do you want to go, Lad?"

"I don't know."

I eased my foot off the accelerator and coasted to a stop at the next corner.

Ladbrooke looked over in alarm. "Why are you stopping?"

"Because I don't know where you want me to take you."

She studied my face a long moment. "Can I come home with you?"

Not knowing quite what to say to that, I shrugged. "I guess so."

I set the car in motion again. Ladbrooke was clearly so cold that that was absorbing most of her concentration. I could hear her teeth chattering.

"How long have you been out there? That could have been dangerous, you know. It's not a night for standing about improperly dressed."

She said nothing.

"What's going on? What happened?"

Still no response.

She didn't seem drunk. By that point, I think I would have preferred to have found her drunk, because it would have explained more.

"Lad, you've got to tell me what's been going on."

"Don't keep at me, okay?" she said.

Back home, I pulled my car into the drive beside my landlord's Ford. I hoped he wasn't going to hear us, because I knew he'd ask me what I'd been doing. He was a good-natured sort and wouldn't mind, but he was nosy.

Ladbrooke followed me inside and up the stairs to my small attic apartment. I put on all the lights as I came in. Lad fell heavily into the first available chair.

"Are you still cold?" I asked.

She had the same colorless look she'd had in January. If she hadn't been drinking tonight, she'd been drinking heavily sometime over the past few days.

When she didn't respond to my question, I went into the bedroom and got the patchwork quilt off the end of my bed. Ladbrooke wrapped it tightly around herself.

"Have you eaten recently?"

She shrugged.

"Look, I'll make some toast. And a hot drink. I think I've got Ovaltine in there. Is that all right?"

She nodded.

When I came back, the exhaustion was undisguised. She kept the quilt up around herself and accepted the drink from me without a word. I set the toast down on the end table and dropped into the other chair.

"So what the hell's going on?" I asked.

"I don't want to talk about it. I'm too tired."

"I don't want your life story, Ladbrooke. Just a quick explanation. I'm feeling pretty uncomfortable with all of this right now. I think I'd feel better if I knew what was going on."

She took a piece of toast and ate it slowly.

I continued to regard her.

Finally, she shook her head. "I'm too tired, Torey. Really, I am." There was a plaintive note in her voice, and I could see she wasn't going to cope with being hassled.

Disgruntled, I got up and went into the bedroom to get some bedding for the couch. I changed back into the T-shirt I'd been sleeping in. As I returned to the living room, I pitched a spare T-shirt in Ladbrooke's direction. "I'm afraid this is all this hotel provides."

Ladbrooke was already asleep by the time I had tidied away the mugs, turned out the lights and brushed my teeth. She had taken the quilt in with her and put it over the top of the heavy down comforter already on the bed. Curled up in a tight ball beneath all these covers, she slept, her breathing deep and noisy. The bedside lamp was still on. The door was left wide open.

I paused a moment and watched her sleeping. Bewilderment overcame me. Initially, I had been irritated with her for all this trouble. Now I felt only confusion.

As I stood, watching her, it occurred to me that I loved her. In the same gut-wrenching way I loved the kids, I loved Ladbrooke. And for the same brutal, aching humanness. Why, I wondered, did I love troubled things so?

Then wearily, I turned away and went into the living room. Rearranging the pillows and blankets, I lay down on the couch in an effort to rescue what little bit was left of the night.

But I couldn't sleep. My mind was in hyperdrive. Every time I would settle down, the events of the previous hour or so reappeared, which, in turn, led me to question my own part in all of this. Suddenly, I had come face to face with the fact that I was involved, whether I'd ever intended to be or not. I hadn't gone looking for involvement, but, like so much else in my life, it had just sort of happened along, and I hadn't particularly discouraged it. I had grown to like Ladbrooke; I wouldn't have wanted to miss out on her company in the classroom. But I knew there had been a therapeutic quality to our relationship. We spent our days in a warm, supportive environment, and it had been easy to extend to her the same kind of gentle caring I provided for the children. I had taken each day as it came and never thought much more about it.

But how had we gotten here? I had vivid memories of sitting on the side of the pool at the spa, telling Carolyn that whatever Ladbrooke did with herself on her own time was her business, that I couldn't care less. How had I gotten from that point to this point? All along I had meant for her to get legitimate help from someone who knew more about the kinds of problems she was coping with than I did. But I'd known she still wouldn't go into treatment for the alcoholism, and because she was never drunk in my presence anymore, I had never pressed the issue. Now, suddenly, I became concerned that I'd done something incredibly wrong. My classroom was, at best, a bizarre form of therapy. Was I hurting more than helping? Should I have forced the matter of traditional therapy? Was I being naïve? Was I being irresponsible? Was I being stupid?

Previously, I hadn't thought so. I had great faith in the healing powers of my kind of milieu. Moreover, I felt any supportive environment would be preferable to empty days full of arguments with her husband and drinking bouts. And my setting was well suited to cope with Ladbrooke's low self-esteem and lack of control. Indeed, she had done very well in there. Neither had I been especially daunted by my lack of expertise in the treatment of addiction. I was comfortable dealing with her other problems, and that had seemed sufficient to me at the time. I was experienced and qualified, both in my own methods and in more traditional therapeutic techniques, so I'd never felt I was overstepping my abilities. As nonconforming as the circumstances were, I'd felt satisfied. Now, suddenly, I wasn't so sure anymore.

Lying on the couch, I stared into the darkness. Three and a half months now, and Ladbrooke gave no indication of letting go of the booze. Was this my failing? Was I, like Tom and everyone else, more a part of the problem than a part of the solution?

CHAPTER TWENTY-ONE

Feeling like something chewed over by a sheep, I dragged myself off the couch when my alarm rang at 6:30. I had to go into the bedroom and rummage through the drawers and the closet to get my clothes for school because I hadn't been thinking clearly enough the night before to get them out then. Sprawled comfortably across the bed, the tension finally gone from her face, Ladbrooke never stirred.

When I returned at 4:30, it was obvious Ladbrooke had only been up a short time. Her eyes were puffy from so much sleep. Her hair was uncombed. Still dressed only in her underwear and my Minnie Mouse T-shirt, she was sitting at the kitchen table with orange juice and an English muffin. She had her feet up on the chair across from her and was paging through a copy of *Time* magazine that had arrived in the mail.

"Hi," she said pleasantly, when I came in.

"Hi. How're you feeling?"

"Okay. A lot better. I was tired."

"So I gathered."

I left the room to take my things in to the desk in the bedroom. I stayed in the bedroom for some time, slowly changing my clothes and steeling myself for what lay ahead.

Back in the kitchen, I wrestled a package of ground beef out of the cluttered refrigerator with the intention of making spaghetti. I didn't know if Ladbrooke was staying for supper or, for that matter, if having just downed breakfast, she was going to be interested in supper immediately afterward. But making spaghetti sauce was fiddly enough to give me the appearance of doing something else when what I really needed to do was drag some sense out of Ladbrooke.

Taking down the chopping board, I began mincing an onion. I had my back to Ladbrooke and I could hear her still turning the pages of the magazine. "We've got to do some serious talking, Lad."

"I'm sorry about last night. I just didn't know who else to turn to. But I'm sorry for causing you such a lot of trouble."

"It's not that so much. I'm glad you did call me in those circumstances. But . . . it's . . . I'm . . ." Words were failing me. I rotated the chopping block and attacked the slices of onion from another direction. "What was going on last night? What had you been doing before I picked you up?"

Silence.

I used the excuse of getting some garlic to turn around and look at her. She was slouched down in her chair like an adolescent.

I turned back to the chopping board and began to pick the papery skin off the garlic cloves. "I'm not just being nosy. I think we've both got to face the fact that I'm involved. If I'm going to start bailing you out of places, if I'm going to be the one picking up the pieces, then I think we've got to acknowledge that I'm involved. And if I'm involved, then I have to know what's going on."

More silence.

I glanced over my shoulder at her. "I don't mind. Being involved, I mean. I don't mind helping you out, but one thing needs to be clear from the onset. It's got to mean change. I don't want to end up just one more prop on the stage."

Continued silence.

I went back to the garlic. Giving one clove a hefty thunk with the back of the knife, I loosened the skin. Making this sauce wasn't a cover for ulterior motives. It was therapy. For me. I thunked the clove again.

"Lad?"

"I was just out."

"Had you been drinking?"

"Yes."

"Last night?"

"No. I had been earlier. In the morning, I think. I don't really remember."

Silence came again. Ladbrooke went back to paging idly through *Time*.

I had hoped she would do some of the talking in this conversation. Tired as I was, I didn't feel like carrying both sides. But she offered nothing. She seemed relaxed and comfortable, sitting there at the table, wearing my clothes, eating my food and reading my magazine. She wasn't refusing to talk; she just wasn't helping things along.

"Has it been a binge, these last few days?" I asked, bringing the onion and garlic to the stove and scraping them into the frying pan.

She nodded.

"What caused it?"

She toyed with the edge of one page of the magazine, flipping it back and forth with the tip of her finger. Slowly, she shrugged. "I don't know. I just needed a drink, that's all."

"I'm sure the last thing in the world your poor stomach needed after that virus was a drink."

"My stomach's been all right."

I got the herbs out of the cupboard and took them over to the stove. Bringing a hand up, Ladbrooke braced her cheek with it and leaned forward, appearing intent on an article about world banking. I finished the last additions to the sauce, stirred it and watched it bubble up. Finally, I turned down the gas and put a lid on the pot, before coming over to the table. Ladbrooke took her feet off the other chair to let me sit down. I turned the chair so that I could lean it back against the wall. I didn't want to be sitting face to face with her.

"We need to puzzle a few things out," I said.

"There's not much to puzzle out. That was a horrible day, plain and simple. I got drunk, plain and simple. It's over, plain and simple."

"Which day was horrible?"

"Thursday. Well, Thursday and Friday both. That bug was awful. I think I was throwing up about every ten minutes for a while. I hadn't been sick like that since I was a kid." She twiddled a piece of hair beside her face. "Tom doesn't have much patience with things like that, with people being ill. He's not exactly Florence Nightingale. He kept saying '*JEEsus*, Ladbrooke, I can hear you all over the house.' As if I were being sick just to annoy him.

"And then he wouldn't take Leslie. He wouldn't come in from the studio. He slept out there because he didn't want to take a chance of catching the bug too. So, there I was, commuting between Leslie and the toilet all night long. Then on Friday, his kids came over. They, unfortunately, weren't the least bit deterred by the bug. I just couldn't cope, Torey. I really couldn't. I needed to get out."

"Why didn't you call me? I could have done something. If nothing else, you could have come over here. Why didn't you let me know it was going like that?"

"I didn't want to bother you."

"It would have been a whole lot less bother than it's been this way, Ladbrooke. And I wouldn't have minded. It would have been better than going out and getting drunk."

She braced her chin on one hand. "I wasn't thinking that clearly."

"So where did you go?"

She shrugged. "Just out."

"By yourself?"

"Yeah, pretty much."

I rose to stir the sauce. Lad said nothing more. Hunched forward, she inspected her fingernails before settling on one to chew.

"Who are the men you go out with?" I asked.

Ladbrooke's eyes widened. She looked over. "What men?"

I looked directly at her.

Averting her eyes abruptly, she lowered her head. A small, sharp silence followed. Then she frowned. "Who's been telling you that kind of shit?"

"No one in particular."

"Who told you? Tom? Have you been listening to Tom?"

I watched her.

"It's just lies."

"Look, it's not something that's going to bother me unduly, if that's what concerns you. But it's something I think I need to know about."

"It's *shit.*"

"Shit it may be, kiddo, but let's not pretend it's not there."

Bleak, angry silence followed, and it was shockingly complete. Only the soft burbling of the sauce intruded.

Still at the stove, I turned, wiped my hands on the kitchen towel and hung it over the handle of the oven door. Then I leaned back against the edge of the drainboard. "Look, we've got to make a decision right now. Right this minute. I'm suddenly finding myself in this with you, neck-deep, Ladbrooke. God knows if that's what either one of us ever intended, but here I am. Now the thing is, you can't have your cake and eat it too. Either I'm involved and you're honest with me and we make a real effort to see things change, or else I'm not involved and you don't go calling me out of bed at two in the morning. You've got to decide which you want, because you can't have it both ways."

Head down, tawny hair obscuring most of her features from me, she began to cry.

"So?"

"Of course I want you involved. You know that."

"So?"

"So what? What do you want me to say, for Christ's sake?"

"So who are the men, Ladbrooke? Where do they figure in this? Are they drinking buddies? One night stands? Or something else?"

No response.

"Is something like prostitution involved?"

Ladbrooke looked up, absolutely horrified. "*No.* God, Torey. How can you ask me that?"

"Because I don't *know.*"

The horrified expression intensified, and she glanced around the room quickly. I think if we'd been anywhere else, if she'd been dressed in more than underpants and a Minnie Mouse T-shirt, she would have bolted at that point. I could hear her breathing, quick and shallow.

"Look, I'm sorry for being blunt like that," I said.

"I'm *not* a whore."

"No."

"Of all the people in the world to ask me that."

"I'm sorry, Ladbrooke. But I needed to know. I picked you up in the wee hours of the morning in some phone booth on the other side of town, and there you were, no money, no proper clothing and no intention of telling me what was going on. I had to draw some conclusion, didn't I?"

"Is that what you really think of me?"

"I asked it as a question, not an evaluation of your character."

"I thought you were my friend."

"I am."

"Shit, with friends like you, who needs enemies."

"Ladbrooke."

"They're my friends. Regardless of what Tom has told you."

I remained silent.

"Just *friends*, Torey," she said, a little louder than necessary.

"Okay," I replied.

"I just need somebody sometimes. I like sex, okay? Is that what you want me to say? I mean, Tom's old. I'm young, Torey. I need a man sometimes. Is that so strange?"

"No."

Silence came. Ladbrooke covered her eyes a moment with one hand and leaned forward. She exhaled heavily. Anger seemed to dissipate into something wearier. Several minutes passed, and she didn't say anything.

"I was with someone Friday night," she said at last. "Usually when I go out, I just take the car and drive. Once last summer, I drove all the way to Denver, 461 miles, just to be alone for a while. To think. To relax. But on Friday I was still feeling too rotten from that bug. So I drove around town and then I got a motel room."

She paused. I returned to the table and sat down.

"I hate motel rooms. They make me feel lonely. So after I was there a while, I got to drinking down in the bar. I was just too lonely."

A sigh. "I ended up getting hold of Bill. I don't know what time it was. I was pretty well potted by then, I'm afraid, because I don't remember much about it. He was just someone to be with. To sleep with. I don't like sleeping alone . . ."

She became progressively quieter and more introspective as she talked. A small pause followed, and she frowned slightly, remaining pensive.

"I don't know. Maybe it is whoring. Because, if I'm honest, I've got to say, I'll make love to anyone if it'll keep him in my bed afterward so that I don't have to go through the night alone."

I watched her.

"That doesn't sound very good, does it?"

"It sounds honest."

She nodded. "Yes, it is honest."

The earlier emotion was gone entirely. Ladbrooke remained in the same position, head braced in one hand, but she just sat, staring at the table. She looked pale and worn. "Anyway," she said, "I got hold of Bill."

"So that was Friday night, yes?"

"Pretty much. Not as exciting as you seemed to think. And Saturday and Sunday and Monday just got swallowed up. I don't know where they went or what I did. That time just disappeared. By yesterday, I'd had enough. We were still at the motel, and it was getting boring. And I was sick a lot. I got to thinking about you and the kids and I wanted to come back to work."

She lifted her shoulders in a slight half shrug. "Nothing special happened last night. We just got into an argument over Bill's driving. He was driving like a lunatic, and I told him the police were going to get us if he didn't settle down. I got really mad at him because he just didn't listen. And I was scared to death something was going to happen. So I told him to stop the car and let me out *right there*. And he did. My coat and my purse were in the back seat, and I couldn't get them. He slammed the door and drove off before I could. But nothing sinister happened. It was all pretty mundane."

Silence.

I looked over at Ladbrooke. I really looked at her, studied her features, and it occurred to me that somewhere along the line, I had stopped seeing her physical beauty. This surprised me, and I wondered at what point it had happened. I now had to search her face to see what had seemed so overpoweringly obvious to me in the beginning.

She caught me staring at her. "What are you thinking about?"

"About you." I refocused my gaze. "You do realize that the time's coming when you're going to have to make the decision to quit drinking, don't you?"

She nodded very slightly.

"That's what this whole thing boils down to. You *must* stop."

"I just couldn't cope, Torey. It was being sick. And Tom's not helping.

And Leslie. And Tom's horrible kids. It wasn't that I meant to drink. I'm *trying* to stop."

"Then why didn't you call me instead of Bill? Why didn't you try to do something constructive about it?"

She lowered her head.

"Tom's not making you drink, Ladbrooke. I know you have a difficult time of it at home, but it isn't Tom. Or Leslie. Or Tom's kids. You're the one picking up the glass. No one is pouring it down your throat except you. *You* are."

Ladbrooke's chin trembled.

I could tell it was time to back off. There wasn't much point to upsetting her again. There was even less point to getting upset myself, and I was going to if we pursued this. Tired as I was, my patience wasn't what it could have been.

"Let's take another tack," I said. "Let's look for ways to prevent this from repeating itself in the future."

Ladbrooke nodded.

"What precisely made this happen, in your opinion?"

For several moments Ladbrooke was silent. Hands pressed against her lips, she stared thoughtfully ahead.

"The extra day," she said finally. "Friday. Being home from work on Friday."

"Why?"

"Tom's kids came over."

"But Tom's kids come over almost every weekend. You don't drink then. What made this time different from all the other weekends when you do just fine?"

Ladbrooke looked into her lap. "You want me to be really honest?"

"Yes, of course I do."

"Well, I don't do just fine most weekends. To be honest," she said very softly.

"Ah."

"I do okay sometimes. It's just that if I'm going to slip, it's going to be then."

"I see. I hadn't realized that. I mean, I hadn't realized you'd been drinking any since that last time in January."

"Just the weekends, Torey. Just maybe—what?—three times? That's not much. Not if you count how many days there are in between. And I haven't really gotten smashed, except for this time. I've kept it pretty much under control."

"That's not stopping though, is it?" I rubbed my hands over my eyes and exhaled a long breath. "What do I have to do to get through to you, Ladbrooke? You have to *stop*. You have to *want* to stop."

"I do want to stop. But I *can't*."

Silence. Her expression was despondent. The silence persisted several minutes.

"I try," she said very softly. "You know what? I've got this little routine worked out to get me from Friday night to Monday morning. Just stupid things. Like, for instance, usually I get up and have a shower, but on Sundays I have a bath instead. I get up in the morning and have this bath and—you know—do things like shave my legs. I'm thinking about Monday and I do this really thorough sprucing-up job on Sunday morning so that—this sounds stupid now that I'm saying it aloud—so that I look nice . . . feel good." She laughed self-consciously. "I mean, I'm sure the last thing in the world you're going to check is whether or not my legs are shaved. But when Sunday comes around, it's crucial to me to do it. And quite often, it's enough to keep me sober Saturday night, because I want to be clearheaded enough to shave my legs the next morning. I feel better if I do it. It makes the weekdays seem a little more within reach, if you know what I mean."

She sighed and braced her head with one hand. "It was getting that bug that did it. I can usually manage two days on my own. But I've got to admit, I don't seem to be able to manage more than that." She shook her head. "It was the same at Christmas. I just couldn't cope with all those days and nowhere to go and nothing to do."

"Ladbrooke, why on earth didn't you tell me this before?"

She shrugged.

"We could have arranged to get together. We could have come up with something. Why didn't you tell me?"

"I was embarrassed to. I mean, it's not your mess. Why should you be responsible for me all the time?"

"You're not going to be able to go it alone, Lad. No matter how much you might want to."

She shook her head glumly. "I don't want to. That's the whole thing. I'm sick of going it alone. I've done nothing but make a mess, going it alone. But I'm not quite sure what else to do."

"Would it help if we got together on the weekends for a while? Not for anything big. Just a chat. An hour or so, maybe, on Saturday afternoon or Sunday morning. Would that help?"

"I feel incompetent. I feel like a baby, needing a baby-sitter."

"But would it help? Would it make you less likely to drink then?"

Slowly, she nodded. "Yes, I suppose it would."

"And if anything unusual crops up, like illness or holidays or whatever, we'll make special arrangements. But the important thing is that we stop you from taking that next drink. Yes? Do you agree?"

She nodded.

"What's the matter?"

She shrugged. "I feel bad, making you do this."

"You're not making me do this. I'm offering to do it, okay? It won't be forever. Just until you get over the hard part."

"I still feel bad."

"Look, you've been a lot of help to me in the classroom. Shoe's just on the other foot, that's all. Don't worry about it. I'm not going to."

She nodded. "Okay."

The water had begun to boil on the stove, so I got up to put the spaghetti in. Ladbrooke, too, rose from the table. She stretched, then came over to throw away a wad of tissue in the garbage. Afterward she left to use the bathroom. I paused then, resting my hands on the sink and looking out into the darkness beyond the window. Through the condensation forming on the pane, I could see snow falling. The sudden solitude was soothing.

Turning away from the window, I went to take things from the refrigerator to make a salad. When Lad returned, I was tearing lettuce into a bowl. Putting her hands under her hair, she lifted it up off her neck and held it there a moment. She was standing quite close to me, and I could feel the whoosh of air as she let her hair fall.

"You want me to do that?" she asked.

"If you feel like it. Here. You can slice these." I pushed a handful of mushrooms in her direction.

Ladbrooke reached across me for the cutting board and knife.

"You know, of course," I said, "that I have no expertise in the area of alcohol abuse."

"Yeah," she replied, her tone unconcerned.

"It's a whole specialty of its own. And it makes me think that maybe you'd be better off if you had a proper professional involved."

"I thought you just said *you* were going to help me."

"I did. But I'm not sure I can do enough. No joking, this isn't going to be easy, Ladbrooke. And I'm simply thinking that you may need someone more experienced than I am."

She gathered up the sliced mushrooms and pitched them into the salad bowl. "I don't want anyone else's help."

"Yes, I know," I said.

"Pretend I'm just one of the kids."

"The thing is, Lad, you're not one of the kids. You're an adult and you've got adult problems. Cripes, you're older than me."

"By what? Two years? Three years? What's three years, anyway?"

"That's not the point."

"That *is* the point, Torey. It's the whole point. If I were one of the children, you wouldn't be saying all this. You'd just get in there and keep trying. What's this garbage about adult problems? Problems are problems. And since when did you have a degree in anybody's problems? You haven't a degree in Dirkie's kooky obsessions, have you? Or in kids whose parents get murdered in Northern Ireland. But you keep trying just the same. I think that's all that matters. That's all I want, Torey. It's enough for me."

I let out a long breath. "I just don't want to do wrong by you, kiddo. I want things to get better for you. And I need some evidence that I'm doing the right thing here."

"Okay. So, I won't drink anymore. I promise. Will that make you happier?"

"*You.* You, Ladbrooke, *you.* Not whether or not it'll make me happier. You. You've got to be doing this for you, or it's never going to work."

She gave a small, slight gesture with her shoulders. "Okay, okay. So, I just won't drink again. All right?"

"And what if you do?"

"I *won't.*"

The timer for the spaghetti went off. Grabbing a colander, I took the pot off the stove and drained it. I remained at the sink, regarding the steaming pasta.

"Okay, look, let's try it this way," I said. "Let's have a compromise, all right? You and I'll try this with just us, like we've been doing. We'll have a good, serious stab at it. But it's the very, very last time I try on my own. Because I just wouldn't be comfortable with more than that. It's the *last* time. If you slip again, Lad, you go to AA. Or a specialized therapist or whatever. But you go to someone else. All right?"

No response.

"Okay? I mean, I'll still support you. We'll still keep trying too, even if you slip. I'm not saying I'm going to walk out on you. I have no intention of that. But if you slip again, we're going to both know it's too big a job for me alone. If you slip again, you go to AA as well. Deal?"

Ladbrooke frowned and looked down at her fingernails.

"Deal, Lad?" I asked again.

"Okay," she muttered. "Deal."

CHAPTER TWENTY-TWO

If someone had given me a magic wand that could grant the chance to work full-time with only one child, the child I would have chosen that year would've been Leslie Considyne. I loved all the rest of the children, but she, ultimately, was the most rewarding in terms of sheer progress. Of all of them, Leslie had the most potential for change.

The extent of Leslie's disturbance became fairly evident as I continued to work with her during our daily half-hour sessions. She fell into that rough category of children that was popularly called "autistic," although by the stricter definitions of that disorder, she didn't quite fit. She had some classically autistic behaviors. Most evident was her peculiar way of relating to people. While she did relate in her own inimitable way, and more successfully than I'd seen a lot of autistic children do, she still seemed unable to distinguish us as separate from the nonliving world. We were objects of Leslie's environment, like chairs or can openers, and just as they had to be acted on to get them to provide their services, so did we. She had amazingly refined methods for extracting from people the behaviors she wanted in order to carry on her life as she saw fit, but they were coldly performed. People appeared to be just a rather trickier class of object to Leslie, one requiring a bit more sophistication to master.

Another typically autistic behavior was Leslie's echolalia. This behavior became much more pronounced as her speech developed. Encouraged to talk, she now did so with increasing frequency, but about 85 percent of it was nothing but immediate echoing. "What's your name?" I'd ask. "What's your name?" she'd reply.

Also in autistic fashion, Leslie could self-stimulate for ages if she came across the right circumstances. Balls were her favorite. Rolling one up a slightly inclined surface to watch it roll down again could occupy Leslie for literal hours. Or simply rolling a ball around under the palm of her hand. She'd quite happily spend a morning doing that.

On the other hand, Leslie had some sharp differences from traditionally defined autistic children. She didn't have the typical aversion to being touched or cuddled. She didn't lack eye contact. She didn't greatly mind disruptions to her environment. And in spite of her disturbed interpersonal relationships, she *did* relate. While it was impossible to know if she did in some way perceive us as other individuals, similar to herself, or just extremely useful objects whose services she particularly enjoyed, she did make it obvious that she knew we were there and that she wanted us there. She showed clear preferences for different people and, in her own way, formed stable relationships.

Whatever the precise etiology, I had little doubt that the majority of Leslie's problems were physiological rather than psychological. In fact, Leslie didn't appear to have any problems I could label as emotional disturbances. She did have some pretty peculiar emotional behaviors, but within the disturbed circumstances of her family life, they were all amazingly adaptive and made good sense. There was little doubt that the Considyne family itself was seriously troubled, but Leslie, within the confines of her handicap, seemed to have a surprising degree of emotional health.

It did become apparent to me, however, that a lot of precious time had been wasted. If Leslie's handicap had been identified when she was a toddler and she'd been given an intensive treatment program, I suspected she could have been functioning at a much more normal level by nearly eight. She was an obviously intelligent child, and several aspects of her learning capacity seemed untroubled by her other difficulties. She quickly learned the alphabet and numbers, followed soon by the processes of addition and subtraction. With enough help, I knew she'd be able to read.

Meaningful speech, however, was a long way off. In teaching Leslie things like the alphabet, I was able to encourage a form of meaningful speech. For some reason, she seemed more able to identify abstract symbols by their names than pictures of concrete objects or even the objects themselves. In the same way, she could readily tell me that five was the sum of two and three, but if I asked her another child's name or even her own, she usually couldn't answer. To encourage speech, I tried to make hers as verbal an environment as possible, but while Leslie began to freely use words and phrases, there was still little genuine communication with her.

As Leslie became more responsive in the classroom, I decided to tackle the issue of toilet training. The other children were very aware of Leslie's diapers and although no one ever said as much, I felt this was a major contributing factor to the others' continuing treatment of Leslie as if she were a young, helpless child. And of course, Leslie's incontinence was a major contributor to tensions at home. For her to progress more rapidly toward normalcy, I felt she had to acquire this socially necessary behavior.

Unexpectedly, Lad didn't greet this announcement from me with much enthusiasm. Tom had never allowed Leslie to wear diapers at home since she was a toddler under the belief that they were "humiliating" to her. Not only had this left Ladbrooke with a five-year-long clean-up job, but it had also shifted responsibility for the toileting act from Leslie to her mother. If there was an accident, Tom got angry with Ladbrooke. Only while discussing my plans for toilet training did Lad admit the intense relief she had felt being in the classroom, because I'd insisted on diapers. The thought of losing this small bit of peace with her daughter troubled Ladbrooke. Consequently, I had taken the occasion of Lad's being ill with the stomach virus and then absent on her binge to start Leslie off. It was a rotten time to do it, as we were still in the thrall of the tummy bug ourselves and I was in and out of the toilets with some of the other children more often than I would have cared to be. And of course, as the following week dawned, I was up to my eyeballs in Ladbrooke's problems, which, added to Leslie's, made me feel as if there were no one else in the world but the Considyne/Taylor dynasty. I was also handicapped by Leslie's diabetes, as it limited my usual technique of stuffing the kid full of drinks and salty foods to require more drinks so that there were a lot of opportunities to visit the pot.

But we managed. I got Geraldine and Mariana to demonstrate for Leslie what it was all about. We spent several fun hours in the toilet stalls, flushing, pulling off toilet paper, inspecting the toilet lid and flipping it up and down. I backed up any type of success with copious amounts of Jerusalem artichoke.

It was an advantage, I think, having five days with Ladbrooke absent in which to tackle the problem, partly because it was a rather puddly experience the first few days, as Ladbrooke had feared it would be, and partly because Lad's presence might well have reminded Leslie too much of home and what she did there. As it was, Leslie became reliably dry in only a handful of toilet-obsessed days. She still needed to be taken to the toilet, because if I waited for her to indicate a need, she was inevitably too late. But that, I figured, would improve, and otherwise, we were all cheered by her progress.

This success in the classroom, unfortunately, did not transfer. Ladbrooke, still recovering from her own problems and quite unsettled through the rest of February, found the whole thing too much to cope with; she was in no shape to implement my approach at home. Moreover, she took my speedy success in her absence as a personal affront. Leslie and I had ganged up on her to prove her incompetence as a mother. Then Tom got into it. What was going on? What was I doing to upset Ladbrooke so much? What was happening to Leslie? We had another one of those irritating conferences where Ladbrooke ended up in tears in the girls' rest room, while Tom and I argued. Thoroughly fed up with the lot of them, I tossed up my hands in despair. And Leslie, little fox that she was, loved every minute of it.

Ideally, I would have put Leslie into diapers at home too, because that would have disarmed her. Unable to annoy and divide her parents, I think she would have conformed fairly quickly. But as things were, I didn't even bother to suggest it. Leslie's toilet behavior was such an integral part of the Considyne family dynamics that I realized I could have little impact. So I withdrew from the situation. Satisfied that Leslie was dry in the classroom, I made no further efforts to see things change at home.

March came at last, with a slow, welcome thaw. I'd grown decidedly tired of winter by that time, and while this March was unlike Wales, with its hillsides of snowdrops and daffodils, I was willing to accept the gray, gritty snow's turning to slush as a sign of spring.

There were other changes too. The relationship between Shemona and Geraldine was breaking down in the same slow, deteriorating fashion as the melting snow. Geraldine had remained static for several weeks. She fluctuated back and forth between her usual clingy, babyish behavior and arrogant imperiousness, wherein she ordered everyone around and demanded the best place, the best piece, the best treatment. Her petty antisocial behavior continued unabated, as did the spiteful episodes of vengeance. Slowly, these began to extend to Shemona, as well as the others. More and more, she and Shemona fought.

In the beginning, I hadn't thought much about the fighting. Most of it was very much of a sibling nature. Moreover, Geraldine was going through a pugnacious phase with everyone and was in almost daily knockdowns with Dirkie and Mariana, so I didn't think much about the odd fracas with Shemona. But as time went by, I realized there was more to their fighting. Shemona, I noticed, was increasingly the provoker. She tended to choose safe locations and safe times, but she openly defied Geraldine. A seat wouldn't be saved for her older sister. A paper wouldn't be shown to her. A treat wouldn't be shared with her. Carefully, Shemona managed to extend the same stony unresponsiveness to Geraldine that she had always displayed with the rest of us. In most children I would have taken this as a step backward, but in Shemona, I reckoned this act of slowly shutting out Geraldine was progress. And it infuriated Geraldine, who, if not watched, was regularly giving Shemona a clop around the chops.

The major reason I did not consider Shemona's increased withdrawal in the classroom as regressive was that she had begun to show definite signs of a strong, stable relationship with Ladbrooke during their time together each day. Shemona, still continually dour and silent with the rest of us, would smile and laugh and play with Ladbrooke.

Once Ladbrooke had become comfortable with the format of the sessions, I'd turned the whole works over to her, allowing her free rein to structure the period as she saw fit. This seemed the only sensible way to assure a natural, free-flowing relationship between them, which was what I was aiming for. Although the two of us discussed what was going on, and particularly the results Lad was getting, I tried not to influence Ladbrooke's natural inclinations. She was reliable enough and I was always near enough to insure there would not be any serious problems. Because I stayed out of the planning, their program took on an atmosphere very different from what it probably would have done if I'd been involved. Ladbrooke had gotten started some weeks earlier using the dressing-up box with Shemona. From there, she'd gone on to regularly styling Shemona's hair and putting makeup on her face. The whole period, day after day, revolved around this. Shemona, wrapped up in feather boas and an oversized black dress, netted hat on her head, fifties-style black patent leather high heels on her feet, would parade back and forth in the gloom of the long, narrow blackboard arm of the room. Loosened up by the privacy and, I suspect, my absence, Ladbrooke responded very uninhibitedly to Shemona, popping silly hats and clothes on herself and letting Shemona play with her long hair. In complete contrast to her normal laconic style, Ladbrooke now carried on nonstop monologues with Shemona, as she helped the child dress or did her hair or face for her. "Ooooh, look at you, Gorgeous. You're a fancy woman now. See? You're fit to walk down Fifth Avenue. Could go shopping in Saks, looking like that. Here, put this on. Aren't you something? Look at yourself in the mirror. Oh, wait a minute. Let me fasten that bit of hair up like this. Oh, that's better, isn't it? *Look* at you!"

It was very easy to listen to them. They were only a matter of feet away from the rest of us, as we sat just around the corner at the table, and Ladbrooke, in her enthusiasm, could forget herself and talk quite loudly. This tended to catch our attention if the activities at hand weren't too interesting—that, and the incessant click-click of Shemona's high heels as she teetered back and forth across the linoleum floor. I certainly had my occasional doubts about what they were doing. The beauty routine, the dressing up, the hair styling, were all light-years away from what my own approach would have been, if I'd been working with Shemona. I doubt I ever would have thought of doing such a thing with her. The other children sometimes verbalized what I was thinking: This is school. How come Shemona gets to play for half an hour every day? But I restrained myself from interfering.

To me, perhaps the most intriguing aspect of these sessions was Ladbrooke and Shemona's choice of a medium that required a maximum amount of physical contact between them. Neither of them could tolerate the ordinary touching that went on in the classroom, yet both ritualized it into their daily routine and approached it with glee. Shemona would shriek with delight when Ladbrooke smeared makeup on her cheeks or brushed her hair or wrapped scarves around her.

During the course of one of the sessions, Ladbrooke produced a mail-order catalogue. She had brought it in earlier and shown it to me. It was an outdated Christmas toy catalogue from one of the large chain stores and had a huge section of ready-made costumes for children. Ladbrooke had thought this might be of interest to Shemona, and now they were together in their arm of the room, where I could hear them leafing through it, the thin pages being turned rapidly, one after another. Ladbrooke was carrying on her usual patter, enthusing over things in the doll section. Then they reached the costumes.

"Oh, look," Lad said. "Look at this one. That would be super, wouldn't it? It looks like a nurse's uniform. We could have ourselves some fun with that one, couldn't we? I could be the patient. Lie down right there. And you could be the nurse and put Band-Aids on me." There was a pause, and I assumed Shemona was indicating something. "And look at this one. And *this* one. Isn't this grand. Look, it's long. And the girl's got high heels on, just like yours in the dressing-up box. What do you think this is meant to be? A ball gown? I think so."

Another, longer pause followed. "I've worn a dress like this," Ladbrooke said. "It was long. And it was done up so. And you know what color it was?"

"Gold?" replied Shemona.

Sudden silence.

I had been working with Dirkie at the table and had been half listening to Ladbrooke's constant monologue, so I heard Shemona's voice. Dirkie did as well. He turned his head toward the corner of the shelving. I paused, listening hard.

Much to her credit, Ladbrooke did not overreact. After all these months of waiting, it would have been understandable if she had. But there was a long, long pause, and then I heard Ladbrooke say, "Well, no, actually it was blue. But it was very pretty nonetheless." The tentative note in her voice gave away her surprise, but she continued on with the catalogue. "Oh, look, Shemona. *Here's* a beauty. It looks like a pink ball gown."

"It's a fairy dress," Shemona said, her clear Irish accent rolling out the *r*'s.

Because we, on the other side of the shelves, had all been doing quiet work, everyone sitting with me was now listening to Ladbrooke and Shemona. Such a small leprechaun voice, yet we all heard.

Mariana looked over and smiled. "Torey," she said in a hushed voice, "do you hear that? Shemona's talking!"

I nodded and put a finger to my lips to keep her and the other children quiet. I didn't want to break the magic spell that Ladbrooke was weaving beyond the steel shelving.

Glancing down the table to where Geraldine was bent over her work, I noticed she alone had gone back to what she was writing.

"Hey, Geraldine," Mariana whispered, "do you hear that, Ladbrooke's made Shemona talk. Do you hear?"

Geraldine shrugged and returned to her spelling workbook. "So? So what?"

And Shemona *was* talking. Unlike the two previous occasions when she had spoken to me, this time it was genuine. For several days afterward, she confined her talking to the sessions with Ladbrooke, but during those periods, she grew bolder and bolder. She not only talked with Ladbrooke, she teased and bantered and made silly noises. I was astonished, listening to her. It was as if there were an entirely different child from the silent, scruffy little thing I encountered away from the safety behind the metal shelves.

Then slowly Shemona began to talk to the rest of us. She seemed to realize that we'd been listening all along and, after a point, no longer felt the need to secrete herself away before speaking. First she spoke with Mariana, who had plagued her mercilessly to talk to her ever since Mariana had heard her speak that first day. Then Shemona began talking to the other children, particularly when they were out on the playground. Last of all, she spoke to me.

With the rest of us, however, Shemona was still constrained. She seldom spoke unless spoken to. I never saw her laugh or tease the way she did with Ladbrooke. If I hadn't overheard her, I doubt I would have ever believed this other side of her existed. But I was unconcerned by this difference between her behavior with Ladbrooke and her behavior with others. The important thing was that Shemona was finally talking.

Perhaps almost as important was the effect that Shemona's decision to talk had on Ladbrooke's morale, coming as it did at such a low point in

Lad's life. I don't suppose there was anything I could have done which would have had the same uplifting effect that this small Irish girl's words had. Despite throwing herself into the classroom activities, Ladbrooke had continued to feel like a fish out of water with us. She loved us, I had no doubt about that, and she loved the work. But the fact remained that she was not a teacher, not a psychologist, not even a trained aide like Joyce, and no amount of effort to focus her attention on the very real help she provided me had ameliorated her feelings of inadequacy. But Shemona had managed what I hadn't: She'd made Ladbrooke feel competent. After the session in which Shemona first talked, Ladbrooke had remained sitting at the small student desk with the mail-order catalogue. When I'd gone around to her, she'd looked up, a bemused expression on her face.

"What do you know," she said in amazement. "I can do this."

CHAPTER
TWENTY-THREE

Ladbrooke was having a brutal winter, despite the supportive environment of the classroom and her genuine efforts to keep herself together. Although Shemona's new-found speech gave a much needed boost to Lad's self-confidence, she still careened from one crisis to another, virtually nonstop. I was sadly concluding that this was not an unusual state of affairs. The more I was with her, the more I suspected that this was simply the way Ladbrooke's life was. The miracle to me was that she had managed to survive thirty-three years of it.

The vast majority of her problems lay on the domestic scene. Tom and Ladbrooke had a relationship that made me shudder. As I grew to know the two of them better, I lost all my admiration for Tom's persistent desire to keep the marriage together, because it was an evil thing that preyed on them both. Rather than patching it up, they ought to have been attempting to drive a silver stake through its heart.

Tom's interest in maintaining the relationship was complex, and I never had a chance to understand it well, but the peculiar kind of indulgent contempt with which he always treated Ladbrooke was hard to miss. He had no perceivable respect for her as an individual and he was disdainful of her instability; yet at the same time, he martyred himself putting up with all her outrageous behavior. My gut feeling was that, as with Leslie, he loved the idea of Ladbrooke and her leonine beauty rather more than he did Ladbrooke herself. Reality never seemed to fit very well into Tom's life. Ladbrooke, on the other hand, had more straightforward reasons for continuing the marriage. It was the closest she had come to a loving relationship. With so few emotional resources, she didn't dare give it up.

From her February binge onward, Ladbrooke and I met late every Sunday morning. It was easiest to have her come over to my apartment. The quiet privacy allowed us the opportunity to talk, and my not having to go out to meet her made the disruption to my own weekend a little less. The first couple of times, I made an effort as a hostess, but it was a setup that was unnatural to us both. We were accustomed to working together and not much more, so in the end, I just kept on with whatever it was I was doing, and Ladbrooke simply joined me at it for an hour or two. As a consequence, she enjoyed such delectable Sunday entertainments as cleaning the oven and shampooing the carpet. We joked about its being occupational therapy. Truth be known, it probably was.

Whatever it was, it worked. Ladbrooke stayed alcohol free. Day by day and then week by week, she managed to wend her way through her assorted difficulties without resorting to a drink. As I grew closer to her, I realized that Ladbrooke had been fairly astute when she'd told me that what she needed most was someone to hold her world together for her when she was no longer able to. For the most part, she seemed to have the intelligence, the insight and the desire necessary for change, but she was like one of those rapidly spinning stars in far outer space, which, with no stable core, eventually spin so fast that they fly apart.

Over the course of the three or four months that Ladbrooke had been with me, I was slowly coming to terms with what I concluded to be Lad's most serious problem: her inability to express herself verbally. While things like her alcoholism and her wretched relationship with Tom were much more noticeable, I began to see them as extensions of her difficulty with talking. Indeed, almost all her other problems could be traced back directly or indirectly to this one area.

In the early days I had assumed the problem was one of shyness. Why else would an intelligent, well-educated adult be so inarticulate? And the symptoms fit that sort of pattern. She avoided people in order to avoid talking to them, and she became tense in even very minor social situations. But as time passed and I grew more familiar with her, I saw that while the symptoms fit, Ladbrooke herself really didn't. She didn't have that withdrawn, acutely self-conscious type of personality associated with shyness. Indeed, on occasion she could be considerably more uninhibited than I was, and I wasn't known for my retiring nature. Moreover, Ladbrooke did not perceive herself as shy. And shyness, to my way of thinking was not something likely to be present unbeknownst to its victim.

This left me puzzled for a very long time. Then, slowly, patterns in her behavior grew more apparent. I'd known all along that tension gave her a massive amount of trouble. The more anxious or stressed she was, the less likely she would be to speak well. And if she did manage to speak at all past her habitual yes, no or I don't know, she would often make a hash of it, saying silly things or things she didn't really mean or didn't want to say or even, occasionally, that made no sense at all. Because she became anxious so quickly in any kind of social situation, even those as mundane as the gatherings in the teachers' lounge, this had been a very easy behavior for me to observe. However, as time went by, I started noticing other, less obvious occasions when Ladbrooke also was not very articulate. Odd things, like background noise, soft music or other people chattering, could give her trouble. Being rushed affected her, even if it was innocent and she was feeling friendly and secure in the situation. Being very tired was yet another cause. I grew able to recognize the nights Leslie had been up frequently by Ladbrooke's confused speech the following morning.

These patterns would have been more obvious to me, I think, if it were not for the few converse situations when Ladbrooke could be surprisingly eloquent, such as the occasion when she'd told me about her childhood Christmas. Because such situations didn't occur often, I had to spend a great deal of time with her before I realized that they, too, tended to happen only in set circumstances: we were alone, the immediate environment was totally quiet, the emotional setting, if not relaxed, was always secure, and lastly, they were always monologues. Ladbrooke never showed the same kind of eloquence in conversation.

Mulling over these patterns, I eventually concluded that Ladbrooke's inarticulateness was not so much the result of an emotional problem as a type of aphasia, a dysfunction of whatever part of the brain it was that controlled expressive speech. From that point of view, a huge amount of her behavior suddenly made sense, and it became easier to understand what was happening to her the rest of the time. For some while, I'd been aware that in many social situations she was having paralyzing anxiety attacks. Now the cycle became clearer. Tense, she became less articulate. Frightened at finding herself unable to say what she wanted, she panicked. The panic destroyed whatever bit of expression she was still capable of. Ladbrooke had found only two ways of coping. Either she avoided people altogether and discouraged further social encounters with her hostile, aloof behavior, or she drank. When drinking, she relaxed. Even if she didn't make much sense, when Ladbrooke had had enough alcohol, she could talk. Or at least not care if she couldn't.

This theory also lent insight into her difficult relations at home. Brilliant in his own right and rapier tongued, Tom was a formidable individual in conversation. I knew this from my own experiences with him, because he regularly outmaneuvered me, twisting and turning my words, switching subjects, doubling back and often simply bludgeoning me with sheer persistence until I found myself agreeing with him, whether I meant to or not. Such elaborate verbal gymnastics were wasted on Ladbrooke. She was defeated before she started, reduced to fuming silence or noisy bursts of temper that communicated nothing.

Theirs was a vastly unequal relationship, the inequality perhaps being the most salient aspect to outsiders. First impressions were of Tom as a domineering father to Lad's sulky, sullen child. However, I came to feel that the inequality was much deeper than that. Ladbrooke wasn't simply being obstinate or petty. It wasn't because she wouldn't talk to Tom as an equal, but rather that she couldn't. Tom's reference on that one occasion to Ladbrooke's being a lioness trapped in human form was a chillingly apt description. Their situation wasn't a matter of maturity vs. immaturity or dominance vs. submission. They were of two different species entirely. Tom's role was one of zookeeper, an indulgent master of something he desired but could not control, while Ladbrooke paced restlessly back and forth within the confines of the marriage, trapped and voiceless.

The rain had been bucketing down all day. The children had had to stay in over the lunch hour, and so everyone was rowdy and unsettled when class resumed in the afternoon. Mariana, in particular, was having a bad day. She hadn't finished any of her morning work. She'd gotten into fisticuffs with Geraldine at lunch and later with Shemona in the girls' rest room. She'd encouraged Dirkie into frantic masturbation under the table. An she'd larked about, annoying me the whole day long. I had had her in and out of the quiet chair several times during the morning, and she was in it again after lunch, sitting on the wooden chair, rocking it back and forth to make an irritating creaking noise. The timer I'd set to the number of minutes she needed to stay in the chair went off with a resounding ring, and Mariana got up.

I was working with Shemona and looked up momentarily from what we were doing. "Okay, Mariana. Your work's right there on the table. Please get started immediately. There isn't much time before recess." I went back to Shemona.

Mariana returned to her place at the table. She opened her folder and, still standing, leaned over her chair and studied the worksheets. Taking her pencil, she went to sharpen it. Then she returned, seated herself and looked over the worksheets again. She glanced to Geraldine, two chairs away, who was listening to a tape through headphones. Mariana made a face. When Geraldine didn't notice, Mariana leaned over, touched Geraldine's elbow and made the face again.

"Mariana," I said, "please get busy."

Mariana looked down at the worksheet she had taken from the folder. She picked up her pencil and began to write but almost immediately put the pencil down again. She got up, went to her cubby, got out her pencil box and came back to her place. Sitting down again, she opened the box and rooted through it. Out came a big green eraser. She started to erase with it but then picked it up and examined it. With one fingernail, she scraped along the edge of the eraser. She rubbed the eraser under her nose, then stopped, smelled it, smiled, smelled the eraser again. Then she began to rub the eraser back and forth on the Formica tabletop.

"Mariana," I said. "Get to work."

Mariana stared at her paper. She twiddled her pencil. She drew little wavy lines down the side of the worksheet. Lifting the pencil up, she examined the point again. Then she started cleaning her fingernails with it.

Annoyed with Mariana's fooling around, I excused myself from Shemona and her work and went over to sit next to Mariana. "What is your problem today?" I asked.

"I don't understand this."

"It's exactly the same kind of sheet you've been doing all week. Here, let's read the directions and go over them so that you do understand."

Mariana haltingly read through the directions.

"So what do they mean?" I asked.

"That I read these words on this side and then these on this side and draw a line between the ones that go together."

"That's right. So what don't you understand?"

She shrugged.

"Then please get busy." I stood up and walked around to see what the others were doing. When I next looked, Mariana was spinning her pencil around and around on the tabletop.

Completely fed up, I grabbed a nearby yardstick and without warning brought it cracking down on the table about six inches from the spinning pencil. Mariana squawked in surprise.

"*Work!*" I said. And she did.

Only moments later, the bell sounded for recess.

It was Lad's and my break, so after herding the children down to the playground, we returned to the teachers' lounge.

"Don't do that again, okay?" Ladbrooke said, as we were climbing the stairs.

"Don't do what?"

"Hit the table like that, like you did in the room."

I smiled. "I was just trying to get Mariana moving. She's been a right royal pain all day long."

"But don't do it again."

"I wasn't going to hit her, Lad. But she's been screwing around all day. The whole point of it was to scare the daylights out of her."

"It's not right," Lad replied.

At that moment we reached the teachers' lounge. Brightly lit in contrast to the gloomy corridor, it was also full of people. Bill and Frank and three of the people from speech therapy were in there, drinking pop and laughing unroariously. The conversation between Ladbrooke and me came to an end.

It wasn't until after school when Lad and I were working together at the table that the subject reappeared. Ladbrooke paused at what she was doing and braced her chin with both hands. A few moments' silence ensued as she watched me writing.

"I remember at school once," she said quietly, "when I was six and in the first grade and we were doing reading workbooks. There were these spaces, and you had to write the words in. And I wasn't doing it right.

"The teacher would walk up and down the aisles, watching us as we worked. She had this long pointer, a blackboard pointer, that she always carried with her, and she'd tap the wrought-iron bit of the desk if she thought you weren't working the way you should be. I was terrified of her doing it to my desk. I wasn't a kid to goof off much, but I was always scared that she might be thinking I was."

Ladbrooke paused. "I was afraid of her. She was always displeased with me. You know how people get, how they sort of sigh with exasperation. She'd do that. She hated the fact I was left-handed. She was forever threatening to tie my left hand to the desk if I didn't stop using it. And then I kept spelling my name wrong. Believe me, never, ever give a child a name with a 'd' and a 'b' right next to one another. Do you think I could remember which was which? I was a dunce at it. And the teacher'd get frantic. She made me stay after school and write pages and pages of my own name. And I was always so scared, because I never had any idea if I was doing it right or not. I just had to do it and pray it was the proper way around."

Another pause, and Lad grew introspective. "That's not what I meant to tell you," she said softly. "I didn't mean to get sidetracked." Pause again. "I guess I just wanted to explain why I was so frightened. I just wanted to be good for my teacher. You know how you are at that age. You want people to like you.

"Anyway, we were doing this particular worksheet. One of the words to put in the blanks was 'carry,' and I'd stuck it in the wrong sentence. The teacher came along and leaned over me and said, 'What word is this?' And I'd answered, 'Carry.' And she said, 'Carry doesn't belong in this sentence, does it? It doesn't make any sense. What does the word 'carry' mean?' And she waited for me to tell her. But I couldn't. I mean, I knew what carry meant, but I couldn't say it. So she asked me again. And again. And again. I was starting to get upset. I wanted to tell her, because

I wanted her to know I wasn't dumb. I *knew*. But I couldn't say it. And she just kept asking and asking, without letting up. I knew I was going to cry and I felt really embarrassed. There was this unsaid thing in first grade that only babies cried, and it was very important to never cry in front of the other kids if you could help it. But she kept saying, 'Come on, Ladbrooke, you're a big girl. You know a little word like that, don't you?' And I *did* know. That was what was so awful. But I couldn't say it; I just sat there like a dumb bunny. Then right out of nowhere, without any warning at all, she brought her pointer down on my desk. Right in front of me, right across my paper really, really loudly. It alarmed me so much, I wet my pants."

Ladbrooke shifted slightly in her chair and drew her arms in around her. She looked over. "To this day I can feel the humiliation of that moment."

"What I did with Mariana wasn't the same kind of thing, Lad. Mariana's not afraid of me. I wish she were sometimes. But she *can* do all the work in her folder. She was just horsing around."

Ladbrooke frowned. "That's not the point."

"What is?"

Still the frown. "I don't know exactly. How to say it, I mean. But it's not whether or not she can do it. Or if she's horsing around. It's treating someone like that."

I regarded her.

She shrugged. "I don't like to think of you doing that kind of thing, Torey. You're a better teacher than that."

Picking up her felt-tipped pen, Ladbrooke returned to her work. I sat a few minutes longer, watching her, and then finally went back to what I'd been doing. We worked in silence for a very long time, perhaps forty-five minutes or more.

"Torey?"

"Yes?"

"Can I ask you something?"

I was still writing. "Yes, of course."

"Will you tell me the truth?"

"If I can."

"Do you think there's something wrong with me?"

Lifting my pencil, I looked over at her. "How do you mean?"

"The way I am." She paused. "I've been thinking about what I was telling you earlier. I can remember so distinctly sitting there and *knowing* what that word meant, but not being able to make myself say it. It wasn't there to say, if you know what I mean. Is everyone like that?" She paused again and leaned forward, her elbows on the table. "Or is there something wrong with me? You've got to be really honest with me, because I think I need to know." She searched my face a moment, but before I could respond, she continued on. "It seems to be the way I think. I mean, not what I think, but how I think. And how I talk. Because, like sometimes, I just . . . it just . . . what? Stops? Freezes? Or maybe it was never there to begin with. I don't know. But I keep watching everyone else and they don't seem to have this kind of problem. You don't. Tom doesn't. Cripes, nothing stops Tom from talking. Is it just personalities, do you think? Am I inhibited or something? Tom says I'm mentally frigid. And although I'd hate to admit it, that's what it feels like sometimes. Is he right? Or is it some kind of deep-down emotional problem that I don't know anything about, like maybe down in my subconscious or something? Like Shemona's got, only different. Is it that? What do you think? You're the expert in these kinds of things. What's your opinion?"

So I told her. I said I thought she had some kind of organic disability that made verbal expression difficult and unpredictable, that this unpredictability had caused a lot of tension and anxiety for her, that the anxiety had magnified the effects of the disability, and that these together had sent out tentacles into many parts of her life. Ladbrooke listened intently, her brow furrowed, her eyes never leaving my face.

"Has anyone told you anything like this before?" I asked.

Pensive for several seconds, she then slowly shook her head. "Not really. I've been told I have emotional problems, that that's what caused it. That psychiatrist I told you about before—the one we saw when Leslie was being diagnosed—said it was just a hysterical reaction. I'd told him about this, about how I felt like I didn't talk as well as other people, and he said I could talk if I wanted to, that I just thought I couldn't. He said I used silence as a defense to keep from facing my problems."

"And what do you think?" I asked.

"I wasn't using it to keep from facing my problems. It *was* my problem."

She fell abruptly silent. Bringing up one hand, she began to energetically chew the thumbnail. Eyes down, she gazed thoughtfully at the tabletop. "On one hand, I've been desperate for years to ask someone who knows about these things. If I'm honest, I've got to acknowledge that's why I ended up volunteering for this job. Because I thought I might find out. I *need* to find out. I need to understand what's going on better. But at the same time, I've been scared to. I've been frightened to death that if I ever did find out, it would just confirm what I've always pretty much assumed the answer was going to be."

"Which was what?"

Tilting her head to one side, she gave a slight shrug and kept her eyes averted. It was an oddly poignant gesture. "That I'm just not very smart.

That I think this way because this is the way dumb people think. And talk. Or rather, don't talk. I've always had the feeling that maybe it's just been some kind of idiot savant thing that I was so good at math and science. Just a fluke, you know? I've felt even more like that since I had Leslie, because I've seen how she can be so gifted in some ways and still be so totally out to lunch. I've just assumed she's gotten it from me."

My heart melted as I listened to her. She spoke in such a soft, matter-of-fact manner. What an evaluation to be carrying around inside oneself.

"You're not dumb, Lad. Idiot savants don't ponder about their condition. They don't hold down research positions at Princeton. There's nothing wrong with your IQ."

She sighed quietly.

"I'm not just saying it. You've asked my professional opinion and that's it. There're plenty of things for you to worry about, but your IQ isn't one of them. Neither is the fear that you've given Leslie her handicap. In her case, I'm afraid Fate was just in a malevolent mood."

Ladbrooke continued to regard the tabletop. She simply stared at it, bracing the side of her head with one hand.

"I'm not saying I have all the answers either, kiddo. No one does in these kinds of things. But having you with me all these months and seeing how things go for you, I'd be very surprised if this wasn't a physical problem. That's not to say there haven't been emotional side effects. It's no secret to either one of us that you're being eaten alive by anxiety on occasion. And there're plenty of other things causing you grief. But for the most part, I think it's your inability to express yourself easily that's setting you up for the emotional problems and not the emotional problems making you unable to talk."

Ladbrooke was chewing her nails again. Removing her hand from her mouth, she examined her fingers thoughtfully. She picked at one. Then cautiously, she nodded. "Okay. If what you say is true, then what? What can be done about it?"

"Well . . ."

She looked over.

"This is the hard part. I'm afraid I don't have any answer. Except learn to accept it. Come to terms with it as a part of your physical self—your body—that just doesn't work quite as well as it should and learn to live with that fact, the way epileptics or diabetics do."

She said nothing.

"Probably the thing to concentrate on is lowering the stress and getting rid of the panic you feel when you find you can't talk as easily as you'd like."

"Yes." She nodded. "Yes, I've got to admit you're right about the panic.

I hadn't realized I was being that obvious. I've tried to keep it to myself because I know it's just in my head. I know it's just me—being stupid. But Jesus, Torey, sometimes I feel like I'm having a heart attack, I really do. I think I'm going to die."

"It happens quite a lot, doesn't it?" I said.

She nodded.

"Has it been going on for a long time?"

Again she nodded. "Yeah. For years and years now." She sighed. "All it takes is strangers."

A small pause came into the conversation. I momentarily lost myself in thought, pondering what it must feel like to experience such agony in the kind of social encounters I normally didn't even give full conscious attention to. Which in turn led me to thinking what hard work her academic accomplishments must have been, not only in terms of her learning problems, but also emotionally.

"How on earth did you do your doctorate?" I asked.

"I was okay with that," she said. "It was all in an area I'm good at, so I never had any problems."

"I wasn't thinking so much from an educational point of view. I was thinking of your oral exams for your dissertation."

"I knew my examiners pretty well. And I *did* know my material."

"I'm sure you did, but it must have been a nerve-wracking experience nonetheless, with your examiners asking questions and your having to defend your research orally. Did you drink?"

A faint, sheepish smile followed. "I took Valium. About fifteen milligrams, as I recall. I was hardly awake."

"I see."

The smile faded, and she shrugged. "That," she said softly, "and I slept with my advisor."

Ah, well, I didn't have much of an answer to that.

"But I *did* know my material. It wasn't cheating. Not really. I'd earned the doctorate. I just needed to make sure I got it, that's all."

CHAPTER
TWENTY-FOUR

Over the next several days Ladbrooke and I spent a vast amount of time discussing her problem with expression. Once the topic was opened, Ladbrooke seemed to have an insatiable need to explore it. Mostly, she wanted to talk about the experience of being trapped inside a brain that refused to cooperate. Episode upon episode came flooding back, and she wanted to relate all of them in minutest detail. What rose from this sudden flood was the poignant specter of an unwilling captive, locked inside a cage no one else saw. Isolated, unable to make herself understood, frenzied by the humiliation of perpetually being thought stupid, she'd grown angry both with herself and with others. And she sought relief where she could find it. Considerably before she mentioned discovering alcohol, she had found another powerful weapon: her appearance.

This was the first time Ladbrooke ever spoke directly of her beauty, the first time she ever acknowledged it as a notable factor in her life. She didn't feel beautiful, she said flatly. An empty box with pretty wrapping. But it was there. It was something to use, something to assuage the terrible helplessness. In the end, I could tell that it had become just one more expression of her frantic anger, as she enticed men to give her love and then despised them because they never saw the worthlessness she felt. Listening silently, I realized that perhaps this was the source of Tom's powerful hold over her. Her beauty hadn't blinded him. He was only too willing to confirm her own opinion of herself.

I could appreciate Ladbrooke's need to recount all of this and found it interesting that, once we got onto the subject, she was anything but inarticulate. Alone with me in the privacy of the classroom, she could reconstruct all those terrible little moments with wrenching eloquence. However, after the first few days of listening to her, I wanted to make sure something constructive came out of it. All this insight wasn't worth much if it didn't change things for the better.

My two main concerns were closely related. The first was to develop some way to help her cope with her anxiety attacks and eventually curb them, as they were considerably more debilitating than her unexpected moments of speechlessness. The second was to get Lad to realize that the methods she'd already come up with to cover the panic and avoid unnecessary interactions were almost as unpleasant to others as her anxiety was to her.

We talked then about relaxation techniques and other methods commonly used with phobics. I reminded her of some of the things I did with Dirkie, who was also prone to panic attacks. But beyond these, I admitted that mostly it was going to be a matter of getting back into social situations and just plowing on through. An inelegant solution, I'd called it, a term used on me years earlier when I'd confronted a phobia myself. I told her about that too. And inelegant as it was, the method worked. If you plowed through long enough, you got over the disabling anxiety.

I also brought up the other matter: the impression she gave people when she tried to save herself from panicky situations. Interestingly, for all her perspicacity regarding her own situation, Ladbrooke had surprisingly little insight into how her behavior affected others. I had noticed this shortcoming on other occasions, particularly in regard to her relationship with Tom, but it was more marked here. On one level she did appear to realize that she projected a cold, thoroughly hostile image. But on another level, she seemed genuinely amazed that people had believed that was how she was. I'm not *really* that way, she'd replied, miffed. Why did everyone insist on taking things so literally? I explained that that was just the way people were, that in general, all of us tend to accept what we see as what's true. But Ladbrooke, still too desperate for understanding herself, had none to squander on other people. So I let the matter drop for the time being.

Toward the middle of March, Tom was taking Leslie and his other two children upstate to visit his mother. They were planning to be gone five days, and Leslie was due to be out of school from Wednesday to Friday of that week. Ladbrooke was staying home, openly grateful to have her work in the classroom as an acceptable excuse. Knowing that Ladbrooke had no commitments over the period, I thought I'd ask her if she wanted to join Carolyn and me for one of our evening swims at the spa. It seemed like a good idea at the time, a friendly gesture. I knew Ladbrooke had been slightly envious of Carolyn's and my frequent evenings together and the silly things we got up to. This seemed a good opportunity to include her. Moreover, I thought we could kill two birds with one stone and provide Lad with a chance to cope in a slightly broader social situation. The relaxed, distracting atmosphere of the swimming pool would be, I hoped, less threatening than that of the teachers' lounge.

After discussing it with Carolyn, I did ask Ladbrooke, who accepted the invitation readily, a surprised smile on her face. I apologized ahead of time for the facilities, which really weren't very spectacular even by my rather undiscriminating standards. And I explained that our routine was pretty much a do-it-yourself affair. I tried to get a mile's worth of laps in before we degenerated into just lounging around the whirlpool and chatting. Carolyn, however, usually felt less energetic and spent most of her time treading water.

I hadn't anticipated any problems when I'd first thought of asking Ladbrooke. The invitation had been extended purely in the spirit of friendship, and I'd counted on Lad's feeling more at ease than in previous social situations and not letting the side down. However, by the time Friday rolled around, I found myself overwhelmed with misgivings. I'd tended to forget how truly unpleasant everyone else found Lad because we didn't interact much with anyone else at school and it had been so long since I'd felt that way about her myself. Now, suddenly, the memories were very vivid. What if Ladbrooke didn't cooperate? What if she kept up her old, bristly, hostile guard and made Carolyn thoroughly unhappy I'd invited her? This thought for my own possible discomfort concerned me much more than the possibility that Lad might grow uneasy herself or panic. Agonizingly tense by the time we arrived at the spa, I found myself wondering how the heck I got myself into things like this when it would have been a lot less trouble to stay home and watch TV.

I can only assume that my anxiety accounted for assorted other silly behaviors on my part that evening. For instance, after years of feeling fairly satisfied with my body, I found myself unexpectedly self-conscious beside Lad. Covertly, I watched Ladbrooke as we changed, and all the while I compared bits and pieces.

Ladbrooke further aggravated things by being in better shape than either Carolyn or I. She went off the diving board into the water and swam away like a fish, while Carolyn and I just stood there, trying to look skinny. This was no small disillusionment to me. Here I was, straight as an arrow, while she abused her body mercilessly—and this was the reward I got?

She then quickly snatched from me the one small gem in my crown. Swimming had been a hard-won skill for me, something I'd learned in later years and had never found particularly natural. Yet, I'd persevered, and the fact that I was one of the better swimmers among the regulars at the spa had always pleased me tremendously. But Ladbrooke was very obviously superior. Joining me for the laps, she effortlessly passed me and was sitting with Carolyn on the edge of the pool when I finally dragged myself out. Generally disgruntled, I returned to the water and kept swimming until at last I was too tired to care about anything.

Afterward, we all sank gratefully into the whirlpool. I leaned back against the jets and let them massage hard-worked muscles. Ladbrooke lowered herself into the deeper part, her long hair spreading out around her in the water, making her look like one of the girls in the Maxfield Parrish paintings. Only Carolyn seemed full of chat. She launched into a hilarious account of her tortuous efforts to get one of the children in her class toilet trained. Always a first-rate storyteller, she proved very funny that evening. The rather poopy humor of the tale left all of us giggling like schoolgirls.

Then Ladbrooke came up on the bench beside me. Leaning her head back against the edge of the whirlpool, she closed her eyes. We all drifted into companionable silence for a few minutes.

Carolyn looked over. "So, Lad," she asked, "what do you think of us? Do you like our kind of work?"

Ladbrooke opened her eyes. She glanced briefly in my direction before looking past me to Carolyn. She nodded.

Carolyn didn't say anything further.

"Yes, I like it," Lad said. "I've learned a lot."

"Would you want to go into it?" Carolyn asked.

"I don't know."

Carolyn smiled amiably. "Well, at least that's honest."

"I kind of like being in there with all that goes on," Ladbrooke replied quietly. "If you know what I mean. It all sounds odd, when you're on the outside, but when you're actually in there, in with the action, it's a lot more exciting than I thought it'd be. It's more . . . more . . . It's more . . ." She paused.

"More honest," Carolyn supplied. "More real. More alive."

Ladbrooke nodded. "Yes, that's what I meant, I think. Alive."

Carolyn grinned. "Yeah, Lad, that's what hooks you. It's like dope. Once you get a snort, nothing else is quite the same."

Afterward in the dressing room, Carolyn apologized for having to hurry. We'd stayed longer than we ordinarily did, and it was Friday night. She had a date at 8:30. Ladbrooke was still drying her hair, so I sat on the long bench between the lockers and waited for her. Coming back over from the dryers, she stood over me and combed her hair, pulling it way out to the side with a wide-toothed comb to reach the ends. Then it would fall, swinging past my face, one section after another.

"What are you doing now?" she asked, as she worked on it.

"Now?"

"Tonight, I mean. Anything? You want to come over chez Taylor and have something to eat?"

"All right," I said.

"I'm no great shakes as a cook. I'll tell you that now. But I can manage something if you don't mind that it's not fancy." She paused to pull hairs out of her comb.

"Okay."

I sat alone in the Considynes' cavernous living room. It was the first time I had ever been inside the house. Ladbrooke had disappeared into the kitchen, and I could hear her banging pots and pans around. So I'd been left to my own devices. Leaning my head back, I stared at the vaulted ceiling.

There was nothing chez about this place; it was definitely château. I'd never really seen anything like it up close. It felt like a church to me, with its massive, hewn beams and pitched roof. The peak of the ceiling must have been twenty feet above me. And way up there along the beams ran little tracks of spotlights that provided a soft, very diffuse form of illumination. It was attractive, but I wasn't sure I'd have cared to carry on my normal life under it.

The fireplace was gargantuan, like the rest of the room. Dividing the living room from the dining room, it had a magnificent stone hearth that ran half the length of the room. Studying it, I was overcome with an unexpected moment's homesickness. My tiny cottage back in Wales had an equally mammoth fireplace, born not of opulence but of the mistaken belief in days gone by that bigger meant warmer. It didn't, of course, because all the heat went up the chimney. I expected all the heat went up this chimney too, although here probably no one noticed. Once the cottage was on my mind, however, I was unable to shake the homesick feelings. So, to keep the evening from being spoiled, I got up and went into the kitchen to see what Ladbrooke was doing.

She wasn't kidding about her cooking ability. I found her scraping a concoction of ground beef and canned spaghetti onto two plates. The incongruity of such food in these luxurious surroundings struck me as amusing, and I smiled.

Lad smiled back. "You like this?" she asked, her voice hopeful.

I nodded.

Opening the refrigerator, she stared into it. "What do you want to drink?"

"I don't care."

"Six months ago, I would have suggested we wash all this down with a bottle of plonk." Her voice was wistful. "That's the kind of drinking I really miss." She looked at me over top of the refrigerator door. "Do *you* want wine? There's some in here." She lifted up a large, half-empty jug of California white. "I don't mind, Torey. Tom drinks it all the time. I don't care if you drink in front of me."

I shook my head.

"I've got that much self-control. It won't make me feel bad or anything. Really."

"No, that's okay. Have you got milk?"

She looked back into the refrigerator. "Milk? What kind of drink's that? I'd feel silly giving you milk."

"Milk's fine, Lad. It's what I drink at home."

We sat down at the table. Very aware of the huge house echoing around us, I was uncomfortable. I would have hated it here on my own. Even with the two of us, we created such a negligible bit of life in the silence that I'd have been happier with more light or some music or something to fend it off.

Ladbrooke, however, seemed unbothered. In fact, she was more relaxed than I customarily saw her. Taking up her fork, she tucked into the spaghetti mixture with undisguised enjoyment.

Then, unexpectedly, she giggled. "This is great. It's just like having my teacher home to dinner."

"I'm not your teacher, Lad."

"You *are*," she said with feeling. She was still smiling, clearly relishing the idea.

Adjusting my napkin, I picked up my fork and began to eat. Ladbrooke, I noticed, was already halfway through. Where she put it, I didn't know, but she usually ate with the appetite of a lumberjack.

When she'd finished, she rose from the table and went into the kitchen. "Do you want some ice cream, Torey?" she called. She returned with two cartons. "There's this kind, let's see, what is it? Raspberry ripple. And this one. Double chocolate fudge." She grinned gleefully. "That one's Tom's, but this one's mine. I *love* chocolate." She scooped a bit off the edge of the lid with her finger and tasted it. "Have some of this. It's nicer than that."

"Okay."

She disappeared back into the kitchen to get bowls. I was left, contemplating the carton of double chocolate fudge. It struck me suddenly how normal this all was, the ice cream, the canned spaghetti, Ladbrooke's obvious pleasure with the evening. And I realized with poignancy that I had almost no knowledge of Ladbrooke in the small, ordinary ways of friendship. Four soul-searing months together and I'd never known she especially liked chocolate.

Ladbrooke returned. Putting bowls on the table, she began to scoop generous helpings of ice cream into them. "Tom hates chocolate. He says it ruins your skin. I don't think it does, but he's always telling me I shouldn't eat so much of it." She shook her head wearily. "I don't know about Tom sometimes. He can be a real pain. And bossy. He treats me like I'm about six years old. Everything's got to be done *his* way. I hope your future husband isn't like that. I hope you have more sense about this sort of thing than I did."

Ladbrooke took the carton back to the freezer while I tried to soften my ice cream slightly with my spoon.

"Why did you marry Tom?" I asked, when she'd sat down again.

She shrugged. Taking an enormous spoonful of the ice cream, she held it, bowl of the spoon upward, and licked it as if it were a cone. Her eyes were on me. "I don't know." Pause to lick the ice cream again. "He was nice." Pause. "I was impressed with what he did—you know—the painting." Another pause. She took up a second scoop of the ice cream. Lifting the spoon, she studied it a moment before licking it. "Tom had a lot of things to offer. You've got to understand, I was young when I met him. I was not quite twenty-three. I didn't have much experience. You get this guy coming along who's rich and famous and really somebody. It's pretty hard not to be flattered when he makes it obvious he wants *you*. It's pretty hard not to do what he wants."

"Were you working then?"

She nodded. "I was still doing my graduate work at Princeton when we first met. I was a couple years from finishing my doctorate. We started out just living together. Tom had an apartment in Manhattan, and I just moved in with him on the weekends, when I wasn't at Princeton. But then after a while he kept wanting to come back here. I'd never been here before, but he made it sound nice. And he kept wanting to come back; his roots were here. I was just getting established about then. But Tom got pretty insistent. He wanted to get married; he wanted everything formal and above board. We had Leslie and I think, deep down, I already knew something was wrong with her; so I thought, maybe I'd better— you know—for her sake. Tom kept telling me that I didn't have to give up the project anyway. He had the jet then, and we thought we'd just carry on like we always had, my living in Princeton during the week and at home with him on the weekends. We were together five years before we ever actually spent an entire week together under the same roof. So I didn't object to the move a whole lot. The way Tom talked about it, the area sounded interesting. And I really liked planes. I was intending to get my pilot's license, so that sounded exciting, flying back and forth across the country."

"What kind of work were you doing on your project?"

"It was experimental work on the geometry of certain molecular substances." She glanced over. "You familiar with Raman spectroscopy?"

I shook my head slightly. In fact, I'd never heard of it.

A rather disappointed expression crossed her face. "I know. It sounds pretty boring, doesn't it? It does to most people. But I really like it. I'm good at that sort of thing."

"I doubt that's the kind of talent you could fake."

She shrugged. "I don't know."

"What made you give it up in the end?"

Another shrug. Scraping the sides of her bowl, she finished the very last of the ice cream. "It got to be too much of a hassle, I guess. I was wrong about its being exciting, trying to commute halfway across the country every week. I mean, there I was, weekdays in New Jersey, weekends here. Tom was always wanting parties and his kids over. Then back to work and long hours and endless meetings over funding and all that. I was continuously exhausted. I was twenty-eight and feeling about eighty-eight. And I was never getting anything done. I never got my pilot's license. I was too busy sleeping on the plane to think about flying it." She paused and exhaled a long breath. "You see, if I'm honest, it was just an ego trip in the beginning. It seemed glamorous to me, to be able to commute all that distance, to be able to afford to commute and all that. But it wasn't worth it. I was too tired to enjoy anything. Leslie was getting worse and worse. Tom nagged me nonstop about what I wasn't doing with him. It was killing me. And it wasn't as if I were Einstein or anything. I was just a junior member of the project. The juniorest. They didn't need me that much. So, when it got too hard, I gave it up."

"Seems a shame," I said. "It sounds like it would have been a fulfilling career."

Her expression was momentarily wistful. "Yes, maybe." Then she shrugged. "But who knows."

We got up and took the dishes into the kitchen. Ladbrooke unloaded the dishwasher. Acknowledging that she did virtually nothing in the kitchen, she admitted to having no idea where most of the things went. So we spent a giggly ten minutes opening cupboards and drawers and just chucking things in. Poor Consuela undoubtedly would not be able to find anything for weeks. Then Ladbrooke made us coffee in a thing that looked like it would require a physics degree to operate.

"I'm going to regret this," she said, as she did it. "It kills my stomach. But sometimes it just tastes so nice."

And it was good coffee, filling the room around us with its dark, robust smell.

"Come on," Ladbrooke said. "Let's take this down to the study. It's friendlier down there." She then led me through unlit halls and down two short flights of stairs to a smaller, much more intimate room. Unlike the rest of the house, which was showroom immaculate, this room betrayed definite signs of being lived in. Shoes, socks, dirty clothes, and, in particular, newspapers were everywhere.

"I'm afraid I'm as lousy a housekeeper as I am a cook," Ladbrooke said, shifting things off one chair. I sat down there. Ladbrooke put her mug on the coffee table and stretched out full length on the couch. Putting her feet up on the far arm, she had her head on the near-side arm, her long hair spilling up and over it.

We said nothing for several minutes. I sipped the coffee, which was hot and strong and tasted wonderful. Ladbrooke remained stretched out. I couldn't see her face from that position but I had the definite impression she had her eyes closed. The silence, warm and intimate, was almost sleepy.

"You know, I lied back there, a bit," Ladbrooke said, her voice quiet.

"Back where?"

"Back there, in the dining room, when you were asking me about why I gave up my work."

"Oh."

"Well, it wasn't a lie exactly. All that commuting and everything *was* hard. But I was being a little stingy with the truth." She had her hands together, fingertip to fingertip, resting on her abdomen. She studied the shape they created.

"It was actually my fault. That's what I wasn't telling you. Not Tom's. Not Leslie's. Not anybody else's. I quit because of something stupid I did." Again she contemplated her hands. "I haven't told anybody about this. I mean, quite a few people knew anyway. But I haven't told anyone else. I haven't told Tom. I doubt I ever will."

Silence slid in around us.

"I guess first I need to explain what it's like doing hard research. Hard, as opposed to soft. Not hard, as opposed to easy. In the hard sciences, it's really competitive. I don't think most people appreciate that. They see it all as ivory-tower stuff, but they don't seem to realize that up there in the ivory tower, folks are killing one another just as mercilessly as everywhere else. Slit, slit, slit at one another's throats. You have to. The money's hard to come by, and the projects are expensive. The project leader has to be one hell of a good politician as well, to get the kind of money that's needed for most really serious research. And to keep it."

She paused.

"There are a lot of scientific awards around, and they're vital. You've got to get them. If you've done something at all notable, you've got to get some recognition for it. It helps you get your money. See, a lot of the big corporations who do the funding, their bigwigs aren't going to understand your research. But they all understand if you beat out the competition to one of the awards. They know you're good then, and they're willing to back you. Plus, in a lot of cases, the awards themselves are worth a sizable amount of money. So people take them very seriously indeed."

Another pause. Ladbrooke sucked in a long, audible breath and held it several seconds before slowly releasing it.

"We were at this awards dinner. My advisor, who was the head of our project, was in contention for one of the awards. We had a very good chance of getting it and we all knew it, so everyone was in pretty high spirits. You see, we were having trouble with our funding. There was another project in California that was quite similar to ours, and one of our sponsors had defected the previous year and backed that project instead. And the administration in Washington had changed . . . It was critical that we find some new sources of support. We needed recognition that year.

"So there we were at that awards dinner, waiting to hear if John was going to win. It was a very highbrow affair. You know the kind—evening gown and gloves and all that. And I'd been drinking . . ."

She paused and several seconds went by before I realized she'd come to a full stop. Expectancy hung in the air.

I said nothing, waiting.

Ladbrooke contemplated her hands, holding them both up in front of her.

"I didn't think I really had a drinking problem then," she said. "I suppose I did, if I think back on it, but it wasn't significantly interfering with my lifestyle. A few people had said things to me about it, but nothing too serious. Or at least I didn't take them too seriously."

Selecting a fingernail, she chewed it, the sound of her teeth audible to me.

"At this dinner . . . I was, what would you call it? . . . flirting I guess, with my advisor, with the man who'd been my advisor when I was a grad student, but who was the project leader then. I really had had too much to drink. I'd been miserably anxious, miserably worried about making a good impression at that dinner, because it was so important. I'd started drinking in the afternoon so I'd be calm enough to get ready. I don't remember how much I'd had by the time I got there, but it was enough. And then, of course, we were all drinking once the thing started. First the predinner cocktail party. And then the wine and all that.

"Anyway, I began flirting with my advisor. His wife was there. All of them had their wives or girlfriends with them, you see. I was the only woman on the project. Five days a week it was just me and the guys. But here, at this dinner, it was all the guys and their sweeties. And me on my own. I didn't have Tom with me. He was back here. He was busy. So I was alone.

"John's wife, of all people, was sitting right across the table from me. That's what got me started, I think. Although God knows. Anyway, I started doing all these silly things to get John's attention, to make him acknowledge me, but he wouldn't. I think it was because his wife was there. I wasn't really jealous of her. I mean, after all, *I* was the one he was sleeping with, so I had nothing to be jealous about. No, what it was, was that he was treating me *like* his wife. Like I was just one of the decorations and not a colleague. I guess what I wanted, if I'm honest, was for him to show the other women I wasn't one of them. I wasn't just a pretty face. I was there because I'd earned a place there. I was an equal. And that's what I wanted, to be treated like that."

Dead silence followed.

"What happened next?" I asked.

Still the silence.

"I'm embarrassed to talk about this," she said finally.

"You don't have to, you know."

"I do have to. I need to hear myself say this. It's like the first time I ever told anyone I was an alcoholic. Some things you just need to hear yourself say."

She let out a long breath.

"What I did . . . and this really makes me sound awful . . . but what I did was this kind of striptease. I thought that for every five minutes that went by and John didn't acknowledge me, I was going to take something off. I thought, if that's the only way he knows how to relate to me, then that's what I'm going to do. I know it doesn't make any sense sober, but it made a hell of a lot of sense to me at that point. I was feeling really angry. And the longer we sat there, the angrier I got. He made me feel like trash. There I was, a full member of the project team. Maybe I was a junior member, but I *was* a member. I'd earned my place. And not by being fucked behind the filing cabinet, either. I'd *worked*. And yet, he was treating me like I was no more than his bit on the side. I kept thinking, if that's the way he wants it, I can play that part too . . ."

"So I did. I had gloves on. I took them off. I had a necklace on. I took that off. I had my hair up. I took the pins out. This little pile of things was accumulating beside me as the meal progressed. And people certainly started noticing, once my hair came down. Then I took the jacket to my evening gown off . . ."

She sat up abruptly. She was blushing. With one hand, she gingerly touched the skin along one cheekbone. Then she put her hands over her face and rubbed her eyes. "I shouldn't have had that coffee. Now I feel sick." Lowering her hands slowly, she pressed her fingertips against her lips a moment before taking them away and looking at them. "See? I'm shaking."

Silence came, and it grew very, very long.

At last she sank back into the cushions on the couch. She sighed. "If you're wondering what happened that night, what happened at that dinner, suffice it to say that a lot of people forgot they'd come for an awards ceremony. I got the attention I was wanting so much."

She glanced over, and I nodded.

"I've got to admit, I don't even remember what all happened. What I do remember is so incredibly humiliating that I hate to even think what I might have gotten up to that I don't know about. I remember John taking me out of the room. And I remember getting sick all over the sidewalk outside, but that's about all, until the next morning, when I woke up in the apartment of this other guy on the project. God knows how I got there. I hardly knew him, which makes it worse, because I can just imagine what might have happened. Anyway, I couldn't go back. Not after embarrassing John and the others in front of everybody. How could I? And I sure never told Tom. In the end, I just withdrew from the project. I came back here, wrote out my resignation and never returned. That seemed the only alternative."

Silence.

Ladbrooke blew out a long breath. "So, now you really know what kind of stupid booby you've gotten lumbered with."

"I can see where that must have been pretty horrific, all right."

Lad sighed again. "It took me two years to come to the point where I could bear even thinking about it. This is the first time I've tried to talk about it with someone else. It was the most embarrassing thing I've ever done."

A rueful smile touched her lips. She cast a long, sideways glance in my direction and caught my eye. "Well, of course there was what I did in your room."

I grinned, and the tension eased off abruptly.

"I suppose what happened in your room wasn't as bad," she said. "At least it was less public. But I think I felt about as bad, because there was no way of escaping from it. I wanted to die then, that time in with you."

She brought her hand up and thoughtfully chewed the thumbnail.

"I don't remember very much about that day. I'd been drinking from about 6:15 in the morning. I hadn't been able to sleep at all the night before, and all I remember was needing courage to face you. Everything else is pretty hazy. Up until I got sick. I sure remember throwing up everywhere. The *look* on your face when I did . . ." She smiled slightly then and looked over. The smile became teasingly affectionate.

I grinned again.

"You were a picture, Torey. You really were."

I blushed.

"And you and those damned floor cloths . . ." She chuckled. "It's probably not funny. I never expected to be laughing about it. Not in a million years. I was so terrified of you. You'd said, 'You're not going to be sick again?' and I'd said no. But I kept thinking, what if I am? I felt paralyzed, sitting there. And you had those floor cloths. You were very gentle about it, but there was no nonsense. There was no doubt who was in charge. I was thinking, it's like I'm just another kid. Which was all right. I think that's the precise moment it occurred to me, really occurred to me, that I needed to do something. Not earlier, not when I was sick—that was just humiliating—but then, with you and your floor cloths. I thought, I need this. I need somebody else to take control for a while. Because I just wasn't making it on my own. I needed to start over. I needed to grow up, because I don't think I ever really did it the first time."

Caught up in my own memories of the day, I was still smiling. "Do you remember threatening me with that lawsuit over my taking Leslie out of your car the day before? When you came into the room that next day, I thought you were going to kill me. No joking. You had death in your eyes. Do you remember that?"

"Sort of. I mean, I don't really. I remember having been angry with you, but that's about it. But Tom's reminded me about the lawsuit business, because we got charged for the call I made to the lawyer."

"You really did frighten me. I got a heck of a scare from that," I said.

"I scared you? You scared the shit out of me. Right from that very first day. Remember that? In the front office, when we couldn't get Leslie out of the car? I was scared to death of you. And remember that first meeting you set up for Tom and me, that first conference? I got so worried over it, I got sick. Tom was furious with me, but I just couldn't go. I couldn't face you. You scared me shitless."

Amazed, I looked over. "Why on earth—?"

She shrugged. "I don't know. Just the way you looked at me. It scared me. I felt like you saw right through me."

"I didn't."

She straightened up, stretched, ran her fingers through her hair, pushing it back over her shoulders. "I think you did," she replied. "And that was what was so frightening. But it's all right. I think I was ready to be seen through."

CHAPTER TWENTY-FIVE

"It wouldn't be like this in Ulster," Geraldine said, as she stared out the window. There was snow again, feet of it this time instead of inches. "Daddy'd have planted our broad beans by now."

"It snows in Ulster," Shamie replied.

"Not like this."

It was a spring snow, deep, heavy and wet, but uncannily beautiful. The drab grays and browns of a fading Western winter had disappeared under what looked like heavy-handed dollops of marshmallow creme. But it was impossible weather for driving. I had managed to make it to work all right, and the Lonrhos had a four-wheel-drive vehicle, but we were it. The buses carrying Dirkie and Mariana couldn't get through, and I didn't know what had happened to Lad and Leslie. I assumed they had been defeated by the snow, like practically everyone else. It was almost ten o'clock and they still hadn't arrived.

"Come on, you lot," I said. "Let's get back to work." The snowfall was proving an irresistible distraction that morning. Everyone kept pausing to look at it. The fact that there were so few of us made it even harder to keep things going as usual. "Come on," I said again and put my hand on Shamie's shoulder to guide him back to his chair.

"We'd have our garden all laid out by now," Geraldine said, as she sat down. "This is a silly place. You never know what's going to happen."

"I like it here," Shamie replied. "You can do lots more things than you can at home." He turned to me. "The trouble with Geraldine is that she thinks everything that happened in Ulster was good and everything that happens here is bad."

"It *was* good," Geraldine said.

"It *wasn't*. It wasn't, Geraldine. Where's your memory?"

"It *was*. We had our garden in by now. Daddy was making our garden."

"Garden?" Shamie cried. "Garden-schmarden, Geraldine. I get fed up with all your talk. Don't you remember it over there? What kind of place it was? We couldn't even go down to the playground anymore. Remember what it looked like after the riots? Was that good? And remember the cellars? Remember Colin in the cellars, making petrol bombs, and how Shemona got down there, got the petrol all over herself and cut her hand? Was that good, Geraldine?"

Geraldine's expression blackened.

"She could have been killed, Geraldine. And she was just a wee child. And your sister. She could have been killed, like Matthew was."

I could see tears glistening in Geraldine's eyes. Her expression had softened slightly; she was obviously most intent at that moment on not crying. She swallowed, sniffed softly, swallowed again. Shamie was watching her closely. His mood wasn't malicious, but I could tell he intended to make his point.

Although the tears hadn't fallen, Geraldine removed her glasses and wiped them from her eyes. She replaced her glasses. "I just want to go home," she said, her voice very small.

Shamie mellowed slightly. "It's nicer here, Geraldine," he said gently.

"I was going to have a wee bit of garden for myself. Daddy said."

"Maybe you can have a garden here. Maybe Auntie Bet'll let you."

"They don't have any garden at all."

"Well, maybe they could make one for you."

Geraldine wasn't going to be placated. She shook her head morosely.

Silence drifted down around us, soft as the snow beyond the window. Shamie looked down at the tabletop and his folder. Geraldine had her eyes squeezed shut to keep the tears back. Beside me, Shemona sat, watching the other two. We were on the opposite side of the table from Shamie and Geraldine and a couple of seats down, so we weren't directly across from them. Shemona, who was nearer to them than I, appeared to be listening intently to the conversation.

Shamie suddenly shook his head, as if still in conversation with someone. Then he looked at me. "I'm glad I'm here. It was no good there. All it was, was fighting."

"There's got to be fighting," Geraldine replied.

"Why? What good does it do? It just kills people."

"You've got to fight, Shamie. You've got to take revenge. People do you wrong, people take away what's yours, you've got to take revenge," Geraldine said, her voice quiet, as if she were stating a known fact.

"Revenge is for God to take. Not us."

Geraldine shook her head. "God's too slow."

Shamie didn't respond. Instead, he grew pensive. Clasping his hands together in an almost prayerful attitude, he brought them up and rested them against his lips. He stared, unseeing, ahead of him. I studied him as he sat. He was a good-looking kid, more beautiful than handsome, with his long lashes and his full, sensual lips. He had an artist's face. It was in keeping with his soul.

"You know what the worst part of it was, over there?" he asked, turning to look at me.

"What was that?"

"You're not free. You walk around free, but you're still not free. I remember once, last summer, when Mammy and Daddy took us for a picnic. We went to County Down, down to the lough, and my mammy had made a lunch and put it in the picnic basket with a blue cloth on it. And we put it on the ground and we had sandwiches and crisps and lemonade. I was watching the swans on the lough. The car radio was on, and we heard on the one o'clock news that the Provies had blown up a Land Rover with soldiers in it near Ballynahinch. We'd come through Ballynahinch. Brid gets travel sick, so we'd stopped in a lay-by there, and Mammy'd taken her over to sick up on the verge. And after we'd heard the news, I was looking out across the water, across the lough, at the swans. I was watching them, but I was seeing these soldiers, these dead soldiers in the Land Rover, with blood on them. Like this dog I saw once. After the riots when Bobby Sands had died. There was a dead dog. I don't know if he got run down or what, but he was dead in the street, lying in his own blood. It was dark, the blood was. Almost black, not red like what comes out of you when you cut yourself. It was blacky-red and soaked into the pavement. Except there were footprints made with his blood, where people had walked over him. Blacky-red footprints going down the street." Shamie shook his head. "I was looking at swans on the water and I was seeing this dead dog's blood."

Then, jarringly, we were interrupted by the noisy arrival of Ladbrooke and Leslie. The classroom door went bang and there they were, red cheeked and cheerful, clumping across the room in heavy boots, leaving a trail of melting snow in their wake. Lad was full of their adventure. They'd been involved in a minor traffic accident on the way to school. While no one had been hurt or even shaken up, it had necessitated tow trucks and police and a lengthy wait at the Mercedes garage. Ladbrooke and Leslie had walked to school from there and arrived, very excited by their experiences.

I regretted their intrusion. The three children almost never directly mentioned the Troubles or spoke of their former life in Belfast. There were odd, fragmented references shot back and forth amongst them, like coded messages, but they seldom included me when talking. And I was uncomfortable raising the topic when it did not come up naturally, partly

because I was at a disadvantage as a foreigner, and partly because there
had been so many traumatic consequences for these children, that I feared
I would lumber in, inadvertantly hurting more than I helped. But Ladbrooke and Leslie were there, wet and noisy and excited, and there wasn't
much I could do about it. Within moments the other children had caught
their high spirits. We went back to talking about snowstorms, and my
quiet interlude in Ulster was gone.

I alone seemed unable to pull myself away from Northern Ireland.
Throughout the day, the conversation kept coming back to me in snips
and snatches.

Out on the playground that afternoon, the children were going mad in
the deep snow. Carolyn and Joyce had come out too. They had only four
children in their class, so the day had taken on a holiday mood. Carolyn
got a game of Fox-and-Geese going with her children in which Leslie and
Shemona happily joined. Geraldine and Shamie, feeling themselves above
playing with preschoolers, kept apart. After constructing a crude snow
fort, Shamie began lofting snowballs at Ladbrooke, who returned fire with
unrestrained precision. Geraldine joined in, in a halfhearted way, but after
getting hit in the cross fire, she withdrew and came over to stand next to
me.

"Shamie likes her," Geraldine said in a rather disgruntled voice. She
seldom referred to Ladbrooke by name.

"Yes, I know."

"You know what else? He keeps that picture she drew, that one she
made on his spelling paper when he got 100 percent. He keeps it in his
bedroom drawer. By his bed. And then he takes it out and looks at it.
Sometimes he *kisses* it." Geraldine made a distasteful grimace. "He's in
love with her."

I smiled down at her.

"I think he's silly. She's a grown-up woman."

"Well, it's all right for him to feel that way."

"He thinks she's beautiful. He thinks she's beautifuller than you are."

"I suspect he's right."

"I don't think so," Geraldine said. "I think you're beautiful, Miss. I
think you're beautifuller than she is. You're nicer."

"Thank you, Geraldine. That's kind of you to say."

We stood together in affable silence, watching the others play. Geraldine took one hand out of her pocket and put it through the crook of
my arm. She leaned her head against me.

"You know what we were talking about this morning," I said, "when
we were talking about Ulster?"

Geraldine nodded.

"Shamie was saying how it was no good, all that fighting, how it wasn't getting anywhere. What do you think? Does the fighting there seem good to you?"

She didn't answer immediately. Then slowly, she shook her head. "No, Miss, it doesn't seem good."

"Does it seem right?"

Another thoughtful pause, then she shrugged. "I don't know. I think maybe it's right. Just because some things aren't good, doesn't mean they aren't right. You have to fight back. When somebody fights you, you have to fight back. You have to take revenge."

"You have to take revenge?"

She nodded.

"Do you think revenge is a good thing, Geraldine?"

She nodded again with no hesitation.

"Why?"

"Because it's justice."

I looked down at her. She was bareheaded, in spite of the cold weather. She was still watching the other children, still holding on to me, still leaning her head against my arm. I regarded her dark, shiny hair.

"What *is* justice, do you think?" I asked.

No answer. She just stood.

"Do you know what justice is, Geraldine?"

"Yes, Miss."

"What?"

"What you take revenge for."

Taking my hand from my jacket pocket, I put my arm around her, drawing her closer to me. She put her arm around my waist. I was silent a moment, watching Shamie and Ladbrooke. They had grown exuberant in their game, and snowballs were zinging back and forth at a remarkable rate. Ladbrooke had a childlike quality about her that allowed her to enter into the kids' games as an equal, and the children always accepted her as such. On such occasions, she could become very free spirited, but it made her noisy. I tried to catch her eye and signal her to move away from Geraldine and me a little, but she was too absorbed to notice.

"I'm not so sure revenge is a good thing," I said to Geraldine. "I think maybe it's just an excuse to hurt someone else and not feel guilty for having done it."

"No," she replied.

"Someone hurts us and it makes us angry, so we want to hurt them back. But then, after we've done it, afterwards, what's been accomplished? Nothing. It's just another name for violence. And it's a particularly wicked kind of violence, to my mind, because it's been thought through first and not just done in the heat of the moment. In taking revenge, one's set out only to destroy, and that seems evil to me."

"But the soldiers kill children," Geraldine replied. "My daddy showed me pictures of children who were shot by rubber bullets. He said the soldiers didn't care if they killed women or babies or little girls. So he said it was right to kill them in revenge."

I pondered what to say.

"He said that because he's my daddy. He didn't want them to kill me."

"But do *you* think it's right to kill in revenge?"

"It's what my daddy said."

"But *you*, what do *you* think?"

Geraldine sighed. She pressed closer to me, sighed again. There was a small silence, cluttered with the noise of the others playing.

"I don't know. I didn't used to think it was right. I used to think like Shamie did—you know—that they shouldn't keep doing all those things, all that hurting." A pause. It grew lengthy. "Then Mammy and Matthew got killed."

"Did that change your mind?"

She didn't answer immediately. "I don't know. I don't think so. It just made it seem more wrong."

I watched Shamie running and laughing.

"Then my daddy died."

"And that changed your mind?"

She nodded. "Revenge is what my daddy wanted. It's what you do when you're a grown-up. You see, you understand everything then. It's what you do. And I'm the oldest now, so I must do it."

Shemona's birthday was at the end of March. In other years, I'd always made a big fuss of the children's birthdays and usually my own as well, just to give us the excuse for celebration. Our special classes were often excluded from participating in the activities that regular classes enjoyed, such as fun fairs, school plays, music programs and the like, and this went a ways toward assuaging the deficit. More importantly, I wanted to celebrate the sheer existence of my children, to give them tangible evidence of their worth. However, with this group, the calendar worked against us. Shamie and Geraldine had early autumn birthdays, which had already passed by the time they joined the class. Mariana's birthday was Christmas Eve. Leslie's was on Easter Sunday. Ladbrooke's was in late July. That left only Shemona and me with birthdays falling on school days, and since mine was in May, Shemona had the honor of having the first birthday we encountered.

Because of the unusual number of out-of-school birthdays, I was uncertain whether or not to make a big event of Shemona's. On one hand, it didn't seem fair to the others if we had a special party just for her. I was also concerned that Shemona might not want all that attention focused so conspicuously on herself. She was a self-conscious child, and I would have been sorry if something meant to please her had been overshadowed by uncomfortable embarrassment. On the other hand, it seemed a nice way to make her feel special, as being the smallest, quietest member of the group, she was often overlooked or excluded from the other children's activities. Plus, we needed some merry-making. In the peculiar constraints of being one of only two classes in the administration building, not only had we no chance to participate in the assemblies, plays and programs that provided variety in a normal school, we couldn't even watch them. Thus there had been no break in routine since the Nativity play.

I broached the subject on Monday. Shemona's birthday was on the following Friday. The children were thrilled with the idea of a party, any kind of party, and assured me they wouldn't mind if Shemona was guest of honor. Shemona, however, as I had feared, seemed overwhelmed by the sudden attention. She ducked her head when I first mentioned her birthday. As the conversation progressed, she brought an arm up to hide her face, looking very much like a small bird, trying to tuck its head under its wing.

Watching her, I decided to ease off the idea of making it a birthday party and concentrate more on its just being a bit of a celebration for us all. Shemona remained withdrawn throughout the entire discussion, and I couldn't see the point of embarrassing her further. So we talked instead of food and games, and the other things we had to celebrate. The children left morning discussion in high spirits, and the prospect of the upcoming party remained a favorite topic of conversation for the remainder of the week.

That afternoon, when Lad and I were leaving the teachers' lounge after our recess break, we found Shemona outside the door. There were still three or four minutes left before the children were due back inside, so it came as a surprise to find her there, especially as she was not supposed to be in the building unsupervised.

"Hey," I said, when I saw her, "what are you doing here?"

She looked up, a rather bewildered expression on her face. She still didn't talk easily to me. Since she was standing outside the teachers' lounge, I could only assume she was waiting for us; however, now that she had found us, she seemed rather unsure what to do. I nudged Lad.

Ladbrooke knelt down to Shemona's level. "Did you want something from us, Shemona?"

Shemona shook her head.

"You aren't really supposed to be here, you know. It's recess time," Lad said. Then she rose and put her hand behind Shemona's head. "Well, come on, let's go back upstairs to the room."

Whatever it was Shemona wanted, we didn't find out then. She walked back to the classroom with us but never said a word.

It wasn't until the following afternoon, when I again found her lurking, this time after school. Ladbrooke was still down on the playground, seeing the children to their rides, and I'd stayed upstairs to put things away. I was in among the stacks in the library where I stored work for the students. Out of the corner of my eye, I caught movement. I turned my head to see what it was and saw nothing. Back again to what I was doing, I started taking down the papers from the high shelf. Movement again. And once more I paused and looked. And once more, nothing. This time I feigned involvement.

Shemona appeared at the end of the aisle. Lunch box in hand, coat disheveled, knees scabbed, socks fallen, hair straggly, stringy and the washed-out color of wax beans, she regarded me. She never looked any different, no matter how new her clothes were or how clean Mrs. Lonrho had scrubbed her before she came to school. She persisted in being one of the grubbiest-looking children I had ever had, sort of a leprechaun version of *Peanuts'* Pigpen. But there was something poignant about it.

"Did you want something?" I asked.

She came down the aisle until she was standing very near to me. She looked up, her head cocked slightly to the side, like a sparrow's.

We regarded one another silently.

"Will there be a birthday cake for me, Miss?" she asked at last.

"If you want one."

"I want a birthday party, Miss."

I smiled. Coming down to her level, I touched her arm. "Did you think it wasn't going to be for you, our party? It is. It's your birthday, isn't it?"

"With a birthday cake?"

"Yes, with a birthday cake."

"With candles on it?"

"Yes."

"Six candles?"

"Yes, with six candles."

"Will you sing 'Happy Birthday, dear Shemona' to me?"

"Yes."

She nodded then, and a very small smile came to her face. "Okay, Miss," she said and turned, went back down the aisle and disappeared out the classroom door.

I felt obliged then to have a real, proper birthday party. Over the lunch hour on Friday, I hung streamers and balloons. It was hard to do with the high ceilings and the metal shelving, but by the time the forty-five minute period had passed, I'd transformed the room into something that, if not designer perfect, was at least festive.

Ladbrooke was providing the cake. I'd hoped she would stay at lunchtime and give me the benefit of her height, putting up the decorations, which would have made the job a lot easier, but she insisted on going home because she hadn't wanted to bring the cake in the morning.

She returned about fifteen minutes before the afternoon session resumed. Setting down the cardboard box she was carrying, Ladbrooke removed the cake. I came over from where I'd been arranging paper cups and plates.

This was no ordinary cake. Indeed, it was quite unlike anything I had ever seen before. It was more-or-less round, covered with bumpy yellow icing and had a very definite angle to it—sort of a cake version of the Leaning Tower of Pisa. Happy Birthday Shemona was spelled out across the top with M&M's.

Ladbrooke regarded it after setting it out on the table. "I made it myself," she said, her voice uncertain.

This was nothing you would mistake for a bakery cake, but I didn't say that.

Ladbrooke continued to study it. She rotated the plate so that the angle of the top layer was not quite so apparent. "I should have bought it." She rotated the plate again. "This looks terrible."

"No, it's okay."

"It isn't, Torey. It looks like a yellow cow pat."

Indeed, it did rather.

"I'm sure it tastes just fine. That's all that matters."

"Do you think she'll mind?" Ladbrooke looked over at me. "I could go out at recess and buy something better."

"No. Shemona's not going to mind. She won't even notice. All she'll see is that you've made a birthday cake for her, and it has six candles on it. That's all that matters."

And it was all that mattered. Cake on the table, juice in the cups, Care Bear plates and napkins, all the trappings were there. We lit the candles and sang "Happy Birthday" to Shemona with loving gusto. She hid her face with her hands and peeked out through her fingers. And she loved every minute of it.

Afterward, we played games, sang songs, dressed each other up with clothes from the dressing-up box, toasted one another and ourselves with orange juice. No one seemed to mind at all that this party was for Shemona and that no one else would have the chance that year to be the center of attention.

In all the years and with all the children I had had, this turned out to be one of the most joyous parties I'd ever participated in. There were no fights, no tears, no disappointments, nothing to dilute the pleasure. As with the Nativity play, it came as close to a completely happy occasion as was reasonable to expect.

This gave me pause to wonder. At one point midafternoon, when the others were slipping hats and coats from the dressing-up box on one another, laughing and squealing and posturing in front of the mirror, I found myself apart, watching them, and I pondered this matter. Why this group? Why should they be so extraordinarily gifted at catching happiness? They were a motley crew by anyone's standards, a duke's mixture of backgrounds, ages and circumstances. There were no especially bright stars among them, no one with outstanding promise. Yet, of all the groups I'd been with throughout the years, it was this small, diverse band who seemed most able to shuck off troubled individuality and come together as a perfect whole.

After the party, Ladbrooke and I were left with the mess. And there was one. We'd gotten pretty high spirited by the end, and there were spills and scraps of food and popped balloons everywhere. I went down to Bill's closet to get a dustpan and broom. Ladbrooke climbed up on the table to start taking down the decorations.

"That was really good fun," she said to me, when I returned.

"Yes, Shemona loved it. Did you see the way she was dancing, there at the end?"

"It was the first birthday party she's ever had. She told me that." There was a brief pause while Ladbrooke stretched up to get a streamer just out of reach. She still couldn't quite get hold of it, so she jumped and snagged it. "They seemed to eat the cake okay. I was worried. I don't know what got into me, thinking I could make one."

"It was okay. It tasted good."

"Well, it's the thought that counts, isn't it?" she said. "I really wanted to do something special for Shemona. And it wouldn't have been the same if I'd just gone out and bought a cake. You know what I mean?"

I nodded.

Ladbrooke smiled down at me. "I had a good time, making that cake. I was up till all hours. You ought to have seen me, there with all the pans out and everything. Consuela thought I'd lost my ever-loving mind. She kept saying, 'I can do it, Mee-sus.' I should have let her. But I was having fun."

She jumped down from the table. Pausing beside me, she leaned down, picked up one of the fallen crepe-paper streamers and began to wind it up. "All the time I was doing it, I was thinking of Shemona, of how excited it was going to make her. I mean, you'd have to make a cake for a kid like that, wouldn't you? You couldn't buy it." Then Lad fell silent. She continued to wind the streamer, but more slowly. "I really like Shemona," she said softly.

"Yes, I know."

She stopped what she was doing altogether then and just held the streamer. She was standing very close to me. If I'd shifted feet, we would have been touching. "I'm going to tell you something really horrible," she said quietly.

"What's that?"

"I love Shemona."

"That's not so horrible."

She began to reel in the streamer again. "It is," she said after a considerable pause, "because I think I love her more than I do Leslie."

I glanced over at her and smiled, but she wasn't looking in my direction.

"If it were anybody else but you, I don't think I'd even dare say that aloud. It's horrible to admit, even to myself, because Leslie is my own child." She paused. "It's just that . . . it's just that . . . well . . . Shemona's so *normal*. I look at her and I see . . . what? I see myself. I remember being five and six so clearly. I remember all those feelings. It's so easy to want to do things for her, to make her happy. It makes me feel good. You understand any of that?"

I nodded.

"But then I just wither with guilt. Because Leslie never makes me feel like that. I mean, my cat's more responsive to me than Leslie is. I feel like she doesn't care if I'm there or not. It could be anybody getting her food for her or wiping her butt. But then . . . I don't know."

"I wouldn't worry about it," I said.

"That's because you don't have any children."

"No. It's because I expect they're entirely normal feelings. And there's nothing particularly wrong with them."

The streamer had tangled at the end, and in the process of shaking it out, Ladbrooke shifted her weight. She was still standing very close to me, and this change of position pushed our upper arms into contact. For the first time, she did not instantly jerk away. She remained against me for a moment. Turning her head, she gazed down at our arms, then she shifted only very slightly to separate us by an inch or two. She continued to gaze in that direction, so I looked down too, wondering if she saw something there. Ladbrooke remained stone still, the streamer motionless in her hand.

Several seconds' silence followed before she glanced up at me briefly, an unreadable expression in her eyes. Then once again she looked down at the space between us.

"I've never touched another woman," she said. Ladbrooke spoke with such quiet awe that it made her sound as if she'd just tried to rape me. She glanced back at my face and caught my surprise. This appeared to disconcert her, and she moved away from me.

"I've never liked women to touch me," she said, her voice still quiet.

I regarded her.

"I've never liked women."

I didn't reply.

"I've never liked being a woman," she said softly. "When I was pregnant with Leslie, I prayed she'd be a boy. I never wanted a girl. I think maybe if she'd been a boy I could have coped better. I think I might have known more what to do with her, if only she'd been a boy."

I continued to watch her.

She turned away. Laying the streamer on the table, she walked around and to the window. Putting her hands deep into her pockets, she leaned forward and gazed out. A silence grew up between us. Taking out a chair at the table, I sat down. I pulled over the half-wound streamer and started doing it myself.

She was nervous as well. She shifted restlessly back and forth, from foot to foot. All the while she kept her back to me.

"Have I ever talked about my mom?" she asked at last.

"Not much."

"She died a couple of years ago. When I was thirty-one."

"Oh."

"We were a small family—just my mom, my two brothers and me. She kept marrying and divorcing, so there were fathers occasionally, but not usually. They never lasted. Usually, there were just the four of us."

I finished the streamer and taped the end. Then I surveyed the table, still cluttered with the aftermath of the birthday party. Rumpled napkins, dirty paper plates, empty cups were everywhere.

"And then she died. Cancer of the stomach. I remember my younger brother, Kitson, calling me and telling me. He'd been with her at the end. I can remember hanging up the phone afterward. I hung it up and thought to myself, well, that's that. I didn't cry. I didn't even feel bad, really. I guess if anything, I felt relief, because at last all the hassles were over."

She turned around and looked at me then. Hands still deep in the pockets of her jeans, she leaned back against the radiator and studied my face.

"I did feel bad, after it sank in, but mainly for myself, because suddenly I felt old. Mortal, you know? There was no generation above me any longer, no one standing between me and death. But as for my mother herself, I must confess, I felt absolutely nothing."

Ladbrooke paused then, her expression growing introspective. She looked down in the direction of her shoes. "I suppose I must have loved her once, but I don't remember when. By the time she'd died, I'd long since stopped. I hadn't seen her in years. All we ever had in common was my father's last name."

Silence washed in around us. I was wondering what had brought up this powerful bit of memory, whether it had been such a minor thing as bumping against my arm, or if it was more directly connected with Ladbrooke's uneasy feelings about Shemona and Leslie. Or both.

Once again she studied me in that very thorough, unabashed way she had. As always, I found myself having to look away, unable to maintain such long eye contact.

"You know, you're actually the only other woman I've ever known. I've never had any women friends, not even any girlfriends when I was younger. We didn't invite kids home, Bobby, Kit and me. You never knew what my mother was going to be up to, so it was just safer not to. Consequently, I never really had friends. I had my brothers, but that was about it.

"And you're so different from my mom. It's not at all like I expected it to be. It's so different. I've never been close to a woman before.

"I was never close to my mother. My brothers were closer, but I never was. She never touched me. She never put her arms around me. She said women didn't do that kind of thing with each other. She said it turned her stomach to think of kissing another woman on the lips. I can remember once trying to kiss her like that. I was maybe ten or something, and she was absolutely disgusted by it. She didn't like to kiss me. She didn't like having to touch me."

Lad shifted feet. She shifted again, then boosted herself up to sit on the radiator. She leaned forward, elbows on knees, chin in hands. Her gaze scanned the room for several seconds, regarding the table, the shelving, the kids' work on the bulletin board. The very soft, rhythmic thud of her jogging shoes swinging against the side of the radiator filled the silence.

"When I was younger, when I was in my early twenties, I used to think about it constantly. I had this professor in my senior year at college. I didn't know her or anything; I never saw her outside class or her office, but I really liked her. She helped me a lot getting into graduate school, and I really liked her. And I remember wanting to touch her. It scared the hell out of me, because I thought I must be a lesbian or something. And I wanted her to touch me. You know, just touch me. You know, put her hands on me. And it scared me shitless."

Ladbrooke paused. Lowering her hands, she regarded them. "I used to try and picture my mother taking care of me when I was a baby. You know, picking me up, holding me, playing with me. I mean, she must have done it. I was just a baby and there was no one else there. But I always wondered if she did it like I remember her doing with Kitson, if she held me like that. Or if it was different because I was a girl."

She was sitting on her hands. "It was probably like me with Leslie. Tom is right, you know. About the way I treated Leslie. He isn't exaggerating. I've been a terrible mother. Because, you see, I couldn't hold her. I really couldn't. And I couldn't bear the thought of nursing her, of having her touch my breasts. I took care of her and stuff. Of course I did. I mean, you have no choice with a baby. But thank God for Tom, for what he did for her, because I just couldn't make myself hold her. I couldn't just pick her up to hold her. I had to put her down, to get her away from me, even if it made her cry."

CHAPTER TWENTY-SIX

April. The long Easter weekend occurred only a few days into the month. I had an old friend from my days in Minnesota coming for the three-day break, and I was anticipating his arrival enthusiastically. We'd been colleagues in Minneapolis. He'd worked as one of my research assistants on my elective-mutism project, and we'd shared almost three years together on the front lines. It had been a good, wildly workaholic period in my life, when all I'd lived for were the kids and the research. Tim had been a major part of the fond memories I had of those years.

The school day had just ended when Tim arrived. It was Thursday afternoon before Good Friday, and after taking the children down to their rides, I'd gone into the teachers' lounge to run off some material for the following week on the ditto machine. When I returned to the second floor, there was Tim, standing in the hallway outside the classroom. I whooped joyfully when I saw him, and he responded with a booming hello, his deep, masculine voice echoing loudly in the empty hall. Then he caught me up in a bear hug that lifted me right off the floor.

"You're early," I said, when he put me down.

"Yeah. The traffic was all right. I wanted to come up and see your room. Hoped to see your kids."

"Sorry, they're all gone. They get out at 3:30."

His eyebrows twitched with sly interest. "Who's she?" He jerked his head toward the classroom door. "The Valkyrie."

I grinned. "My aide."

Tim rolled his eyes. "How do you get them? Where do you find people that look like that? You're always going around with a horde of tall, blond women behind you."

I laughed. When I'd worked in Minnesota, I'd had another research assistant, who, if anything, was taller and blonder than Lad. She, like

Tim, had been with me several years. Cindy and I had been christened "the Amazons" by one of the more roguish male psychiatrists in the department, and the nickname had dogged us the rest of our time together.

"I hardly had a horde, Tim. You're thinking of Cindy, aren't you? She makes one. Lad makes two. That's not what I'd call a horde."

He grinned. "I only wish *I* had your knack. That's horde enough for me."

"She's married, Tim. Forget it."

Opening the classroom door, we went in. I introduced Tim to Ladbrooke, who was working at the table. They'd already met, because he'd come into the classroom while I was downstairs, and she'd aimed him in the direction of the teachers' lounge, but he was quite happy for a formal introduction.

I sat down at the table to staple the dittoes together, as I needed to have them ready before I could leave. Tim meandered around the room, looking at the children's work on display and asking about them. Lad, I noticed, didn't go back to work. She'd been designing some math worksheets for Shamie and now just sat with the pencil and ditto master lying in front of her. Finally, she shuffled them all together.

"I think I'll go now," she said.

"Don't feel like you have to leave, Ladbrooke," I replied, surprised. "Tim's just a friend."

Ladbrooke rose from the chair. "No. I need to get home. I've got tons to do."

I looked up at her. I hadn't meant the day to end like this. Not having anticipated Tim's arrival in the classroom, I'd left things between Lad and me until the end. I needed to talk to her to make arrangements for the long weekend. We were still getting together every Sunday, and this was going to be the first major disruption to that routine since the February binge. She'd stayed dry since then, so I wanted to make definite plans to get her through the three-day break. I'd had no intention of letting her get away without settling this matter.

She put her things away in the filing cabinet and went to get her jacket. Tim was aware something was going on; he glanced back and forth between us. Finally, I got up.

"If you'll excuse us a minute," I said to him, and went out into the hallway with Ladbrooke. I shut the door firmly behind us. "Look, what do you want to do about this weekend?" I asked her.

She had a reserved expression on her face. There was distance between us. I'd noticed that on other occasions when I'd had friends stop by the classroom. "I can make it okay this weekend," she said.

"Let's get together."

"Sunday's Leslie's birthday. Tom's mother'll be down."

"Well, Saturday then."

She shook her head. "No, let's just leave it. I want to try it on my own. I'll be okay."

"You're not going to interrupt anything, Lad. We can go out if you don't want to come over with Tim there."

"It's just three days, Torey. I can manage. Don't make me feel like I can't."

Silence came between us, and we regarded one another for a long moment. Then Ladbrooke zipped her jacket and turned. "Anyway, I'll see you."

I reached out and caught hold of her arm. "If there's any sort of problem at all, call me, Ladbrooke." Her muscles tensed under my grip, but I didn't let go. "I mean it. This is platonic between me and Tim. If you call me, you won't be interrupting anything."

She nodded but remained poised to go.

I kept my hold a moment longer, wanting to tell her not to do anything stupid, not to ruin all these weeks of hard work, but I held my tongue. It wouldn't sound as if I had much faith in her, if I said that. So I let go and just said good-bye.

When I came back into the room, Tim looked over, his expression questioning. That'd always been his most striking characteristic: He never missed a thing.

I shrugged. "It's a little different this time. She isn't Cindy. She's one of the kids."

It was a great weekend. I hadn't seen Tim in almost three years, but back together, it was almost as if we had never been apart. We spent the entire three days reminiscing like a couple of little old grannies, reconstructing and reliving the years we'd spent sharing a cramped, windowless office that had still borne the scars of its former life as a shock-treatment room.

Ladbrooke never rang. Except for talking about her situation with Tim during a conversation on Sunday afternoon, I hadn't thought about her throughout the long weekend. And even when Tim and I had been discussing her, it had been in a detached, professional manner, the way one does when sharing case notes with a colleague. I hadn't had time to think of Ladbrooke herself at all, until Monday morning, when it occurred to me as I was standing in front of the mirror and brushing my hair that I hadn't heard from her. The thought was accompanied by a sinking feeling. I just knew I wasn't going to see her when I got to school. But I was wrong, because there she was, looking particularly well scrubbed with her long hair pulled back into a ponytail and her sleeves rolled up. From the extent to which she had her work spread around her at the table, she'd clearly been in for some time before my 7:30 arrival.

"You look busy," I said, and took off my jacket to hang it on the hook.

"It's just the stuff I hadn't gotten around to on Thursday. I thought I'd better get in and do it."

And then, between us, the unasked question. And it stayed unasked. We made small talk. We got the materials out. We prepared the room for the children. I went down for a cup of coffee, stopped by to say hi to the gang in the front office, had a moment's chat with Frank. Ladbrooke ran some dittoes. But neither one of us volunteered any information on the weekend.

After school, Carolyn brought us some gerbils for the class. Hers, in her classroom, had a prodigious sex life, resulting in a phenomenal number of offspring, and she was unloading them on everybody. I'd been out of the room when she'd come up with them and returned to find Ladbrooke cooing into a box. Dismayed because Carolyn had not asked me if I wanted them, especially this close to the end of the school year, I huffed off to rummage around in one of the storage rooms to find some kind of cage. At last I located an absolutely filthy one. Running a sink full of soapy water, I attempted to clean it up. Ladbrooke sat at the table with the gerbils, lifting them out of the box, caressing them with her fingertips, pressing furry little heads against her cheek.

It took me about thirty-five minutes to deguck the stupid cage, by which point I had some choice words for Carolyn. The whole time I worked, Ladbrooke played with the gerbils.

"You wouldn't want to take those creatures home with you?" I asked, the sarcasm not too disguised.

But that sort of wit was wasted on Ladbrooke. Nose to nose with one of the animals, she smiled at it. "No, Tom'd kill me. He doesn't like little mousy things."

I thunked the dripping cage down onto the table. "Well, here. Chuck some of that shredded newspaper in, because I'm as ready for them as I'm ever going to be. Are they both the same sex? Did Carolyn say? They'd better be."

Ladbrooke rose up with the one she'd been playing with still in her hand. She picked up the cardboard box containing the other one with her free hand. Apparently sensing a return to captivity, the one she was holding made its break for freedom. Like a little furry pinball, it shot out of Ladbrooke's hand and across the table. Before she could catch it, it had gone off the end of the table, down onto the floor and was away under the shelves of the library.

"Oh, for crying out loud, Ladbooke!" I yelled.

Catching a frantic gerbil in a room with five rows of industrial shelving is no mean feat. Even with two of us, the gerbil persisted in outmaneuvering us. I'd been very annoyed initially. It was late in the day; cleaning the cage had been unpleasant work; and I hadn't wanted the gerbils in the first place. Having to spend twenty minutes chasing one of the damned things was not my idea of a good time. However, as the two of us scrambled after it, the humor of the situation overcame me. It was like a scene out of the Keystone Kops, and I was soon in hysterics.

"I've got him cornered, Torey," Lad finally said. She was down at the far end of the last row of shelving. "He's back under here. Bring the cage."

Grabbing the cage, I went down the aisle and knelt beside her. Prone, with her chin on the floor, Ladbrooke reached under the shelving unit.

"I've got him!" she cried triumphantly, grinning, as she pulled the gerbil from under the shelves. I held open the cage door, and in the animal went. With a gasp of exaggerated exhaustion, Ladbrooke flopped back against the wall. "Whew!"

I sat down, cross-legged, with the gerbil cage in my lap. We'd exerted ourselves in the chase; Ladbrooke's forehead glistened with perspiration. My heartbeat was still fast. It had all been made worse because we were laughing so hard toward the end.

Ladbrooke was still smiling. She shook her head. "You'd never know we were grown women," she said.

"We'd have caught it in half the time if we hadn't been laughing like a couple of hyenas."

"You started it," she said.

"Me? Who let the cussed thing go?"

"Yeah, but you started laughing, you nitwit. If you hadn't started, I wouldn't have."

I grinned.

There came between us a gentle silence. Putting the cage on the floor, I prepared to stand up.

"What am I going to do without you?" Lad asked. Her tone was affectionate.

I rose and lifted the cage. "Probably not bust a gut chasing gerbils. You know, I'm half mad at Carolyn. I never said I was going to take any of these. She knew better than to bring them up when I was in the room."

There was silence. I held the cage high and peered in at the two animals, busily rearranging the shredded newspaper.

"I mean it, Torey," Ladbrooke said, and the tone of her voice had changed. "How am I going to survive without you?"

I looked down at her.

"We've got nine weeks left. I was counting them over the weekend. There's only nine weeks till the end of school."

The shift in mood was so abrupt it was wrenching.

"How am I going to survive? How am I going to make it, when you're gone? That's only two months."

Our physical positions accentuated her words. She'd remained sitting on the floor, her arms around her drawn-up legs. I was standing over her, my pale shadow cast across her face.

"Things'll be different in two months," I said.

She regarded me, unconvinced.

"Two months is a fair amount of time for some things, Lad. You'll feel differently about it than you do now. Besides, I'm not about to leave you in the lurch. I wouldn't; you know that."

"I don't want to go back to my life the way it was," she said quietly. "It was okay then because it never had been different. But now I want it to be like this. I'm happy now. In a lot of ways, this has been the hardest year of my whole life, but it's been the best too. I'm happy."

"Good, I'm glad."

She looked up again. "I don't want to end up with these months being the only happy ones ever."

"They won't be." I reached a hand down to her to encourage her to get up. "Come on, Lad."

She remained sitting. "I don't think you understand what it's like."

Putting the cage on the floor, I sat back down myself.

She didn't continue.

"Was it a hard weekend?" I asked.

She bit her lower lip and did not look over at me. Slowly, she nodded.

"Did you drink?"

"No."

"Good job."

"I made it. I made it through the entire weekend. But just barely."

I smiled. "But you did make it."

She still wasn't looking at me. "All this weekend did was scare me, Torey. All I kept thinking was, if this is what three days is like, what's it going to be like after June?"

"You're still expecting too much of yourself, Lad."

"Three days? When *can* I expect three days of myself?"

"It's not the time that's important. It's the expectations. You're expecting three days at home to be like three days in here, and they're not going to be. It's going to go in stages, and the first stage is always going to be just getting through, which emotionally, is going to feel like very, very little improvement over not getting through at all. But despite how it feels, it's a huge step, maybe the biggest step. You're doing okay, Lad. Don't keep making these situations into tests. We'll sort things out by June. Don't worry about it."

"What are you going to do? Stay here? Take me with you? 'Hi, Ken, don't mind me. I'm just a little someone Torey's brought along on the honeymoon.' " She smiled, saying that, her tone more good-natured than antagonistic, but I knew she wasn't joking.

"Trust me a bit longer, would you? Let me do the worrying. There're nine weeks left. Let's not ruin them panicking over Week Ten."

She nodded. "Yes, okay." She shifted position in preparation to rise. "But I expect that'll be much easier for you than for me."

I had to admit Ladbrooke's future was occupying my mind as well. The long Easter weekend had brought the issue to the forefront during my discussion with Tim, although for some time I'd been mulling it over. Tim had said the obvious thing to me. If she still needed therapy, she needed a new therapist. That was all there was to it. Ah, I'd replied, if it were only that easy. Was making up my dittoes, baking birthday cakes and having endless, patient conversations with Dirkie over the color of cats, therapy? And if so, should I pack her off to the mental health clinic or to the university to get a special education degree? And was fetching her home at two in the morning or eating her canned spaghetti, therapy? Or was it simply friendship? And what, in fact, had Ladbrooke needed more? Tim had smiled then in a thoughtful way. What was therapy anyway, he'd replied, except professional friendship? This comment caused the two of us to grow philosophical, and we digressed into discussing the kind of world we'd ended up in, where one had to buy caring relationships.

Still, nine weeks *was* a fair amount of time. I wasn't being facile when I'd said that to Ladbrooke. A lot could happen. And the time had already come, I thought, when I could talk her into accepting alternate forms of help, if necessary. But that image of Ladbrooke sitting in my shadow was one to haunt me for a considerable time afterward. I wished I did have the power to make her happy, to keep her happy.

On Tuesday morning all three of the Irish contingent were in foul moods. Obviously, there had been some sort of scrap going on before they got to school, because they came in irritably silent, and there was much slamming and banging of things into cubbies. I asked Shamie what was going on, and he told me to ask Geraldine. I asked Geraldine, and she said it was none of my business. I asked Shemona, and she refused to answer.

Shemona seemed the most affected. As the morning wore on, she grew weepy and unwilling to leave her chair at the table. She wouldn't talk to either Ladbrooke or me. When I knelt beside her mid-morning, she cowered away.

"Are you feeling all right, lovey?" I asked.

"Tell Miss you're okay."

"Geraldine . . . I can talk to Shemona by myself, thank you."

Shemona's face dragged down in a grimace of tears.

"Tell Miss you're okay, Shemona, or she isn't going to leave us alone."

"*Geraldine.*"

"What it is, Miss, if you must know, is her toe. Shemona has a poorly toe."

"Oh," I said with some surprise. "May I have a look at it?"

Geraldine let out a long, world-weary sigh, implying a very particular type of denseness on my part. "She's not going to show it to you, Miss. She won't even show it to Auntie Bet. I'm the only one she shows things to, because I'm her sister."

I turned Shemona's chair so that she was facing me and bent to remove her shoe. "Here, let's take your shoe off, Shemona. Let's see what's the matter."

Shemona began to cry in earnest then and shifted quickly around in the chair so that her feet were back under the table again.

Across from us, Shamie groaned audibly. "I'm bloody sick of this toe," he said. "Auntie Bet took her to the doctor's last night, and she wouldn't show him her toe either. She had a proper, screaming fit right in the doctor's surgery. And we were supposed to go to McDonald's afterward for our tea, but we didn't get to, did we? Because you acted so daft at the doctor's."

"Shemona didn't want him to see her toe," Geraldine replied.

"Why ever not?" Shamie asked. "What did she think he was going to do? Cut it off?"

"Hey," I said, and frowned in Shamie's direction. "That's not going to help."

"Well, I'm getting fed up, having all my fun ruined. She's getting dafter by the minute, her and Geraldine both. I've got it all the time, here and at home too. Twenty-four hours a day of these wee girls' daftness."

"Well, she's not going to talk to a doctor, is she?" Geraldine retorted. "Shemona never talks in places like that."

"She doesn't talk because you make her not talk. You don't *let* her talk. You don't let anyone talk. No one can get a word in edgewise," said Shamie.

"Bloody, stinking liar. Shemona won't talk at the doctor's because he's a man. Shemona doesn't like men."

"And you know why, Geraldine?" Shamie asked, his voice grown loud.

He turned abruptly to me. "You know why Shemona doesn't like men, Miss? Because of Geraldine. Geraldine scares her. She keeps telling She-mona the men are coming. That they're going to come and burn our house down."

This proved too much for Shemona, who bolted off the far side of the chair, knocking it over in her haste. She ran around the corner of the shelving and disappeared in among the aisles of the library. Frantic sobbing filtered through the stacks of journals.

"There. See what you've done?" Geraldine said. "Are you happy now, Shamie?"

"I didn't do it, you did."

"*Stop!*" I said in a voice that left no doubt that I meant it. And everyone did, instantly. Even Lad and the other children, some distance from us, froze. The sound of Shemona's weeping engulfed us.

Geraldine regarded us with an unreadable expression on her face. She had half risen from her seat, leaning forward on the table, and now she remained in that position, motionless. For a long moment, she glanced from me to Shamie and back to me again, and I didn't have a clue as to what she was thinking. Then, in a slow and deliberate fashion, she pushed her glasses back up on the bridge of her nose and sat down.

"I think you and I have some talking to do later," I said to her, quietly.

"I've got nothing to say to you, Miss."

Rising, I went to find Shemona.

Ladbrooke had already gone to her. Crouched at the far end of one of the aisles, her arms protectively up over her head, Shemona was sobbing hysterically.

"Can you manage things for a while?" I asked Ladbrooke. "I want to take her down to the lounge, if no one's there. I'll try to be back before lunch."

"Don't worry if you're not. We'll be okay," Lad replied and returned to the others.

I struggled to carry Shemona the distance from our room to the teachers' lounge, two long corridors and a flight of stairs away. As tiger-fierce as ever, she wasn't going to accept this activity easily. I had to put her down twice to renew my grip. And the entire distance, she screamed like a trapped banshee. Mercifully, the teachers' lounge was empty, because I don't know where I would have gone otherwise. It would have been almost a physical impossibility for me to have moved her much farther on my own. Managing to get the door open and pull us inside, I collapsed with her onto the floor and pushed the door shut with my foot. For several minutes thereafter I did nothing other than contain her. She writhed and wriggled, struggled and fought, bit and scratched and kicked. And screamed. I had never come across a small kid with bigger lungs than Shemona had.

Slowly, slowly, slowly, she wore down. She began to choke over her screams and then gagged. I pushed her forward onto her stomach in case she vomited and then tightened my hold so that she couldn't move any longer. At last she collapsed forward onto the floor and lay there, cheek pressed against the linoleum. She gasped noisily for breath.

I let go. Rising up, I dusted myself off, then bent and picked Shemona up. Carrying her to the sofa, I set her down gently and brought over the box of tissues. Shemona shuddered, her body racked with hiccuping spasms from the tears. Her face had gone red and blotchy. Her nose ran. The jerk-and-snuffle aftermath of her explosion lasted nearly as long as the incident itself. Shemona just couldn't quite get herself back together. I sat, waiting, and watched the hand on the clock jump the minutes. When she was finally quiet beside me, I handed her one last tissue.

"Here. Take this and blow your nose."

She did.

"Now, lie down. I want to look at your foot."

She shook her head.

"Lie down, Shemona. Here. Put this pillow right there and then you can put your head on it and your feet in my lap. Lie down."

"No."

"You can put off your auntie and your uncle and the doctor and everyone else by acting like this, but you can't put me off. You've met your match, kiddo. Now lie down."

She looked back at me, sizing me up. I couldn't believe she had any energy left to resist with. I hardly did.

Finally, she acquiesced. Adjusting the throw pillow on the sofa, she lay down with her head on it and cautiously put her feet into my lap. I began to undo the laces of her jogging shoe. Carefully, I removed her sock.

She had an ingrown toenail. The swollen skin around the nail was tight and shiny. All the thrashing around we'd done earlier must have been agonizing. Not knowing what the problem was, I'd not removed her shoes as I usually did when one of the children lost control. Now I was glad I hadn't, because it would have resulted in excruciating pain. Pressing gently around the toenail, I saw pus come up.

"You stay right where you are for a minute. I'm going to go down to the office and get some antiseptic cream and things for this. I'll be right back." I rose.

"Is it going to hurt?" Shemona asked, her brow puckering.

I smiled. "It hurts already, doesn't it? I'm going to try and make it better."

When I returned, Shemona was still lying just as I had left her on the couch. She was sucking her thumb.

Lifting her feet, I sat back down again. I propped a pillow under the infected foot in my lap and began to clean the toe with a piece of gauze. "I'll try very hard not to hurt, but I need to clean this off. You tell me if I do hurt, and then I'll try to be more careful. Okay?"

Intent on not causing any more pain than was absolutely necessary, I worked very, very slowly with gauze and bits of cotton to clean away the pus. We didn't talk for some time. The thumb sucking became less noisy. Shemona relaxed back against the pillows and turned her head. I noticed out of the corner of my eye that she was surveying the room now. She looked at the worktable, up at the ceiling. Then I clipped a small V in the toenail to relieve the pressure on the sides of the nail. That made her flinch, and she looked back to my face, but she didn't speak.

"Did that hurt? If it did, I'm sorry." I smiled reassuringly. "I'm almost done."

Back we went into silence.

My thoughts returned to the argument earlier in the classroom. I pondered it as I worked.

"Shemona, what do you remember from before? From before you came here?"

She didn't answer.

I glanced over. "Do you remember the fire at your house in Belfast?"

An almost imperceptible nod.

Taking a piece of clean cotton, I swabbed the toe with antiseptic. "Can you tell me about what happened that night?"

"There was a fire," she said, her voice soft. "I woke up. Our brother was crying."

"Was your brother sleeping in the same room as you?"

She nodded. "Yes, Miss."

"And then what happened?"

"Matthew was crying. And I couldn't find him. I got out of my bed to go to him, but I couldn't find him."

Taking up the roll of gauze, I made a bandage. "Then what?"

"I was scared. I couldn't find the light. I was scared of the dark, so Mammy was supposed to leave a light on for me, but there wasn't one. I couldn't see anything. There was smoke, and I couldn't breathe and I couldn't find Matthew."

"So what did you do?"

"I started to cry. I tripped over something and I fell and I started to cry. I couldn't find anybody. I kept saying, 'Mammy? Come here, Mammy!' But I couldn't find her."

Shemona's eyes were on my face, the fear naked in them. Her features puckered. Gently, I reached a hand over to touch her cheek. "That must have been very scary."

She nodded. The thumb returned to her mouth.

"What happened after that?"

"I don't know," she said around her thumb.

I glanced over and smiled before returning to bandaging the toe.

"I remember after the fire," she said.

"What do you remember?"

"We were outside," she said. "It was dark and I still had my nightgown on. There was a man in a cold, black coat."

"Your daddy?"

"No, his coat was cold. He was carrying me. He put me in a big car."

"A fireman?"

"I don't know."

Silence.

I finished with her foot. Cupping it gently, I raised it and kissed the bandage. "There. Better now?"

She made no effort to get up. Instead, she remained on her back on the couch and kept her feet in my lap. Her eyes never left my face. "Do you want to tell me more about it?" I asked. "About the fire?"

"I don't remember more."

"I see."

She kept the tip of her thumb in her mouth. Slowly, her gaze drifted upward from my face toward the ceiling. She seemed for a moment to be looking at something specific, and then her expression grew more inward.

"Our Matthew went to play with Baby Jesus," she said softly, "in His palace. And Mammy went too, to take care of Matthew, because he was just a wee lad still."

"So that left you and Geraldine and your daddy."

"Yes," she said, nodding.

"What happened then?"

"We lived with Daddy for a while. We had chips and fried eggs for our tea every night because Daddy didn't know how to cook anything else. Sometimes we had baked beans too. And I was going to be a schoolgirl. I had my satchel. Daddy bought it for me. But then we went to live with Auntie Meg, and I didn't get to be a schoolgirl. And then we went to live with Auntie Aileen. And then we went to live with Auntie Cath. And then we came here. And we're still here."

"What about your daddy? Where's he?"

"He got lonely for Mammy."

I nodded.

Silence came then. Shemona gazed into space, her eyes unfocused.

"Do you know how the fire started at your house that night? Did anyone talk to you about it?"

"No."

"Does Geraldine talk about it?"

She shrugged.

"What about the Troubles? About the Provies and the men your daddy used to do things with? The things Shamie and Geraldine talk about sometimes. Do you understand what they're saying?"

"I know there's fighting, but I don't know why. I don't know why everyone can't be friends."

I smiled at her.

She continued to lie with her feet in my lap. I rested my hands gently on her legs, and for the first time, she did not pull away from my touch.

"What kinds of things *does* Geraldine tell you?"

A slight shrug.

"Does she talk about your old home and your mammy and daddy much?"

"Sometimes."

"Does she tell you other things? Things that frighten you?"

Another shrug. "I don't know."

"Do you believe the things Geraldine tells you?"

"No, not always. Geraldine talks a lot of rubbish. Like Shamie says."

"Yes, I think maybe that's so."

"Sometimes, I wish I was Shamie's sister and not Geraldine's," Shemona said, her tone surprisingly heartfelt.

"Why's that?"

"Shamie's nicer to me. He doesn't get so cross. He lets me play with his things and Geraldine doesn't. But *she* plays with *my* things, without even asking. Like yesterday, she took my new crayons and she broke one. And she didn't even say she was sorry."

What struck me in listening to this was the absurd ordinariness of everything in the midst of such extraordinary circumstances. She could have been any six-year-old talking, just then.

"You know what Geraldine says?" Shemona asked.

"What's that?"

"That I've got to do everything she tells me to. She says I got to always obey her and do whatever she wants."

"Why does she say that?"

"Well, so she can take care of me. That's what she says. But really, it's so she can boss me around. And I don't like it."

"So do you do as she says?"

There was a slight pause. I looked over at her.

"Sometimes," she said. "And sometimes I don't."

"What happens then?"

"Geraldine gets cross."

"Are you afraid of her then?"

"A little. She can beat me up. And she takes my things sometimes."

"Do you tell your Auntie Bet? Or Uncle Mike?"

Shemona shook her head.

"Why not?"

She didn't answer. A sudden little silence slipped in around us. The thumb, which had remained poised at her lips, slid back into her mouth. She sucked softly for a few moments.

"What does Geraldine tell you about men, Shemona?"

No reply.

"Are you afraid of them, like she says?"

"Yes, Miss."

"Why?"

"She says that bad men are coming at night, like before. She says that's what happened at home. She says they put petrol bombs through the letterbox and that's what made the fire. She says it was the bad men who fought with Daddy. They made everything happen. They made the fire. They made us not have a mammy and daddy anymore. They made us come over here. And if I'm not good and do as she says so she can take care of me, then they're going to come over here too."

"And what do you say to her when she tells you all this?"

"I tell her Auntie Bet and Uncle Mike don't have a letterbox. They've got a mailbox down at the end of the drive. But she says it doesn't matter. They'll find an open window or something. They'll still come if I don't do what she says so she can take care of me."

"Do you believe her, Shemona?"

There was no answer, but I watched as tears puddled up in her eyes. Then very slowly, she nodded. "Yes, Miss," she replied in a tight, tiny voice.

"Shemona, sweetheart, come here. Come sit on my lap. I want to tell you some secret things, and I need you very close so you can hear."

She rose up then and crawled onto my lap. I wrapped my arms around her, pulling her in against my body. For a moment she remained tense and then, with an audible sigh, she pushed in closer, her face in the soft folds of my pullover.

"Geraldine is trying to be a good sister to you. She loves you and she wants things to be better for both of you, but she's just a little girl herself, and she's been just as scared by all that's happened as you've been. So she doesn't see things very clearly. What she's telling you *isn't* the truth,

Shemona. It's the way Geraldine feels. I think she believes it's true, but it isn't. No men are going to come and put petrol bombs in your house. Geraldine's confused. It won't happen here, not at your Uncle Mike's house."

Shemona sucked energetically on her thumb.

"When you want to know the real truth about something, you need to ask a grown-up. You need to talk to me or to Ladbrooke or your aunt or uncle. Not Geraldine. Because Geraldine doesn't always know what's true. And here's the secret. You've got to remember it, remember that I've told it to you, because it's *very* important. Do you want to know this secret?"

"Yes, Miss."

"It's this: What's happened to you in Belfast is over. It was horrible, but now it's over and it's not going to happen again. You're here and you're safe with Auntie Bet and Uncle Mike and their family. And you're going to stay safe. So if Geraldine tells you something scary about that time in Belfast, if she tells you that you have to do as she says or else those things'll happen again, then you tell her *no*. You're in on the secret now. You know it can't happen again, because it's *over*. That's the truth, Shemona. Those days are gone and they won't come back."

With one finger, she gently wiped the unfallen tears out of her eyes. Then pressing against me, she clutched my arm and pulled it tighter around herself.

CHAPTER
TWENTY-SEVEN

✳ I left the discussion with Shemona convinced of one thing: the need to separate the two sisters. As it was, they were together virtually twenty-four hours a day, which gave Geraldine far too much opportunity to tyrannize her younger sibling. Although I was increasingly impressed with just how durable and resilient Shemona actually was, it was expecting too much of her to continually fend off Geraldine.

My first thought was to place Shemona in a regular kindergarten class, but this was dealt a body blow by the discovery that Shemona was, in fact, still not talking to anyone else, anywhere, other than in the classroom. I was dismayed to discover this and irritated with myself for not having followed up things more closely. I'd talked to Mrs. Lonrho several times in mid-March when Shemona had first begun to talk, but she had never recontacted me, and I had never gotten back to her in the intervening weeks. When I'd heard nothing, I'd just assumed Shemona's speech had carried over. No one had intimated that it hadn't, but then I'd never asked.

So where from there? It probably wasn't a good idea to cause a major upheaval by placing her in a new class and simultaneously expecting her to speak as well, not with everything else that was going on. So I contemplated the limited alternatives.

One afternoon, I had a fit of complete exasperation. Why had it taken me so long to reach this conclusion? Why hadn't we coped better with the lack of speech? How was I going to place Shemona? Where could I put her? I cursed our stupid setup, here in the administration building. If we'd been in a regular school, as we should have been, it would have been a much simpler matter, even if Shemona had been unwilling to talk. I could have mainstreamed her for a few hours or put her in a resource room or something. It wouldn't have been the major production that this was turning out to be.

Ladbrooke let me rattle on. "What about Carolyn?" she asked, when I paused for breath. "Would her room work?"

"No, they're all preschoolers. And they're all subnormal."

"Yes, but she plays with them at recess and doesn't seem to mind that they're younger or handicapped. And she talks to them."

I hesitated.

"She *does* talk to them, Torey. I mean, wouldn't that be better, to be in there, where she's already comfortable? Maybe just a couple hours. For art or music or something."

I nodded slowly. "Maybe it would."

And it was. I talked to Carolyn on Thursday evening, and she was quite interested in the idea. By the middle of the next week, Carolyn, Frank and I sat down with Mr. and Mrs. Lonrho and confirmed the change. By that Friday, Shemona was ready to go down with Lad for a morning in Carolyn's class.

The only drawback to this switch was, of course, the lack of an appropriate curriculum. Carolyn's children, while close to Shemona's age, were much less advanced. Many of them weren't toilet trained or able even to manage their clothes. Most of the school day was devoted to learning basic self-care skills Shemona had long since mastered. I wasn't unduly bothered by this as there were a lot of other advantages to Carolyn's room, beyond her convenient proximity. She had a beautiful selection of toys and trikes and trays for sand and water play. And the other children, while not as bright as Shemona, were, for the most part, friendly and sociable. Most children Shemona's age were kindergartners, who only went half days anyhow, and as Shemona would return in the afternoons to my room, I felt she would be getting sufficient academic input. So I was satisfied, as were the Lonrhos, which was the most important.

The biggest surprise was Shemona's completely undisguised relief at this change. Although I had known that she was under pressure in our room, not only from her relationship with Geraldine, but also from trying to keep up with children three and four years older than she was, I had not been aware of how heavily it must have weighed on Shemona. She'd never once intimated that she disliked our room or wanted out, but once she *was* out, she made no secret of her delight to be somewhere else.

I suspect Shemona's biggest pleasure came on Friday of the following week, when she came back to class with a large construction-paper badge with the word "Helper" written across it. She explained to Lad and me that now she was a big girl in Miss Berry's class and had to help with the other children. She had to show them how to do things the way big girls do them, and this was her badge, so they'd know to come to her for help. Carefully unpinning it, Shemona stowed it in her cubby. Each morning when she arrived, she brought it over to have it repinned on her clothes before going downstairs. That single small kindness on Carolyn's part perhaps best epitomized the whole experience. At last Shemona was somewhere where she was biggest, smartest and most capable. She was also somewhere she could just play, and I think that was something that Shemona, in her short life, had not had enough of an opportunity to do.

Stung by my ineptitude regarding Shemona's failure to generalize her speech to home, I made sure the Lonrhos were included in every aspect of this new development. I rang Mrs. Lonrho at every turn. We also tried to create parallel changes at home for Shemona. She and Geraldine changed rooms, for instance. Shemona went in with the Lonrhos' younger daughter, four, while Geraldine went in with their twelve-year-old. I suggested that Mrs. Lonrho and her husband make a concerted effort to spend a regular amount of time with each girl individually. I also thought it might be best not to leave the two sisters alone together unsupervised, at least for the time being.

Interestingly, within days of these changes at school and at home, Shemona started, of her own volition, to speak to her aunt and uncle. Over the next few weeks she broadened her talking to include virtually anyone who spoke directly to her. This confirmed in my mind the suspicion that her mutism, at least in part, had been controlled by Geraldine. In the beginning, when Shemona had first ceased talking, perhaps that was a reaction to the traumatic events surrounding her, but its long duration I credited to Geraldine.

In regard to Geraldine herself, I anticipated—indeed, hoped for—some kind of interaction between the two of us as a result of all that had happened. Of course, I wanted it to be a positive interaction, such as mine with Shemona, so that we could at long last face some of Geraldine's demons together and exorcise them, but I would have settled for a negative one. Even an out-and-out confrontation was better than the emotional no-man's-land we seemed to have drifted into. I was sure Geraldine knew she'd lost control of Shemona on that morning Shemona and I had gone down to the teachers' lounge. Shemona's circumstances had changed so rapidly after that that Geraldine couldn't have missed the connection. She was canny enough to have worked everything out, so I stayed alert and prepared, but Geraldine made no move.

Geraldine was not unaffected, however. Tension grew up between the two of us. She became surlier in the classroom, less able to cope with her schoolwork, less cooperative with the other children. She did nasty little destructive things, like breaking Mariana's colored pencils or tearing up Dirkie's cat drawings. And she began to bait Ladbrooke mercilessly, taking out on her all the anger I suspect she felt for me, but she made no overt moves whatsoever toward Shemona or myself.

In the end, I felt it would be best to bring the issue to a head; since Geraldine seemed unwilling to confront me, I attempted to make her talk. I cornered her and asked her directly if there was anything she wanted to say to me. I took her around into the privacy of the blackboard arm of the room and coaxed her along. I chatted casually on the playground with her. I aimed morning discussion in her direction. I queried her when we were working individually. But Geraldine remained unwavering. No, Miss, she'd always reply, I've nothing to talk about. She had an air about her of a fox run to ground—wearily alert and slightly desperate—but she wasn't defeated. I may have caught Shemona, but she made it patently clear that I hadn't yet caught her.

The time was coming to consider the future placement for all the children. We had only about a month and a half left before the school year let out. I had no doubt now that Shemona was going to be ready for regular first grade in the autumn. We were once again working on a plan to reintegrate Shamie into the nearby junior high. He was going over for just two classes three times a week, and this was fairly successful. They were both nonacademic classes, and he got on quite well with the teachers and other students. So I felt a normal placement for him, too, was quite likely. The only other student in the class who looked like possibly being able to return to the mainstream was Mariana. She was the dodgiest of the three. She still had absymal academic skills for her age, but she had made steady, albeit slow, progress all year long. At nine, her reading skills were only those of a seven-year-old and her math skills were even lower, but when she'd arrived in the classroom in September, they had been nonexistent, so she'd improved quite a lot. I didn't expect that Mariana would ever be a scholar, whatever the setting. Her IQ just squeaked into the normal range, and what she was doing academically was probably consistent with her abilities. In fact, of all the children in the room, she alone was probably working up to her potential. So I thought it best she return to a normal setting. My kind of room could do no more for her academically than a resource room could in a regular school, and socially, she was held back here. Admittedly, Mariana was still a bit rough around the edges. We seemed to have gotten reasonable control over her more outlandish behaviors, such as the sexual precocity, but she was still distractable and impulsive. She would need a mature, organized, experienced teacher, and so I set about looking for one.

This left me with Dirkie, Geraldine and Leslie. All three would need continuing full-time self-contained special education. Frank had already contacted Mrs. Samuelson, the woman who was to take my place in this classroom. I'd talked to her on the phone, and we'd made arrangements for her to come spend some time in the class during early May to acquaint herself with her future students. Frank and I explored other possibilities for these three, but as things stood, all of them were due to return to this same room.

Dirkie had remained forever Dirkie throughout the school year. He had made some academic progress, but otherwise, there had been almost no change in his condition. He was squirrelly as ever, still obsessed by his cats and long hair, still spending much of his day hooting happily to himself from under the table. It was unfair to both Dirkie and ourselves to say we were no more than a holding pen for him, because he clearly got a lot out of the classroom experience and thoroughly enjoyed himself in the process. And of course, he gave a lot too. He had a cheerful, engaging personality, and I would have been genuinely sorry to have missed this time with him. But in realistic terms, he was unlikely ever to find himself in a normal classroom in a regular school, just as he was unlikely to find a future outside the sheltered caring of his foster parents.

Geraldine had proved to be my most enigmatic child that year. When she'd first come, I'd badly misjudged her. I'd had no idea she was as disturbed a girl as she eventually showed herself to be. Assessing her now, from several months' vantage point, I knew she was and undoubtedly always had been, the most unbalanced child in the group. Nothing gave me the feeling there was anything organic or intrinsic about Geraldine's problems. Hers was a genuine psychopathology, which, fortunately, was a fairly rare phenomenon in a class such as mine.

On numerous occasions I pondered what might have been responsible for the extent of Geraldine's disturbance. Could she have tolerated life in what was essentially an emotionally disturbed city if it hadn't meant the death of her parents? Could she have tolerated the death of her parents if it hadn't meant disruption and separation from everything she knew? Or would she have been a problem child in any setting? The whole matter was academic anyway, a passle of what-if's that no one, not even Geraldine, had the answer to. But I couldn't help wondering anyway. What Geraldine's future would be like was equally unknown. In my opinion, she certainly needed to be confined to a self-contained room. Deep in my gut I couldn't shake the feeling that she was potentially dangerous. We knew so little about her, about what she felt, or even if she did feel, that it seemed wiser to keep her in a restricted setting until we understood better.

Of all the children, it had been Leslie who'd made the greatest gains over the course of the year. By April she was functioning at a surprisingly high level, considering how she'd entered the class in the autumn. There was still loads of room for improvement, and she was still what could only be called a severely handicapped child, but she had made heartening progress. Her academic skills, which I'd only worked on since the turn of the new year, were galloping ahead. She could read the same primer as Mariana, albeit in a lilting sing-song voice that gave no sense to the words, but she had mastered the concept of reading. By the same token, she could perform basic arithmetic. Socially, her gains had been slower, but still remarkable. She talked now, virtually nonstop. The majority was straightforward echoing, either of what had just been said to her or else regurgitated from earlier conversations. She also took to reciting things she'd read. I often heard her, while playing alone, reeling off lists of ingredients, such as one finds on the sides of cereal boxes. I loved this new-found noisiness in Leslie. It made her charming and alive, unlike the silent ghost we'd had earlier. Leslie remained toilet trained in class but made only very slow progress toward it at home. Even with us, it wasn't very reliable and was the first thing to go if Leslie was under stress. So I mentioned in my notes to the new teacher not to be surprised if Leslie wasn't dry at the beginning of the new school year. She could be and she would be, with persistence. And insistence.

Of course, in spite of all this progress, there was still a lot of work to be done. Leslie was now given to explosive tantrums when really frustrated. She could be sulky and uncooperative, and she had Neanderthal views on sharing, of the walk-softly-and-carry-a-big-stick variety. On the whole, she had the emotional finesse of an average two-year-old and was going to require an enormous amount of kind, but very firm and consistent handling on the part of her next-year's teacher. But all in all, I felt Leslie had done phenomenally well over the course of the eight months in the class.

Throughout the third week of April, I held parent conferences in an effort to discuss the future placements I had in mind for each individual child. It took two full after-school afternoons to get through with the Lonrhos alone. Then on Wednesday afternoon, I saw Mariana's mother. Dirkie's foster parents came on Thursday, and Friday afternoon I allocated to Tom and Ladbrooke.

Tom and Ladbrooke's conference was scheduled fairly late in the day because Tom had prior commitments that Friday. Consequently, he wasn't due at school until 4:30. Ladbrooke appeared to find the hour between the time the children went home and Tom's arrival a trial. She couldn't settle at her work, couldn't even stay seated at the table. Up and down from her chair, back and forth across the room, first putting away the toys, then straightening up the cupboard under the sink, then back to the toys, over to water the plants, out to the toilet, back to feed the gerbils, over to the filing cabinet. It was distracting me, as I sat at the table and tried to sort through Leslie's work. Then, hands in pockets, Lad paused a moment in front of the window and stared out. It was a sunny day, breezy and brisk for the time of year, but brilliantly clear.

"I *hate* these conferences," she muttered.

"I can tell."

She turned around and came over to the table, but instead of sitting down, she remained standing. I was trying to organize all the materials regarding Leslie I had collected over the course of the year and had little piles growing up around me of anecdotal records, charts, graphs, worksheets. Lad watched me.

"I thought, as the year went on," she said, "these conferences would get easier."

"I'm not springing anything new on you, kiddo. I suspect I'm not even springing anything new on Tom. This is all more or less a formality."

"I know it."

"Then it's probably better just to relax. Nothing's going to happen."

She nodded. Hands still stuffed deep in her pockets, she continued to stand over me. "Torey?"

"Yes?"

"Would you do me a favor?"

"What's that?"

She didn't reply. I continued what I was doing for a few moments longer, but when she still didn't speak, I looked up.

"I'm trying to think what I want to say," she muttered.

"Oh, okay." I went back to my work.

"I need you to talk to Tom for me," she said finally.

"How so?"

"I need to . . . I need you to . . . well, I don't mean *you* to talk to Tom. *I* need to talk to Tom. But I need you here."

"You want me with you while you talk to Tom?"

She nodded. "When I need to say something to him, it never gets said. He bullies me out of it. But I need to talk to him." A pause. "Things really aren't very good at home at the moment."

"I'm not sure I'd feel comfortable getting between you and Tom. I'm not a marriage counselor, Lad."

"I'm not asking you to be. I just want to talk to him. Things have got to change between him and me, Torey, and I need to say that to him. He won't listen to me if I say it at home. He won't take me seriously, but he will here, with you. You don't need to say anything yourself. Just be here. For me." She smiled self-consciously. "For moral support."

"I'm not sure I'm comfortable with this, Lad."

Her brow puckered with concern. "Please?"

Tom arrived a few minutes after the appointed time and seated himself beside me at the table. Nerves had gotten the better of Ladbrooke again in the interim, and she'd been up and around the room, so when she sat down again, it was away from both of us at the far end of the table.

This conference was indeed just a formality. Ladbrooke had ferried home most of the news of Leslie's progress as it happened, so Tom knew most of what I had to say. He and Ladbrooke had already discussed Leslie's return to this class in the autumn. However, I preferred the chance to talk to Tom and show him Leslie's work myself.

As always, Tom showed intense interest in what Leslie was doing. He went over each individual chart, each note I'd made. He examined her folder. He studied her worksheets. At one point I noticed him giving particular attention to one paper. Silence had come to us while Tom was looking through the materials, and now he seemed absorbed in this one item. Very gently, he touched Leslie's name. It had been written in red crayon in bold, childish letters. He traced the beginning *L* with one finger.

"When did she learn to write?" he asked.

"She's been making letters for some time now, but she's just mastered her name in the last three or four weeks."

He smiled in a soft, enigmatic way.

Since all the material to be covered was more or less a foregone conclusion, everything was said and done in about half an hour. When I closed the folder, Tom reached for his coat.

"Tom?" Ladbrooke said.

He had already risen and was turning to push the chair in when she spoke. He looked over at her.

"Tom, I've got to talk to you."

A questioning expression came to his face. He glanced quickly to me and then back to her. "What do you want?" he asked, perplexed.

"I want to talk to you."

"Here? Now? What about?"

Ladbrooke nodded. "Sit down, okay?"

Another glance to me. "What does she want?" he asked, bewilderment clear in his voice.

"For you to sit down, I think," I said.

He sat, his coat still on.

"I want things to change," Ladbrooke said.

"What is this?" Irritation was creeping into his tone.

"I want things to change, Tom."

"What's going on here? I came in to talk about Leslie. What is this? Some kind of ambush?"

"You did come to talk about Leslie. Now we're done, so you're going to talk about me."

"Oh, Jesus."

"I want things to change, Tom."

"I want things to change, Tom," he mimicked. "You've said that about six times now, sweetheart. I'm not deaf yet. I've heard you. Now come on. Get your coat and let's go."

Lad's brow furrowed. She had her hands clasped together in front of her, the thumbs pressed against her lips. She didn't move a muscle.

Tom turned to me. "Is this your idea? Have you put her up to this?"

"No," interjected Ladbrooke quickly. "*I* put me up to it. Because I need to talk to you, Tom. I never can do it at home. You never let me get a word in edgewise."

Shaking his head wearily, Tom ran a hand over his face. "You want to haul all the dirty laundry out again in front of strangers, Ladbrooke? What is this thing you've got about discussing our private lives in public places? It's a perversion of yours."

"I just want to *talk*."

Tom sighed.

"Things are changing, Tom. You don't seem to be able to realize that. They're changing, and you're going to have to change too."

"Things haven't changed, Ladbrooke. Nothing's changed."

"*Everything's* changed!"

"Oh? Like what, for instance? Name one thing that's changed."

Dead silence.

"Like what, Ladbrooke?"

Still silence.

I glanced over at her and suspected by her expression that she'd gone tongue-tied. What a hell of a time for it, I was thinking, because there wasn't much to be done to get her started again.

"Like *what*?" Tom asked a third time.

"Lay off me, Tom. I'm *thinking*."

"Oh, God help us."

Silence.

Again I glanced at Ladbrooke, who was bent forward, regarding her bitten nails. I tried to send her ESP messages. *Tell him you're not drinking anymore. Tell him how well you're doing with Leslie. Tell him about going down to the teacher's lounge on your own.* But she said nothing.

The tension, which had momentarily grown acute, eased off, and boredom set in. I could appreciate where this kind of behavior wouldn't be very conducive to difficult, much-needed conversations.

"Me," Ladbrooke said at long last. "I've changed."

"How?" Tom's tone had lost its acerbity. He sounded only tired.

"I don't know how. But I have."

Once again the silence. No one seemed to know quite what to say.

"So, what do you want out of me?" he asked.

Ladbrooke brought up a finger and nibbled at the nail. Then she took it out, examined it, bit it again. Finally she looked over. "I want another baby."

This was about the last thing in the world I had expected to hear. By the look on Tom's face, it had hit him that way as well. He looked stunned.

"Before I'm too old to have one, I want another baby."

"Good God, you're only thirty-three. That's hardly menopausal, Ladbrooke."

She didn't reply.

"What the hell would you do with another baby anyway?" he asked.

Ladbrooke looked over at me. "This is why I wanted to talk here with you. So you can see this. He treats me like I'm six years old. He never lets me say anything, anything I feel. And if I do, he just puts me down for it."

"I'm letting you say it, aren't I? I'm just asking you what the hell you've said it for? The last thing in the world you need, Ladbrooke, is another baby. Look at your last one."

"That was just something that happened. The next one isn't going to have Leslie's problems. It isn't going to happen twice."

"It wasn't something that 'just happened,' Ladbrooke. Nothing 'just happens.' Don't delude yourself. You're no mother. You never took care of Leslie. Don't try and pretend you did. You don't know hell's bells about loving a child."

"I could do better this time."

Tom rolled his eyes.

"I *could*. If you didn't keep telling me how lousy I am at it, maybe I'd be a better mother. I didn't know *how* last time, that's all. But I can learn, can't I? Maybe I could do it."

"And maybe you couldn't. What then? 'I'm too old to be Mommy again? My nursing days are over?' So let's not hear such drivel."

"I'm *changing.* I *am.* Whether you like it or not."

Snorting, Tom looked away. "Oh shit, Ladbrooke, you haven't changed and you're never going to."

"You talk to me like I'm a child and I'm sick of it. I want to be treated like an adult. Because I *am* an adult."

Tom sighed.

"I mean it. I'm not going to put up with it anymore. *That's* what we need to talk about. I'm an adult and not a child, and you're going to have to start treating me like one."

"Is this your handiwork?" he asked, turning suddenly to me.

"*No!*" shouted Ladbrooke, leaning forward across the table toward him. "Fuck it all, Tom, I'm right here! Talk to *me.*"

There was a sudden, piercing silence. Tom rotated very slowly in his chair until he was facing Ladbrooke with his entire body, and for a long moment, he did nothing but regard her. Ladbrooke shrank back. She'd come way forward, her hands on the table, but now she pulled back, pulled her arms back and finally wrapped them around herself.

"I love you," Tom said, his voice unexpectedly tender. "I love you and Leslie. What more do you want out of me, Ladbrooke?" He continued to regard her.

Lad lowered her head. I realized instantly that she was going to cry, and it was the last thing I wanted her to do just then. I didn't know if this was a regular tactic that Tom used, but it was astonishingly effective. And it made me hate him.

Without saying another word, Ladbrooke rose and left the room. Dead silence followed the quiet snick of the latch as the classroom door closed behind her. Tom, in the next chair, still had his back to me.

I toyed with a pencil on the table. "She's been working hard to change," I said softly. "After all this trouble, she seems to have finally gotten a good grip on the drinking problem. She's been very conscientious about attempting to control her other problems. I can appreciate the fact that she's still a very long ways from perfect, but she is trying, Tom. It's going to be fairly hard on her self-esteem if you don't give her credit for the ability to change."

Tom turned back in his chair and leaned forward on the table. "I pretty much reckoned this was your handiwork," he said, his voice quiet and unemotional. "It's got your fingerprints all over it."

I didn't reply.

"She does nothing but talk about you. It's gotten to be a bit of a joke around our place. She's always on about how you say this and you say that. How you never make her feel guilty for Leslie. For her drinking. For all that other crap."

A quiet pause.

"But damn it, Torey, she *is* guilty. She *has* hurt Leslie. She's hurt me."
He looked over.

I nodded.

"Yet, you're telling her it's not her fault."

"I'm telling her the past is over."

"It's the same thing."

"She's a good person, Tom. You know that as well as I do. She deserves to be treated like a good person. Like someone who would not intentionally hurt the people she loves, because I don't think she would."

"But so much of this *has* been her fault, and you keep telling her it isn't."

I shrugged. "Because I can't see much point in telling her it is. She can't change what's already happened. She can only change the future."

Tom shifted in his seat. He regarded his hands as they rested on the table. Then, slowly, he turned his head and looked at me. He gave me a long, searching look before speaking. "What you don't seem to realize, Torey, is that I never necessarily wanted her to change. She's always been difficult, and things have always been hard for us, but I liked her the way she was. Untamed. Not quite like other people."

He sighed heavily. "In fact, I've got to admit, you're the person in all of this that I'm the most angry with," he said, his tone still quiet. He didn't sound so much angry as just weary. "You've come along and almost singlehandedly destroyed my life. Do you realize that? When you meddled in all these things, did you stop to think about that at any point? The effect it would have on *me*? I mean, first it was Leslie. Now it's Ladbrooke. You've left me with nothing. You've taken away everything I loved best."

"But they weren't happy. All I did was try and make it a little better for them."

"But is it better? Have you made it better?"

I shrugged slightly.

"Can you ever judge that about other people's lives?"

CHAPTER TWENTY-EIGHT

At last, spring. There in the higher reaches of the Rockies, real spring with its warm, fitful weather and floral-scented air hadn't come until late April. Even at that point it was a bit unreliable; we had snow showers on the twentieth. But the grass had finally gone green and the tulips were up.

I loved this time of year. I loved recess time, the perennial games of marbles and hopscotch that appeared in that season, as predictably as the tulips. I loved the noise of the children's voices then, a fuller, more exuberant sound in contrast to the thin, sharp noises carried on cold winter air.

That particular day was stunning. It was Thursday of the last full week of April, a clear, cloudless day in the low seventies. Although Ladbrooke and I had morning recess duty, Joyce had opted to come out as well. She was across the playground from us, near the sandbox, where most of her children were. Leslie was there too, busily loading a small truck with sand and dumping it. Geraldine and Mariana had tied a jump rope to one of the basketball supports and were taking turns jumping, chanting out a jump-rope rhyme that I remembered saying myself as a girl. The rhythm of their voices floated across the playground toward us. Shamie had brought a baseball and bat to school that morning and spent his time throwing the ball up, trying to hit it and then chasing after it. Ladbrooke and I retreated to the deserted swing set, where we both sat on swings, idly pushing them into motion with our feet and chatting. I was saying to her how my own best memories of childhood schooldays had been of springtime recess periods. The only thing to mar my nostalgic recollections and the general peace of the morning was a couple of carpenters who had come to repair something in one of the basement rooms. Bang, bang, bang went their hammers, a jarring intrusion into our conversation.

Shemona wandered over to us. She stood a moment, swinging around one of the support struts and watching us. Then she approached Lad's swing and took hold of the chain on one side. "Can I swing with you?" she asked.

"Yes, sure," Lad replied, and I believe she thought Shemona was going to get into the next swing over, but Shemona didn't. Instead, she climbed up on Ladbrooke's swing, standing on it, a foot on either side of Lad.

"Okay," Shemona said, "you push now."

Ladbrooke launched the swing gently, and for a few moments they swang back and forth. Then, after the swing had come to a stop again, Shemona sat down. She was on Lad's lap, face to face with her, Shemona's small hands just below Lad's on the chains. She was wearing a light cotton dress, and her long, bare legs extended out behind Ladbrooke on the swing. She smiled again. She must have been only inches from Ladbrooke's face.

"Push again, okay?"

Lad smiled and launched the swing again. Shemona leaned back to keep the motion going and then it was teamwork. They managed between them to get the swing quite high, pumping back and forth, locked in one another's smiling gaze, long hair flowing first in one direction and then the other. Then Ladbrooke stopped pumping and let the swing slow down naturally.

"Do it again," Shemona said.

So again they went, swinging for several minutes, back and forth, back and forth. There was magic in watching them, in watching their faces, and in the rhythmic movement of their bodies. Then once again Ladbrooke stopped pumping. The swing glided soundlessly back and forth, the arc growing gradually smaller until at last they were even with me.

"Do it again," Shemona said.

"No, that's enough."

"Do it again, please? Please?"

"No, I'm tired. That's hard work. I'm a weary old woman."

"No you're not," Shemona replied with a giggle. "You're not old."

"I'm older than Torey."

"No you're not. She's the teacher."

"I'm still older. I was born before she was. I'm the oldest person out here."

Shemona laughed. "No you're not. She's the teacher, so she's the oldest."

Ladbrooke grinned.

"So do it again. Please? Swing with me."

"No, that's enough."

"Please? *Please?* Please, Miss?"

They were still sitting, face to face, both still holding onto the chains suspending the swing, but at that point Ladbrooke took her hands down and surrounded Shemona. Both continued smiling, their intimacy candid and relaxed.

"You know something," Ladbrooke said, as she encircled Shemona with her arms. "I have a name. And it isn't Miss."

Shemona reached up and touched Lad's cheek with her fingers.

"I'd rather you called me by my name than Miss. Do you know what it is?"

"Yes," replied Shemona.

"What?"

She ducked her head and her smile grew coy.

"What?"

Shemona leaned very close to Ladbrooke until they were touching, forehead to forehead. "Mommy," she said.

"Well, yes, I'm Leslie's mommy."

Shemona sat back a little and locked her arms around Lad's neck. "I want you to be my mommy."

Lad smiled.

"You could be. I don't have a mommy *or* a daddy. You could go to a court and adopt me."

Lad smiled again, her expression affectionate. "That would be nice, wouldn't it? I'd love to be your mommy. But I don't think it's very likely, is it? I've already got a little girl. And you've already got your aunt and uncle. I don't think they'd be very happy with me if I took you away from them."

"But they're not my mommy and daddy. I want to be *your* little girl. Leslie wouldn't care. She could be my new sister."

It was about then that Mariana and Geraldine wandered over. Geraldine sat down on one of the free swings, but Mariana came up to Ladbrooke. She touched Lad's long, loose hair. "Can I swing with you like that?"

Ladbrooke, I think, sensed the need to ease out of the conversation with Shemona. She gently put her hands under Shemona's armpits to help her down. "Let's give Mariana a turn." Mariana clambered on. Considerably stronger than Shemona, she was more able to help Ladbrooke pump the swing, and the two of them sailed above us.

"Come on, Shemona," Geraldine said, getting up. "Come do the jump rope with me."

"No. I don't want to. I want to stay here."

Geraldine's brow furrowed. "Come *on.*"

"No, I said."

"I want you to turn the end so I can jump. Come on."

"No, I'm staying here. I want to swing again."

Geraldine impatiently put down the jump rope and came over. She grabbed hold of Shemona's arm. Shemona jerked it free.

"Geraldine," I said, "Shemona doesn't sound like she wants to jump rope. Let her be, please."

Determination colored Geraldine's features, and she lunged at Shemona, knocking her down into the sand beneath the swings. I was at them instantly, pulling them out of the way of Mariana and Ladbrooke's swing, still in motion.

Geraldine, angry with Shemona, angrier, perhaps, with my interference, screamed. Even though I had hold of her, she managed to pull herself free and attack Shemona again. Pushing the younger girl down, she leaped on top of her, yanking Shemona's hair. But Shemona was no easy victim. She furiously returned the attack, and the two of them rolled away through the sand like tiger cubs.

Ladbrooke was desperately trying to stop her swing and extricate herself from Mariana. I could grab one of the girls but not both, particularly with the obstacle course created by the swings. Finally, Lad was there as well, and between the two of us, we managed to pull the sisters apart. Neither was hurt. In fact, neither was even crying, although they both raged noisily at one another.

"Okay, okay, you two," I said. "Settle down. Recess is almost over anyway. So settle down."

"Yes, go back to your retard class! Back to your baby class! Back where you go wee in your nappies!" shouted Geraldine.

"Better than being in with you!" Shemona screamed back. "I *hate* you! You're worse than having no sister at all!"

"I hate you too!"

I struggled to aim Geraldine in the general direction of the door.

"You just wait, Shemona. It's going to be different next year, when we get back to Belfast."

"I'm not going back to Belfast," Shemona retorted.

"Yes, you are."

"No, I'm not! I'm *never* going back to Belfast. Never, never, never! So there."

We'd made it to the doorway of the building by then, and Joyce came over to relieve Lad of Shemona, but the girls were still screaming angrily back and forth at one another.

"You're going back! You're going back!" Geraldine shrieked.

"I'm *not*! You can't make me. Nobody can make me. I'm never going back."

All the way down the hall they shouted, until Joyce finally dragged Shemona through their classroom door and Lad and I pulled Geraldine into the stairwell. It was at that point that Geraldine finally began to cry.

"We *are* going back," she wept. "Shemona and me. We're going back to 38 Greener Terrace after school gets out. When it's summer. We *are.*"

As we went up the stairs, I tried to pull her close to me, but she was having none of it. She pushed herself free, bolted up ahead of the rest of us and into the classroom to take refuge among the library stacks. Ladbrooke went to settle the other children, and I stopped at the head of the aisle where Geraldine was. She was sitting on the floor, hunched up, hands covering her face. I came down the aisle and knelt beside her. Gently, I put a hand out to touch her shoulder.

"Go away!"

"Here, come sit with me."

"Go away, bitch."

"Let's talk about things, okay?"

"Go *away.*"

I sat down on the floor beside her. For several minutes I said nothing at all. Geraldine kept her head down, hidden from me by her hands. She didn't seem to be crying.

"I think maybe it would help if we talked about things, Geraldine. Would you like to come sit with me? Or would you prefer we went somewhere more private?"

"Go away. What's the matter with you? Can't you hear me? I don't want to talk to you." She raised her head then to look at me. "I *hate* you. When are you going to realize that?"

I nodded slightly.

"I hate you. This is all your fault. You've ruined everything, you and her in there. Why should I want to talk to you?"

"In what way have we ruined things?"

"Can't you see? Shemona's not going back now, is she?" Tears returned to her eyes. "What am I going to do now, you bitch? You've ruined everything."

Afternoon recess rolled around. It was Carolyn's turn for duty, but Lad decided to go out as well, since it was such a beautiful day. I needed to have a word with Bill about getting some clean chalkboard erasers, and it was always easier to catch him during breaks than after school, when he was off cleaning, so I declined the offer to join her. I did mention to Lad, however, to keep an eye on Geraldine and Shemona. Geraldine had soon settled down after the morning's turmoil and gone back to her normal routine. After lunch, when Shemona had returned to our class, there was no evidence that either remembered the morning's fracas. But they always seemed more combustible in the unstructured setting of the playground, and on several occasions, they had rekindled a morning's argument in the afternoon.

Bill had a little office-cum-workshop on the ground floor. It also housed the boiler, so there was a tangle of pipes and trailing bits of lagging tape that needed to be ducked around and under. Perched on the edge of his desk, balancing the two clean erasers on my knees, I was talking with him about our local high-school sports team when all the commotion became audible. Carolyn's voice came through the clearest. She was shouting my name.

"I'm in here, Carolyn," I called, opening the door to Bill's room.

"Torey? Torey! Come down here, quickly!"

There was panic in Carolyn's voice, something I'd never heard before. I responded with alarm, running the length of the corridor to meet her at the stairwell. "What's going on? What's happening?"

"Oh God," she was saying, "oh God, oh God, Torey, come down here."

There was complete chaos in the basement hallway. Both Carolyn's and my children were tearing back and forth in panic. Some were crying. Some clamored for attention.

"Where's Joyce? Where's Ladbrooke?" I asked, fear clutching my voice.

Ignoring the children, Carolyn pushed her way through to the room beyond her own where the carpenters had been working. They weren't in there at the moment; I knew because they'd been upstairs having coffee in the teachers' lounge when I'd gone in to find Bill. Carolyn opened the door and beckoned me in before closing it firmly behind me to keep the children out.

At the far end of the room were Ladbrooke and Geraldine. They were kneeling on the floor, but I couldn't see what was going on because their backs were to us. Ladbrooke, hearing the door, turned her head. Her face was colorless.

"Oh, my God," I said, when I came abreast of her and saw what had happened. Geraldine had her left arm extended across the hardwood floor, the palm of her hand upward. A huge, six-inch nail had been driven straight through the palm, nailing her hand right to the floor.

"Joyce has gone to call an ambulance," Carolyn said.

"Go get Frank," I said. "Get somebody for the kids. Get them out of the hallways."

I looked at Geraldine. Her face was perfectly blank. No tears, no look of pain, nothing. I wondered if she was in shock. Kneeling down beside her and Ladbrooke, I reached a hand out to feel her forehead. Then I looked over at Lad. "What happened?"

"I just found her. We were out on the playground, and I looked around and she was gone. So I came in to see where she was. And she was here. She had the hammer and she was just hitting the nail with it, just hitting and hitting and hitting." Lad's voice was shaking. As I rose back to my feet, I rested my hand momentarily on her shoulder. That, too, was shaking.

I didn't know what to do. There was surprisingly little blood, although certainly I had no idea of how much blood to expect in this situation. Indeed, it was almost more grisly for lack of blood. But I didn't know what to do; my first aid course had never covered anything quite like this. I didn't think we ought to try anything with the nail or the hand, but I was unsure whether or not to do something for Geraldine herself. It would be hard to get her into any kind of shock recovery position with her hand nailed to the floor.

Frank appeared, his face filling with the same look of revulsion the rest of us had had on first seeing Geraldine. Like me, he immediately touched her face. He encouraged her to try and lie down, which she did manage to do. Then he rose and turned to me.

"Joyce and Katy have the kids. They're all together in Carolyn's room and they're fine, so don't worry about them."

The ambulance arrived within a few minutes, and in came three big burly men in black shirts. They carried an assortment of equipment and surrounded Geraldine. Ladbrooke, who had never released her grip on Geraldine's arm throughout, now finally eased back and stood up. She paused a moment to stretch stiff muscles and then moved behind Carolyn and me. I knelt to reassure Geraldine.

After considerable discussion, the medics decided to remove part of the flooring and take it along, rather than attempt to separate the nail from Geraldine's hand then and there. This necessitated locating the carpenters, who were still obliviously drinking their coffee in the lounge. One appeared shortly after with a small handsaw and knelt down to begin cutting through the floorboards. The wood was oak, part of the original turn-of-the-century flooring that had by and large been covered by linoleum on the building's other stories. It made the going very slow work indeed with a handsaw. All throughout, Geraldine remained silent and motionless, her face growing paler and paler.

Finally, the small square of wood came free. Geraldine still did not lift her arm, but one of the medics did. Another scooped up Geraldine herself. Frank had departed earlier to call the Lonrhos. He was going to accompany Geraldine in the ambulance to the hospital and wanted her family there at the other end.

I went upstairs and out the front door of the building to the ambulance with Geraldine and the medics. It wasn't until we actually reached the vehicle and the men started bringing out the stretcher that Geraldine showed any real sign of life.

"Miss," she cried out suddenly. "Don't let them take me, Miss. Miss! Miss!"

The ambulance men laid her gently onto the stretcher, and I bent down to reassure her. She clutched at me with her uninjured hand.

"You're going to be okay, lovey. Mr. Cotton's going to come in the ambulance with you and ride along to the hospital. And your Auntie Bet will be there at the other end. Everything's going to be all right. They'll take good care of you."

"No! Don't leave me, Miss! Please, don't let them take me!"

I hugged her. I clutched her upper torso, pulled her against me and hugged her. I kissed her face. Frank was there then and he gently unlocked Geraldine's fingers from my shirt. The medics lifted the stretcher into the ambulance, and Frank climbed in beside it. Geraldine made no further sound.

Frantic about the other children, I returned as fast as I could to Carolyn's room. Carolyn still wasn't in there and neither was Lad. Poor Joyce, and Katy from the office, had tried to create some kind of order. There were games and toys out, and when I arrived, Joyce was trying to get the children to sing along to a record, but about half of them were up, moving aimlessly about the room. Of mine, only Shemona was actually singing. Shamie and Mariana sat glumly at a far table. Leslie was on the floor, her expression entirely blank. Dirkie was squeezed under the small sand-tray table.

"Come on, you lot," I said from the doorway. My children rose and came over. "Thanks, Joyce. Thanks, Katy."

Joyce nodded wearily.

"What's happened to Geraldine?" Shamie asked when we were in the hallway.

"She's been hurt. She was in where she shouldn't have been, playing with the carpenters' tools, and she's hurt herself. Mr. Cotton called an ambulance, and they've taken her to the hospital. I don't think it's very serious. I think she'll be okay again quite soon, but we'll have to wait to hear more."

"What did she do?"

"She hurt her hand."

Upstairs, I opened the door and turned on the lights. Glancing up at the clock above the chalkboard, I was shocked to see the time. I hadn't realized just how slowly the men had been working to free Geraldine. There were only about twenty minutes left until the end of the school day. That was much too short a time even to get a decent discussion going. Casting around for something to calm the children down and allow me the opportunity to talk to them each individually, I suggested they take a big box containing the crayons and felt-tipped pens down, and we would make pictures.

"What of, Miss?" Shemona asked.

"Anything you want, sweetheart. What do you feel like drawing?"

"Can I make a picture of my brother?" she asked. "Of him before they took him to the hospital?"

I nodded.

About halfway through the remaining time, I heard the classroom door open. I rose from my chair and went around the corner to see who it was. Carolyn stood just inside the door. When I appeared, she beckoned me over, pulling me into the hallway, out of the children's hearing. Her expression was distraught.

"You need to go in with Ladbrooke," she said.

"Where is she?"

"In the bathroom. She's really upset."

"I can't just now. I've got the kids."

"She's sick to her stomach, Torey. She's throwing up in there."

"I'm sure she's okay. She has the world's touchiest stomach, and you just sort of have to ignore it. I'm sure she's going to be all right."

Carolyn shook her head. "You need to go in there and do something."

"Carolyn, I can't. I've got the kids. And the kids come first. *You* go in there and stay with her if you think she needs somebody now. I'll be in as soon as I can. It won't be that long."

From the expression on Carolyn's face, I think she was speaking as much from her own need as Ladbrooke's. Lowering my head, I took a deep breath and held it a moment before expelling it slowly. We were suddenly coming apart at the seams, all of us, Carolyn and myself included. I took a second deep breath.

A look of helplessness crossed Carolyn's features, and she let her shoulders drop. "This is awful," she said softly, then there was a brief moment's silence before she turned and left.

Back inside the classroom, the children were all sitting silently, watching for my return.

"Who was that?" Shamie asked.

"Miss Berry."

"Where's Ladbrooke?"

"She isn't feeling very well at the moment."

His gaze narrowed. "What's going on anyway? Why's everyone acting so funny?"

"Everybody's just a little upset by Geraldine's injury. It caught us unawares. We weren't expecting her to get hurt and, because we care about her, it's upset us all."

"Is she dead?"

"No. No, of course not." I smiled reassuringly at him. "No, don't worry, love. Like I said, she isn't even badly hurt. It just startled us, that's all. But she'll be quite fine again soon, I'm sure."

There was a moment's silence. Shemona had continued to color throughout most of Shamie's conversation with me but at that point she put down her crayon and looked up. "I've seen a dead person before, Miss," she said. "Outside our church after Mass. He was laying on the pavement. He had blood coming out of his head. Right there. He was dead. And I saw him."

Shamie nodded. "So did I."

As soon as I had taken the children to their rides, I returned to the building. Sprinting up the stairs two at a time, I headed for the second-floor girls' rest room.

Ladbrooke was still inside one of the toilet stalls at the far end. The door to the stall was open, and she was sitting on the floor with her head back against the beige metal panel separating that toilet from the next one along. She had that horrible grayish cast to her skin that I'd previously associated with excessive drinking but now realized was probably more a result of the vomiting. She had clearly been crying, although by the time I came in, she was dry-eyed. She looked up when I approached. Her eyes had a dull, jaded look. Crossing her arms over her drawn-up knees, she lowered her forehead onto them.

I knelt down in the doorway of the toilet stall. Her hair had fallen forward, so I reached a hand out and gently put it behind her shoulder.

"What a day this has been," I said softly.

Ladbrooke didn't respond.

"That must have been dreadful for you, finding Geraldine like that. This is the wretched part of this work, the part they never tell you about in the job description."

Still no response.

I sat down on the tile floor, crossing my legs Indian-style and resting my elbows on them. The day was certainly taking its toll on me too.

Lad turned her head. Still resting it on her crossed arms, she turned just enough to look at me. I smiled, a rather inept response for the moment at hand.

"It was like seeing Jesus, nailed to the Cross," she said, her voice hoarse. Then she gazed past me to the metal door of the toilet stall.

"What exactly happened?" I asked.

"I couldn't find her."

"She'd just left the playground?"

Ladbrooke nodded slightly. "I went to see where she was. I thought maybe she'd gone to the toilet, but I wasn't sure, so I went to check. But I couldn't find her. So I started to look. And then . . ." She sat back, although she kept her legs drawn up. "I looked through the door to that room as I was going by. I just glanced in, not expecting to see her there, because, see, I thought she might have gone to the auditorium. The kids do that once in a while if you don't watch them. So I just happened to glance in, and there she was. I saw what she was doing. It stunned me so much, I just went tearing in to stop her. I didn't think about anything else, like going back to get Carolyn, which is probably what I should have done. I just ran in and jerked the hammer out of her hand. And held on. I was afraid to let go, Torey. I was afraid she'd do something worse to herself if I didn't hold onto her. I didn't know what else to do. But then I was trapped there with her. The door had shut behind me. I just went in without thinking about propping the door open. And nobody could hear me. I yelled for help. I yelled for Carolyn, for Joyce, for you. For somebody to come help me. But nobody seemed to hear, because nobody came."

"Oh, lovey," I said.

She swallowed. There were tears in her eyes. "I wanted to stop her, Torey, but I didn't know what to do."

"You did okay, Lad. You did what you could."

I could hear her rapid breathing.

"I hope you're not feeling this was your fault, what Geraldine did," I said. "It wasn't. It's Geraldine's own problems coming to a head, and I suspect it's been coming for a long time now."

"I should have stopped her," Ladbrooke said, her voice low. "If only I'd been a few minutes earlier . . . I mean, I did notice that she was gone from the playground. I thought it was just the toilet, so I didn't do anything at first, but she didn't have permission."

"No, don't think like that. It's only destructive at this point."

"But I wasn't doing anything out there. It wasn't as if I'd been busy. I was just leaning against the wall. It was sunny and . . ."

"Ladbrooke, don't. It wasn't your fault. How many thousands of times do we let the children go off the playground to use the toilets or get a drink or whatever? She could have done this, whether she had permission to go in the building or not. You can't hawk over them every minute. That'd be more destructive in the end than this was. You did okay, Lad. I'm sure I wouldn't have done any better if it had been me down there instead. It was just one of those dreadful things."

Silence came. Ladbrooke brought her thumb up to chew the nail but didn't. Instead, she rested the tip of it in her mouth, the way Shemona did when she tried to stop herself from sucking it. The silence grew deep and introspective.

"Can I tell you about something?" Ladbrooke asked after several minutes' silence. Her eyes remained unfocused, her expression distant.

"Yes, of course."

"You know, my brother Bobby . . ." and then she stopped.

Silence.

"What about him?" I asked.

She looked over at me, searched my face a moment and then looked away. Still she didn't immediately respond.

"Bobby and I were close. We were only eighteen months apart. Less, actually, because my birthday's July 21st and his is New Year's Day."

I nodded.

She looked at me. "I get the feeling sometimes that you don't think I've ever been close to anyone. That I'm not very good at close relationships." She paused. "Maybe I'm not in some ways. Maybe you're right. But I was close to Bobby. I loved Bobby.

"See, I think it was growing up in our family that did it. You had to be close. What's that adage? Comrades in adversity, or something. That was us. He was the only other person in the world who understood what it was like."

She stretched her legs out in front of her and leaned back against the metal divider.

"Anyway, Bobby had an apartment near Asbury Park. That's in New Jersey, down on the shore. And I was at Princeton on the project. I used to go over there all the time to see him. His apartment was really near the beach and we used to go down there all the time, walking, looking for things. You know, sort of beachcombing. It was just something we liked to do.

"Bobby was never a talker. Nobody in my family was. But he was easy to be with. I could just be myself and not worry. I came over once or twice a week, just to get away from Princeton. To get away from Tom sometimes too. I hid out with Bobby quite a lot.

"He had plenty else going on. He was an electronics engineer, and he was doing okay. He was into research too. And he had a girlfriend. Her name was Sarah. I'd met her a few times. I don't think they were really serious. Just enjoying themselves."

Ladbrooke fell silent then. There was a moment's expectancy, as if she was still mid-thought, but then it passed, and a more complete silence came down around us.

I regarded her, trying to discern why she'd stopped talking.

She shifted position, pushing her hair back behind her shoulders.

"What next?" I asked.

"I went over this one time," she said, her voice soft. Pulling her knees up, she hugged them. "It was September. A really clear day, you know, the kind you get in the fall. I was late. I'd said I'd be there by four, but then we had this meeting and I stayed longer than I'd meant to. Nothing special, but it made me late. And then the traffic was bad because it was a Friday. Still, I didn't think anything about it. I hadn't bothered to call him or anything. You see, usually I'm very punctual, but Bobby never was. He was terrible. He'd be, like, half an hour late somewhere, and that'd be early for him. No sense of time at all. So he wasn't the kind to say anything if I was late. Usually, he never noticed.

"Anyhow, I got there about 5:30, I guess. I parked the car and went on up to his apartment. But when I got there, the door was locked. Now, this really surprised me because, normally, Bobby never locked the door if he knew I was coming. I had a key, but he usually left it open for me. His car was in the garage, so I'd assumed he was in. I couldn't figure out why he'd locked his door."

She paused.

"What I thought, see . . . was that he probably had Sarah in there. I thought they were in there, you know, making love or something, and he'd locked the door to keep me from barging in on them. So I decided to ring the bell. I rang and rang and rang. But no answer. So I thought he must have stepped out for a minute. There was a cash-and-carry down on the corner, so maybe he'd gone there. And I let myself in. All the lights were on. There had been a record on the stereo, but it was finished playing . . ."

She was silent a few moments, all her muscles rigid.

"It's funny, you know, the way your mind works. The things you remember from an event. It's always the little things, isn't it? Little, tiny, unimportant things. Like I remember looking at the record on the stereo. It was Bach. Bach's "Sheep May Safely Graze." And then I went out to the refrigerator to get something to drink. I was really thirsty and wanted something like a Coke, but all there was in there were a bunch of cans of that horrid cheap stuff that comes in flavors. You know, like black cherry and strawberry . . ."

"Lad, what happened?"

"I mean, what I remember is *that,* that stupid assortment of soft drinks in the refrigerator. Feeling really irritated that Bobby could never get in anything decent that I liked . . ."

She glanced over very quickly and our eyes met in that split second.

She looked away. A long, intense silence followed. Her eyes filled with tears. They welled up, shimmered briefly on her lashes and then slowly trickled down over her cheeks.

"What had happened?" I asked.

"He'd killed himself. I went in to use the bathroom, and there he was. Hanging in the shower. And he'd left a little note on a piece of paper, lying on the edge of the bathtub. It said . . ." Her voice broke. "It said, 'Sorry, Laddy.' And that was all."

Forehead on her drawn-up knees, she began to cry.

"He'd only been dead about an hour. That's what the coroner said. If I'd only not been late that day . . . Why hadn't I at least bothered to call? Why did I stand outside the door all that time instead of bothering to get my key out? Why did I go stick my head inside the goddamned refrigerator first?"

"Oh, Lad, I am so sorry."

Ladbooke looked over at me. Her jaw was tight in an effort to control the tears, so momentarily she could not speak. She looked down, then back over again.

"Hold me, okay?" she asked, her voice almost inaudible. "Would you?"

And I did. In the dingy confines of the toilet stall, I reached over and pulled her against me and held on as tightly as I could.

CHAPTER TWENTY-NINE

It took us a considerable amount of time to get out of the girls' rest room and back into the classroom, and even then, we were both in a sorry state. My discomfort, however, was inconsequential compared with Ladbrooke's. She sat at the table, drinking water out of my coffee mug and looking as if she had just survived a war. It was almost 5:30, but I didn't have any of the necessary preparation work done for the next day, so I took a couple of aspirin and then sat down with my plan book to get on with things. Folding her arms on the tabletop, Lad lay her head down on them and closed her eyes. She remained like that throughout the time it took me to do the plans.

Finally, I rose from the table and went to put my work away. "I need to get something to eat," I said, as I slid the plan book back into the filing drawer.

Ladbrooke straightened up. She rubbed her face and her eyes. "Don't leave me alone just yet, okay?" She didn't look up. "This has been a bit too much for me today. I don't think I'm going to cope with it, not without having a drink."

"Do you want to come with me? I've got to get something to eat, because my head is killing me. Do you want to come too?"

She nodded.

"Ring Tom first, though."

"Why?"

"Just to let him know where you are. Then we'll go get something to eat."

"He won't care where I am."

"Just do it, okay?"

We went to a small, self-service restaurant that specialized in soup and sandwiches. I wanted a place where we could relax and not be hurried, but I was reluctant to go home. After the tumultuous afternoon, I wasn't up to an evening entirely on my own with Ladbrooke. I needed other people around and the reassurance of normal life.

The restaurant was ideal: dark, quiet and fairly empty. The booths, while large and comfortable, still afforded me a view of the other patrons and the serving area without infringing on our privacy. Lad took a bowl of soup and a glass of milk, while I wolfed down soup, three sandwiches and dessert to appease an adrenaline-crazed body. Afterward, we relaxed in companionable silence while I had a cup of coffee.

"You know," Ladbrooke said after a while, "the thing that hurt me the most about Bobby's suicide was that I never saw it coming. I never had an inkling. I wasn't just saying it; we *were* close. But he never said a word to me about it, never said he was depressed, never said things were going badly for him."

"I can imagine it must have been a shock."

She nodded. "I kept asking and asking myself why. I still do, sometimes. *Why?* Everything seemed to be coming together so well for him. He had a job he loved. He was earning a good salary. He had Sarah. So why did he do it?"

I shook my head.

"That eats at me, even now, even after—what?—almost six years. It always made the guilt worse to cope with, because I thought it was my fault for not seeing it coming, not preventing it. That, or God forbid, even worse. I mean, what if it was just intended as a gesture, if he'd just needed help and didn't know how to ask for it? And if I'd gotten there that day when I'd told him I would, then . . . maybe it would have been enough to . . . I don't know. I suppose it's useless to keep thinking about it."

"It's useless to keep blaming yourself for it."

She nodded wearily. "Maybe so. But it's next to impossible not to. I even dream about it sometimes, about coming just in time . . . but even in my dreams, I never save him."

A small silence came between us.

"I told you Bobby wasn't much of a talker. I wonder now if perhaps he didn't have the same kind of problem with expression as I do. He was better at getting on with people, but he never talked easily. In a way, that was nice, because he was the only person I never felt I *had* to talk with. But now, of course, I realize he must have had a whole lot more going on inside his head than I ever knew about. The sad thing is, if I didn't know about it, chances are no one else did either."

She sighed. "What I still can't figure out is why he did it *then*." She looked over, glancing in my direction but not directly at me. "You have to sort of understand about our family. We had a really rough childhood, Bobby, Kit and me. Not in the physical sense. Nobody abused us. But emotionally . . ."

I nodded.

"Kit never did manage. He had problems right from the start, both in school and at home. He was taken into care once, when he was about nine, because he got into trouble with the police. Even now he's not gotten himself together. He's been in and out of jail and detox centers all his life. But Bobby and me, we always managed to do all right. We kept each other going. We called ourselves the Two Musketeers when we were little. Not too original, I know, but that's what we were. We used to make these blood pacts with one another—you know, one for all, all for one. We got really serious about it and cut our fingers and all that. I mean, it was silly. He already *was* my blood brother. But it worked for us. It got us over the rough bits and kept us going. We survived."

Ladbrooke grew thoughtful.

"So I keep asking myself, why did he commit suicide then, when he'd finally made it, when he was finally free? If he was the kind of person to do that sort of thing, why hadn't he done it earlier when he had all the reasons?"

"That's impossible to say."

"Bobby's killing himself completely devastated me. For a long time, for like a year or more, I was absolutely numb. And then everything just fell apart. I lost all faith in myself. To have missed seeing something that catastrophic coming, to have misjudged someone I knew so well and loved so much—how the hell could I possibly trust my judgment on anything else?" She paused. "When I discovered I didn't know Bobby, I suddenly felt like I didn't know me any more either."

She exhaled a long, slow breath.

"I spent a lot of time thinking about suicide myself after that. Before, it had never really occurred to me, but then suddenly, it didn't seem like such a bad idea. My biggest obstacle was not having the courage to actually do it. I made the plans. God, I made the plans at least a hundred times, and on each occasion, I fully intended to carry them out. But I was always too big a chicken in the end, which, like everything else in my life, left me feeling like shit."

A quiet, grim silence wrapped itself around us. Ladbrooke just sat, her thoughts absorbing her. I glanced around. The restaurant had emptied further. There were only about half a dozen people there.

"Bobby's doing that destroyed the whole image I'd worked up of us. I'd always thought of us as a couple of *real* survivors, the kind of people who can always make it, in spite of the odds. I used to get by on that quite a lot. Things'd go wrong, something awful'd happen, and I'd manage to keep going because I had this image of myself as a real survivor. But it was an image I'd built up from childhood, from Bobby and me sticking together through thick and thin, from all the Two Musketeers junk. It wasn't an image of *me*; it was an image of *us*. Both of us, together. Because that's why we survived. Then, all of a sudden, wham. He didn't survive. And my world fell apart.

"I couldn't believe it. You see, he was always better than I was. He was smarter. He was really well liked; people got on with him. He never drank. I was the one who was constantly screwing up, not him. He was the strong one. And then . . . and then, I mean, what hope is left after that? What's the point of trying?"

"But you *are* a survivor, Lad," I said.

"I don't know. If you're drowning and someone saves you, it doesn't mean you won't drown the next time you fall in the water."

"But I don't think you will."

She shrugged noncommitally.

"You *have* survived, Ladbrooke, and that's been no mean feat, by the sound of it. You're a great deal stronger than you give yourself credit for."

"I wish I felt like it sometimes."

Eventually, Lad came home with me, and I made a place for her to sleep on the couch. Beyond that, we were both too worn out to do anything other than collapse in front of the television. Ladbrooke, stretched out on top of the bedding on the couch, fell asleep during the ten o'clock news. I turned off the set and went in to have a long soak in the tub to ease still-tense muscles along my back.

Tired as I was, I was unable to fall asleep immediately. The events of the day kept replaying themselves. However, my thoughts were haunted mostly by Bobby, whom I'd never seen, not even in a photograph, yet could visualize with heart-wrenching clarity. I wasn't seeing a twenty-six-year-old suicide victim, but rather a little boy, undoubtedly like so very many of the little boys I'd encountered in my career. He was the small, quiet one in the back of the classroom. He was the kid we forgot at the fairgrounds because we didn't even realize he was missing. He was the boy who continually came and pressed his face against the window of my classroom door but who always disappeared before I opened it. That was Bobby, the child no one quite managed to notice.

I visited Geraldine in hospital the following afternoon. Although her injury was not serious, there was some concern about possible nerve damage; thus, the doctors had decided to keep her for a period of observation. She was in a room with three other children. When I first came into the room, it took me a moment to recognize her. She wasn't wearing her glasses, and it completely altered the appearance of her face. She looked innocent, an attribute I hadn't previously associated with Geraldine.

"Hi, punkin," I said. "How are you?"

She smiled when she realized it was me. I don't think she could see very far without her glasses.

"Here, I've brought you something." I handed her a small package.

"What is it?"

"Open it and see."

For a few moments she struggled one-handed to open the gift and then looked up. "Could you help me, please?"

I reached over and held it for her while she undid the wrapping. It was a very small stuffed lion. She smiled at it and cuddled it against her cheek. "Thank you, Miss."

"I thought of you, when I saw that," I said. "Brave as a lion. You were yesterday, you know. With all those men working over you. And going in the ambulance with Mr. Cotton. You were very brave."

She squinted slightly, regarding my face. "I was afraid you'd be mad at me."

"No. It was a rather unfortunate thing to have done, but I'm not mad."

"Is Ladbrooke coming to see me?"

"Well, not today, I think. But if you're still here on Monday, I'm sure she'll come."

"Is she mad at me?"

"No. You frightened her. I think she was more scared than you were, but she isn't angry. Neither of us is."

Geraldine looked down at the toy lion. She stroked its mane tenderly.

Sitting in the chair beside the bed, I watched her. I felt a desperate need to talk to her. With sudden, distressing clarity I was having to face the fact that somehow, somewhere along the line, she had slipped away from me.

"I wish I'd known that you felt so very unhappy yesterday afternoon," I said quietly. "Perhaps if I'd known, I could have done something to help."

Geraldine shrugged slightly. Most of her attention still appeared to be on the lion, which she was petting over and over again.

I glanced at the other children in the room. They weren't being noisy or intrusive, but this wasn't a very private place. Lowering my head, I studied my hands for a moment. Would it be better to wait until another time, until she was well again, until we had more privacy? Or had I lost too many chances already, waiting for a "better time" to come along?

Geraldine did not look at me.

"Can you tell me why you did what you did?"

She shrugged. "I don't know."

"Was it Shemona saying she was never going back?"

"I don't know."

"I can appreciate where that must have hurt you a lot, her saying that. Sometimes things kind of pile up, and something hurtful like that can push us into doing things we ordinarily wouldn't have done."

Geraldine continued to regard the toy lion. "Like I said, Miss, I don't know."

I looked over. "Maybe we can try again. This was an unpleasant thing to happen, but now that it has, it's probably better to put it behind us and concentrate instead on what we can do to keep you from feeling like you need to do that sort of thing again."

She shrugged.

Silence came between us. Geraldine lifted the lion up to eye level and regarded it a long moment before finally reaching over and setting it on the table beside the bed. She then folded her hands in her lap. When I didn't speak, she glanced briefly in my direction, catching my eye. She looked down then at the bandage on her left hand.

"I'm to see a skytrist now," she said. "Did Auntie Bet tell you?"

"Yes."

"His name's Dr. Morris. I have to see him. It's not a choice."

"I'm sure that will help."

Geraldine shrugged. "I don't know. It'd be better if Auntie Bet used the money to just let me go home. That'd help me more."

Of the other children, only Shamie questioned what had happened to Geraldine's hand. Living with her, he had, of course, much more opportunity to know it was a self-inflicted injury. No doubt the adults in the household had discussed the matter, and perhaps even Geraldine herself had said something. I didn't know. However, it was clear the episode preyed on him. Finally, during a quiet moment the following week, I called him aside.

"What's wrong with her, that she does things like that?" he asked.

"I think that there've been a lot of things in Geraldine's life that have been hard for her to accept," I said.

"But why can't she? Shemona's accepted them. I've accepted them. Why can't Geraldine?"

"All things aren't the same for all people, Shamie. Geraldine misses Belfast. She misses her home and her family and the way things were before. We need to have a lot of compassion in something like this, because Geraldine has had so much to adjust to. That's why your aunt and uncle and the people at the hospital have decided that maybe Geraldine needs a little more help getting things straightened out. That's why she's going to be seeing Dr. Morris."

We were in the chalkboard arm of the room at the small student desk. Shamie sat, sprawled over his chair in a glum, almost recalcitrant pose, as if he were there to be reprimanded. "She's ruining everything," he said, his voice disgruntled.

"How so?"

"I just want it to be peaceful. But she's ruining everything. She goes around yelling and screaming all the time. She says how nothing's ever as good here as it was in Belfast. Nothing makes her happy."

I didn't respond immediately, not knowing how to. I lowered my head and studied my hands while considering what to answer. When I next looked over, I saw tears in Shamie's eyes.

"She's just like my brother Colin," he said, his voice low.

"In what way?"

"Oh, she just is. The way she thinks." He brought up a hand to wipe his eyes. "She wants things to be the way they aren't. You know. Not real. She thinks everything's going to be perfect, just if. If we were back in Belfast. If she was back at Greener Terrace. If. It doesn't matter how you do it or what you do or who gets hurt, just so you can have what you want. That's the way she thinks. And that it'll all be perfect, when whatever it is happens. That's all that counts."

"And your brother thinks that way too?"

More tears came to his eyes. They clung to his long lashes. He nodded.

"Is Colin in the IRA?"

Again Shamie nodded. There was a pause. "Well, he's in prison now. Him and Brendan both." Shamie sniffed softly. "My daddy was always shouting at him. There was always shouting in our house. My daddy works with the dad of the fellow who got killed. He knew him. My daddy kept saying to Colin that he was just another man's son."

Shamie straightened up in the chair and leaned forward. "But it never made any difference to Colin. All he cares about is the republic. That's all he talks about. If Ireland was united tomorrow, I don't know what Colin would do. Everything he's ever done has been based on hating the Brits."

"And now you feel that Geraldine is the same as Colin?" I asked.

Shamie nodded. "She is. There's still yelling. There's still fighting. I might as well be home. At least my mam was there."

"Do you want to go back?"

This brought the first sign of serious tears. He lowered his head and his mouth dragged down into a grimace, but he still did not weep openly. I rose and came to kneel next to him. I put my arm around his shoulders, and he willingly accepted comfort. I held him close for several moments, until the tears abated, then, rather than returning to my chair, I simply sat down on the floor beside him. This put me physically lower than Shamie, and he had a hard time avoiding my eyes.

"*Do* you want to go back?"

"I can't."

"Why not?"

He didn't answer.

"Are you still worried about the Troubles? About something happening to your family?"

He shook his head. A small silence slipped in, and Shamie regarded his hands in his lap.

He glanced at me, then back to his hands. He shook his head a second time. "I always thought Colin talked rubbish. I always, always did. It just can't be right, people killing each other like that. But then . . . then the Brits arrested Uncle Paddy. And well, then what happened, happened . . ."

A long pause followed. And then he said, "What if Colin's right?"

I looked at him.

"If we all took up arms and defied them and made them reunite us, maybe it would all stop. Maybe Colin's right. What if he is? What do I do then?"

CHAPTER
THIRTY

✴ Five weeks left. In the classroom, final arrangements were getting underway. Mrs. Samuelson was formally hired, and she came over for three days during the first week of May to see the classroom and the things we were doing. And, of course, she met Dirkie, Leslie and Geraldine, all of whom would be staying on with her. She was a pleasant woman in her mid-forties, who fortunately was unencumbered by long hair or cats.

I pushed Shamie out of the nest. He had been attending his nonacademic classes three times a week for some time, but I finally got him to go to the junior high half days. This time, with lots of encouragement, we were successful. Our classroom, however, felt empty with both him and Shemona gone in the mornings.

Mariana was confirmed for third grade in a school not too far from her home. Although I did not personally know her classroom teacher, she had come on good recommendation from the resource teacher in that school, whom I knew and respected. So the placement seemed as good as we could hope for. Mariana went over for two half days to acquaint herself with the setup, and I spent an afternoon after school with her new teacher, passing all the pertinent information on to her.

Shemona was slated for first grade in the Catholic school that her cousins attended. Although there was no chance for her to visit the class while it was in session, Ladbrooke and I took her over in the afternoon after school was out, and we all met several of the sisters who would be involved with Shemona and her new teacher. Shemona was pleased that two of her three cousins who were in the school had had this same teacher, so we felt considerable confidence in the placement.

On the whole, I felt happy with everyone's proposed future. Most years things didn't work out so neatly. I was always stuck with one or two who didn't seem to fit in anywhere, but with this group, it all looked promising, which made the upcoming end easier to face.

The square peg in the round hole, of course, was Ladbrooke.

I had devoted a fair amount of my spare time to thinking about Ladbrooke and what to do with her. Tim's suggestion of introducing a new therapist had remained the most sensible alternative, but sensibility still did not govern a lot of what Ladbrooke did. I suspected that she would be more likely to accept the idea of therapy and a new therapist now than she would have been earlier in the year, but I knew it was still an issue needing very diplomatic handling. As it turned out, it was Carolyn who brought the matter to a head. She stopped by the room one afternoon after school with a whole armload of brochures, which she promptly dropped onto the table in front of Ladbrooke and me.

"I thought you could use these," she said to Ladbrooke. They were course prospectuses from the nearby university.

"I've got to get six credits in this summer if I want to have my master's done by January. I was thinking of taking an overview course on emotional disturbance." Carolyn looked over at me. "Even if I never teach E.D. kids, I'm thinking that after that incident with Geraldine, it might be helpful to know more."

I nodded.

"Anyway, I thought I'd drop these by. You might as well have them, Ladbrooke."

Lad's expression was questioning.

Carolyn smiled in a friendly fashion. "I mean, I assume you're going to want to get some certification." Then she turned to me. "She is staying on, isn't she? We're not losing you both, are we?"

"I haven't quite decided," Lad replied.

"You could get quite a bit of course work done over the summer, if you wanted. That's how Joyce is doing it. And I'll be there. We could have our own contingent," Carolyn said cheerfully. "And we could have a car pool. It's sixty-four miles round trip. But if we were all going, we could split the driving."

Ladbrooke nodded.

"Anyway, I've got to run. See you two around."

I looked over at Lad after Carolyn had left. "Does she know something I don't?"

"Don't feel bad. She seems to know something *I* don't." And Lad burst into giggles.

A small silence followed while Ladbrooke pulled over a prospectus and opened it. I remained sitting but didn't go back to what I'd been doing. It occurred to me once again with poignancy how blinkered my relationship with Ladbrooke still was. Busily plotting her future with the same detached concern I had for the children's well-being, I had never asked her about her intentions regarding the actual work we'd been sharing. How did we spend all this time together, I wondered, and never talk about things like that?

"You *are* good at this," I said.

Ladbrooke didn't look up from the brochure.

"It'd make sense, your going for certification now." I snagged one of the course listings and pulled it over in front of me.

"I never said anything to give Carolyn this idea."

"I suppose Carolyn was just assuming that you liked it, considering the time you've spent in here. And she could see for herself that you have an aptitude for it, because you do."

"No," she said, her voice quiet. "I wouldn't want to do it without you. I stayed for you, Torey. If it had just been the work, I probably would have walked out the moment Dirkie told me I had big tits. I'd have walked out and never come back. I was terrible at all of this."

"You weren't."

"I *was.* Don't try to flatter me. Maybe I'm okay now, but I was terrible then. And I knew it."

I didn't reply.

"I just stayed to be near you and the children. The chemistry in this place was phenomenal. You could feel it coming in the door. I just wanted to be part of it." A slight, self-conscious smile touched her lips. "And after a while, I just stayed to prove I could, to prove I was worth all this trouble, but I've never really belonged."

"Of course you've belonged, Ladbrooke. What a thing to say."

"No, you don't understand what I'm saying. You *let* me belong. I've loved it; I've felt really good. But it isn't mine. You and the kids made it alive. It would never live for me on its own."

"So what are your plans?"

"I want to go back to my own work."

I looked over.

She smiled in a faintly apologetic way. "Have I disappointed you?"

I shook my head. "No. To be perfectly honest, I haven't even managed to think that far ahead. I haven't got much future sense."

"I don't know what I'm going to do exactly, but I've definitely decided I want to go back. This here, like you're always saying, is real. This is the real world in here. God knows, my stuff's all in the ivory tower, but it's what I'm good at." She smiled gently. "And it would be so wonderful to be back with something I feel competent at."

A long silence followed. Ladbrooke gathered the brochures and prospectuses up into a pile and set them to one side. Then she returned to what she'd been doing before Carolyn had come in. I picked up my pen but did not resume work. Instead, I just sat, staring at my plan book.

"Lad?"

"Hmmm?"

"I've been thinking?"

"What about?"

"Do you remember James McCann? He was the psychiatrist who came down from that project on the reservation. He observed in the classroom for those few days in January."

"Yes, I remember him."

"He's a super therapist. I've seen his work. I've seen videos of him in therapy. And he's a personal friend of mine . . ."

She knew what I was leading up to. She lowered her head a moment and touched her eyes, as if she had a headache. Then looking over at me, she shook her head.

"I haven't even said anything yet," I protested.

"No."

"He's *good*. You'd like him. You got on well enough with him when he was here. He's no different in private."

She shook her head.

I frowned.

"Look, Torey, I've thought about it quite a lot and I've decided I'm not going to see anyone."

"Laa-ad," I moaned.

"I think I can manage. I mean, I know things were rough. I know I was a mess, but they're a lot better now. And I think I can cope with them on my own."

"He's really *very* good. You'd like him. You'd like his style."

"But it's not going to be the same, is it? Some therapist. Sitting around talking in some dinky office for an hour a week. It's not going to be like in here, is it?"

"It doesn't need to be," I replied. "It just needs to help. You've done so well. I don't want us to have come all this way just to lose everything we've gained."

She studied my face. "You are a funny person. You've got so much patience, but you've got no faith at all."

"I've got faith."

"No, you don't. You've got no faith in me whatsoever. You don't think I can do it. Just like you didn't think I could make it through the Easter weekend. Just like in February, when I said I'd stop drinking. You had no faith in that either."

"I've got no expectations. That's different from no faith."

She shrugged. "Whatever you want to call it."

I fell silent.

"Now you're upset."

"I'm not upset," I replied. "I'm just trying to figure out what next."

"Listen, here's how I'm planning it. I'm going to get hold of my old advisor back at Princeton. I want to get back into the spectroscopy work; that's what I'm interested in. I suspect our old project's kaput by this time. It nearly was when I left it, so I don't expect to get back on that. But I thought I'd talk to John and see what's around." She paused. "It means having to ask him for references . . ."

She smiled then, dipping her head to catch my eye. "See how far I've come? I never thought I was ever going to be able to face those people again in my life. Now I think maybe I can. I know I can. Or at least I'm willing to try."

I smiled back.

"So aren't you proud of me?"

Still smiling, I nodded.

"And if something's going on, if John can put me onto something, then I'll go back to work."

I nodded again.

"And if I can get back to work, I'll be okay. I'll have something to do and I'll keep myself together. I wouldn't be here to see a therapist anyway."

I didn't know what to say. Here we were, taking opposite sides of the same discussion we'd had in early April. Then, it had been Lad protesting and me reassuring. Now the roles were reversed. Had things changed that much in four weeks? Or was this simply a new example of Ladbrooke's old tactic of making a good offense the best defense?

"What about Tom?" I asked. "What about Leslie and everything at home?"

Lad took a deep breath and let it out slowly. "Well, I was just coming to that," she said softly, her voice flat. "I'm thinking maybe I'll go back East and work a while. If not Princeton, then probably M.I.T. I'm thinking I'll get my work sorted out first, and then I'll take a look at this thing with Tom."

"By 'this thing,' do you mean your marriage?"

She nodded.

A pause came, and she looked over, searched my face for a moment or two and then looked down at her work. She raised her shoulders as if to shrug but then slowed the gesture down, keeping her shoulders up several seconds before finally dropping them.

"I don't know, Torey. I guess the only way to say it is that I've pretty much concluded that Tom and I can't stay together. At least not for the moment. I won't stay sane if we do. I still love him. And I know he still loves me. But I'm not sure we're meant to live together. I'm not sure we're good for each other."

As I listened, I had an absurd recollection of her conversation about Bobby, of her telling me how stunned she'd been to think she knew him so well and yet had missed all the internal activity that had led up to his suicide. I was having the very same kinds of startled feelings. All these plans for major change turning over in Ladbrooke's head, and I hadn't had a clue she was thinking them. Being with her so continually and having become so much at home with her still largely laconic nature, I'd grown overfamiliar with her silences. It had become too easy to assume that there was never anything going on behind them.

"I don't think Tom likes the new me," Ladbrooke said, her voice resigned. "It's been sort of a hard conclusion for me to come to, but I think that's what it boils down to."

"When are you planning to implement all this?" I asked.

She shrugged. "June, I suppose. I've been drafting letters, but I haven't sent any." She glanced over, a sheepish expression on her face. "I was hoping you might help me, that you might look at the letters and tell me if they're okay. You're a lot better writer than I am."

I smiled.

She smiled back. "I've got to confess, it's still hard to do. I'm afraid I couldn't find the guts to phone John, not right out of the blue. But I am up to writing a letter, if I can make it sound, well, professional."

Still a little overcome by this deluge of information, I didn't know quite what to say.

"You told me back at Easter that nine weeks was going to be enough. Remember that? I didn't believe you then, but you know, maybe it is going to be enough."

"Good; I'm glad," I said.

She studied my face a moment. A slight smile touched her lips. "You're not any good, are you, about not being in control."

Sadly, the episode over Geraldine's hand did not prove to be the catalyst for change that I had hoped it might be. Despite its bringing about much-needed psychiatric intervention and also acutely focusing my attention on my own lack of communication with Geraldine, nothing altered. She returned to school during the first week of May, her hand still in a large bandage, and went on much the way she always had.

My children all went down to the gymnasium over the lunch period and ate with Carolyn's children, where they were supervised by two aides specifically hired for the lunch hour. This period was considered sacrosanct by Carolyn, Joyce, Ladbrooke and me. Unless all hell broke loose, the children were the responsibility of these two lunch aides. The two women employed in this position were big, burly and experienced and could handle most crises that came their way, so we generally enjoyed a trauma-free forty-five minutes to ourselves. But the ultimate punishment for any of the children was first to be reported to us by one of these lunchtime Brunhildes and, if that didn't improve things, to be sent up to the class-room. Dirkie was our worst culprit in this regard and had been sent up to spend the rest of his lunch hour with Ladbrooke and me on a handful of occasions.

On Thursday of the week Geraldine returned to class, Lad and I were eating our lunches as usual. Ladbrooke was trying to wrestle open one of the incorrigible milk cartons that the dairy supplied us with and, in the process, spilled most of the contents across the table. She left the room to go get paper towels from the girls' rest room and returned with a dismayed expression.

"Something's going on down there," she said, and set the paper towels on the table.

"Where? In the lunch room?"

She nodded. "Somebody's screaming blue murder."

"One of ours?"

"Sounds like it." She bent to wipe up the milk.

Within moments noise approached our door. I put down my sandwich and went to see what was going on. One of the aides had Geraldine by the collar of her dress. In her other hand was Geraldine's lunch box.

I held open the door to let them in. "What's going on here?"

Geraldine wasn't crying, just hollering. "I didn't do it! I didn't do it!"

The aide shoved Geraldine in ahead of her and around the corner of the shelves to the table, where Lad and I had been eating. She pushed Geraldine into a chair. "Look at this," she replied, flicking open the latch on the lunch box. Out fell a huge collection of cookies, candy bars, cupcakes and the like. The box had been crammed completely full of them.

"Where did all this come from?" I asked.

"She's stealing them off Miss Berry's children again. She's got a regular little racket going. We've gotten after her and after her for doing this kind of thing, and I'm fed up with it. I told her if I caught her doing it one more time, she was going to have you to answer to."

I looked at all the things.

"She traps the other kids. Outside in the hall and in the bathroom, mostly. She makes them give her these things out of their lunches or she beats on them. Regular little mini-Mafia going here."

"I didn't do it!" Geraldine screamed, and she lunged across the table. Picking up Ladbrooke's milk carton, she pitched it viciously in the direction of the aide. It missed and milk went splashing across the floor.

Dragging Geraldine over, I yanked out the quiet chair and shoved her into it. "You sit there until you've settled down. Then we'll discuss all this." After seeing the aide out, I returned to my half-eaten lunch and sat down. Ladbrooke was on the floor, mopping up what had been left of her milk. She rolled her eyes when I looked over.

Geraldine fumed and fussed, determined to disrupt our lunch as much as possible. I didn't like having to sit there and eat, because I was providing a ready-made audience for her antics. Disgruntled, I wrapped up the other half of my sandwich and stuffed it into my lunch bag. Ladbrooke, also trying to avoid encouraging Geraldine's behavior, stood around the corner, leaning against the filing cabinet and cramming the remains of her salad into her mouth. I nudged her aside and opened the top drawer to put away my lunch.

"Come here," I said to Geraldine, as I came back around the divider. She rose from the quiet chair and approached me at the table. "So what is this?" I asked, "What happened?"

"Nothing."

"No, not 'nothing.' Mrs. Anderson found all these things in your lunch box and they don't belong to you. I want to know why you took them and what we're going to do about it."

Geraldine shrugged.

I waited.

"Shamie took my two cookies away from me. Last weekend. When we were sitting outside having our snack, he took my two away from me and ate them."

"You're saying you've taken, what, let's count them—nine, ten, twelve, fourteen things away from Miss Berry's children because Shamie took two cookies away from you last weekend?"

"It wasn't fair he took them. They were my cookies. Auntie Bet gave them to me."

"Do you think it's these children's fault that Shamie took your cookies?"

"No."

"So that reasoning doesn't quite make sense to me."

"They're retarded, those kids."

"Which means they need our special help, doesn't it? Rather than our taking advantage of them."

"But they're stupid."

"That's really immaterial, Geraldine. The fact we need to examine is that you were doing something wrong. You're bullying people who are weaker than you are. You're using fear and force to take things that don't belong to you. And this isn't the first time, is it? You've been caught doing this kind of thing again and again."

"But they're stupid."

"That's *not* a reason to take advantage of people. How would it make you feel if someone did that to you? If a bigger child stopped you in the hallway and demanded that you give her a nice piece of your lunch every day?"

"There aren't any bigger kids here."

"No, I know there aren't. But I want you to use your imagination. Imagine how you'd feel if someone forced you to give up your cookies and cupcakes every day. Would you like it?"

"Well, like I already said, Miss, Shamie took my cookies off me last weekend."

"So how did it make you feel?"

"I hated him. It was unfair."

"And how do you suppose it makes these children feel when you take their sweets away from them? Don't you suppose they think it's unfair too?"

"They're just retarded."

"Geraldine, they're people. They feel just like you and I do. And how do you think they felt?"

She looked me straight in the eye. "I don't care, really."

Disgruntled, I sighed and looked away. Expelling a long breath, I shoved my hair back from my face and rubbed my eyes. Then I looked back at her. "Can you see that there was something wrong with what you did?"

She shrugged.

"Is that yes? Or no?"

She shrugged again, the gesture more defiant.

I sighed again. "Well, Geraldine, the fact of the matter is that it *was* wrong. If you can't tell that, then you're just going to have to take my word for it. And I can't let you keep doing it. I can't allow you to hurt other people. You know that already."

"You're just taking their side. You always do. You take everybody's side but mine."

I regarded her. She sat, slouched down in the chair, arms wrapped tight around herself, eyes averted. I hated this kind of interaction with a child, where there was no communication whatsoever.

"I'm going to have to take a more serious course of action, Geraldine. I don't know how many times you and I have talked about taking things that don't belong to you, but it's been too often. In the beginning, I assumed maybe you just didn't know how wrong it is, but now I can't believe that anymore. You *do* know. You're choosing to keep doing it."

"Okay, so I'll sit in the stupid quiet chair," she said with glum annoyance.

"No, I don't think the quiet chair is going to do the trick this time. I think first you and I need to go back downstairs so that you can give each child back his or her sweets. And then, I think you need to give them something of yours. If you take from them, it's only fair to have to give them something in retribution."

Concern colored her features.

"You brought in that packet of My Little Pony stickers this morning. I think we ought to take those down and give one to each of the children you've stolen from."

She was aghast. "Those are mine! Auntie Bet bought those for *me*, to go in my sticker album. That's not fair!"

"I think it is. You took things that didn't belong to you, that other people wanted to keep. This is a fair way of making up for it."

Geraldine began to cry.

Rising from my chair, I put a hand on her shoulder. "Come on. Let's go get the stickers."

Geraldine wept all the way down to the lunchroom and all the way through the process of returning the sweets and passing out the stickers. At the start, she was simply angry and raged noisily against her helplessness in the situation, but after a while, I think the tears fed upon themselves. She got going and she couldn't stop. As we headed back to the classroom, she was still crying and sullenly attempted to pull away from me when I tried to put my arm around her shoulders. But she didn't quite. She reached the extent of my fingertips and went no farther.

We'd come to the end of the corridor and started up the stairs to the second floor. I paused on the landing. "Shall we sit down a minute?" I asked.

"Where?"

"Here." I indicated the steps.

"What for?"

I shrugged slightly. "Just to have a few minutes."

She nodded.

And so we sat, side by side, on the first step leading up from the landing. Geraldine had a huge wad of tissues in her hands, and she kept folding and refolding them, searching for dry places. I reached my arm over and put it around her shoulders, but a small space remained between us as we sat.

My intention had been to give her a few minutes to compose herself before we launched into the rigors of the afternoon. I also wanted the opportunity to talk to her. Ladbrooke never meant to be intrusive, but there were moments when I felt a desperate need to be totally alone with a child, and this was one of them. I wanted to reassure Geraldine of my regard for her. I needed to clarify my actions, to insure she understood that I hadn't done what I did simply in order to dominate or humiliate her, but rather that it was my responsibility to see she followed certain rules. This had been one of our problems all along. Despite considerable evidence to the contrary, Geraldine never seemed able to accept that any rules applied to her. Nor could she understand that my predictable response to rule breaking was anything other than acutely personal attack. So I wanted a few moments of privacy to sort everything out between us.

However, once I had the privacy, I suddenly found myself with nothing to say. We sat in silence perhaps five minutes or more.

Then, when I didn't say anything, Geraldine turned her head and looked up at me. It was a slow, deliberate movement. She didn't speak; she just looked up at me, her eyes searching my face. Then she lowered her head. The tears, which had ceased, began again with an abrupt sob. Without a word, she leaned against me and buried her face in my lap.

Gently, I touched her hair.

Where had all our chances gone? Things had never been perfect between the two of us, but they had been no worse than with so many other children. What had happened to us? When had we ceased working together and become opponents? When had I lost her? Because hard as it was for me to acknowledge, I knew I had.

CHAPTER
THIRTY-ONE

Ladbrooke went into a period of remarkable stability. We no longer met over the weekends; we hadn't since Easter, but she now handled them as a matter of course. In the classroom she was providing mature, reliable assistance with the children. She would go down to the teachers' lounge on her own occasionally, and while not friendly, her silence was acceptably neutral. She had developed a fairly pleasant relationship with Carolyn and now joined us regularly at the spa for a swim. Even in conversation, she was more at ease. She still clutched, sputtered and lost her words occasionally, but it interfered with her fluency less. Most importantly, however, she had made it three months without a single drink.

Despite this progress, or perhaps because of it, Ladbrooke's and my own relationship went on the skids. The difficulty materialized virtually out of nowhere in the early days of May and overshadowed a fair proportion of the otherwise pleasant springtime activities taking place. Ladbrooke's suddenly announced plans for her future appeared to be the first herald of this change. I was genuinely caught off guard, and this seemed to intrigue Ladbrooke. Throughout our time together, Lad had found entertainment value in catching me unawares. She liked proving that I wasn't as unshakable as I appeared and she preferred staying a little unpredictable herself. This'd always lent some tension to the relationship and on occasion had created a faintly competitive edge, as we attempted to determine who could outwit whom; however, I'd never been particularly concerned about it. To me, it was simply one of the many normal forces ebbing and flowing subtlely in a dynamic relationship. Then in May, Ladbrooke's behavior changed aburptly. She grew positively enthusiastic about keeping me unsettled. What had hitherto been subtle became trenchant.

Lad's favorite tactic was to confront me with my own emotions. "You're upset now." "You wanted it your way." "I've disappointed/angered/irritated you." And so on. These became bywords to our conversations and were all the more annoying because she was almost always right. Moreover, the emotions she remarked on were generally ones I was not thrilled to have exposed. She also enjoyed playing devil's advocate. This was a totally new behavior, and I fell very hard for it the first few times by getting quite upset. The topics she chose were invariably sensitive and controversial, such as my feelings over Northern Ireland or similar political issues, or ones which brought into question my authority, such as my choice of discipline in the classroom. Whatever stance I took, she chose the dead opposite and would debate with me in a very serious fashion indeed. I was surprised by how hurt I could feel when I believed she actually meant what she was saying. Then, once I was wound up, she'd shrug or laugh and say she hadn't meant any of it at all, not really; she just wanted to see how I defended myself on the issue. Then I'd feel even worse than when I'd thought she was serious.

Ladbrooke was generally not sadistic in these attacks. While she obviously intended to push things as far as they would go, she didn't like me to get genuinely upset. If I did, she'd immediately back down and apologize profusely. In my saner moments, this gave me hope that she wasn't out to hurt me personally and this was just one of those irritating stages, but the verbal jousting was persistent and the comfortable acceptance which had been a part of our relationship for so long was momentarily eclipsed.

Understandably, when not under siege, I devoted a considerable amount of time to thinking about this change. Despite its negative appearance, I suspected it augured growth. The time, I think, had finally come when Ladbrooke was unwilling to let me stay in charge of things. I'd carried her long enough, and she was now wanting to take her own weight. Doing this necessitated shaking up both our roles. To put herself on equal footing with me, she had to knock me down to size first.

From an intellectual point of view, I could appreciate such a theory. Considering all the factors, it made sense, and it matched my previous experience. Moreover, it was a necessary stage of growth. The problem was, it was miserable to be on the receiving end of such behavior. The other times I had encountered something similar had been in my work with older adolescents, and it had been no picnic with them. But with Ladbrooke, it was pure hell. She was experienced and intelligent, giving her a fully equipped armory with which to work; she knew me well enough to be able to really get under my skin; and she'd had Tom all these years to sharpen rapiers with. Worst, there was no escaping her. For the first time, I could see real sense in the traditional client/therapist setup. An hour a day, once or twice a week, I could probably have handled with aplomb. All day, day in, day out was killing me.

In the end, I decided the best solution would be to give both of us more space.

I'd had a hectic morning before coming to school one day and hadn't managed to make myself much of a lunch. It ended up being no more than a plain peanut butter sandwich and a bruised banana. Sitting at the table at lunchtime, I regarded it with dismay.

"Let's go to Enrico's for lunch tomorrow," I said.

Ladbrooke lifted an eyebrow.

"This is rotten. Look at this. I can't eat half this banana. I'm in the mood for something decent."

"Here. You want some of this?" She held out her container of salad. "Give me the plastic wrap from your sandwich. I'll put some on there."

"No, that's okay. I'm just saying I'm ready for a change."

Ladbrooke wrinkled her nose.

"I love Mexican food," I said, "and I'm really sick of sandwiches. I never have time in the mornings to make anything better."

"I do mine the night before. Do you want me to do yours as well? I wouldn't mind. It wouldn't be any trouble."

"No, I'd rather go to Enrico's."

Lad came too, that next day. I had assumed she would. Despite her still clumsy social skills, she liked company. She wouldn't have been happy staying in the room on her own, and since her relationship with most of the rest of the staff had improved steadily throughout the year, I trusted Enrico's would not prove to be the anguishing experience it had been in November.

The first lunch hour passed flawlessly. Only six people from the school went to Enrico's that day because there was a meeting Frank and some of the special-services staff needed to attend instead. That meant we could all sit together at one table. Conversation flowed without interruption. Lad talked mainly with Carolyn and Katy from the office. I caught up on the latest gossip about upcoming school-board elections from two of the secretaries. Returning to school afterward, I felt more refreshed than I had in ages.

There was less concern the next day. Lad sat next to me, as she had the day before, but I paid no attention to what she was doing. Neither of us knew most of the people sitting at our table. There were the men from driver's education and someone from career services. Carolyn came late, so she sat at a different table. But Frank was with us and all three of us got into a conversation about Mrs. Samuelson.

It wasn't until the third day that we ran into trouble. Mariana had a dental appointment, and her mother was late picking her up, so Lad and I didn't get to Enrico's until almost 12:30. Virtually everyone else was there already, as were a considerable number of other people. As a consequence, there was no room for us to sit together at the same table. So Ladbrooke joined Carolyn and the office girls, while I joined Frank and the people from speech therapy. I didn't think too much about it at the time; I was too concerned with snagging a waitress to take my order, as we didn't have a lot of time to spare.

Afterward, when I was in the rest room, Carolyn stopped me. "You better go rescue Lad," she said. "She's gone cold as a fish again."

I groaned.

Back out in the restaurant, I took my soda water, which was all I had remaining from my meal, and came over to the table where Lad and Carolyn were sitting. I pulled a chair over from an adjacent table and sat down near Ladbrooke. She was encased in grim, bristly silence. Her food was virtually untouched.

For a few moments I chatted with one of the secretaries and finished my drink, waiting to see if Ladbrooke could pull herself together on her own. When it became obvious that she wasn't going to manage it before we needed to leave, I thought I'd better give her an out.

"You want to walk back? It's such a nice day. Seems a shame to ride."

She nodded. Putting her napkin on the table, she rose and made preparations to leave.

Outside, the sun was warm and very bright in contrast to the darkened interior of the restaurant. I squinted as I reached the doorway, but smiled because the day was simply glorious. I paused to take in deep breaths of apple blossom–scented air. But Ladbrooke was having none of it. She started down the steps and off across the parking lot without looking back.

We walked for a few minutes without talking. Ladbrooke was setting the pace. She had a long stride and was walking in a no-nonsense manner that was going to get us back to the school sooner than if we'd accepted a ride with someone. I had to work to keep up with her.

"Carolyn told me you were having problems," I said.

Ladbrooke scowled. "What did she say that for?"

"Because I think she thought you were."

Ladbrooke quickened her pace. In a few moments I wasn't going to be able to talk if I wanted to, because I was going to need all my breath just to keep up with her. I was almost having to run.

"If there're problems, Lad, there're problems. No big deal. But there's no point in pretending they're not there if they are."

"There weren't any problems. I've already said that."

We'd come into the schoolyard.

"I just don't want to go there, that's all," she said. "I'd rather eat in the classroom." She mounted the steps to the door and pulled it open. I followed her in. Within moments, we were back in the room.

"Well, I'd rather not," I said. "It's a good break, getting away from the school for a while. I feel better for it."

She shrugged. "So you eat there. I'll eat here."

"Lad, don't be impossible."

"You're getting as bad as Tom. I think I'm going to be glad to be away from you too. You treat me like a child. I don't need you to do everything for me. I'm quite capable of eating a lunch on my own."

The temptation at that moment was to point out that if she was intending on taking off for the East Coast in a few weeks' time, it would probably be profitable to learn how to make casual conversation with acquaintances in a restaurant. But I didn't say it, realizing I would be talking more from my own frustration than from a need to make a point. Instead, I turned away and started to take the children's afternoon work out.

"See, now you're angry with me," Ladbrooke said.

"I'm not angry, but I'll tell you what. I *am* getting frustrated. Do you know what you've been behaving like lately? I can't do anything right by you. I'm damned if I do and damned if I don't."

She regarded me, her expression unreadable.

"Do what you bloody well please, Ladbrooke. If you want to sit here on your own and eat your lunch, be my guest. If you want to go down there and sit like Grim Death, then do that. If it's no problem for you, then God knows, it's certainly no problem for me. Do whatever you want. Just lay off me."

She gazed at me for several seconds. "See," she said quietly. "You *are* angry."

I nodded. "Yes, I am."

At recess, Ladbrooke approached me on the playground as I leaned against the brick wall and watched the children.

"Look, I'm sorry about earlier," she said.

"That's okay."

She pulled her hair around over one shoulder and then leaned back against the wall beside me. "I did panic a bit at lunch. I don't know why. It just came over me as I was sitting there."

"Well, don't worry about it."

We watched Shamie and Mariana playing a makeshift game of baseball. Shemona was running back and forth to fetch the ball for them, as they took turns hitting at it.

"I felt dumb," Ladbrooke said quietly. "I felt worse because I knew Carolyn knew. I could feel her watching me. I wanted to scream at her after a while."

"You probably should have. She needs to mind her own business sometimes."

"I wanted to sort it out on my own. I didn't want her to tell you. God, that was the last thing I wanted, you two gossiping in the ladies' room."

"We weren't gossiping, Lad."

"Well, you know what I mean."

I scanned the playground, counting heads to make sure all the children were still there. Carolyn had gotten a new boy, and he kept wandering off. I spotted him at the far end. Standing against the wall was very hot, so I pushed myself off to let the air circulate. Lad looked over at me.

"I'm still going back," I said. "To Enrico's, I mean. I really do feel I need that break in my day."

Ladbrooke looked down at her hands.

"You're welcome to come. You know that. But I'm not going back to sandwiches in the classroom."

"You're still upset, aren't you?"

"No, I'm not. I just think the time's come for me to have a change of scenery."

Ladbrooke frowned and didn't say anything further.

The next morning I arrived as usual at 7:30, got my cup of coffee, sat down at the table and started to organize myself for the day. Within a few moments, the classroom door opened and someone came in. This surprised me. I was one of the few people to come so early, which was why I did it. It usually guaranteed me an uninterrupted half hour to myself.

I sat, waiting for someone to appear but heard instead the familiar rumble-bump of Ladbrooke's putting her things beside the filing cabinet. She opened the bottom drawer and took out her jogging shoes. I craned my neck to see around the divider but couldn't quite.

"You're early," I said.

She came around the corner then, still in her sock feet, the shoes in her hand. She stopped across the table from me but remained standing.

"I got drunk last night," she said.

I thought for a moment she was going to burst into tears.

"I've gone nearly three months. Through hell and high water. And then I took one shitty drink and blew it all."

"Sit down, Lad."

She remained standing. "What's wrong with me, Torey? Why can't I stop?"

"Nothing's wrong with you. It's just very hard to do."

"I only wanted one drink. That's all. Just one. Why couldn't I stop at one?"

"Lad, sit down."

Pulling out the chair across from me, she fell into it. Her shoes made a resounding thud as she dropped them to the floor beside her. Despondently, she braced her head with both fists. I regarded her, and there was silence around us.

"Do you know why it happened?"

"I just felt like a drink, that's all."

I studied her, as she sat across from me, her posture reflecting her despair. The obviousness of her disappointment kept me from asking her why she hadn't managed to take any of the numerous preventive measures we'd come up with over the months to help her avoid that first drink. I could sense that this had caught her as much unawares as her announcement of it had caught me. After all the traumas she'd managed to ride out, I was perplexed that she had succumbed here and now in the middle of the working week.

"Was it Tom? Did you and Tom have an argument?"

She shook her head. "Tom wasn't even home."

"Did his kids come over?"

Again she shook her head.

"You just felt like a drink?"

"Yes."

Folding my arms on the table, I leaned on them. "Is it me, Ladbrooke?"

She glanced over briefly and our eyes met. Then she looked away again. She shook her head. "No."

Silence followed.

"You and I have been having an uncomfortable, confusing few weeks, haven't we? It's getting to me too. I've been feeling under a lot of pressure from you."

"From me?" she asked, surprised.

I nodded. "I feel like I can't do anything right around you. If I try to help, you don't want me to. If I don't help, you're angry with me because I haven't. I give an opinion on something, and you disagree. I make a decision, and you tell me it's the wrong one. That's been hard on me."

Ladbrooke was watching me. Chin braced in one hand, she gazed at my face. Tears had filled her eyes but they remained enmeshed in her lower lashes and did not fall.

"I can't imagine that you're not aware that this has been going on," I said. "I kept hoping it was just a stage and would pass, so I didn't say anything; but now I think maybe it's time for us to talk. My feeling is that the pressure's getting a bit too much for you too."

She looked down at the tabletop.

"What's behind it? Are you afraid of the end?"

"Not really."

"Is it the pressure of working to a deadline like we're doing? Do you feel like I'm pushing you out too fast?"

She shrugged slightly and kept her head down. "I don't feel like you're pushing me out."

I nodded.

Another slight shrug. "What I do feel like is that maybe you don't care if I go."

"Oh."

She looked over. "I still can't figure you out."

"What do you mean?"

"You never protest. You never say you're sorry that it's all coming to an end. We've all sweated blood in here, but it's just business as usual with you. Get Shemona placed. Get Shamie into junior high. Get Ladbrooke to make small talk at Enrico's. Maybe you're so used to all this by now that it doesn't matter to you anymore."

"Does it seem like that to you?"

"You're so damned objective about everything. I can never tell when something really matters to you and when it doesn't. You always seem to care terribly about everything, and yet, at the same time, I don't see how it *can* be caring, because it doesn't affect you."

"It's not quite like that."

"It seems like it to me. Like yesterday, I knew what was going on in your head. It was just get me back to Enrico's, get me talking, make a socially acceptable person out of me so I can go off and live a good life and you can notch up one more success on your tally. You didn't really care that I was so unhappy, that it'd scared the shit out of me and all I wanted was some support."

"Hey, Ladbrooke, hold on. Yesterday you were telling me you didn't want me to help, that you were angry with me for interfering. Now you're saying you're angry with me because I didn't help you enough. Which do you want? It's sort of difficult for me to do both."

Tears sprang up again and again did not fall, but her entire jaw tensed to keep them in check. A long, very pointed silence followed.

"I don't know what I want anymore," she said at last, her voice shaky. "Everything seems to be in a state of flux. My opinions, my feelings, my

thoughts, nothing's the same. Sometimes I just want to do things by *myself*.
I don't want everybody to keep paying such close attention to me."

"I think you're having fairly normal feelings, Lad. I think we've come
to the point where you're going to feel a bit ambiguous about my intervening. That's a positive sign, not a negative one. That's growth. It's your
life, not mine, and ultimately, you're going to want to take sole charge
of it again."

With one finger, she flicked the tears from the corners of her eyes.
"We've managed to get this conversation off you again, haven't we? You're
like trapping a shadow. You really are."

I smiled slightly.

"I need to know about *you*, Torey. Can't you understand that? I can
handle the end coming. Maybe I don't like it, but it's a fact of life. I can
come to terms with it. However . . ." She paused. Gazing down at the
tabletop, she ran her fingers along the edge. "What I can't seem to shake
is the feeling that this is all just a job for you, that it's nothing more than
some sort of high-class assembly line, processing people through, getting
them to turn out more acceptable than when you got them."

Ladbrooke lifted her eyes to meet mine. "I've got to understand what
you really feel, because, otherwise, nothing is going to make sense. I've
survived all this hell these last few months because I felt it finally mattered
to someone that I did. I felt I had some value, that you cared. But if it's
all been just a job for you, then it's been kind of a hollow victory, hasn't
it?"

I was silent. I looked away and then down. I studied the fake wood
grain of the Formica tabletop and did not speak for several minutes.
Ladbrooke, chin in hand, watched me intently.

"This *is* a job, Ladbrooke. There's no denying the obvious. I would
never have been here in the first place, never have even met you, if it
hadn't been for someone's hiring me with the specific intention that I
come in here and do the kinds of things you've watched me do over these
last nine months. It is my job; it's what I've been trained to do. But I
don't like to think of it as processing people. What I'm working with,
what I'm 'processing,' are problems. I'm contracted to get rid of problems
interfering with people's lives that they themselves can't get rid of on their
own. I go in; I do what I can in the time I'm given to accomplish that.
And when my time's up, I leave, because that's what the contract says.
I don't get very emotional about the problems; if I did, I wouldn't be very
effective. But I don't like to think I seem the same way about the people.
For you and Shamie and Shemona and all the others, I *do* care, Ladbrooke.
I love you. Otherwise, you'd be right. There wouldn't be any point in it."

She looked down at her hands.

"Don't confuse yourself with your problems, Lad. You're not your problems. Don't go back to drinking to discover that."

She shrugged slightly. "I don't know why I did that."

"Well, I think it was one of those things like we all do sometimes and wish afterward we hadn't. Probably, it's best just to acknowledge it's happened and leave it at that. You've been doing a super job, Lad. Pick up where you left off and go on."

"You know what I keep wondering?" she asked, her eyes still down.

"What's that?"

"I keep wondering what it's going to be like without those problems. What's my life going to be like?"

She paused.

"I watch you getting ready to finish with the kids . . . I know you're probably never going to even see any of them again, and still, you go on like normal, even after all this intense togetherness." Again she paused. She continued to study her hands in her lap. "I mean, I wouldn't want it to go on like this forever, with everything so intense. I'm tired of it. I've felt at times like there's been both of us in here under my skin with me, and there just isn't room. I want to be my own self again. But still, over and over, I find myself wondering what it's going to be like without this, when you've packed up and gone. I wonder, are you even going to miss me?"

I did smile then. I smiled and covered my eyes with one hand and kept smiling.

"What's so funny?"

"I'm not laughing, Lad. This is amazement—at how two people can spend all this time together and still not figure one another out. Yes, of course, I'm going to miss you. How could I not miss you?"

She smiled self-consciously at the tabletop.

"The thing is, it's not going to be the end, is it?" I said.

"What do you mean?"

"I mean, that's what all this hassle's been about over these last few weeks, hasn't it? The time's come for the changeover. You're not going to be just another kid anymore. You're going to be my friend."

CHAPTER
THIRTY-TWO

My birthday came during the fourth week of May. It fell rather inconveniently midweek, but I decided, what the heck, we'd have a party anyway, middle of the week or not. The only two special occasions all year had been the Nativity play and Shemona's birthday, so this provided one more needed break in routine.

Celebrating my birthday, rather than one of the children's, was better because, while the focus of the party was pleasantly familiar, no one was going to get a nose out of joint over preferential treatment. So we opted for all the trimmings: balloons, streamers, silly hats and games.

I gave over the whole of Tuesday to the party. We now had only four children in class in the morning anyway, so I let them do the decorating, which led to considerable noisy chaos. Leslie and Dirkie enjoyed the atmosphere tremendously but didn't contribute much in the way of concrete help, so this left everything to Mariana and Geraldine. They reveled in their new-found authority, commanding the rest of us like two despots.

We blew up balloons, cut streamers and made Chinese lanterns. Mariana and Geraldine hopped from table to chair to radiator to bookcase and back again, taping things up. Then we made a small assortment of no-bake cookies and bars, and chocolate-dipped bananas to be frozen in the ice compartment of the refrigerator in the teachers' lounge. Toward the end of the morning, the four children sat down to make party hats.

"This has really been fun," Mariana said. "We ought to have parties more."

"If we had parties more, they wouldn't be as good," I said. "We couldn't afford to spend time like this very often."

"How come?" Mariana asked.

"Because we wouldn't learn anything," Dirkie said. "If we spent all our time having parties, we wouldn't learn, and you come to school to learn."

"We're learning. I learned how to make a Chinese lantern this morning," Mariana said. "Besides, I didn't mean have a party every day. I just meant more often than we're doing now."

"There isn't time now," I said. "The school year's almost over."

Silence enveloped us as everyone grew involved with the activities.

"I'm lucky," Geraldine suddenly said.

Mariana looked up. "How come?"

"I get to stay in this class. Me and Dirkie and Leslie. We're going to be in this class next year. But you won't."

"Well, I'm going to third grade," Mariana replied, her voice injured sounding.

"So?"

"So I'm going to be in a real class. With a real teacher."

"She's real," Geraldine said, jerking her head in my direction.

"No, she isn't," Mariana replied. "And this isn't a real class."

"So?"

Mariana couldn't think of an answer to that.

Geraldine raised her head to look over at me. She smiled. "I'm lucky. I'm going to be in here."

When Ladbrooke came back from lunch, she found me on my hands and knees in the depths of the library.

"What are you doing?" she asked.

"Hiding peanuts for the treasure hunt."

"You're really getting elaborate, aren't you?"

I stood and dusted off my knees. "They're good kids. I want them to have a good time." And I smiled. "Besides, it's my birthday."

"Well, come on out here then and look at your birthday cake."

Ladbrooke set the box on the table. "Now, don't look for just the minute, okay? Turn around. This is going to stun you, believe me."

When I was given permission to turn back, she was holding a piece of paper in front of the cake. "Ta-da!" she said, and pulled it away.

"Gosh, it's great," I said and it was. A tall cake with rather passionately pink icing, it had my name written across it in bold white letters.

"I've been practicing. Besides, it's angel food. They're really easy to make. You don't end up with two pieces you've got to stick together, like with other cakes."

"You're getting pretty good at this."

"Well, I could only get better, believe me. But I think I did all right this time." She smiled at the cake. "You're another one like Shemona. It just wouldn't have done to have bought you a cake at the bakery."

And then it was party time. Everyone put on silly hats. Music went on the phonograph. And the party started.

We played endless games. I blindfolded the children and gave them each a plate of food, which they had to taste and try to identify, then remember and write down afterward. We had chocolate chopping, a game I'd come across in Wales, where the children, divided into teams, had to run, put on a series of clothes, then get to a plate containing a large bar of chocolate, cut a bit off with knife and fork, eat it and get back to the next team member. Lad and I joined in, our dubious talents divided between the two teams, but it was Leslie and Dirkie who gave real hilarity to the thing. While alight with the spirit, neither had a clue as to what was actually happening, which necessitated having other team members accompany them to try to get them through the motions. At one point, Leslie, Shamie and Shemona were all laughing so hard that none of them could stand.

Coming back from recess, we all sat down at the table for cake and ice cream.

"Miss," Shamie asked, "can I put my record on now?"

I nodded.

Shamie got up and went to his cubby. When he'd arrived at lunchtime, he was carrying an LP he'd brought especially for the party. It was a recording of Irish folk music, and he'd thought I might like to hear some.

Carefully, Shamie removed the record from its sleeve, dusted it with his shirt cuff, then set it gently on the turntable. After lowering the stylus, he returned to the table and sat down with us, while the air around us filled with thin, foreign sounds.

"This is *céili* music," Shamie said. "When *we* have a party, this is the kind of music we play."

"Yes," said Geraldine enthusiastically, "and everybody dances."

"The party itself is called a *céili*," Shamie said. "We had them down at the church hall in Friday nights. Curran Maris and Sean Michael O'Flannery would play their fiddles. Sometimes my daddy would too. And everyone dances. It was nice."

We listened to the music as we ate.

"Oh, there's 'The Top of Cork Road,'" Geraldine said, as a new piece of music began. "I can dance a jig to that. You can too, can't you, Shemona?"

Shamie looked over at me. "Could they do jig for us, Miss? Geraldine and Shemona? If I set the needle back to the beginning, could they dance to 'The Top of Cork Road'?"

"Yes, sure."

All three leaped up enthusiastically.

"You ought to have a dress on, Geraldine," Shemona said, touching her sister's shorts.

"This is okay. Shamie, are you ready? We are."

He nodded and lifted the stylus.

It was an eerie experience, sitting at the table with the sun streaming through the window, the sticky sweet cake and the melting ice cream in front of us, the trappings of an ordinary American school all around us, and seeing those two girls dance. The music was thin and reedy, coming from violins and some kind of pipe. Shemona and Geraldine stood side by side, both facing us, arms and hands down against their bodies. They were in the sunshine, which came through the window onto them like a spotlight. And they began to dance.

I had never seen an Irish jig. It was the sort of thing one went through life hearing about, yet never seeing, which gave it a false familiarity. In fact, it was a much different dance than I'd imagined. Although fast, it was very self-contained. The girls remained in a stiff posture throughout, with only their feet moving. But the feet made up for it. Toe-heel-turn-kick-toe-heel. It was an individual dance not meant for partners, so they never acknowledged one another's presence.

Shemona's hair was made paler by the sunshine. Long and unkempt as ever, it bounced around her as she moved. But Geraldine, more than her sister, was given a new aura by the dance. Shemona always had a little wildness about her, but Geraldine, plain and ordinary in everyday life, was transformed. Her eyes fixed on some unseen spot beyond us, her expression turned inward, she danced to music I don't think the rest of us heard. She obviously knew the steps much better than Shemona. I saw Shemona glance to her sister's feet occasionally to check, but Geraldine danced with no hesitation, her upper torso disciplined against the movement, her feet flying.

The rest of us sat, entranced. There was something ethereal about their dancing. The reedy Irish music transposed against this distinctly American afternoon undoubtedly had something to do with it. But the girls did too. They danced so naturally there in the sunshine, like leprechauns momentarily freed from the tedium of reality.

When the music stopped, Geraldine collapsed in mock exhaustion. Shemona collapsed in giggles. The rest of us clapped.

"That was really good," Ladbrooke said. "That was fantastic."

"Do you dance like that all the time?" Mariana inquired.

"Not all the time," Shemona said. "But we do sometimes at home. When we feel like it. When Shamie puts the record on."

Geraldine came over to us. She ran her hand along Ladbrooke's shoulder to come to rest on mine. Standing behind my chair, she draped her arms on either side of my neck and hugged me, her cheek against mine.

"That was lovely dancing, Geraldine. Thanks for doing it for us."

She kept her face pressed against mine. "See," she said gently. "There's some good things about Northern Ireland. It's not all bad there. I just wanted to show you we had good things too."

And then it was June. That last week was a waste, as far as schoolwork was concerned. Only Dirkie and Leslie continued to concentrate, simply because neither of them managed to understand the end was so near. Shamie's new love was baseball. He had joined a local team for the summer, so that was all we heard out of him. Geraldine was going to day camp with one of her cousins. Shemona was slated for a week of Bible school at her church, shortly after school finished. She was rather unsure what this was and obviously considered it a dubious treat compared to Geraldine's lofty tales of the swimming and horseback riding she intended to do at camp, but Shemona, desperate not to be outdone, managed to make it sound quite grand. Mariana's grandmother was coming from California for a visit, and Mariana assured us Granny would take her to the park *every* day and buy her chewing gum, as well. She and Geraldine made elaborate plans to see each other over the summer vacation. Dirkie's enthusiasm was over an upcoming trip to Disneyland with his foster family. I didn't find out until later that it wasn't taking place until August, because Dirkie spoke of it as if it were happening the week after school let out. Only Leslie had nothing to contribute to this excitement, but her summer, too, was planned. She was enrolled in the school district's special summer school program, to encourage her continuing progress.

Ladbrooke was telling me about the program as we were working after school. It was Tuesday and our last day was Friday, so we were involved in the slow task of taking inventory and then packing everything away for good. She was on the floor, boxing up audiovisual equipment and tapes. I was up on a chair, removing all the things I'd stored on the upper shelves of the outermost steel shelving unit.

"How are your plans coming?" I asked. She'd brought in the letters she'd wanted me to help her with, and they'd been mailed some ten days earlier. She hadn't said anything to me about them in the interim.

"All right."

"Have you heard anything from your advisor?"

"Not yet. He's probably still picking himself up off the floor after getting my letter. But I did hear from this other colleague I was telling you about. The one up at M.I.T."

"What's he say?"

"Same as I expected. About how everybody's cut back and how tight everything is. He was positive enough, I guess, in his way. He thought I could probably get in if I tried hard enough, but he wasn't sure I could get back directly into spectroscopy research. Not at first anyway. A lot's going to depend on my references, I'm afraid. So it all comes down to John."

"What's Tom think about all this?" I asked.

She shrugged. "I don't know. He's not happy, if that's what you mean. But I reckoned you'd probably guessed that. As to what he's thinking, I just don't know."

"Is he trying to stop you?"

"Well, he can't, can he?"

I looked down at her.

She glanced up then and shrugged. "Maybe that was half the problem," she said. "He never could."

We worked a while in silence before I finally got down from my chair and took the things I'd cleared from the shelf over to the table.

"What about Leslie?" I asked.

Ladbrooke grimaced.

I lifted up an apple carton and began putting things into it that were mine and needed to be taken home.

"I don't know," she said. "I want her with me, but I keep thinking maybe she should stay with Tom."

"Tom told me about Leslie's not being his child."

Ladbrooke looked up in surprise. "He did? When was that?"

"Ages ago. In January, I think."

Ladbrooke was silent a moment. "You know, Torey, I'm always amazed at some of the things you get people to tell you."

I set the loaded box on the floor.

"I never thought Tom would ever tell anybody about that. Even his mother doesn't know."

"Is it true?"

"Yes," she replied. "Leslie's John's child."

"Are you sure?"

"I think it was the diabetes that really confirmed it for us. Neither Tom nor I have any history of that in our families, but John's a diabetic."

I looked over. "There's still the long shot that she might be Tom's, isn't there?"

Lad shook her head. "I don't think so." She briefly glanced over. "You see, mostly, Tom's impotent."

"Oh."

I went back to my packing. We didn't speak for several minutes.

"Is it going to make any difference to Leslie's future?" I asked. "I mean the fact Tom isn't her true father."

Ladbrooke shook her head. "No. He's her true father. Maybe his genes aren't hers, but his heart is."

She frowned down at the things in her lap. "I want her with me. She *is* my daughter, and I do love her. When I go, whenever that is, I want to take her, but I keep wondering if that's right. Do I want her just because I know it'd destroy Tom? Or do I really think it would be best for Leslie? Do I really think I'd be the better parent? I feel like I *am* a better mother now than I was. I know more what to do. I can control her better. So maybe that's not so far out. Maybe I am the better choice. But then, maybe not. Tom adores her. She adores Tom. And Consuela. What would happen to her relationship with Consuela? Consuela's like family to Leslie. She's been there practically all of Leslie's life, and I've got to admit, she's probably given Leslie more stability than Tom and I put together." Ladbrooke looked over. "How do you decide these things, Torey?"

"I don't know."

She shook her head slowly. "In some ways my life seems so much better. I mean it. It really is. But in others, it's gotten worse. Well, no, not worse. That's not the word I'm looking for. Harder. It's gotten so much harder. I see all the sharp edges now."

CHAPTER
THIRTY-THREE

And then it was the end. As was my tradition, we had a picnic on the last day. I arranged for packed lunches for the children instead of the usual hot ones sent from the neighboring school. Ladbrooke and I supplied pop and potato chips. Mrs. Lonrho sent cookies. Dirkie's foster mother sent delightful little treats made to look like monkeys with candy eyes and licorice whip tails.

Most years I held the last-day picnic in a nearby park, but here there was no nearby park, and I thought that if we had to go to the trouble of packing everyone into cars, we might as well go somewhere worth the trip. So Lad and I decided to take the children out of town about ten miles to a historic fort once used by the cavalry to defend the area against Indian attacks. Nestled up in the foothills of the mountains on a broad plateau, it was surrounded by a large recreation area. So once everyone had arrived on Friday, we packed up the picnic things and loaded Lad's and my cars full of screaming, wriggling children.

The day was not as sunny as the previous few weeks had been. It was overcast with high, thin clouds and, although it was still very warm, a strong westerly wind was blowing.

The kids were all heady with end-of-school freedom. This had been a good place to bring them because it was spacious enough to absorb their energy. They ran, screaming and yelling, back and forth across the hillside.

The children's excitement evoked enough recollections of my own childhood exhilaration over the last day to keep me in high spirits as well, but there was still one part of me always standing back. I kept watching them, all of them, Lad included, as if from a great distance, as if looking down the wrong end of a pair of binoculars and seeing not just the warm, windy present, but all the days and weeks and months telescoped together. At one point, Shemona came running up to me, and I was very aware of seeing her not as she was, in her pastel-striped sundress and bare feet, but as she had been, clutching Curious George in the Nativity play, swinging with Ladbrooke on the playground swings, dancing to "The Top of Cork Road" with Geraldine. Again and again and again throughout the day that happened to me. All the little moments of the year came crowding in around me like so many tiny ghosts.

For all her traumatic anticipation of the day, Ladbrooke appeared to be feeling only the joy of it. She was as free spirited as the children were. She had a marvelous way of being able to loosen up and completely throw off the usual shackles of adulthood, and this day proved to be one such occasion. She absolutely delighted the children with her silly behavior. She showed Shamie how to throw his Frisbee into the wind to make it come sailing back. She boosted Shemona, Mariana and even Dirkie up onto the ramparts of the old fort. At lunch we had small containers of Jell-O, and Ladbrooke did horribly rude things with hers, such as blowing into it with a drinking straw, the kinds of things an eight-year-old would have been scolded for. The kids loved it, of course, and laughed so hard that Geraldine sprayed the table with a mouthful of pop. Later, Ladbrooke took out a ridiculous-looking hat and presented it to me from all of them. It was a blue baseball cap with fox ears sticking out of the top of it, and she insisted on my wearing it throughout the rest of the day, popping it back on my head whenever I took it off.

We all explored the fort, waded in the reservoir, chased endlessly after things being blown away by the gusty, persistent wind. Then, finally, the end of the day approached. The children were still all wildly tearing up and down the broad hillside where the picnic ground was situated, terrorizing the ground squirrels that lived in burrows amid the sagebrush and buffalo grass. Since we needed to leave soon in order to get back in time to meet the children's rides, Lad and I had begun clearing up and putting things away.

Coming around to the side of the picnic table where I was, Lad loaded a handful of paper plates and cups into the cardboard box we were using to transport our belongings. Then she paused.

"There's something I've been meaning to do," she said to me, and smiled.

Before I could ask her what, the children were on top of us. Squealing with excitement, Mariana slid under the picnic table and came out between us. Dirkie bounded up over the top of the table.

"Hey, you guys, cool it," I said.

They were all laughing.

I looked back to Lad. "You were saying?"

"I was saying, there's something I want to do before we leave." And she stepped over to put her arms around me in a friendly hug. But as she reached me, Mariana exploded up from under the picnic table again, bumping headlong into us. All three of us went down with a bump on the grass.

"Dog pile!" screamed Geraldine, when she saw us go down, and every single one of the children piled on top of us.

"I got you! I got you, Teacher!" Dirkie screeched.

"Me too! Me too!"

I was at the bottom of the heap, flat on my back, the prickly buffalo grass coming up in a yellow clump beside my face. Slowly, one by one, they began to get off. We untangled ourselves until only I was still lying on the ground, with Shemona sitting astride my legs. She moved up to sit on my stomach. Leaning forward, she put a hand on either side of my face. She brought her face down very close to mine, so that our noses almost touched.

"I love you, Miss," she said with an easy, confident smile. "Miss Hayden. Torey Hayden. That's your name."

I nodded. "And I love you too, Shemona."

She was still smiling. "Yes, I know it."

Ladbrooke had separated from us, and I saw her over at a nearby picnic table, talking to a man there. He was a tourist, quintessentially dressed for the part in madras shorts, sunglasses and a terry-cloth fishing hat. I rose and dusted myself off. When she saw me get up, Ladbrooke looked over.

"You all stay there a minute," she called. "I'm going to get him to take our picture. All of us together." She held up her camera.

"Did you hear that?" I said to the children. "Don't go wandering off now."

Dirkie was cramming cookies into his mouth. He wasn't even bothering to take bites of them. One, two, three he shoved in whole.

"Hey!" Shamie cried, annoyed. "Those aren't all yours." He pulled the box from Dirkie's hands.

"Me too. I want one," Mariana said, and grabbed the box from him.

"Come on, you lot, don't fight," I said. "Ladbrooke wants to get a picture."

"I want to sit next to you, Teacher," Dirkie said.

"*I* want to," Mariana said, pushing Dirkie aside.

"Hey now, let's get this organized," I said. "There's room for everyone."

"No, there isn't. I want to sit here, but he's in my way."

"You get up on the table. You too, Geraldine. We can't all sit in a line, anyway."

"Where's Ladbrooke going to be sitting?" Shamie asked. He had the box of cookies open again.

"Lad and I'll sit here on the bench. You there, Shamie. Shamie, please put those cookies away. Now you there, Dirkie. Leslie here. And Shemona in front. Geraldine and Mariana, you two up there behind me and Lad."

"I have to go to the bathroom, Miss."

"Hold it, all right? This won't take that long."

"Here, Miss, put this on." Shamie took the cap with the fox ears from the cardboard box.

"Oh, I don't think I'd better wear that," I replied. "Ladbrooke wants a nice picture of us."

"No, Miss, please wear it."

"Yes, Miss, do," said Geraldine.

Mariana grabbed the cap from Shamie's hands and bounded up onto the picnic table to reach over and place it on my head. "You'll look nice with this on, Teacher. It makes you a foxy lady."

Ladbrooke's camera, like everything else about her, was not straightforward. The man from the other table couldn't understand how to operate it. He couldn't figure out Ladbrooke's light meter and kept pointing the camera skyward to get a reading.

The children grew restive as we waited. Leslie sat down on the ground and refused to get up. Mariana popped the box-eared cap on and off my head half a dozen times. Shemona reminded me with some urgency that she needed to use the toilet. At last the man seemed to understand what he needed to do, and Ladbrooke joined us. She squeezed in between Shamie and me on the picnic bench and pulled Shemona in closer.

"Leslie, stand up," I said. She wouldn't. So I reached down and pulled her up, taking her on my knee to keep her from complaining.

"Are you ready?" the man asked.

"Just a minute. Here, move in a bit, Dirkie," Lad said.

The man with the camera brought it up and focused it. "Get closer. I can't see you all."

We squeezed together. Lad put her arms around Shamie and me.

"Are you ready?"

"Is my hair okay, Teacher?"

"It's fine, Mariana. Just keep your head down so that the man can see you in the viewfinder."

"Okay. Now, are you ready?" he asked.

"Smile. Everybody, smile."

Click.

EPILOGUE

More than five years has escaped with eye-blink speed since that windy June afternoon. Throughout these years, Ladbrooke and I have remained close friends. I see her during virtually every trip I make to the States, and she has spent considerable time with me and my family here on our small farm in the misty upper moorlands of North Wales.

Following the end of the school year, Ladbrooke did go back to her work in the East. She and Tom were divorced about eight months later, and she has since remarried. Her new husband, a gentle, self-effacing man with a well-developed sense of humor, is also a physicist and is involved in work closely allied to Ladbrooke's current research. Two years ago, Ladbrooke gave birth to a healthy baby girl. Six weeks later, so did I.

Ladbrooke still struggles occasionally with the ghosts of her past, and her new marriage and her relationship with her young daughter have both been seriously challenged as a result. However, for the most part, she is living a positive, productive life. During our most recent visit together, we got to talking about the personal accomplishments we were most pleased with. Ladbrooke was unequivocal about hers. One is that she was now capable of preparing any family meal herself—without a can opener. The other is that she has not had any alcohol since that night in May so long ago.

Tom and Ladbrooke shared custody of Leslie for about a year after the divorce in an arrangement that did not suit anybody. Since then, Leslie has lived full time with Tom and sees her mother only rarely. The question of her paternity has never been raised. Leslie has progressed well within the limits of her handicap to become a charmingly amiable girl, who shows promise of being able to live, if not on her own, at least independent of her family when she reaches adulthood.

Dirkie remains very much his old self. Still living with his foster family, he now attends a special workshop for severely handicapped adolescents and young adults, where he will probably continue for several more years. While he will always need to live at home, it is hoped that the skills he is acquiring will lead to sheltered employment and a chance of increased self-care.

Mariana went off to third grade the following autumn and was fairly successful. At the end of that school year, her family moved, and we have since lost track of her.

Shamie has grown to a strapping six feet three inches, and with his dark, gentle good looks and his enchanting manner, he's become a real lady-killer. Although never much of a student, Shamie found his niche on the sports field as he progressed through junior high and high school, and he now attends a nearby university on an athletic scholarship. He has also distinguished himself in the community for his compassion. Since his mid-teens, he has been deeply involved in volunteer work in a local hospice for the terminally ill and has been commended recently for his prodigious efforts to raise money for better facilities at the hospice. Although Shamie has chosen to remain with his aunt and uncle, he goes back to Belfast to visit his family on a yearly basis. His feelings for his country have mellowed, and he now hopes to return permanently after his schooling is done.

Shemona, almost a teenager now, was formally adopted by her aunt and uncle when she was seven. She has adapted well to her new family and her new life. She now looks as American as her cousins, and there isn't even a hint of the burry Ulster accent remaining. Shemona has never returned to Belfast in the intervening years and now says she has no real desire to do so. The events there are over and gone for her, as are most of the memories. She can only dimly recall her real parents, her brother and 38 Greener Terrace.

Geraldine returned for another year in the special class without noticeable improvement. In fact, toward the end of that period, she became increasingly self-destructive and was finally committed to residential treatment. After three months, her family decided it would be better for Geraldine if she could return to live in Northern Ireland, which she did shortly before her tenth birthday. Living with Shamie's parents only three doors down from her old home, Geraldine was still unable to find peace. After a year, she went back to the Lonrhos. Sadly, this, too, did not work, and she returned yet again to Belfast to live with one more branch of the extended family. By this time Geraldine was an adolescent and had grown very difficult to control. As a last resort, she was taken into care and now lives in a children's home in County Tyrone. I've not seen Geraldine since the summer we parted, although barely sixty miles separates us across the Irish Sea. All the information I've had on her comes from Shemona, via Ladbrooke, or from Shamie, who visits Geraldine on his trips home. Latest word is that the authorities are trying to find a permanent foster home for her. I sincerely hope they succeed, because I fear otherwise Geraldine may find the familylike bonds she is so desperate for in the ideologies of terrorism.

This remarkable group has thus far proved to be my last class. I returned to Wales and was married within two weeks of our June parting. My husband and I and our young daughter now live on a smallholding, where I divide my time between writing and being wife, mother and farmhand.

When I came back from my honeymoon, I found a large envelope from Ladbrooke waiting for me, which contained a copy of the photograph taken of us that last afternoon. It's a friendly, natural picture. Lad and I are sitting close together on the bench, with the children pressed in around us. Geraldine and Mariana are up on the table behind Lad and me, Geraldine's arms draped over my shoulders. Dirkie and Shamie sit beside us. Leslie's perched on my knee. Shemona stands in front. It isn't a particularly flattering photo of any of us, except Leslie, who is smiling beatifically into the camera. Dirkie has his eyes closed. Shemona looks blank. Shamie has a hand up to avoid Lad's blowing hair. I have the blue fox-eared cap pulled down on my head, the visor almost obscuring my eyes, my expression giggly. Lad is wearing a broad, cheesy smile, like a kid in a school picture. And up behind her is Mariana, making horns with her fingers. But somehow, the magic's still been caught. All the faces are open and friendly and leaning in toward one another. Ladbrooke looks quite ordinary. The kids all look like kids anywhere.

It's the way I'll always want to remember things.